MOVING SUBJECTS

EDITED BY
TONY BALLANTYNE AND
ANTOINETTE BURTON

Moving Subjects

GENDER, MOBILITY, AND
INTIMACY IN AN AGE OF
GLOBAL EMPIRE

UNIVERSITY OF ILLINOIS PRESS
URBANA AND CHICAGO

© 2009 by the Board of Trustees
of the University of Illinois
All rights reserved
Manufactured in the United States of America
I 2 3 4 5 C P 5 4 3 2 I
∞ This book is printed on acid-free paper.

Library of Congress Cataloging-in-Publication Data
Moving subjects : gender, mobility, and intimacy in an age
of global empire / edited by Tony Ballantyne and Antoinette Burton.
p.   cm.
Includes bibliographical references and index.
ISBN-13 978-0-252-03375-9 (cloth : alk. paper)
ISBN10 0-252-03375-2 (cloth : alk. paper)
ISBN-13 978-0-252-07568-1 (pbk. : alk. paper)
ISBN-10 0-252-07568-4 (pbk. : alk. paper)
1. Body, Human—Social aspects—Cross-cultural
studies—Congresses. 2. Sex role—Cross-cultural studies—Congresses.
3. Colonization—Congresses. 4. Imperialism—Congresses.
5. Globalization—Congresses.
I. Ballantyne, Tony II. Burton, Antoinette M.
GT495.M68   2009
306.4—dc22   2008019205

Contents

Acknowledgments

This collection grew in part from a conference convened by Tony Ballantyne at the University of Otago in the fall of 2004 that was designed to think about what histories of gender, mobility, and settler colonialism can and should look like. It is also the fruit of a set of long-distance collaborations that have given transnationalism new meaning for the editors and the contributors alike. Tony would like to thank the University of Otago History Department for the funds that made the initial conference possible and the chair of the department, Professor Barbara Brookes, for her support of this initiative. Sue Lang, Frances Couch, and Kyle Matthews each played a key role in the organization and running of the conference. Tony would also like to acknowledge the love and support of Sally, Evie, and Clara. Antoinette would like to thank the Bastian Fund at the University of Illinois and the sponsors of the William Evans Fellowship at Otago for their support, as well as Paul, Nick, and Olivia for their love and patience.

Both editors would like to express their gratitude to Joan Catapano at the University of Illinois Press, who has been very supportive of this project from the outset. They would also like to thank the anonymous readers for the Press who provided detailed and constructive responses to earlier versions of the texts gathered here. Finally, a particular vote of thanks is due to the volume's contributors, who have embodied the ideals of collegiality and collaboration, as they have offered valuable feedback to the editors and responded so constructively to each others' essays. They have made the production of this volume a great pleasure.

Note on Orthography

Many of the essays collected here deal with non-European language materials. The scientific linguistic transcription of these languages from South Asia, Australasia, the Pacific, and North America follows a wide variety of conventions. In order to avoid a text that is weighed down with a range of diacritic systems, the authors have simply glossed all significant non-European terms to avoid any ambiguities that might arise from the absence of diacritics.

MOVING SUBJECTS

TONY BALLANTYNE AND
ANTOINETTE BURTON

Introduction

THE POLITICS OF INTIMACY
IN AN AGE OF EMPIRE

Capturing intimacy and its histories has become a preoccupation among scholars, especially among students of former European empires. Ann Stoler's recent exploration of the "tense and tender ties" of imperial governance and colonial knowledge production has helped to galvanize interest in the affective dimensions of global and transnational power. Her work has been central in shaping an emergent terrain of historical inquiry around the question of how "sentiments of a private nature"—to quote Haiti's minister of finance under the American occupation there in 1918—have not just facilitated imperial ambition, but serve as the very grounds for the creation and maintenance of imperial power.[1] Though it is too rarely acknowledged, recent interest in the recesses of the imperial body politic also owes a debt to several generations of feminist scholarship, which has problematized the presumptive dichotomy of public and private. This feminist work has also rigorously historicized the cultural and temporal contingencies of colonial domesticity—a domain that, despite even the efflorescence of research on house and home, remains comparatively undertheorized, at least compared to its correlative "public" stage, the imperial state. Nor should we neglect the impact of theoretical engagements on the problem of intimacy in the aftermath of Michel Foucault. These have been produced most often at the convergence of interdisciplinary projects and political exigencies, as Ann Cvetkovich's *Archive of Feelings*—a meditation on the everyday trauma

I

of queer communities made available in public culture—so powerfully demonstrates.[2] If the impulse toward intimacy is, pace Cvetkovich, a kind of therapeutic response to the relentlessly "sensational life" of late capitalism,[3] it ought also to be read as symptomatic of the challenge of reimagining the relationship between the social life of self and the global life of violence in an age of aggressive Anglo-American imperialism. In offering a set of genealogies of this contemporary challenge across a range of spaces during the high noon of an earlier (and arguably foundational) global order, our collection aims not so much to capture imperial and colonial intimacies as to materialize the histories of a variety of moving subjects who utilized a wide range of intimate opportunities and practices to negotiate, contest, and reconfirm the boundaries of rule.

Crucial to such a project is a reconceptualization of space as a technology of imperial power and anticolonial agency. To be sure, critically imperial histories over the past two decades have insisted on the importance of space and place in the imaginations of empire builders, colonial settlers, and native subjects, whether comprador elites or subalterns. Whereas a long-established tradition of imperial history approached empires through the lens of either economics or the elite politics, more recent scholarship has identified the culture of space as an object of analysis and as an interpretive grid for reinterpreting the colonial and imperial pasts. This diverse body of work has been particularly concerned with how the "rule of difference" and its regimes were constituted through the languages of popular politics, in domestic arrangements, in various forms of texts (from travel narratives to textbooks), and in the complex movement of commodities, ideas, and people across imperial systems.[4] The imperial past is no longer primarily accessed, in other words, through ledger books or parliamentary debates. Nuanced analyses of a range of cultural spaces— from the classroom to the hospital, the asylum to the family album, the nursery to the archive—have made it possible to understand how and why imperial power operated through the colonization of spatialized domains brought into the purview of the colonial state and its reformist agendas. Indeed, dominion meant precisely the deterritorialization and subsequent reterritorialization of all manner of public and private spaces. That is to say, empire was a *self-consciously* spatializing project, with colonizers attempting both to impose their own topographies on conquered space and—to the extent they were aware of or interested in local apprehensions of space on the ground—to unmake preexisting maps of native communities or refashion them to suit their own political, economic, and military ends. Historians have certainly been alive to this phenomenon: whether implicitly (as in Mrinalini Sinha's concept of "imperial social formation") or explicitly (as in recent monographs by Philippa Levine and Tony Ballantyne), the spatialization of empire has become an indispensable consideration for historicizing the material and symbolic operations of imperial ideologies and colonial practices.[5]

But as Doreen Massey has recently observed, the race for space in recent humanities scholarship has also tended to rob space itself of some of its more promising analytical possibilities. Space has, in the first instance, been largely imagined as "an expanse traveled across," emerging as a surface rather than as a constitutive factor in the creation and maintenance of social, political, and cultural relations.[6] Many of the contributions here break with this inherited view of space and instead imagine imperial locations as power-saturated sites of cultural conjuncture and contest: what Massey terms "meeting-up places." Moreover, as Massey also argues, the rush to embrace postmodern and postcolonial interpretations of the power of place has tended to produce a working notion of space as "the realm of the immobilized."[7] Our collection takes aim at this presumption by illustrating that imperial spaces did not emerge from either self-evident or static geographies; nor did they exist in mutual isolation. Acknowledging what Manu Goswami calls "the lived unevenness" of both imperial and colonial spaces, the essays here understand empire as the ground of consistently territorialized mobility—that is, to borrow again from Goswami, as the site of "a complex movement of accumulating interconnections within a specific global field."[8]

It is worth lingering on this proposition, since despite the emphasis on transnational flows and counterflows even in "new" imperial histories, space in this literature tends to work either as a surface across which people and things move or as the fixed site on which power and its capillaries are deployed and circumvented. These seemingly contradictory uses of space add up, ironically, to an evacuation of its radical potential for historical interpretation, in part because historians have tended to borrow the apparatus of spatiality wholesale from geographers rather than using it instrumentally so that it enables critical interrogations of the archive and serves the attendant analytical purposes of a critically antiimperial imperial history. What we are endeavoring to imagine here, then, is a somewhat more dynamic, even kinetic model: one where the ground or space itself is ever moving, and those operating on it find themselves routinely adjusting themselves—whether by choice or otherwise—to its perpetual motion. At one level, this approach echoes Eugene Irschick's insistence on the dialogic nature of colonial societies, whereby cultural formations were produced out of "the heteroglot and dialogic production of all members of any historical situation."[9] As valuable as this insight is, we reach beyond Irschick by insisting on the profoundly asymmetrical social relations produced out of colonialism *and* by arguing that these relations must be anchored in a critical reading of space that remains attentive to local contexts as well as the networks and exchanges that worked over long distances—especially *intracolonial* distances (New Zealand to Fiji as well as London to the Cape, for example) that were both created by and helped to produce what we now recognize as the globalizing forces of empire.

As an alternative to prevailing ideas about space, ours is no less metaphoric than other iterations when it comes to conjuring the territorial dynamics of empire. For all the kinetics involved in imperial space-making, the majority of subjects to be found in the following pages did not, of course, literally feel the ground moving beneath their feet. But whether they were agents of empire or its unwilling objects, the servants, aristocrats, fugitives, and fur-traders who appear here acted not as if the ground they inhabited—be it regional or translocal—were static, but as if its rifts and fissures, its uneven and unstable surfaces, were part of the regular (albeit anxiety-inducing) business of empire. Either in reaction or in anticipation, they seized on the intimacies of the leper colony, the colonial bureaucracy, the letter, and the bedroom in their capacity as *moving* subjects. What Elizabeth Vibert evocatively calls "the cold space[s] of empire" were animated, in short, by the collusions and collisions of imperial bodies with colonial power and colonial bodies with imperial regimes—fractious and chaotic encounters that, we contend, sponsored historically specific, and often politically unsettling, forms of intimacy across a variety of interconnected worlds.

As crucial as it is to rethink space in the historiography of colonial modernity, it is equally urgent to continue to extend the parameters of intimacy and to nuance its social, political, and cultural meanings—work begun by Stoler and her interlocutors, but in need of particular attention in the context of Anglo-American empire of the nineteenth, twentieth, and twenty-first centuries. Clearly the body is one place to begin when it comes to historicizing the domain of the intimate, and never more so than in colonial contexts, where bodies were the objects of coercion, discipline, and violence in ways not simply analogous to processes in the metropole but constitutive of them as well. Attention to bodies reveals the flesh and bone of empire, what Michael McDonnell calls in his essay on the family history of one métis community in the Great Lakes region "the connective sinews" of colonial desire, as practical policy and as fetish. We must also recognize that bodies furnish evidence, however ephemeral, of the failure of colonial hegemonies. As Ramón A. Gutiérrez has so eloquently written, "bodies [have] talked back, fought back, and actively resisted the technologies and regimes of their colonial lords"—thereby revealing the gap between aspiration and accomplishment when it came to conquest on the ground.[10] Our contention here is that more specifically as *mobile* subjects, all manner of bodies gave rise to an equally prolific set of intimacies that colonial regimes had to anticipate in order to create and sustain the kind of social order that would yield the labor, rent, and resources on which they depended. Our collection makes a case not simply for the necessity of a spatial analysis of imperial formations, but for the indispensability of an investigative approach that links space to movement through the messiness of the body and its attachments, which Adrienne Rich aptly calls "the geography closest in."[11]

As editors of a recent collection, *Bodies in Contact: Rethinking Colonial Encounters in World History* (2005), we argued that as a heuristic device and a subject in its own right, the body needs to be historicized in order to understand its global proportions *and* its role as an agent at the intersection of colonial and world histories.[12] The circuits of connectivity and disjuncture—the uneven development of the body as a subject of colonial histories in a global field—that this collection makes manifest continue that project, resuturing the intimate to modalities of imperial power and thereby providing intimacy with a deeper, more tentacled historical account than perhaps it has heretofore had. We intend this volume as a reorientation of the growing literature on globalization and its intersections with imperial and colonial histories, especially in light of what Ania Loomba has called the "overworlding" of the non-West.[13] Most examinations of the globalizing work of empires, particularly examinations of imperial "networks" or "webs," have focused on the mobility of ideologies, the exchanges of ideas, and the political debates that energized the extended public sphere fashioned by imperial print cultures. Conversely, studies of "intimate frontiers" or the "tense and tender ties" of empire have conceived of the intimate as operating as a profoundly localizing domain. In this view, crosscultural sexual relationships are seen as forces that "connect" or "anchor" white men into non-European communities and as enabling the emergence of both creolized and mestizo reworkings of Europeanness. In this scenario, mobility becomes the property of colonizers, and stasis the preternatural condition of the indigene. The local, in turn, is rendered as static and comes to represent the immobility of "primitive" cultures and civilizations, which are relentlessly acted upon by those subjects who colonize via settlement or the sword, with little attention to the structural connections between sexual intercourse and possession on the one hand and territorial expansion and security on the other. Whether consciously or not, work that advances these equations is in danger of reproducing imperial convictions about self and other, in part because of the methodological presumption that in the context of empire, the local is that which does not move and the native is the stationary object on whom intimacy is bestowed, visited, forced. Even and especially when intimate relations are interpreted as consensual, the agency of the indigenous subject (usually female, though not always) is rarely apprehended, let alone recognized as a subject of historical inquiry in its own right, a maneuver that arguably fixes it both outside time and determinedly in place: that is, in the no-man's-land of the historical imagination.[14]

Of equal if not greater concern is the way this story of the "localization" of European men and the possibilities of crosscultural emotional relationships has begun to be viewed as emblematic of imperial social formations that were unproblematically cosmopolitan, comparatively innocent of imperial power and, even more instructively, putatively "preracist."[15] Such a position has been forwarded most recently in William Dalrymple's White Mughals, which reconstructs the world of the East India Company's James Kirkpatrick, who converted to Islam and married the aristocratic Khair un-Nissa in Hyderabad in the late eighteenth century. Dalrymple's study has been enthusiastically received, especially in England, where the book has been read variously as a genealogy of imperial cosmopolitanism, a celebration of multiculturalism, and, in some sense, a recuperation of possibilities fashioned by empire building—again, apparently innocent of the sexual violence and coercion of empire. But, as Durba Ghosh reminds us, the political stakes attached to crossracial intimacy in both the past and present have varied greatly across time and place.[16] While stories of East India Company officials marrying local women in the eighteenth century in India might be feted by a British literary and social elite at the turn of the twenty-first century as emblematic of a British imperial cosmopolitan tradition, the racial and religious politics of intermarriage in working-class Bradford, Oldham, or London's East End have been and remain fraught—through a succession of imperial, postcolonial, and neoimperial ages.[17] Meanwhile, in South Asia itself, the history of interracial marriage in the colonial period elicits considerable moral, religious, and political discomfort, and attempts to recover these histories are often viewed with suspicion.[18]

A rather more critical version of the localization paradigm has driven recent work on intermarriage in Britain's Pacific empire. In contrast to Dalrymple's evocation of a cosmopolitanism borne out of crossracial intimacy, historians of colonialism in Australia, New Zealand, and the

Pacific have identified intimacy as a crucial instrument of colonization. Here intermarriage has figured as a key means by which white men gained access to the resources and land of indigenous communities. Judith Binney has contended, for example, that interracial relationships on the New Zealand frontier operated within a colonial "war-zone" and that marrying into indigenous communities allowed white men to pursue the "covert purpose" of gaining property rights.[19] Within this historiography, intermarriage is identified as diluting traditional lineages, as promoting migration away from ancestral lands, and as working as a key force in the fragmentation of long-established social formations. In other words, historians have argued that rather than merely existing as the space of intimacy, the localization of white men through intermarriage into indigenous communities played an instrumental role in allowing and extending white settlement. Such intermarriage is widely viewed, in short, as being a foundational technology of imperial rule, hardly innocent of the micro- and macropolitics of imperial ambition and desire, however imperfectly realized.[20] In the Australian context, of course, questions of intimacy are very much embedded in the historical debate over the "stolen generations"—the large numbers of indigenous and mixed-race children who were taken from their Aboriginal parents and placed under the care of whites as part of both humanitarian and state-sponsored efforts to "modernize" indigenous society.[21] An influential cohort of Australian historians has seen these interventions in indigenous social relations as instrumental to a broader state project that was genocidal in its aims and impact.[22] Thus, in Australasia, "histories of intimacy" have come to stand at the very heart of historical understandings of the brute realities of white settlement and colonial rule. The very different sensibilities of this work on intimacy and colonization in the southern Pacific and Dalrymple's *White Mughals* remind us of the divergent political stakes attached to the history of "race mixing," as well as the very different roles intimacy played in the development of various social colonial social formations.

The essays gathered here reassess the localization paradigm through their sensitivity to the complex relationships between intimacy and mobility in, across, and around a variety of imperial terrains. Among other things, our collection asks not just how intimacy was constructed but also how it was *embodied* across the restless world of empires, a world that depended on the circulation of capital and commodities, the exchange of systems of governance and surveillance, and the movement of laborers, slaves, soldiers, and settlers. Conversely, we inquire as to how various forms of mobility shaped a wide range of intimate relationships, including the connections between masters and servants, agents of empire and indigenous leaders, colonial ethnographers and the non-European objects of their gaze. To what extent was what Karen Chase and Michael Levenson have called "the spectacle of intimacy" legible to the makers of imperial politics?[23] To what extent indeed was its visibility one of the exigencies of colonial reform policies; and how did bodies on the move both capture and elude the gaze of those in charge of policing them? Given the ways imperial regimes were invested in governing the "unruly and unfulfilled passions" of their subjects, both European and native, how did the presence of mobile intimacies—whether state-sanctioned or transgressive—challenge the prescriptive norms of colonial powers throughout the imperial world?[24] Under what conditions did the domain of the intimate—imagined as private but always already unfolding in the various hybrid publics of colonial contact zones—serve as a carrier of some of the most spectacular and quotidian forms of violence, all in the name of civilization and uplift? How, in other words, did violence itself come to represent the territorial limit of imperial regimes of the most intimate kind, even as the intimacies of imperial violence reveal, to us, the impossibility of marking off the domain of the private as radically separate from that of the (imperial) public? And, not least, how do we assess the kinds of agency that subjects moving across these geographies of intimacy manifest without falling prey to facile, identitarian, and intersubjective notions of agency itself, and without essentializing "native" response (or worse, imagining native agency only as response)?

Not surprisingly, perhaps, a critical mass of contributors here focus either directly or indirectly on sexuality and more specifically on conjugality. These essays reconstruct a multidimensional field of intimate bodily matters that colonial regimes proved at times incapable of controlling, whether legally or in rhetorical terms, despite and of course because—as in the case of interracial marriage—they had serious political ramifications for the imperial body politic. And yet as Mary Renda has noted in her response to Stoler's "tense and tender ties" thesis, it would be a mistake to read the body and sexuality as either equivalent to or coterminous with the intimate—or we would add, the self—per se. Like Stoler, we acknowledge the importance of Foucault's insight that sexuality has operated as a particularly important "dense transfer point" in power relations; but we also acknowledge the broader investigative possibilities that attention to the body and/or the history of intimacy has the capacity to yield for a nuanced understanding of both individual and collective agency.[25] As Matt Matsuda and Vicente Rafael have worked to historicize the phenomenon of love and empire, we attempt to do the same with the pleasures and anxieties—indeed, the anxious mobilities—of imperial and colonial life. The figures enumerated in these essays were people who moved through a variety of "tender scenes," exchanging what Rafael calls "white love for brown affection." In so doing, they experienced the perpetually disorienting unevenness of those transactions—and enable us, in turn, to see the limits of an often-presumed "white-other" boundary.[26] Our emphasis is more deliberately on the domains that sexual intimacy opens onto—like Rafael and in keeping with the work of feminist historians, we reject, both implicitly and implicitly, the notion that the private and the public are segregated one from the other—and we more purposefully nominate mobility as a constitutive factor in the social life of sentiment and its multiple articulations. For after all, bodies are not inscribed with meaning only through sexual desire. They have historically been made and given meaning through various political, economic, and social-cultural processes, including, but not restricted to, reproduction, work, conversion, legislation, and travel. All of these obtained in the context of constant flux and motion—and in the presence, or under the threat, of imperial violence, whether real or imagined, and with enormous historical consequence for individual subjects acting in their own interests or against them, whether purposefully or not.

If the essays gathered here are consistently alive to the multiple contexts and contestations of affect, then, they insist on the links between intimacy and intimidation as well. Pushing the frontiers of intimacy beyond the sexual, a number of the essays that follow track the geographies of imperial and colonial intimacy into courtrooms, onto docks and ships, even into the offices of colonial bureaucracy. In so doing they reveal how far the reach of the "imperial erotic" might extend.[27] They also illuminate intimate worlds as globalized and globalizing fields of coercion: as "local" domains constrained and remade by the power of the imperial state and its agents and—to a lesser degree—constraining the full material and/or rhetorical force of the jackboot, the gavel, the blood-quantum test, and the gun. In the process, they demonstrate that the local is a matter of standpoint and scale, a question of vantage point as well as of structural location, a mechanism for fixings subjects in space. In this sense the global view purports to have a magnifying effect on the local—when in fact that view more often than not establishes the scales of hierarchy and value against which locals are then measured. If the intimate comes into view most often as the local, and does so typically through the distorted and distorting lens of violence, it is in fact rarely either wholly local or entirely subject to the modalities of rule, territorial or otherwise. To borrow from Shani D'Cruze and Anu Rao, the intimate is one of the enabling grounds on which imperial power, in all its *translocality* and instability, has historically operated.[28] Here we employ the term *translocal* as a way of dwarfing the global: as a means of recognizing the spatial logics and the spatializing violence that global visions can and often do produce. Not least, we offer it as a corrective to how the binary of local-global can distort our apprehension of how gender operates, especially where the local (as in Dalrymple, quoted earlier) is taken to be coterminous with the feminine, the supine, and the stationary. The stakes of resisting such a gendered territorial logic are undoubtedly high. For the space of intimacy makes gender legible and heterosexuality normative most often when it is taken to be "simply local." Insisting on the translocality of imperial spaces—*and on the fact that subjects gain subjectivity precisely by moving in and through them*—has the potential, we think, to render the gender politics of global systems more complex and the intimacies of empire more available to critical analysis as well.[29]

We want to underscore that in staking these claims, our aim is emphatically not to herald the domain of intimacy as some kind of pure space, at one remove from the variety of forces—political, socioeconomic, and of course military—through which the British Empire, for all its complexity on the ground, routinely attempted to discipline the objects of its rule. To the contrary, appreciating the material conditions under which global empires were—and are—created and sustained by a host of "moving subjects" helps to refigure imperialism not merely as a territorial project but as an exercise in affect management with high stakes: an intimate business at all levels of power and hegemony, and especially so given the plethora of subjects constantly on the move in and through the spaces of empire. Nor do we wish necessarily to suggest that the intimate is *the* or even a primary means through which colonizer and colonized have negotiated their encounters, in part because to do so is merely to invert the highly gendered binary of rationality versus affect that undergirds modern imperial rhetorics and practices, of the twenty-first-century as well as the Victorian kind. Histories of intimacy and its shifting ground open up new ways of apprehending imperial power, but they do so in conjunction with other forms and objects of analysis, not in place of them. In addition to being material, histories of intimacy are perforce relational, even when they trace ruptures and disjunctions. By excavating a wide variety of historically contingent relationships between space and intimacy, the essays here offer something more modest than a whole new paradigm for thinking about the politics of intimacy in the age of empire. They provide a range of *new vantage points* on the role of intimacy in shaping some of the most significant outcomes of imperial social life—vantage points that underscore the multiple contingent spaces from which and through which the affective bonds of empire drew any number of imperial agents and colonial peoples into their orbit, spinning new and unlooked-for examples of the fractured and fragmented character of imperial power.

Although our contributors write from a wide array of archival sources, nearly half of them are working either in or from the antipodes; and if we count those who focus on Canada and the United States, we have a majority of pieces that capitalize on the particular "angles of vision" on the British Empire that are available from colonies of white settlement.[30] The connections between intimacy and mobility are particularly striking in settler colonies, whether in North America or Australasia, because of the centrality of migration and demographic domination as instruments of colonization. Unlike other imperial formations, such as the plantation colonies of the Caribbean or the military-garrison state of British India, settler colonialism ultimately rested on the transplantation and settlement of large white populations, a process that was dependent on both the alienation of indigenous land and the orchestration of the movement of settlers over vast distances from their European "homelands" to the colonies. In effect, indigenous communities were "swamped" by the settlers, some of whom sought to recreate home and its intimacies, some of whom stumbled into intimate relations, and some of whom exploited their own compatriots and/or native peoples purposefully, carelessly, or both.[31] In 1860, the Kai Tahu Maori leader John Paratene imagined colonization as a "rising tide" that was submerging Maori land, an image echoed by another Maori leader, Wi Naihera, who described the process of settlement and colonization as "when the waves rolled in upon us from England."[32] That metaphor of engulfment captures the new, intrusive forms of both intimacy and social distance—the ebb and flow of imperial power relations—that colonized peoples quickly came to understand as characteristic of the imperial orders they were compelled to grapple with.

In the context of such new imperial orders, mobility and intimacy operated at the forefront of colonial processes, but were woven together in a range of different domains and discourses as well. Acknowledging the embeddedness of intimate spaces in many aspects of social and cultural life, our contributors address intimacy in the context of commercial transactions, political struggles, martial law, domestic service, and literary production—events high and low that played out in "private" relationships as well as in the imperial public sphere; in the recesses of hospital wards as well as bedrooms; in the context of open-air marriage ceremonies and personal diaries; in the lives of an earl's daughter, a grave digger's son, a Hawaiian leprosy victim, and a London "gypsy." These authors presume that intimacy "does not work within the same territorial and jurisdictional logics that demarcate privacy," in part because they recognize that the dichotomy of public versus private is one historical effect of exigencies of imperial social order as a spatial project itself.[33] In the end, this collection argues that histories of empire must not only take account of the politics of space but also understand how and why mobilities of the most intimate kind framed the very bases on which imperial power was designed and enacted. Thus these essays figure the intimate not merely as a domain of power but as one of the technologies available to colonizer and colonized alike in the struggle over colonial territory, imperial goods, and the meanings of global aspiration—from the American West to Fiji, from Portuguese India to colonial New Zealand, from Hawai'i to eighteenth-century London. These essays map new cartographies for the history of intimacy in the age of empire: cartographies of sociality and association, of conversion and coercion, of desire and disavowal—of the wide range of affective relations, in short, that animated British imperial ambition, its unwilling subjects, and its boosters in their many guises.

The book begins with a set of essays that operate from very particular vantage points—Captain Cook's first contact, whaling stations, a Nova Scotia mission, the Yorkshire moors, letters exchanged between Charlotte Brontë and Mary Taylor, steamships crossing the Pacific, a conference in Hawai'i—that in turn open onto gendered worlds of travel and migration, exile and adventure. The essays in part 1 rematerialize the full range and analytical potential of intimacy, examining the ways it structured and was structured by the greatly extended spatial domain of imperial systems. Rachel Standfield's chapter on the initial moment of contact in Poverty Bay, where Cook's ship *Endeavour* landed on the east coast of New Zealand's North Island, makes indubitably clear the costs—in terms of historical nuance, narrative cogency, and interpretive power—of casting the colonial encounter as merely intimate, rather than as fully enmeshed in the social relations of violence that constituted, in this case, a very early Antipodean "endeavor." Her account of the death of the Maori warrior Te Maro reveals how quickly the triumph of a voyage across long distances was telescoped into a very local event—a series of beach-side murders—as well as how Joseph Banks's close readings of Te Maro's body established a morbidly intimate discourse in which scientific collection, territorial security, and ethnographic knowledge were bound up one with the other. Here mobility is the very sine qua non of such intimate violence: it is precisely the "daring" attempts of Maori to escape and resist—their determination to control the shifting ground of an emergent imperial outpost—that is used to justify both their killing and the subsequent intrusions into their corpses and, ultimately, their homelands as well. Standfield is especially insightful when she argues that for all the vulnerability Europeans may have experienced in the face of such intimate encounters of empire, such vulnerability was productive rather than inhibiting of violence. Without diminishing the force of physical violence to which Maori were subject, her analysis insists on the ways that force legitimated Banks and others as intimate observers of indigenous bodily forms and functions—from the characteristics of the Maori dead to their dances, their tattoos, their familial relations. Although imperial claims to authority about these domains was quickly naturalized as the right and privilege of the conquering power, we have an opportunity to see here how such intimate knowledges were mobilized from the very first moment of contact.

With David Haines's essay, our attention shifts from the role of intimacy and violence in producing imperial knowledge in first contact situations to the role of conjugality in consolidating crossracial relationships on imperial frontiers. Haines reconstructs the place of sexual relationships between Euro-American whalers and Ngai Tahu Maori women in the development of shore whaling during the 1830s and 1840s on Banks Peninsula, on the east coast of New Zealand's South Island. Haines focuses on the trajectory of Joseph Price, an English sailor who traveled widely in the Pacific before establishing a whaling station at Ikoraki on Banks Peninsula in 1839. He highlights the importance of sexual relationships in Price's Pacific sojourn, paying particular attention to Price's relationship with his "local" wife, a Ngai Tahu woman named Akarie. Haines demonstrates both the precarious position of whalers' indigenous wives and the importance of such relationships to the Ngai Tahu communities of Banks Peninsula, who had suffered heavy military defeats at the hands of northern tribes and who lagged behind kinspeople who had established important connections with Europeans from the 1790s. Drawing on Gayatri Chakravorty Spivak's essay "The Rani of Sirmur," an influential reflection on the production of colonial knowledge and the multiple silences that structure imperial archives, Haines highlights the fragmentary nature of the archival remains left by the whalers and the profound challenges confronting historians who wish to reconstruct the agency, not to mention the subjectivity, of the indigenous women who were so central in the development of extractive industries at the margins of empire.[34]

From the intimate spaces of the whaling station we turn to those of the mission station in Elizabeth Vibert's account of the life and times of Murdoch Stewart, a Scottish missionary who emigrated to Nova Scotia in the 1840s and left a rich and evocative memoir of the affective ties of family life thousands of miles away from home. Vibert's aim is to "unpick the full, fine fabric of colonial domestic lives," and in Stewart's memoir she recovers the bathos of how the loneliness of exile combined with the exigencies of missionary manhood to produce a life history documenting Stewart's painful struggle with familial longing and disappointment. The dynamic of fraternal admiration and muted competition Vibert is able to conjure through Stewart's writing about his brother Donald powerfully evokes his tortured pathway to acceptable masculinity via the intimate histories of natal family life. In many respects, Donald both shadows and structures the memoir's narrative plot, which rises and falls on memories of his small kindnesses and exemplary deportment, breaks off with Murdoch's arrival in Cape Breton, and resumes woefully with the news of Donald's death. To be sure, Murdoch Stewart chronicles, almost dutifully, his encounter with the settlers—though never one with the native Mi'kmaq presence—and with the small community of Scots who offered him Christian fellowship. But as Vibert suggests, it is Murdoch's soulful preoccupation with his brother's example that in effect substitutes for the intimacies he apparently could not find in either his work or in his family of choice (wife and children). The distant and eventually deceased metropolitan brother is the affective center of this colonial archive, which offers us merely a glimpse of how the "wilds" of colonial settlement shaped the emotional lives of those of its subjects who felt stranded in and by empire.

In marked contrast, the correspondence between Charlotte Brontë and her friend Mary Taylor demonstrates that in other contexts, affective centers are very much on the move in this period, sustained by long-distance correspondence that has the capacity to conjure presence as well as absence, the feel of metropolitan life and the smell of colonial docks, the rhythms of literary celebrity and the mundane routines of commercial life on the edges of empire. Charlotte Macdonald's accomplished essay brings the interconnected world of friendship between two Victorian women into bold relief, tracking what she calls "the intimacy of the envelope" across "the highway that empire made possible" between Yorkshire and Wellington at what was to prove the beginning of Brontë's legendary literary career. Macdonald effectively localizes the story of Brontë's celebrity, not merely by routing it through the affective circuits of her correspondence with Taylor but also by rendering it coeval with the story of Taylor's own career as an independent woman of commerce at midcentury. So we get to see Brontë's rising fortunes from afar, as Taylor did, "in the midst of [the] barrels and goods" that surrounded her as she read about the success of her friend's novels both in newspapers that came into her shop and through Brontë's own missives to her. Among the many insights of Macdonald's analysis is her observation that the intimacies of reading need to be understood as part of the connective fabric of empire, not simply acting "outside the limits of time and space" but enabling each woman to defy the parameters of both. For as Mary so eloquently put it, "I can hardy explain to you the queer feeling of living as I do in 2 places at once . . . the separation is as complete as between the things in a picture & the things in a room. The puzzle is that both move and act & [I] must say my say as one of each." This simultaneity of worlds that Mary, was able to experience through her intimate epistolary ties to Charlotte is quite extraordinary, especially as she appears also to have recognized the kinetic relationship between the "puzzle" pieces—the interconnected world of empire that she and Charlotte inhabited—that moved and acted in concert with and against the grain of her own speech acts via letter. For all that these intimacies occurred between pages and in the imaginations of the two women, Macdonald is remarkably skilled at evoking the material worlds of home and away in which such imaginative affections were forged and sustained without at the same time romanticizing their friendship. This is in part because she is at pains to show how that friendship is "a relation of multiple strands rather than a continuous surface to cross." By representing their intimate bonds as filaments moving in time and space rather than as a flat surface on which they rest, Macdonald mobilizes the very model of critical spatiality our collection aims to offer as a counter to more conventional modes of thinking about place. Even more edifying, she does so by drawing directly, and with interpretive élan, from the translocal field that Brontë and Taylor themselves left us evidence of.

Frances Steel's study of the shipping and maritime culture of the Fijian port of Suva returns us to the dynamic of mobility and fixity by opening with an account of the wharf: the stationary site where so much of the movement of empire's material goods and peoples occurs but that in Steel's hands is a prismatic vantage point from which to view the ever-shifting terrain of imperial communication, transportation, and commercial networks. If the wharf is also a partly indigenized space, occupied in this instance by Fijians, Steel insists that it must be read for the temporalities it reveals. For Suva is, in her view, as much a moment in/of social relations as it is a space of encounter—a claim that echoes

Mary Taylor's image of the puzzle, with pieces that move simultaneously in one direction (in space) and another (in time). Unlike Taylor, whose labor is petty bourgeois, Suva's workers lay hands on the goods and barrels of empire—a fact that, in conjunction with the exigencies of translocal capital, requires them to move through the interconnected world of empire and back and forth between ports of call in Australia and New Zealand as well. Unsurprisingly, given the histories of orientalism and primitivism particular to the Pacific, Suva's laborers were viewed—by everyone from passing tourists to the more anchored employees of the Union Steam Ship Company—as weak and dangerous, as savages and vagrants. The linguistic and ethnic diversity of these "natives" was, moreover, frequently invisible to European "locals," who scarcely appreciated the vectors of labor, migration, and conjugality that brought Tongans, Samoans, and Rotumans as well as men of mixed Fijian and European ancestry to ports like Suva—a reminder of how the shifting ground of Britain's global empire was inexorably shaped by indigenous mobility as much as by its imperial variants, if not more so. The space of intimacy in Steel's essay is the recruitment ground, where the mobile men of the Pacific region were conscripted. Though most of them never were able to come close to the branch office, Steel shows how the Union Steam Ship Company's agent Alex Duncan lived in fear of that particular "official business" space being breached by traders—a breach of commercial and racial sovereignty that posed significant risks to the political economy of social distance on the ground, even as it testified to the perils of endeavoring to manage moving subjects like manual laborers at one remove.

The final essay in part 1 assesses the connections between travel, race, and politics. Fiona Paisley offers a rich cultural reading of performance of racial identities at the 1934 Pan-Pacific Women's Conference in Honolulu. Focusing on the figure of Elsie Andrews, the pakeha[35] leader of the New Zealand delegation to that conference, Paisley examines the uses of intimacy in interwar "cosmopolitan" feminism. In both the formal and social occasions that made up the Honolulu conference, the pakeha members of the delegation emphasized their knowledge, in reality hastily acquired en route to Honolulu, of Maori culture, dance, and language. The New Zealand delegation's presentation to the conference was a carefully choreographed affair, with a bilingual address in which Andrews began by speaking in Maori and Victoria Te Amohau Bennett, a pioneering Maori feminist from an influential Anglican family, concluded by offering an English translation for the international audience. While this address was in keeping with the conference's main concerns, as it emphasized the bonds of "sisterhood" that linked both Maori and pakeha to women from around the world, it drew considerable attention because of the prominence it gave to indigenous language and performance traditions. As Paisley argues, this emphasis on the significance of Maori culture was crucial to both Andrews's own self-fashioning as a pakeha, a person who was to some extent transformed by her intimacy and knowledge of things Maori, and in the presentation of New Zealand as an exemplary site of interracial amity and cooperation. Of course, the Hawaiian location where this intimacy was staged underscored the mobility of elites like Andrews and Bennett even while the performance of the New Zealand delegation contained Maori as a "local" phenomenon. As Paisley notes, indigenous Hawaiians recognized the standing and influence of Maori women like Bennett, thereby puncturing Andrews's attempts to position herself as guiding Maori women into the "global" world of internationalist politics. And, of course, emphasizing interracial harmony and friendship for an elite international audience unfamiliar with the details of New Zealand's colonization in the cosmopolitan Pacific was in almost certainly easier than making such claims at "home," even as the presence of Maori in Hawai'i opened up the spatial possibilities of the Pacific itself. Paisley's essay ends by underscoring the unevenness of the global political terrain aspired to by feminist internationalists and the power dynamics that shaped that uneven ground as well. Although the New Zealand delegation to the Honolulu conference emphasized the intimacy and hence the equality that supposedly linked Maori and Pakeha, when Andrews returned home, she was convinced that Maori culture had to be "saved" by pakeha humanitarians and activists like herself; the friendship staged before the world was ultimately displaced at home by the responsibilities of a settler maternalism.

Part 2 focuses on the sexual encounters at the heart of migration and colonial contact. Our invocation of an economy of affect follows from Sarah Ahmed, who has asked challenging questions about how emotions "move between bodies," both individual and national, not just as the possession or property of subjects but as an interpretive grid through which self and home, love and the nation, are reproduced in and for audiences at various levels of the imperial social order.[36] The essays included here examine the role of conjugality in such economies and offer critical reassessments of existing readings of empire and intimacy in the contexts of colonial war, imperial commerce, genealogies of marriage, mixed and otherwise, and debates over national-imperial sovereignty. We begin with Michael McDonnell's lively account of Angelique Langlade's family history, which tells the tale of several mestizo generations in North America's Great Lakes region (or *pays d'en haut*). The families whose stories Langlade gave voice to (via an almost accidentally recorded oral interview) faced a variety of "strategic crossroads"—racial, territorial, commercial, and historiographical—that tell us much about how the intimate experiences of conjugal space shaped political, economic, and cultural outcomes. As might be expected, the men and women of the Langlade family served as cultural brokers and economic mediators in the largely fur-trading economy of the region for over a century and a half. Within this context, interracial marriages facilitated the creation of a middle ground, a joint Algonquian-French empire based on the incorporation of both Indians into European society, and Europeans into Algonquian families. These social arrangements allowed some players in the regional trade to navigate across a wide swath of territory (from Duluth to Marquette to southern Ontario) as well as across several communities of natives (the Ojibwa, the Ottawa, and others). And as McDonnell notes, for the Indian, French, and métis people who inhabited the *pays d'en haut*, the political boundaries of the eighteenth- and nineteenth-century imperial order were less confining in terms of their experience as moving subjects than received understandings of imperial regimes might suggest. Indeed, these people were often used to facilitate mobility and persistence within and across those boundaries: they roamed far and wide both topographically and in terms of their conjugal lives. What remains striking is the extent to which, by all accounts, stories like those of Angelique's family remain limited in historical accounts, in part because many works on crosscultural encounters end at the American Revolution and in part because long *durée* family histories like hers are rare enough. In addition to providing evidence of how the intimacies of *metissage* impact the life of a family and in turn link a series of spaces contrapuntally with dominant maps of the Great Lakes before 1900, the narratives of the Langlade men and women retold here allow Native American history to move into new, heretofore invisible terrains, both temporal and spatial.

The essays that make up the remainder of part 2 offer a remarkable opportunity to examine the phenomenon of conjugality at work in public and private in a range of colonial and imperial spaces. As Paul D. Barclay has observed in his study of interethnic marriage in colonial Taiwan, there are currently two explanatory frameworks for the pattern of mixed marriage offered by scholars of the phenomenon in the Americas, Africa, and Asia. One is the "middle ground thesis," which has been advanced nominally by Richard White and emphasizes the accommodationist regimes of early modern settlement with respect to "the customs of the country." The other is what Barclay calls a more "metro-centric" model that "emphasizes European anxieties about racial mixture."[37] On offer in the trio of essays that follow McDonnell's is a ratification of those two frameworks and a reorientation of them as well. For the Cherokee case detailed by Kerry Wynn, Katherine Ellinghaus's comparative aboriginal/ Native American research, and Christine Skwiot's Hawaiian account all sketch the emergence of sexual relationships at the margins of empires that transgressed racial boundaries, producing new cultural affiliations that crisscrossed the divide between colonized and colonizer. At the same time, however, each of these authors also reveals colonial regimes' concern about those relationships and the efforts of these regimes, in the U.S. west, in Hawai'i, and in Australia, to order and police these relationships. What is salutary about each of these cases, then, is the ways they move beyond the "accommodationist" and "anxiety" models to trace the centrality of the intimate in the political culture of colonial regimes, where debates about sovereignty routinely drew on those models but in the main tended to absorb them into larger discussions about the governability of the body politic. In this sense, seeing like an imperial state (to borrow from James Scott) meant exploiting a universe of meanings about intimacy, an agenda that allows us to appreciate how much those apparently antithetical models have in common—if only as the lineaments of emergent imperial protocols for the juridical subject on the move.[38]

Kerry Wynn's reading of the spectacle of conjugality in the American West highlights the pivotal role of intimacy in generating a symbolic repertoire and the languages of politics within a colonial situation that featured populations locked in the kinetic embrace of mobility and incarceration. Here, the expansion of the sovereignty of the United States into the West and the incorporation of Oklahoma into the Union were, together, framed by supporters of Oklahoma's statehood as a marriage. Wynn argues that in effect this imperial possession-taking was naturalized when it was imagined as a "union" between Oklahoma Territory and Indian Territory. This initiative to collapse the boundaries of the Cherokee nation and alienate Cherokee sovereignty was strongly resisted by many Cherokee leaders who wanted to reaffirm and protect the boundaries of the two nations. In Oklahoma and elsewhere in the American West, marriage, both symbolic and real, became an invaluable instrument of colonization, a potent way of accessing indigenous land and enlarging the boundaries of an imperial nation-state.

Christine Skwiot's examination of early twentieth-century Hawai'i also places intimacy at the heart of its reading of the cultural appropriation and political struggles of the colonial order. Skwiot is attentive to ways that intimacy figured in the Hawaiian world, specifically through

genealogies that defined social identities, access to resources, and political power. She attends equally to the ways American interests both
appropriated these forms of knowledge and deployed them to legitimate
colonial rule. Indeed, she reads genealogies as intimate knowledges, intimate histories, that exercised tremendous political leverage precisely
through their affective power in debates that went to the very heart of
convictions about the parameters of sovereignty, dominion, and rule.
Specifically, she demonstrates the ways the Hawaii Promotion Committee mobilized the genealogies of Nakuina and Princess Abigail Kawaa-
nanakoa, both daughters of *ali'i* wives and haole sugar-planter husbands,
as part of their project to depict colonial Hawai'i as the "consensual
outcome of a long history of crosscultural marriage and governance"
at a moment when, as Noenoe K. Silva has shown, powerful Hawaiian
voices contested the legitimacy of American rule.[39] That struggles over
the double meanings of "consensuality" were framed through accounts
of intimate family histories is just one indication of how powerfully the
affective grammars of empire shaped—and continue to shape—the global
fortunes of anticolonial resistance. It is also a testimony to how embedded such grammars were in the many modes of imperial re/production
that mobility enabled and in the practices of rule that mobility could
sometimes thwart.[40]

Last in part 2 is Katherine Ellinghaus's study of intimacy and American
empire in a comparative context. By tacking back and forth between the
United States and Australia, she offers a comparatively rare examination of
the divergent state practices and popular understandings of intermarriage
between whites and indigenous peoples in Australia, where intermarriage
was understood as a way of "diluting" and "absorbing" native blood, and
the United States, where intermarriage between Native Americans and
Europeans was seen as an important means of elevating the indigenous
peoples and preparing them for the exercise of political rights. Central to
her story is the connection between conjugality, race, and citizenship, a
set of linkages with far-reaching contemporary resonances; for she offers
a persuasive reminder of the political stakes attached to intimacy within
multiethnic societies. Ellinghaus insists that assimilation, a central ideology for the management of racial difference in the early twentieth century,
was not simply a means of managing cultural difference, but functioned
as a central instrument in nation-making—differentially perhaps in the
two white settler contexts, but always structured by the sentimental logics and rationalizing exigencies of the "frontier" empire.

In part 3, we engage the phenomenon of particular bodies on the move
and the often triangular routes through which intimacies can be tracked

(Portuguese/British/Indian; Gypsies/Londoners/Britons; Canadian/French/ Aboriginal). The essays here are linked by a concern with the ways intimacy erupted into the public sphere of print and politics and generated fierce debates over the governance of intimacy within multiracial imperial contexts. Part 3 opens with Adrian Carton's assessment of the connections between crossracial intimacy and the construction of whiteness in early colonial India. Carton offers an analysis of the cultural forms that emerged at one important node—Portuguese India, especially Goa—within the new global systems that emerged out of European states' aggressive search for new sea-lanes, markets, and colonial possessions from the late fifteenth century on. Charting the contestations over and reshaping of cultural boundaries in India between 1500 and the late eighteenth century, his essay highlights the power of whiteness not simply as an imperial discourse but also as a set of devotional and affective attachments in the early modern period—and in so doing, echoes the call of Irene Silverblatt and others that we be mindful of how we periodize modernity as well as attentive to the pre-Enlightenment histories of imperial forms, whether bureaucratic or representational.[41] As his evidence suggests, while early modern literary texts produced from within Europe dwelt on the fantastic possibilities and monstrous consequences of miscegenation, on the distant frontiers of European maritime empires, "inter-racial intimacy was not spectacular and extraordinary but absorbed into the politics of everyday life." The establishment of intimate relationships across the boundaries of race and religion and the development of culturally mixed family groups was an essential element of the Portuguese colonial project in South Asia, providing a robust social foundation for Portuguese commercial activity and colonial governance. Most important, perhaps, Carton directs us to the importance of religion in managing cultural difference. The Catholic Church accepted the children produced out of the marriages between Portuguese men and local women, and in most cases these mixed-race children also enjoyed the rights of Portuguese subjects. He notes that even though this mixed-race community was marked as different by their physical appearance, its members were routinely identified as "European" and "Catholic" in the records produced by the Portuguese, underscoring the centrality of Catholicism as a symbolic field for the definition of whiteness within this specific context.

As the essays in part 3 illustrate, the scandal of intimate imperial spaces derived in large measure from the boundaries—physical and identitarian—that the subjects at hand willfully traversed. Carton notes that the term "Portuguese" itself was quite capacious in early modern India, as it signified a Christian community defined by faith rather than biological race (and as such encompassed Europeans other than those from Portugal, such as Danes or the Dutch, mixed-race Eurasians, and various "Europeanized Indians"). Carton's essay concludes by sketching how this cultural order was transformed by the growing ascendancy of the English East India Company in the late eighteenth century. Early agents of the Company in India married "Portuguese" Catholic Eurasian women and were willing to have their children baptized as Catholics, but by the 1780s English suspicions about the political loyalties of South Asian Catholics had deepened and few Company men made this marriage choice. Interracial and interdenominational intimacy were eroded as the Company's authority as a territorial power produced a new concern with the policing of racial boundaries and the articulation of a clear cultural divide between ruler and ruled. As Durba Ghosh has argued elsewhere, "the grammar of racial categories" is always a dynamic one: rarely linear or progressive, it depends on the contingencies of imperial rule and operates selectively when it comes to the consolidation of whiteness especially.[42]

Dana Rabin's essay takes up a different iteration of this dynamic racial grammar, directing our attention to an eighteenth-century scandal of intimacy "at home" in Britain. She explores the ways space, cultural difference in manifold forms, and social standing were produced in a dramatic set of mid-eighteenth-century legal proceedings. The focus of Rabin's essay is the alleged kidnapping of Elizabeth Canning, an eighteen-year-old servant, from her home in the East End of London in 1753. Canning alleged that Mary Squires, a "gypsy," had arranged her abduction and imprisonment with the aim of turning her into a prostitute and that Squires was aided by Susannah Wells, a reputed brothel keeper. Rabin traces the fevered public debate over these allegations and reconstructs the path of the case through the legal system. By historicizing how metropolitan anxieties over difference played out in both the legal and cultural domains, this essay underscores the very real stakes attached to discourses of difference within England and especially within London, its multiethnic and religiously diverse metropole. Like the category of the "Europeanized Indian" of Carton's essay, the "gypsy" in Rabin's story is (to cite Stuart Hall) a floating signifier. A stock character with genealogies that predate the eighteenth century, its fungibility as an affective touchstone is directly proportional to the mobility of (here) the highly sexualized, ex-centric female subjects linked to it.[43] By stressing the connections between mobility, race, and sexuality, Rabin is able to highlight both the deeply felt anxieties about the "vagrancy" of gypsies and the broader concerns about personal identity and integrity produced by the economic and demographic forces that were transforming British society in the second half of the eighteenth century.

She rightly insists that these concerns were particularly focused on presumptively white, "native" women who were seen as the guardians of national character, embodiments of the virtue and chastity that marked the English off—or so they believed—from both colonized peoples and the cultures of the continent.

Both Carton and Rabin are concerned with the ways empire building called established understandings of status into question and generated new discourses that attempted to regulate and order the multiple forms of cultural difference that were the fundamental demographic reality of empire—often at the site of scandalous encounters, sexual and otherwise. Kirsten McKenzie approaches these questions from a different vantage point as she examines the place of authority and servitude in the Cape colony at the turn of the nineteenth century. Her essay focuses on the fortunes of Lady Anne Barnard and her servant Samuel Hudson in southern Africa, exploring the deep anxieties over rank and the dramatic social reversals that were part and parcel of colonial life. While the colonies offered opportunities for financial gain and political advancement, the instability and precariousness of colonial societies presented many risks as well. Hudson, for example, left Barnard's employ and initially prospered, owning a farm, a house, and a hotel in Cape Town, and fifteen slaves. But his fortunes reversed abruptly as the family business collapsed; Thomas, his brother and business partner, committed suicide, and Samuel was declared bankrupt. At the heart of McKenzie's story are the ways the political significance of intimacy, whether in the form of patronage in the political sphere or in the quotidian forms of closeness associated with domestic labor, was radically transformed between 1790 and 1830. Aristocratic political dominance, which had been grounded in long-established patterns of patronage and complex social networks, was not only called into question by "scandalous" radicals arguing for the rapid transformation of the franchise but was also increasingly displaced in the political sphere by new models of bureaucratic governance.[44] McKenzie's examination of how Lady Anne Barnard and Samuel Hudson navigated these shifts as they played out in southern Africa reminds us of the complex ways intimacy was threaded through the structures of family life, labor, and political activity—and how their eruption in the historical record is linked precisely to the mobility of differently disruptive subjects of empire.

Whereas McKenzie traces the importance of the intimate in determining social status and political power, Adele Perry's essay demonstrates the analytical possibilities of the intimate when it is not read simply as a synonym for conjugality but rather as encompassing the wide processes of family formation, processes that embrace domesticity, child-rearing, love, and various forms of companionship. Perry's arguments are grounded in her analysis of a trial that brought intimate questions to the forefront of public life in mid- to late-nineteenth-century British Columbia. Here we see in vivid detail how the pathologies of white settler colonialism mapped onto the wider webs of intimacy sponsored by the encounter between aboriginal family formation and the hybrid worlds invariably produced by empire. The trial of Mary Ann M. and her cousin for the poisoning of Mary Ann's father, James—and the print culture coverage of the trial in local newspapers—allows us to grasp in concrete terms some of the explanatory limits of conjugality as an analytical category. To be sure, and as Perry acknowledges, the project of modern empire has been a reproductive one. But as she also illustrates, Mary Ann circulated in a series of social worlds in which child-care, labor, and "the shared maternal territory" of the Fraser River operated as dense transfer point for affection, violence, and power. If conjugality and heterosexual sex are not exactly beside the point, they emerge in the public scandal of the trial as just one of many nodes on the network of colonial intimacy. Not least, Perry reminds us of the multidimensional nature of British Columbia's multicultural landscapes—with African Americans, Chinese, and Hawaiian Kanakas living, working, fighting, and dying alongside white settlers and aboriginal peoples, thereby complicating any facile binary of colonizer versus colonized, male versus female, or heterosocial versus homosexual. Indeed, precisely because of the mobilities that structured people's access to land and livelihood, their solidarities and practices worked in kinetic tension with the realities of colonial political economy and the petty inequities (pace Perry) of colonial power—yielding traces of the variety of sexual practices sponsored by the collision of moving subjects with the reterritorializing force of imperial rule.

The final essay in part 3, Michelle Moran's analysis of leprosy in colonial Hawai'i, raises a series of issues that are of considerable importance to thinking about the history of intimacy under modernity: the authority of Western medicine, the power of the state to police communities as a whole as well as the bodies of individuals, and the spaces within which resistance can be articulated. The essay's starting point is the colonial state's effort to locate and round up indigenous Hawaiians suffering from leprosy during the 1890s. This initiative was resisted by many Hawaiians, most notably by a man named Ko'olau of the Kalalau Valley, who shot and killed Louis Stolz, a health agent and deputy sheriff, in June 1893. Stolz's death and Ko'olau's ability to initially evade capture (along with his wife and son) aroused the anger of government officials and haoles, while it was celebrated in the narratives produced by Hawaiians. Moran uses these multiple narratives to make clear the colonial state's anxiety about the mobility of Hawaiians as well as the centrality of intimate relationships and kinship connections in Hawaiian attempts to resist imperial power and "modernizing reform," especially when its object was the native body imperiled—and arguably rendered scandalous, at least visually—by contagion. As important, she reconstructs the political significance of leprosy in colonial Hawai'i, stressing the divergence between indigenous understandings of the disease (which stressed the importance of the community as a whole caring for the afflicted) and the colonial state's efforts to isolate the infected while attempting to protect the image of Hawai'i as an "island paradise." If leprosy was a scandal, a literal and figurative blot on the imperial body politic, the terms of that scandal were inverted by indigenous appropriations—a phenomenon that enables us to see with particular vividness the extent to which intimate matters and their political consequences had space-specific valences unanticipated by the panoptical ambitions of imperial rule.

Taken as a whole, the essays collected here demonstrate the multidimensionality of intimate matters under a variety of modern colonial regimes. As diverse as these regimes were territorially and politically, they all recognized the risks to settlement and ultimately to dominion that moving subjects—whether in pursuit of intimate attachments or in flight from them—posed. Rather than capturing intimacy in or for imperial history, what we endeavor here is to suggest some of the counterhistories of colonialism that attention to the intimate domains at the interstices of political economy and cultural life can yield—historicities that both originate from and exceed the intimate as a category of analysis, an investigative modality, and an interpretive framework. This is somewhat akin to figuring intimacy as a rejoinder to rather than as the supplement of the imperial or the global or even the translocal—a dialogic approach recently offered by Geraldine Pratt and Victoria Rosner, and with which this collection seeks company.[45] Our hope is to contribute to an ever-expansive set of narratives about the colonial past that counter those persistent claims to rationality and objectivity undergirding contemporary manifestations of colonial power. Since the intimacies of global imperial violence remain among the most spectacular justifications for total war and total empire, we believe that critically engaged, historically situated genealogies of them are necessary for challenging the logics through which they are simultaneously rationalized, disavowed, and repackaged as the foundations of newly aggressive and determined forms of twenty-first-century imperium.

Notes

1. See Ann Laura Stoler, "'Tense and Tender Ties,'" *Journal of American History* 88, 3 (2001): 829–65. Quotation from Mary Renda, "'Sentiments of a Private Nature': A Comment on Ann Laura Stoler's 'Tense and Tender Ties,'" *Journal of American History* 88, 3 (2001): 882.

2. Ann Cvetkovich, *An Archive of Feelings: Trauma, Sexuality and Lesbian Public Cultures* (Durham, N.C., 2003).

3. Ibid., 285.

4. Partha Chatterjee, *The Nation and Its Fragments: Colonial and Postcolonial Histories* (Princeton, 1993); Patrick Wolfe, *Settler Colonialism and the Transformation of Anthropology: The Politics and Poetics of an Ethnographic Event* (London, 1999).

5. Mrinalini Sinha, *Colonial Masculinity: The "Manly Englishman" and the "Effeminate Bengali" in the Late Nineteenth Century* (Manchester, England, 1995); Tony Ballantyne, *Orientalism and Race: Aryanism in the British Empire* (New York and London, 2001); Philippa Levine, *Prostitution, Race, and Politics: Policing Venereal Disease in the British Empire* (New York, 2003).

6. Doreen Massey, *For Space* (London, 2005), 4, 9–12.

7. Ibid., 63.

8. Manu Goswami, *Producing India: From Colonial Economy to National Space* (Chicago, 2004), 107 and 280.

9. Eugene F. Irschick, *Dialogue and History: Constructing South India, 1795–1895* (Berkeley, 1994), 8.

10. Ramón A. Gutiérrez, "What's Love Got to Do with It?" *Journal of American History* 88, 3 (2001): 866.

11. Adrienne Rich, *Blood, Bread and Poetry: Selected Prose, 1979–1985* (New York, 1986), 212.

12. Tony Ballantyne and Antoinette Burton, eds., *Bodies in Contact: Rethinking Colonial Encounters in World History* (Durham, N.C., 2005).

13. Ania Loomba, "Overworlding the Third World," *Oxford Literary Review* 13 (1991): 164–92.

14. For the homoerotics endemic to the history of the colonial encounter in the Pacific, for example, see Lee Wallace, *Sexual Encounters: Pacific Texts, Modern Sexualities* (Ithaca, N.Y., 2003). For attention to the supine position of women in the local/global paradigm, see Geraldine Pratt and Victoria Rosner, "Introduction: The Global and the Intimate," in "The Global and the Intimate," special issue, *Women's Studies Quarterly* 34, 1–2 (spring/summer 2006): esp. 16.

15. For an account of medievalists' attempt to reckon with "race studies," see Thomas Hahn, "The Difference the Middle Ages Makes: Color and Race before the Modern World," *Journal of Medieval and Early Modern Studies* 31, 1 (winter 2001): 1–37. For a different take, see Ania Loomba, *Shakespeare, Race and Colonialism* (New York, 2002).

16. Durba Ghosh, "National Narratives and the Politics of Miscegenation: Britain and India," in Antoinette Burton, ed., *Archive Stories: Facts, Fictions and the Writing of History* (Durham, N.C., 2005), 27–44.

17. It is revealing to note that while many Britons of Afro-Caribbean descent (26 percent) marry white partners, powerful pressures against intermarriage op-

erate within British South Asian communities. In the mid-1990s, only 1 percent of British men of Bangladeshi origin, 2 percent of Pakistani origin, and 4 percent of Indian origin had married white partners. Also see Richard Berthoud, *Family Formation in Multicultural Britain: Three Patterns of Diversity* (Colchester, England, 2000).

18. Ghosh, "National Narratives and the Politics of Miscegnation."

19. Judith Binney, "'In-Between' Lives: Studies from within a Colonial Society," in Tony Ballantyne and Brian Moloughney, eds., *Disputed Histories: Imagining New Zealand's Pasts* (Dunedin, New Zealand, 2006), 93–118.

20. Angela Wanhalla, "Marrying 'In': the Geography of Intermarriage on the Taieri, 1830s–1920s," in Tony Ballantyne and Judith A. Bennett, eds., *Landscape/ Community: Perspectives from New Zealand* (Dunedin, New Zealand, 2005), 73–94.

21. Anna Haebich, *Broken Circles: Fragmenting Indigenous Families, 1800–2000* (Fremantle, Western Australia, 2000). Also see *Bringing Them Home: Report of the National Inquiry into the Separation of Aboriginal and Torres Strait Islander Children from Their Families* (Sydney, 1997).

22. A. Dirk Moses, ed., *Genocide and Settler Society: Frontier Violence and Stolen Indigenous Children in Australian History* (New York, 2004); A. Dirk Moses, "An Antipodean Genocide? The Origins of the Genocidal Moment in the Colonization of Australia," *Journal of Genocide Research* 2 (2000), 89–106; and the collection of essays collected by John Docker and Ann Curthoys in *Aboriginal History* 25 (2001).

23. Karen Chase and Michael Levenson, *The Spectacle of Intimacy: A Public Life for the Victorian Family* (Princeton, 2000).

24. Quotation from Ann Marie Plane, *Indian Marriage in Early New England* (Ithaca, N.Y., 2002), ix.

25. Michel Foucault, *The History of Sexuality*, vol. 1, *An Introduction*, trans. Robert Hurley (New York, 1980), 103; Stoler, "Tense and Tender Ties."

26. See Matt Matsuda, *Empire of Love: Histories of France and the Pacific* (New York, 2005), and Vincente Rafael, *White Love and Other Events in Filipino History* (Durham, N.C., 2000), quotation from 74. We are grateful to Adele Perry for pressing this point.

27. Anne McClintock remains the baseline for discussions of the erotics of imperialism; see her *Imperial Leather: Race, Gender and Sexuality in the Colonial Contest* (New York, 1995). More recently, Nerissa S. Balce has addressed the erotics of the American empire through its embodiment of the Filipina; see her "The Filipina's Breast: Savagery, Docility, and the Erotics of the American Empire," *Social Text* 87, v. 24, no. 2 (summer 2006): 89–110.

28. Here we would like to acknowledge the work of Yongtao Du, who uses the term *translocal* differently but sympathetically. See Du, "Locality, Identity and Geography: Translocal Practices of Huizhou Merchants in Late Imperial China" (Ph.D. diss., University of Illinois, Urbana-Champaign, 2006).

29. Shani D'Cruze and Anupama Rao, "Violence and the Vulnerabilities of Gender," *Gender and History* 16, 3 (2004): 495 and 499.

30. Ballantyne and Moloughney, *Disputed Histories*, 9–24.

31. James Belich, *Making Peoples: A History of the New Zealanders, from Polynesian Settlement to the End of the Nineteenth Century* (Honolulu, 1996).

32. W. A. Taylor Papers, vol. 5, p. 26, and vol. 10, 114–15, Canterbury Museum, Christchurch, New Zealand.

33. Pratt and Rosner, "Introduction," 20.

34. Gayatri Chakravorty Spivak, "The Rani of Sirmur: An Essay in Reading the Archives," *History and Theory* 24 (1985): 247–73.

35. "Pakeha," the Maori word routinely used to describe non-Maori peoples, especially those of European descent, in New Zealand, is probably derived from "pakepakeha," an eighteenth-century word that designated fair-skinned supernatural creatures.

36. Sarah Ahmed, "Affective Economies," *Social Text* 79 (2004): 117–39.

37. Paul D. Barclay, "Cultural Brokerage and Interethnic Marriage in Colonial Taiwan: Japanese Subalterns and Their Aborigine Wives, 1895–1930," *Journal of Asian Studies* 64, 2 (2005): 323–34.

38. James Scott, *Seeing Like a State: How Certain Schemes to Improve the Human Condition Have Failed* (New Haven, Conn., 1998).

39. Noenoe K. Silva, *Aloha Betrayed: Native Hawaiian Resistance to American Colonialism* (Durham, N.C., 2004).

40. Thanks to Adele Perry for urging us to consider this point.

41. See, for example, Irene Silverblatt, *Modern Inquisitions: Peru and the Colonial Origins of the Civilized World* (Durham, N.C., 2004).

42. Durba Ghosh, "Who Counts as 'Native'? Gender, Race and Subjectivity in Colonial India," *Journal of Colonialism and Colonial History* 6, 3 (2005), muse. jhu.edu/journals/journal_of_colonialism_and_colonial_history/v006/6.3ghosh. html.

43. Stuart Hall, *Race: The Floating Signifier*, DVD (Northampton, Mass., 2002).

44. Zoe Laidlaw, *Colonial Connections, 1815–45: Patronage, the Information Revolution and Colonial Government* (Manchester, England, 2005).

45. Pratt and Rosner, "Introduction," 17–18.

PART I

Vantage Points:
Moving across
Imperial Spaces

1 *Violence and the Intimacy of Imperial Ethnography*

THE *ENDEAVOUR* IN THE PACIFIC

Intimacy is increasingly central in historical writing on empire building, and much recent scholarship on the connections between empire and the intimate places particular emphasis on affective relationships between colonizers and colonized. Ann Laura Stoler's influential essay "Tense and Tender Ties," for example, defines intimate domains as "sex, sentiment, domestic arrangement, and child rearing."[1] Her work focuses strongly on the sexual and affective aspects of the intimate, looking at the relations between colonizing men and colonized women and the families they created, as well as attempts by colonial authorities to control such private spheres of life. Conversely, C. A. Bayly has focused on the realm of "affective knowledge" that emanated from the "creation of moral communities within the colonial society by means of conversion, acculturation or interbreeding."[2] Bayly stresses that this affective knowledge was a crucial means of gaining important information about populations under colonial rule. Such approaches, as well as others in this collection, analyze affective relationships that regulated colonized bodies through a subtle yet pervasive system that was refined over years of colonial rule.

While I am appreciative of the intellectual and political work undertaken in recent examinations of intimacy and empire, this chapter shifts the focus away from affective relationships to the brute realities of violence, examining the cultural and intellectual consequences of conflict. In first encounter situations, coercion and violence, rather than affection, were central in shaping crosscultural relationships. In examining a series of early encounters between Europeans and Pacific peoples, I examine the connections between violence and intimacy in the production of European knowledge about "native" peoples through the discipline of ethnography. Like Adrian Carton, I am interested in the "local nodes" of encounter within the globalizing order of European exploration and empire-building, but whereas he explores Portuguese India, I focus on the first Pacific voyage of James Cook in the ship *Endeavour.* Cook navigated through the waters of the Pacific and along the east coast of Australia during 1769 and 1770. His primary purpose was to observe the transit of Venus in Tahiti, staying on this island for three months in 1769, after which he charted the islands of New Zealand, beginning in October 1769, before crossing the Tasman Sea to explore the eastern Australian coastline during 1770.

This chapter contends that violent crosscultural encounters allowed British explorers to produce particular forms of ethnographic knowledge regarding Maori society, especially the nature of Maori men. One of the most striking things about the ethnographic accounts of Maori that were produced out of the *Endeavour* voyage was the dominance of a discourse of masculinity, which dwelt at great length on the qualities of indigenous men, their bodies, and their behavior. This discourse abstracted behavior in very specific and violent crosscultural encounters, at a very specific period of Maori history, to become essentialized information about Maori as a whole. The tattooed, athletic, and seagoing young men who clashed with the crew of the *Endeavour* were seen as indicative of the whole society, as embodiments of a "warrior race," a race connected to its land and eager to protect its resources and power.

In this essay I focus on the meeting of bodies in situations of conflict and on the role of violence as a strategy to manage the crosscultural encounter. I wish to suggest that in the context of the imperial ambition, the British used violence to assert their so-called superiority over the people they met on their voyages. This essay thus follows from Ramón A. Gutiérrez's response to Stoler in the *Journal of American History,* where he simply enquires "What's love got to do with it?"[3] Gutiérrez suggests an approach to intimacy that looks closely at subjection and resistance in the imperial context and continues the quest of feminist scholars to analyze the place of power in the construction of gender and race. Subjection is important to my analysis here, not only in the way reaction to subjection shapes colonial knowledge about indigenous peoples but also in the way we remember histories of subjection. I wish to suggest that some recent histories tend to reify earlier representations of indigenous peoples by not adequately interrogating their basis in particular ethnographic accounts, and hence not recognizing the imperial strategies of coercion and domination employed in Pacific exploration.

My focus on power and violence is at odds with some recent work on empires that stresses European vulnerability when encountering indigenous peoples. Vanessa Smith, Jonathan Lamb and Nicholas Thomas, for example, in their anthology *Exploration and Exchange*, say they are suspicious of "gross totalities" resulting from an assumption of calculated imperial force in histories of travel writing, and they highlight the multiple ways Europeans were "at sea" in the South Pacific.[4] The anthology collects material from the Cook journals with travel writing penned in different contexts, placing Cook alongside voyagers acting with limited resources and no state support. Cook was, of course, employed by the British government to enlarge British knowledge of the Pacific and, if possible, to lay the foundations for an expanded British presence in the region. Even though he might have been "at sea," Cook was a powerful agent of empire, and his actions and perceptions had profound and lasting consequences for Pacific peoples. Similarly, Linda Colley's recent work *Captives* focuses on European vulnerability at the edges of empire, analyzing the capture of whites, while ignoring the vast numbers of racial others, the most obvious group being slaves removed from Africa, whose status as commodities and producers was crucial to the growth of empires, and the development of capitalism itself.[5] But even if we accept the vulnerability and instability of the European self in the intimate encounters of empire, I would argue that such instability was often productive of more, rather than less, violence. The *Endeavour* crew, confronted and challenged by Maori when they tried to intimidate them, responded with aggression to subjugate a "dangerous" indigenous population. While the authors of the *Endeavour* journals highlighted their own vulnerability, they typically did so in order to justify the violence that they often turned to as a first, rather than last, resort.

Thus, in the first encounters on the beaches of New Zealand between the agents of the British empire and the indigenous population, intimate encounters of a violent nature predominated over the sexual kind. This experience in New Zealand contrasts strongly to the British experience in Tahiti, where the voyagers stayed for three months to observe the transit of Venus before sailing to New Zealand, as well as in Australia, which they explored directly after their encounter with Maori. Representations of Tahiti were dominated by discourses of a sexualized and feminized "native" body, while in Australia indigenous bodies are relatively absent from the journal accounts. In each of these cases, the indigenous people responded differently to British tactics of intimidation and threat. As Mary A. Renda has suggested, "if a given episode of colonialism deployed the building blocks of earlier colonial models, surely the colonized as well as the colonizer brought alternative building blocks, alternative deployments, to the interaction."[6] By reading the British ethnographic descriptions of these three indigenous peoples we can trace their alternative, culturally embedded, responses to the crosscultural encounter, written into imperial texts as an essentialized understanding of the different peoples. These ethnographic accounts became influential documents in the archives of European knowledge relating to the Pacific, and were important in shaping British colonial relations with the respective indigenous peoples. Possibly the most crucial aspect of these accounts was the articulation of different modes of property ownership, and as I will show, British explorers saw important connections between organized indigenous resistance to European intrusion and notions of ownership and systems of political organization. And of course, British assessments of the presence, or absence, of indigenous property rights had profound implications for the nature of British colonial ambition. Imperial ethnography did not simply produce textual images of difference but rather had important material effects for its indigenous subjects.

James Cook, his botanist and naturalist-historian Joseph Banks, and the rest of the crew of the *Endeavour* set foot on the North Island of New Zealand, near the mouth of the Turanganui River in Poverty Bay, on October 9, 1769. Te Maro, a chief from the Ngati Oneone *iwi* (tribe), was shot and killed as the British stepped ashore that afternoon. Te Rakao, a chief of the Rongwhakaata *iwi*, was killed, and a number of Maori men were wounded in an exchange on the beach the next morning.[7] A number of men out fishing in their canoes were killed later that day as Cook decided to detain them by force to prove his friendly intentions toward them. Three boys in the same canoes were taken and were kept on board the *Endeavour* overnight.

All of these events are documented in the journals Cook and Banks kept while they were on the *Endeavour* voyage. That voyage was initiated by British strategic and scientific interest in discovering new land and resources. These texts were not simply the product of inward reflection but were entwined with British imperial aspirations. At the request of the joint sponsors of the expedition, the British Admiralty and the Royal Society, both Cook and Banks made specific comments about the suitability of the lands they saw for British settlement, and both men were also tasked with the systematic description of the new discoveries made, be they discoveries of land, plants, animals, or people. The descriptions both men produced were instrumental to the initial stages of extractive industries exploiting Maori resources. (The intimate relations developing from these industries are the subject of chapter 2 here.)

When a party of the British voyagers first went ashore at Poverty Bay on their first afternoon in New Zealand, they left the ship's yawl on the beach in the care of the crew's "boys" and headed across the beach to search the country for supplies. They had seen Maori on shore, but the locals had left when the British landed, only to return and head for the boat. Feeling in danger of being "cut off," the officers rushed back, as soldiers in the pinnace fired twice at the Maori men, with no effect. The third shot killed Te Maro.

Te Maro's companions had to leave his body on the beach, leaving Banks to observe and describe the chief in his journal, the first ethnographic information he collected about New Zealand. Banks offered the following account of the body of Te Maro: "he was shot through the heart. He was a middle sized man tattowd in the face on one cheek only in spiral lines very regularly formd; he was coverd with a fine cloth of a manufacture totaly new to us . . . his hair was also tied in a knot on the top of his head but no feather stuck in it; his complexion brown but not very dark."[8] This detailed and precise account was enabled by violence. Bernard Smith has noted how the artists on the voyage profited from the subjugation of the local people that allowed them to form friendly relations with their subjects for portraiture.[9] The relationship between Bank's ethnographic information and the violence of that first afternoon is here even more direct, with his information collected from a corpse.

Banks could identify and "know" Te Maro through his fleeting encounter with his dead body and began to construct an account of Maori through this observation. Violence in general, and death in particular, made possible a pliant, indigenous subject that could be scrutinized intensely, in much the same manner as the plants and animals also collected by the voyagers. Te Maro's corpse can thus be seen in the sense of a "body-as-contact-zone" as identified by Tony Ballantyne and Antoinette Burton, being the first casualty, as well as the first ethnographic subject, of the British encounter with Maori, a site for the display of superior British firepower as well as for the collection of scientific information.[10] Joanna Bourke has discussed the personal nature of intimate violence where combatants can be identified and known.[11] At the frontiers of empire, death allowed the production of ethnographic knowledge of a particularly intimate kind.

The following morning, however, Banks's role in the next encounter with Maori was less the detached observer and far more active, indeed violent. On October 10, Cook decided to go ashore again, "with the boats man'd and arm'd," when he saw a number of Maori on the beach. The officers read Maori reluctance to cross the Turanganui River as a "sign of fear," but Banks wrote: "As soon almost as we appeared they rose up and every man produced wither a long pike or a small weapon of well polishd stone about a foot long and thick enough to weigh 4 or 5 pounds, with this they threatened us and sign to us to depart."[12]

The British did not depart, however, in the face of this *wero*, the ritual challenge Maori communities issued to all newcomers, a confrontational form of greeting strangers used in situations of both peace and war.[13] They instead chose to make a display of their superior firepower: a "musquet was then fird wide of them the ball of which struck the water, they saw the effect and immediately ceased with threats."[14] At this juncture, Tupaia, the Ra'iatean man traveling with the ship, discovered that he could understand spoken Maori, and communication was established. Tupaia tried to bargain for provisions, offering Maori iron in exchange, on the condition that the indigenous men would put down their weapons. When they refused, Tupaia announced his opinion that this was a sign of "treachery" and warned the British "to be upon our guard for they were not our friends."[15]

Having been shown the power of European weaponry, Maori were keen to trade weapons. The British would not give up their arms, although they were keen to establish trade in other articles, as these were crucial to their attempts to control the crosscultural encounter. Maori, also keen to control the traveling men who had landed on their beaches, tried to take a sword when the visitors refused to barter with them for it. They succeeded in taking Mr. Green's "hanger," at which point Banks felt compelled to act: "It now appeard necessary for our safeties that so daring an act should be instantly punished, this I pronounced aloud as my opinion, the Captn and the rest Joind me on which I fird my musquet which was loaded with small shot, leveling it between his shoulders who was not 15 yards from me."[16] Following this exchange, Te Rakao, a chief of the Rongowhakaata *iwi*, was killed, and two other Maori men wounded. It was the characterization of Maori as "daring" that Banks used to justify this violence, normalizing the use of force within the journals.

Recent historical analyses of the Cook voyages tend to downplay the British use of intimidation and violence. Two of the most important recent works are those written by Anne Salmond and Nicholas Thomas.[17] Both of these works repackage the imperial archive for a modern audience. Thomas writes of the first day's conflict in New Zealand: "the rudimentary properties of the first sustained encounter between Maori and Europeans had emerged: Europeans would meet, fairly consistently, with Maori hostility; and they would admire Maori . . . they would be awed by other arts of Maori warriorhood."[18] Thomas recognizes only Maori aggression, following the journal accounts, which stress Maori "insolence" but efface British threat and intimidation.

Anne Salmond's work *The Trial of the Cannibal Dog: Captain Cook in the South Seas* attempts to restore Polynesian peoples to their rightful place in the colonial archive of Pacific exploration, as agents who were instrumental in crosscultural encounters. She focuses on Maori as a formidable foe, people who put up a worthy fight against the British voyagers. This approach, however, tends to reify, rather than question, the construction of the trope of Maori masculinity created in the British journals. Brian Keith Axel reminds us to consider that "documents pertaining to pre-colonial history have never had a life outside of colonial history."[19] It is within the context of European vulnerability as mobile subjects that such intimate association with indigenous people can quickly escalate to violence.

On his men's return to the *Endeavour* following the confrontation on the banks of the Turanganui River, a frustrated Cook decided to employ other violent means to prove his "friendly intentions," as he put it: namely kidnapping. The captain hoped that by forcing Maori into intimate association with the British voyagers within the confines of the ship he could get them to recognize the benefits to be derived from compliance and cooperation with a "superior" people. Cook targeted fishermen returning to shore on the assumption that they would be unarmed. Tupaia called to the fishermen that they should approach the ship and would not be hurt. Instead of complying, however, the Maori men tried to escape, and Cook ordered guns to be fired over their heads, "thinking that this would either make them surrender or jump over board." Again the Maori men would not comply, as they "took to their arms or whatever they had in the boat and began to attack us, this obliged us to fire upon them." The men were killed and the three boys captured.[20] The capture of these three young men proved productive of ethnographic enquiry, as they were minutely observed for their reaction to European people and things while kept within the restricted space of the *Endeavour*. The boys were brought on board the *Endeavour*, and Banks recorded that "they squatted down, expecting no doubt instant death."[21] They were not killed but instead were clothed, fed, and shown around the ship, and Banks observed them closely, watching their reactions for signs of their humanity.

In the European-controlled space of the ship, these young men could be shown benevolence. As Steel's analysis of indigenous men under colonial rule shows, Fijian men were transformed from dangerous "savages" into valuable laborers as they were brought within the disciplined order of the ship and the port town. These young Maori men were also perceived as less threatening when confined. They were treated so well, according to Banks, "that they seemd to have intirely forgot every thing that had happned, put on chearfull and lively countenances and askd and answerd questions with a great deal of curiosity."[22] Out of the initial situation of violence and death a relationship with the children developed that was to help the *Endeavour* voyagers to form a connection with the local Maori people. The next day about fifty people traveled to the *Endeavour*, coming on board to trade. This pattern of contact echoes Bill Pearson's reconstruction of the development of crosscultural relationships in Tahiti. Pearson describes how at the first meeting European explorers "pacified" the Tahitians, used their superior weapons to intimidate them, following with displays of "conditional benevolence" to secure ongoing cooperation with the "natives."[23]

So ultimately the willingness of the British to use violence in these encounters may have led to increased, and more peaceful, contact, but it still remained for Cook to justify his actions to his patrons back in England. The fear of violence in the face of its constant presence in the first contact situation is nowhere more apparent in the journals than in Cook's justification for killing these men, immediately after he narrates the event in his journal. He writes that he is "aware that most humane men who have not experienced things of this nature will cencure my conduct in fireing upon the people in this boat." His justification, however, stresses the threat posed by Maori, who did not surrender as he expected: "Had I thought that they would have made the least resistance I would not have come near them but as they did I was not to stand still and suffer either my self or those that were with me to be knocked on the head."[24]

Here Cook was responding to James Douglas, Lord Morton, president of the Royal Society. In his "*Hints* offered to the consideration of Captain Cooke, Mr Banks, Doctor Solander, and the other Gentlemen who go upon the Expedition on Board the *Endeavour*," Morton condemned violence against any people who might be encountered on the voyage. Morton stressed that indigenous people were right to defend themselves and resist European intrusion into their "quiet possession of the country." He asserted that "sheding the blood of these people is a crime of the highest nature," given that all people were the "work of the same omnipotent Author."[25]

Cook's justification has another dimension if we consider the example cited in Lord Morton's *"Hints"* when discussing previous incidents of indigenous people "wantonly killed without any provocation." Morton cited reports of the slaying of a man killed when swimming out to a ship, concluding that if "this account was true then there was not the colour of a pretence for such a brutal massacre:—a naked man in the water could never be dangerous to a Boats crew." Cook had to rationalize his killing of these four Maori in the light of Morton's text, and thus we can read his defense, penned in Poverty Bay, as a dialogue with the Royal Society's president, safe in his metropolitan scientific community, unprepared for the dangers faced by the voyager when confronting the New Zealand "savage" at the edge of the known world.

This justification of violence as necessary to protect a vulnerable crew differed markedly from depictions of violence during earlier encounters of the *Endeavour* voyage. During the crew's three-month stay in Tahiti, there were some violent clashes, but relations with Tahitians generally had a peaceful cast. Cook's crew arrived two years after the first European visitors, who had come on the British ship *Dolphin,* captained by Samuel Wallis. When Wallis arrived at Tahiti in June 1767, many of his crew, including Wallis himself, were stricken with scurvy and desperate for fresh supplies. As the *Dolphin* sailed into Matavai Bay on June 24, thousands of Tahitian people came off shore to the ship. The Tahitians attacked the *Dolphin* with a barrage of stones, to which the British responded with musket fire and the great guns, smashing the canoes. Relating the story to Banks, Tahitians later estimated the loss of life as "hundreds and hundreds."[26]

This use of violence by Wallis and his men paved the way for the relatively peaceful contact between Cook's crew and the Tahitians. Pearson has linked the sexual accommodation of Tahitian women, which was to become the dominant motif in representations of Tahiti, to the overwhelming military defeat inflicted on the Tahitian people by the original British voyage.[27] There were moments of violence during the *Endeavour's* stay in Tahiti, but the representation of these differs significantly from first encounter in New Zealand. Sydney Parkinson, an artist on the voyage, wrote of the shooting of Tahitians on April 16, 1769, in a way that characterized the indigenous population as innocent and meek. On this day the officers were taking a walk and "enjoying the rural scene" when they heard gunfire, "and presently saw the natives fleeting into the woods like frightened fawns." Running to the scene the officers witnessed "several of our men, who had been left to guard the tent, pursuing the natives, who were terrified to the last degree."[28] This is the account Parkinson

provides of the incident: "A sentinel being off his guard, one of the natives snatched a musket out of his hand, which occasioned the fray. A
boy, a midshipman, was the commanding officer, and, giving orders to
fire, they obeyed with the greatest glee imagineable, as if they had been
shooting at wild ducks, killed one stout man, and wounded many others.
What a pity, that such brutality should be exercised by civilized people
upon such unarmed ignorant Indians!" When Banks heard of the affair,
he was highly displeased, saying, 'If we quarrelled with these Indians, we
should not agree with angels'; and he did all he could to accommodate
the difference."[29]

This violent scene had much in common with conflicts between
Maori and the British at Poverty Bay a few months later, but these conflicts' descriptions in the voyage journals and impact on understandings
of indigenous people in these respective places were utterly different.
Much of this difference can be traced to representation of class. In the
Tahitian example recorded by Parkinson, the killing is perpetrated by
sailors, with the man in charge being only "a boy, a midshipman." The officers, not being personally involved in the confrontation, could distance
themselves from it and represent it as morally wrong. In his "*Hints*" Lord
Morton particularly advised the officers to check the "petulance of the
Sailors, and restrain the wanton use of fire arms." The killing of indigenous peoples was to be avoided, and the violent tendencies of the lower
classes had to be checked. In later incidents in New Zealand, the officers
were generally the ones involved in conflict, and the officers' depictions
of violence were considerably different from the visions of Lord Morton
or Parkinson. Far from being innocent as angels, Maori were depicted as
a warlike, masculine people to be respected as worthy foes.

The depiction of Maori society as a warrior culture that developed
out of the encounter at Poverty Bay and that was consolidated as a result
of the impact of subsequent violent meetings on the *Endeavour* voyage
came to dominate the more general ethnological accounts of Maori that
Cook and Banks produced at the end of the sojourn in New Zealand. In
these reflective texts, Maori willingness to confront and challenge the
British in very specific and violent circumstances was abstracted to become essentialized information about Maori character and culture. Banks
described the culture of perpetual war that he understood to be a feature
of Maori society. He based this assessment on his description of Maori
weaponry, which "tho few [in number] are well calculated for bloody
fights and the destruction of numbers." Banks was convinced there were
no defensive weapons or missiles, "so that if two bodies should meet

either in boats, or upon the plain ground, they must fight hand to hand and the slaughter be consequently immense."[30]

This account of weaponry drew on information Banks had gleaned from his encounters with Maori at Poverty Bay. The trading relationship established after the kidnapping of the young men had allowed Banks to start his collection of Maori weapons. At the time he had written that one of the men "sold his patoo patoo as he called it, a short weapon of green talk." Having made a drawing of the shape of the weapon, Banks concluded that it was "intended doubtless for fighting hand to hand and certainly well contrivd for splitting sculls."[31] The relationships facilitated by the death of the fishermen and the kidnapping of the young men enabled Banks to collect weapons, giving him "proof" both of Maori "ingenuity" and their warrior culture. The detailed descriptions of Maori material culture, especially weaponry, produced by the *Endeavour*'s officers and naturalists underpinned an assessment of Maori culture as relatively sophisticated and complex.

Banks also described tattooing, which he again linked to war and masculinity. The naturalist surmised that facial tattooing was designed to make Maori "look frightfull in war."[32] The first description of *moko*, as I suggested earlier, was derived from observation of Te Maro's dead body. His corpse provided the initial basis not just for Banks to describe tattoos but also for him to assess their significance. The predominance of depictions of a Maori warrior culture and of their resistance to the British presence on the New Zealand coast convinced Cook and Banks of the cultural capacity of Maori. The role of war in the development of human societies was recognized within Enlightenment thinking, most notably by Adam Ferguson in *An Essay on the History of Civil Society*, published in 1767. Ferguson believed that civil society "could scarcely have found an object, or a form" without warfare, and that defending one's society gives "its most animating exercise, and its greatest triumphs, to a vigorous mind."[33] Duncan Forbes has summarized Ferguson's position: "War plays a positive rôle in the building of states, and social cohesion demands hostility to other societies; unlike purely private quarrels, war calls for the exercise of many virtues and praiseworthy qualities; it cannot be regarded as wholly evil, unnecessary and destructive; it is an integral part of the progress of civilization. There is something here of 'conflict sociology.'"[34]

Thus Enlightenment understandings of social organization and universal history recognized the political and cultural significance of the kind of warriorhood that Cook and Banks reported on from New Zealand. The ability of Maori communities to organize themselves and challenge the British testified to a certain degree of political sophistication, as well as a robust, manly culture. But British observers not only respected Maori society for the value it attached to warfare but also valued the way peace with the British was concluded. Maori were seen to recognize British technological superiority as crosscultural relations became less violent and moved on to a tense form of "peace." Cook wrote: "all their actions and beheavour towards us tended to prove that they are a brave open warlike people and voide of treachery."[35]

As we have seen, Pearson has suggested that British violence was used to demonstrate intercultural "superiority," and once the indigenous people recognized that advantage and deferred to it, then the British were happy to display "conditional benevolence." Maori were respected because they noted this benevolence and were honest in future dealings. Cook, again, recognized this: "After they found that ours Arms were so much Superior to theirs and that we took no advantage of that superiority and a little time given to them to reflect upon it they ever after were our very good friends . . . we never had an Instance of their attempting to surprize or cut off any of our people when they were ashore, oppertunities for so doing they must have had at one time or a nother."[36]

For Banks and other British reporters, Maori dances such as *haka* also embodied the martial spirit of Maori culture. In his ethnological account Banks described *haka* as follows: "The War Song and dance consist of Various contortions of the limbs during which the tongue is frequently thrust out incredibly far and the orbits of the eyes enlargd so much that a circle of white is distinctly seen round the Iris: in short nothing is omitted which can render a human shape frightfull and deformd, which I suppose they think terrible. During this time they brandish their spears, hack the air with the patoo patoos and shake their darts as if they meant every moment to begin the attack, singing all the time in a wild but not disagreeable manner and ending every strain with a loud and deep fetch sigh in which they all join in concert."[37] The performance of *haka* and other dances were described as designed to create "artificial courage," which "will not let them think in the least."[38] The term "artificial courage" is linked to concepts of savagery that stressed the inability of less civilized peoples to control their emotional responses. The difference between the two martial cultures of the British and the Maori was the supposed ability of the British to control and temper their violence and use it strategically.

The effects of this artificial courage were linked to the practice of cannibalism, which was understood within the specific context of Maori warrior culture. Cannibalism, of course, was often understood as indicative of the limits of humanity, as representing people at their most savage. Louis Montrose, analyzing depictions of cannibalism in Jan van der Straet's 1580 drawing of Vespucci's discovery of America, writes that "elements of savagery, deceit and cannibalism central to the emergent European discourse on the inhabitants of the New World are already in place. . . . Of particular significance here is the blending of these basic ingredients of protocolonialist ideology with a crude and anxious misogynist fantasy, a powerful conjunction of the savage and the feminine."[39] In New Zealand, however, Maori cannibalism was linked to warrior culture and was heavily implicated in a gendered discourse, as identified by Montrose, but was connected to masculinity. As such, it could be more readily understood and accepted by the British—as an act of war, albeit an uncontrolled, "savage" one. Thus Banks described how he was unwilling to give credit to stories of cannibalism but had become convinced that Maori "eat the bodies of such of their enemies as are killd in war."[40] Banks's contextualization of the practice of cannibalism within a culture of war has the effect of explaining the practice rather than automatically placing it outside the bounds of humanity.

When the authors of journals did describe Maori women, they defined them in relation to Maori men, and saw women as a "civilizing" influence on Maori men. Banks wrote that Maori women "were plain and made themselves more so by painting their faces with red ocre and oil which generaly was fresh and wet upon their cheeks and foreheads."[41] Banks described that while Maori were "implacable to their enemies" they seemed "mild, gentle, and very affectionate to each other." In the Banks text, Maori women become symbolic of a universal system of gender relations, as women were "formed by nature to soften the Cares of more serious man." Maori society proved for Banks that "as well in uncivilizd as the most polished nations Mans ultimate happiness must at last be plac'd in Woman."[42]

As Ballantyne and Burton have discussed, documents such as travel narratives that were "produced by men and . . . reflected their concerns" underpinned the erasure of women from imperial histories.[43] The substitution of the figure of a universal woman for the particular characteristics of Maori women and gender relations in New Zealand further marginalized women in an interpretative framework that was already structured around a powerful discourse on masculinity. In many ways, the *Endeavour* journals produced the condition for subsequent erasure of Maori women, as later imperial, colonial, and postcolonial texts constantly reiterated the equation of Maori in general with the young, athletic, and fearless warrior.

This rendering of Maoridom as defined by a warrior culture had significant implications for British conceptions of indigenous property rights and attachment to land in New Zealand. Gananath Obeyesekere has suggested that Cook "created an image of the fearless, independent Maoris who had their own ideas of sovereignty and nationhood."[44] An articulation of property rights can be most clearly seen in the comparison to encounter in Australia, where the lack of confrontation by Aboriginal people and the elusiveness of indigenous bodies was read as lack of concern to defend land and the absence of meaningful political organization.

Where the mobility of indigenous communities in Australia and their strategic use of withdrawal as a mechanism for controlling crosscultural relationships were read by Cook and other Europeans as evidence of the Aborigines' limited capacity for civilization, Maori settlement patterns and forms of architecture were seen as proof of their progress toward true civilization. Even before any encounter with Maori took place, the British voyagers sighted a *pa* (fortified village) from the decks of the *Endeavour.* Banks wrote that "many conjectures were made" about the purpose of the building, but most concluded that it was for a "park of Deer or a feild of oxen and sheep."[45] As the voyage progressed this initial idea was revised, and Cook wrote with admiration of Maori skill in building *pa.* He wrote when visiting the remains of a *pa* that its "Situation is such that the best Engineer in Europe could not have chose'd better for a small number of men to defend themselves against a greater, it is strong by nature and made more so by Art. It is only accessible on the land side, and there have been cut a Ditch and a bank raised on the inside the whole seem'd to have been done with great judgement."[46]

Whether they were perceived as elaborate pens for livestock or for military purposes, *pa* could be read as an embodiment of John Locke's connection of property ownership to the enclosure and cultivation of land. The construction of *pa* for fortification and defense was an important signifier to the British of Maori advancement. The significance of pa to Maori society was, however, not unchanging. It was a historically specific development due to the increasing stability of *kumara* (sweet potato) cultivation in the north of New Zealand, which enabled the construction of larger and more powerful political alliances and coincided with, or perhaps even allowed, intensifying internecine conflict.[47]

British observers read these Maori strategies of response, their ritualized challenges to the voyagers and their willingness to fight, as well as the presence of these fortification as signs of Maori communities' attachment to their land. Banks characterized Maori social structures and their martial spirit as creating relationships of landowning, which I believe to be a vital record of ownership that influenced the form of the future British colonial project in New Zealand. While Maori cultivation of the land was also fundamentally important in stadial theory of human development—which suggested that societies progressed through successive stages of development from hunting-gathering to pastoralism, then agriculture, then commerce—the idea that the Maori would defend land was crucial to the British assessment that they possessed notions of property ownership. After the kidnapping of the young boys at Poverty Bay, Banks wrote: "God send that we may not there have the same tragedy to act over again as we so lately perpetrated: the countrey is certainly divided into many small principalities so we cannot hope that an account of our weapons and management of them can be conveyd as far as we in all probability must go and this I am well convincd of, that till these warlike people have severly felt our superiority in the art of war they will never behave to us in a friendly manner."[48]

The importance of this reading of the division of the country into "many small principalities" can be seen in the comparison to Australia, where Banks concluded the lack of challenge from Aboriginal men indicated a thinly populated, undefended country. On the first sign of the British landing in many parts of the east coast, Aboriginal people would move off the land, vacating it during the time of the European visit. The British could often see people from the *Endeavour*, but when they landed, the Aboriginal people had left.[49] There were signs of recent Aboriginal presence, but no people to establish relationships with. There was some violence between Aboriginal people and the British, for example when two Eora men opposed a landing at Botany Bay and were shot at by Cook's men, or when a group of Aboriginal men set fire to the British camp at Endeavour River.[50] In general, however, Aboriginal strategies of withdrawal gave rise to a number of assumptions on the part of the British about population and land ownership. Banks wrote: "This immense tract of land, the largest known which does not bear the name of a continent . . . is thinly inhabited . . . at least that part of it that we saw. . . . At Sting Rays bay where they evidently came down to fight us several times they never could muster above 14 or 15 fighting men, indeed in other places they generally ran away from us. . . . We saw only the sea coast: what the immense tract of inland countrey may produce is to us totaly unknown: we may have liberty to conjecture however that they are totaly uninhabited. The Sea has I beleive been universaly found to be the cheif source of supplys to Indians ignorant to the arts of cultivation."[51]

In contrast to the Tahitian response of sexual accommodation or Aboriginal strategic use of withdrawal and observation, we have seen that the dominant Maori response in the face of the British presence was to confront and challenge the voyagers. The resulting clashes on the shores of New Zealand shaped the journal accounts of the *Endeavour*'s crew and officers, which were dominated by a discourse of masculinity and represented Maori as inherently warlike. Not only did this use of confrontation shape the emerging trope of Maori masculinity within the European imagination but also it had important consequences for the ways Europeans characterized the sophistication of Maori culture. As a "warrior race" of agriculturalists, Maori were seen to have the capacity to embrace Christianity, civilization, and commerce. British intellectuals and Colonial Office officials agreed that Maori were a sovereign people, an understanding that meant that the British colonization of New Zealand could only proceed lawfully once that sovereignty was alienated. While the colonization of Australia was underwritten by the legal notion of *terra nullius*—which simultaneously denied indigenous political rights and erased the cultural presence of Aborigines as it asserted that Australia was an "empty land"—the formal settlement of New Zealand was grounded in the Treaty of Waitangi, signed in 1840. Even as that treaty facilitated the formal incorporation of New Zealand into the British Empire, it protected chiefly authority and Maori property rights, as well as giving Maori the rights of British subjects. The profound divergence between Maori and Aboriginal histories owes much to the very different political rights that were granted under British rule to these colonized peoples, rights that were molded by a body of imperial ethnographic knowledge that was profoundly shaped by the texts produced out of Cook's first Pacific voyage. It is in these texts that a potent set of connections were drawn for the first time between masculinity, warfare, and cultural capacity, a set of cultural understandings that have continued to mold crosscultural understandings in Australasia into this supposedly postcolonial age.

Notes

1. Ann Laura Stoler, "Tense and Tender Ties: The Politics of Comparison in North American History and (Post) Colonial Studies," *Journal of American History* 88, 3 (December 2001): 829.

2. C. A. Bayly, *Empire and Information: Intelligence Gathering and Social Communication in India, 1780–1870* (Cambridge, 1996), 7.

3. Ramón A. Gutiérrez, "What's Love Got to Do with It?" *Journal of American History* 88, 3 (December 2001): 866–70.

4. Jonathon Lamb, Vanessa Smith, and Nicholas Thomas, eds., *Exploration and Exchange: A South Seas Anthology, 1680–1900* (Chicago, 2000), xvi.

5. Linda Colley, *Captives: Britain, Empire and the World, 1600–1850* (London, 2002).

6. Mary A. Renda,"'Sentiments of a Private Nature': A Comment on Ann Laura Stoler's 'Tense and Tender Ties,'" *Journal of American History* 88, 3 (December 2001): 886.

7. Anne Salmond, *The Trial of the Cannibal Dog: Captain Cook in the South Seas* (London, 2003), 116–17.

8. J. C. Beaglehole, ed., *The Endeavour Journal of Joseph Banks: 1768–1771* (Sydney, 1963), 1:400.

9. Bernard Smith, *Imagining the Pacific: In the Wake of the Cook Voyages* (Carlton, Australia, 1992), 93.

10. Tony Ballantyne and Antoinette Burton, *Bodies in Contact: Rethinking Colonial Encounters in World History* (Durham, N.C., 2005), 407.

11. Joanna Bourke, *An Intimate History of Killing: Face-to-Face Killing in Twentieth-Century Warfare* (London, 1999); see esp. chap. 2. Writing of the "warrior myth" in the twentieth century, Bourke describes a desired golden age in which combatants could identify each other, in contrast to the anonymous killing of the world wars and Vietnam conflict. She identifies hand-to-hand combat as central to this myth, and I will return later to the importance of Maori weaponry, designed exclusively for this purpose, as important to depictions of the Maori as a warrior society.

12. Beaglehole, *Endeavour Journal of Joseph Banks*, 1:401.

13. Anne Salmond explains that "early observers of these encounters remarked that it was almost impossible to distinguish peaceful overtures from warlike ones"; *Hui: A Study of Maori Ceremonial Gatherings* (Auckland, New Zealand, 1975), 132.

14. Beaglehole, *Endeavour Journal of Joseph Banks*, 1:401.

15. Ibid., 1:401.

16. Ibid., 1:401–2.

17. Salmond, *Trial of the Cannibal Dog;* Nicholas Thomas, *Discoveries: The Voyages of Captain Cook* (London, 2003). Glyndwr Williams has concluded that these two "books on the Cook voyages . . . can claim to be the most important since Beaglehole's biography of 30 years ago"; "'As Befits Our Age, There Are No More Heroes': Reassessing Captain Cook," in Glyndwr Williams, ed., *Captain Cook: Explorations and Reassessments* (Woodbridge, Suffolk, England, and Rochester, N.Y., 2004), 243.

18. Thomas, *Discoveries*, 87.

19. Brian Keith Axel, "Introduction: Historical Anthropology and Its Vicissitudes," in Brian Keith Axel, ed., *From the Margins: Historical Anthropology and Its Futures* (Durham, N.C., and London, 2002), 14.

20. Cook suggested that there were "two or three" men in the canoes; Banks states that four men were killed. J. C. Beaglehole, *The Journals of Captain James Cook on His Voyages of Discovery*, vol. 1, *The Voyage of the Endeavor, 1768–1771* (Cambridge, 1955), 170; Beaglehole, *Endeavour Journal of Joseph Banks*, 1:403.

21. Beaglehole, *Endeavour Journal of Joseph Banks*, 1:403.

22. Ibid.

23. W. H. Pearson, "European Intimidation and the Myth of Tahiti," *Journal of Pacific History* 4 (1969): 199–217.

24. Beaglehole, *Journals of Captain James Cook*, 1:171.

25. Ibid., 1:514.

26. Beaglehole, *Endeavour Journal of Joseph Banks*, 1:307.

27. Pearson, "European Intimidation."

28. Sydney Parkinson, *Journal of a Voyage to the South Seas* (1784; reprint, London, 1984), 14–15.

29. Ibid., 15.

30. Beaglehole, *Endeavour Journal of Joseph Banks*, 2:26–27.

31. Ibid., 1:407.

32. Ibid., 2:13.

33. Adam Ferguson, *An Essay on the History of Civil Society*, edited by Duncan Forbes (Edinburgh, 1966), 24.

34. Duncan Forbes, introduction to ibid., xviii.

35. Beaglehole, *Journals of Captain James Cook*, 1:281.

36. Ibid., 1:282.

37. Beaglehole, *Endeavour Journal of Joseph Banks*, 2:29.

38. Ibid., 2:12.

39. Louis Montrose, "The Work of Gender in the Discourse of Discovery," *Representations* 33 (winter 1991): 5.

40. Beaglehole, *Endeavour Journal of Joseph Banks*, 2:30.

41. Ibid., 1:417.

42. Ibid., 2:12.

43. Ballantyne and Burton, *Bodies in Contact*, 411.

44. Gananath Obeyesekere, *The Apotheosis of Captain Cook: European Myth-making in the Pacific* (Princeton, 1997), 134.

45. Beaglehole, *Endeavour Journal of Joseph Banks*, 2:399.

46. Ibid., 1:198.

47. L. M. Groube, *Settlement Patterns in New Zealand Prehistory* (Dunedin, New Zealand, 1965), 52; see also Peter Cleave, "Tribal and State-Like Political Formations in New Zealand Maori Society, 1750–1900," *Journal of the Polynesian Society* 92 (1983): 62.

48. Beaglehole, *Endeavour Journal of Joseph Banks*, 2:407–8.

49. Ibid., 2:52, 88, 76; see also Alan Frost, "New South Wales as *Terra Nullius:* The British Denial of Aboriginal Land Rights," *Historical Studies* 19, 77 (1981): 513–23.

50. Beaglehole, *Journals of Captain James Cook*, 2:305, 361.

51. Beaglehole, *Endeavour Journal of Joseph Banks*, 2:274.

2 In Search of the "Whaheen"

NGAI TAHU WOMEN, SHORE WHALERS, AND THE MEANING OF SEX IN EARLY NEW ZEALAND

> Thursday, 14th July 1842. Gave to Richard's Whaheen 10 regatta shirts, 4 pairs cotton socks, 1 white trousers, and 5 pairs lambs-wool hose to get daubed.
>
> —James Barry, "Remarks, at Peraki Whaling Station, July 1842"[1]

Historians have long remarked on similarities between shore whaling in New Zealand and the North American fur trade. The analogy is often based on what we might call the economics of culture contact. Both industries exposed stable, subsistence-based native populations to the dynamics of expanding capitalism, and both relied heavily on indigenous labor and cooperation, requiring Euro-Americans to forge strategic alliances and agreements with local tribes. Hence both are now synonymous with a period of mutual reliance and relatively benign race relations, a "middle ground" before the later colonial excesses associated with large-scale white settlement, the expansion of commercial agriculture, and the alienation of indigenous land.[1]

In the last twenty-five years, fur trade scholars have shifted their analysis from economic to social concerns, revealing the previously hidden lives of native women who married European traders "after the custom of the country," raised large mixed-blood families, and effectively mediated between cultures.[2] This turn to the social has not occurred as quickly or extensively in the scholarship on shore whaling, but as the editors of this collection suggest in the introduction, historians of Australia, New Zealand, and the Pacific have recently begun to explore issues relating to sexuality and intermarriage.[3] Following Ann Laura Stoler's call for historians of empire to engage in explicit crosscolonial comparisons, the time is now ripe to place histories of shore whaling and fur trade "intermarriage" in creative tension, so as to further understand the transimperial workings of intimacy and gender in early colonial resource industries.[4]

This essay examines sexual encounters involving shore whalers and women of Ngai Tahu, who were the dominant *iwi* (tribe) in New Zealand's South Island at the time of first contact. It is divided into four parts. The first part explores sexual encounters with indigenous women from the perspective of Euro-American sailors, focusing on the memoirs of Joseph Price, an English seaman who roamed the South Pacific before establishing a shore whaling station in southern New Zealand. The second section offers an insight into the indigenous perspective on such encounters, examining Ngai Tahu experiences on Banks Peninsula, on the east coast of the South Island. The third part is a detailed case study of shore whaling "marriage," deconstructing Joseph Price's account of his ten-year relationship with Akarie, a Ngai Tahu woman who lived with Price on shore stations at Otago and Ikoraki, Banks Peninsula. The final section gives a close reading of the Peraki Log, which records eight years of shore whaling operations at Peraki, another Banks Peninsula station, and contains several references to the role of Maori women in shore station life.

Ngai Tahu women had a role in ensuring their husbands' commercial success that was broadly similar to that of native women in the fur trade, despite the smaller scale and duration of New Zealand whaling. In both industries, "marriage" to indigenous women gave Euro-American men access to land, natural resources, and extensive kin networks; equally, both forms of intermarriage represent attempts by native communities to monopolize the benefits of ongoing trade by encouraging Europeans to remain among them. The key difference, however, is in the representation of affect and economic advantage in the colonial archive. Whereas the letters and diaries of North American fur traders and company officials explicitly acknowledge the economic advantages of unions with indigenous women, evidence of the benefits conveyed by marriage alliance with Ngai Tahu women in the writings of shore whalers is limited to statements about sexual hospitality, companionship, and domestic service. This archival silence, which is exacerbated by the high mobility of both European whalers and southern Maori communities at this time, can be partially overcome by using the methods put forward by Gayatri Chakravorty Spivak.[5] It nevertheless forces us to contemplate intimate colonial relationships that cannot be shown to be "tense" or "tender" but remain indifferent and perhaps unknowable. Like "Richard's 'Whaheen'" (from *wahine*, woman), they appear in brief flashes of detail before melting back into the surrounding landscape.

A British Sailor's Account of "Native Hospitality"

Shore whaling was one of numerous extractive industries to flourish in precolonial New Zealand, part of a wider set of global commercial and imperial networks through which Europe and America expanded their influence in Australasia and the South Pacific. In the late eighteenth and early nineteenth centuries, several thousand European seafarers were drawn to New Zealand's shores. Some came to restock their ships with wood and water, and trade with Maori for pork and potatoes; others sought specific commodities such as sealskins, timber, flax rope, and whale oil for London, Canton, and Calcutta markets.[6] Many, however, came for the sole purpose of rest and recreation, which included the sexual companionship of Maori women and young girls, euphemized in their logbooks as "native hospitality." Men like Joseph Price, an English sailor who spent most of the 1830s aboard whale ships and trading vessels in the South Pacific, came into regular and repeated sexual contact with Maori and other island women. In Price's memoirs, recorded fifty years after he first entered the Pacific, sexual encounters with indigenous women appear as one of the central and organizing features of the masculine culture of maritime resource exploitation.[7]

Joseph Price left London in March 1830 at nineteen years of age.[8] He was a ship's lad from Newcastle upon Tyne, an English port city famed for producing some of the world's finest sailors. Three months after arriving in Sydney on a convict transport carrying female prisoners to the Australian penal colonies, Price joined the crew of the *William Stoveld.* He spent the next sixteen months aboard that vessel, cruising for sperm and right whales in New Zealand waters. In August 1831, he jumped ship at Port Underwood in Cook Strait, stowing away on the *Vittoria,* a flax trader seeking *Phormium tenax* on behalf of a Sydney rope maker. Unlike whaling, the flax industry relied wholly on Maori villagers to harvest the flax plants and prepare them for shipment. This necessity led some flax traders to live as agents among Maori communities, supervising flax production and liaising with merchant ships.[9] Others, like the crew of the *Vittoria,* made more fleeting visits, coasting from one settlement to another and negotiating trade at each stop according to the available surplus. It was in the context of such negotiation that Joseph

Price found himself walking overland from Port Cooper on Banks Peninsula to visit Kaiapoi *pa* (village) on the Canterbury plains. Kaiapoi was at that time the most populous Maori settlement in the South Island, home to more than one thousand people. Price described his experiences at Kaiapoi and at nearby Akaroa, on Banks Peninsula, as follows: "We remained two nights in Kaiapoi, and were treated by the natives most hospitably. Their hospitality extended itself as a favor to accommodate us not only with fish and potatoes, but also with a female bed companion for each of us, but unfortunately for myself my inamorata happened to be about eighty years of age, and consequently not the most desirable of companions . . . we remained in Akaroa for a week, and as in Kaiapoi experienced the greatest hospitality from the Natives, but in this case I was more fortunate in my choice of companion than at Kaiapoi, getting as my mate a rather attractive specimen of the female Maori. In exchange for kindnesses of this kind an old cotton skirt or a quid of tobacco would be considered ample, nay munificent consideration."[10]

Price's language indicates that he understood the sexual welcome as something offered in the name of hospitality, intended, like fish and potatoes, to improve the terms of trade and encourage the traders to return. Although he marveled at what he could get for "an old cotton skirt or a quid of tobacco," the people of Kaiapoi and Akaroa were more likely concerned with obtaining their share of the two hundred muskets and ten cases of gunpowder loaded on board the *Vittoria* as it left Sydney.[11] Ngai Tahu were at that time feuding with a group of northern tribes led by Te Rauparaha of the Ngati Toa *iwi*, a feud that culminated soon after Price's visit in a series of raids that left the region almost deserted by the mid-1830s. In such a context, the ability of the chiefs to control the sexuality of their female kinsfolk, to gain muskets and thus enhance their fighting ability, was of great importance.

After returning from New Zealand to Sydney with a cargo of "beautifully dressed" flax, Price was again engaged on a sperm whaling expedition, this time as a boat-steer on the *Caroline,* evidence of his growing skill and experience in the whaling industry. He spent the next twenty months "cruising among the Islands of the South Pacific," before the *Caroline* returned to take in wood and water at the Bay of Islands. "Here," Price crowed, "I had different luck to my Kaiapoi experience, being entertained by a sprig of about 15 summers."[12] But the sexual welcome was not always as amicable as Price's memoir makes out. The log of Edward Tregurtha, who was captain of the *Caroline* during Price's time aboard, tells of a stopover in the Solomon Islands, where a group of naked women came to the beach and "by lascivious motions" invited them to go ashore on shore. The *Caroline*'s chief mate was suspicious, warning his captain to be on guard, and no sooner did he reach for his tomahawk when "suddenly a yell was made and 8 or 10 men tried to haul the boats on shore." A second incident, during another visit to the Bay of Islands, shows that Maori "ship girls" were also capable of outstaying their welcome. Here Tregurtha records that "upwards of seventy" Maori women "located themselves on board with the Officers and the crew," until their demands on the ship's food supplies became "such a nuisance" that Tregurtha had to "put all hands on an allowance of biscuit . . . so that it could not be procured without my knowledge."[13]

In *Empire and Sexuality*, Ronald Hyam asks provocatively whether Maori women who "throw themselves at British sailors and demand sex" can justifiably be considered victims of exploitation. Hyam uses evidence from the New Zealand frontier to refute what he sees as feminist claims that "native women had always to do the bidding of the white man because the structure of power relations in an empire left them no alternative."[14] Although questions of indigenous agency are important, and will be considered later, Hyam's focus on who exploited whom may distract us from an equally important task, that of exploring the ways sexual commerce and hospitality were woven into the imaginative and spatial fabric of European empires. Price's account of the "female bed companions" provided at Kaiapoi and elsewhere suggests that in his eyes, "sexual hospitality" was simply one of the commodities on offer from his Ngai Tahu hosts. This reflects an imperial ideology in which indigenous women were seen as natural resources, available like flax, whale oil, and sealskins for colonial exploitation.[15] Maori, unsurprisingly, saw things differently. Trade with Europeans had a very immediate material significance, but it does not follow that Maori women were considered chattels in their own society.

Maori Perspectives toward Sexual Encounters with Sailors

In New Zealand, as elsewhere in the Pacific, sexual encounters featured prominently in first contacts between Maori and Europeans. Maori quickly realized that sex, like trade and the violence discussed by Rachel Standfield, could be utilized to control and take advantage of the newcomers. Indeed, sex and trade soon became almost inseparable in frequently visited places like the Bay of Islands, where sailors on arrival would negotiate a "sexual contract," exchanging items such as muskets and powder in return for the company of a Maori woman for their entire three- to five-week time in port.[16] Most observers described these short-term liaisons as simple prostitution, but their significance to Maori was more complex than such terminology allows. As Damon Salesa observes, payment often occurred according to the Maori concept of *utu* (reciprocity, balance), according to which "satisfaction might lie with the larger group, and not only with the individual."[17] Concern for chiefly rank and local rivalry could outweigh considerations of material gain, as when the daughters of chiefs were reserved for captains and ship's officers, or female slaves captured in intertribal warfare were subjected to mass prostitution as a means of revenge and humiliation.

Crosscultural sexual relationships of longer duration occurred initially almost entirely on Maori terms, as families sought to incorporate the European newcomers into their *whakapapa* (genealogy, line of descent). Adult heterosexual unions were an important feature of Maori society, ensuring stable communities and fulfilling a genealogical requirement that parentage be well established.[18] Within this highly gendered culture, the institution of marriage was used strategically as a way of cementing alliances, avoiding conflict, and healing old wounds. Ngai Tahu, for example, became the dominant *iwi* in the South Island through integration in the seventeenth and eighteenth centuries with two preexisting kinship groups, Ngati Mamoe and Waitaha, a process symbolized by intermarriage between the families of the tribal leadership.[19] Echoes of this kinship system, governed by what anthropologist Gayle Rubin refers to as "the exchange of women," can be identified in later patterns of sexual contact and intermarriage between Ngai Tahu women and Euro-American sealing and whaling crews. However, as Rubin acknowledges, "kinship systems do not merely exchange women. They exchange sexual access, genealogical statuses, lineage names and ancestors, rights and *people*—men, women, and children, in concrete systems of social relationships."[20]

The Ngai Tahu sexual economy did not develop at the frenetic pace or on the same competitive scale as that of the Bay of Islands, even though Maori in both regions experienced European contact from the late eighteenth century. Australian sealing vessels began depositing gangs in Dusky Sound and Foveaux Strait from the 1790s, some leaving groups of men ashore for as long a year. A small number of sealers left their gangs and dwelt among southern Ngai Tahu and Ngati Mamoe communities, forming long-term sexual relationships with local women.[21] Although their southern relations established important trade links with sealers and visiting whaling ships, Kaiapoi and Banks Peninsula Maori remained largely isolated from the effects of contact until the early 1830s, apart from the occasional visiting flax trader such as Joseph Price. It was this relative isolation and their lack of access to new technologies that led the Ngai Tahu in the Banks Peninsula region to suffer a series of military defeats by a group of heavily armed North Island tribes in the early 1830s, wiping out the local flax industry and leaving the area virtually deserted.[22] Significantly, shore whaling began in 1837, providing Ngai Tahu in the area with an opportunity to form alliances and personal relationships with Europeans at a time when the local population was still very much recovering from these traumatic events.

Shore whalers were particularly reliant on the patronage of local chiefs, who provided access to land and protection against attack from neighboring tribes. In such an environment, personal ties across the culture divide assumed a greater importance, especially the mutual recognition of authority and status by Maori chiefs and trading and whaling masters.[23] Sex and companionship between indigenous women and Europeans were integral to establishing these connections. Although Maori women who lived on the shore stations were frequently described as whalers' "wives," these longer term liaisons initially bore little resemblance to the Western institution of marriage, often imposing ongoing duties to a wider kinship group on the often unsuspecting pakeha. According to one observer, at the beginning of each season each whaler "went with such of their comrades as were well known by the natives to the different villages in the neighbourhood, for the purpose of procuring a helpmate during the season." There, "bargains were struck between the experienced headsman or boat-steerer and the relations of the girls selected." In exchange for her companionship, "the whaler's part consisted in a payment made on the completion of the bargain, and in a certain degree of indulgence to the begging visits of his new relations during the season."[24]

Ngai Tahu on Banks Peninsula therefore had much to gain in both material and strategic terms from engaging in the sexual economy. The sources are however all but silent on the less positive aspects of the exchange. Very little is recorded about the nature of crosscultural relationships, but traces of violence, coercion, mistreatment, and abandonment can be found at the margins of the archive. Intimate encounters such as those described by Joseph Price were also vectors through which syphilis, gonorrhea, and other new diseases were introduced into the southern Maori population, in a period when the tribe was reduced to as little one-fifth of its original size by sickness and war. There were, of course, also numerous long-term relationships of genuine affection, some of which were later formalized as Christian marriages by local missionaries. Nevertheless, as Atholl Anderson has demonstrated, the overall trend in the southern South Island was of Ngai Tahu women relocating to shore whaling stations in ever-larger numbers to live with their pakeha spouses, rather than Europeans living among Maori communities. According to Anderson, the loss of fertile young women to European partners and their subsequent removal from Ngai Tahu villages was "probably a more important cause of population decline by 1840 than any other."[25]

Maori notions of *utu, whakapapa,* and marriage alliance thus existed in tension with an emergent colonial reality, in which sexual contact and intermarriage led ultimately to migration away from ancestral lands, social fragmentation, and the dilution of ancestral lines.[26] Although these are sometimes simplified into two "types" of intermarriage, the one displacing the other, it is possible to identify cases where binding kinship ties persisted well into the colonial era. Conversely, there were some early "marriages" in which Maori women were removed from their communities and dwelt solely among pakeha sealers and whalers. These contradictions are compounded by an absence of data, making generalizations about an archetypal form of crosscultural intimacy very difficult unless contained to a particular region or example, such as that of Joseph Price and Akarie. I have chosen Price and Akarie to illustrate that many shore whaling "marriages" were short-lived and transient, abandoned by Europeans after their economic and social utility declined. It is important, however, to acknowledge that one could equally construct archetypes out of men such as William Gilbert, Phillip Ryan, and other Banks Peninsula shore whalers who formed long-lasting, affectionate relationships with Ngai Tahu women that remained long after the whales had gone.

Price and Akarie: "My Maori Housekeeper and Wife"

Joseph Price's enthusiastic descriptions of sexual encounters at sea stand in stark contrast to his near-silence when discussing Akarie, the Ngai Tahu woman who lived with him for ten years on shore whaling stations at Otago and Banks Peninsula and who is mentioned only three times in his memoirs. In 1836 Price returned to New Zealand as chief officer of the *Harriet,* a small Australian vessel engaged to supply shore whaling stations on the east coast of South Island by the Weller brothers, of Sydney. The next year, he returned to Otago and "remained there whaling three winters," in charge of three separate whaling stations on behalf of the Wellers. "Here," he recalled, "I picked up with a native girl named Akarie who acted in the dual capacity of house-keeper and wife."[27] Price was silent on how he met Akarie, although his status as station head on the Weller brothers' whaling stations would have made him important and attractive to local Ngai Tahu who were seeking access to the new economic opportunities associated with the whaling stations and their maritime networks. Although Akarie's precise background is unclear, she is remembered today by some of her Ngai Tahu descendants as "a woman of standing in her tribe, considered a rebel by her elders who frowned on her behaviour."[28]

Marriage alliances with local women were a common condition of original settlement, intended by Ngai Tahu to permanently bind the whaling enterprise to its hosts, and to the region. In Price's case, however, "marriage" to Akarie failed to keep him at Otago for long. Whales were becoming scarce in the region after six years of unsustainable fishing, whereas the waters surrounding Banks Peninsula remained relatively untouched. In November 1839, Price shifted north to establish a whaling station at Ikoraki, taking with him "my Maori housekeeper and child and some other necessaries."[29] His depiction of Akarie as housekeeper, wife, and mother—in that order—shows the importance placed on domesticity in shore whaling relationships, over and above the discourse of "hospitality" described earlier. As Lisa Norling observes in her study of New England whalers' wives, the role of the shore-bound spouse reflected prevailing European notions of marriage, in a period when "the family was still a hierarchy and the husband was still clearly in charge."[30] Indeed, although white women were a rare sight on whaling stations, the few who accompanied their husbands to New Zealand played much the same role.

After Price's first season at Ikoraki, the Wellers went bankrupt, but he continued whaling in his own name for seven years, with considerable success. In 1843, he was reported to have taken "more whales than any Fishery in New Zealand."[31] During the seven years he lived with Akarie at Ikoraki, Price would often disappear to Sydney for up to six months at a time, all the while leaving his "Maori companion and child" at the nearby Oashore station. In Sydney, according to his interviewer, Thomas Quealy, he would "get rid of money at the rate of £600 to £900," although "he was very sore to be asked anything about how he did it." Indeed, during one of these off-season trips to Sydney, Price married Jane Scott, an Englishwoman, at St. James Church in 1848, but again he refused to answer Quealy's questions "about his 1st and 2nd wifes . . . as I seemed to have offended him . . . he would not give me another scrap."[32] Price's disavowal is revealing, given his frank description of previous sexual liaisons. It suggests that at the time of Quealy's interview in 1893 he was uncomfortable admitting his past affective relationship with a Maori woman, or perhaps still experienced a sense of shame for abandoning Akarie in favor of a European wife.

As Ballantyne and Burton point out, crosscultural sexual relationships have been seen by Hyam and others as "forces that 'connect' or 'anchor' white men into non-European communities."[33] If we take Price's imperial career as archetype, it becomes clear that in some cases the "localizing force" of shore whaling intermarriage was very weak indeed, here losing out to the economic incentives of a highly mobile industry, and later the superior cultural claims of formal European-style marriage, to an English bride. The unstated importance of Price's relationship with Akarie was not that it facilitated his long-term integration into the Ngai Tahu community; rather, it was his marriage that helped him gain an economic foothold at a time when Ngai Tahu still held power over European access to their lands and resources. This illustrates how affective values, such as companionship and domesticity, can obscure the unspoken role of intimate crosscultural relationships in securing indigenous cooperation, enabling settlers' access to natural resources and ultimately converting the "middle ground" into Europeanized economic space.

But to focus solely on Price's agency and mobility is to risk repeating another important criticism of Hyam's "sexual opportunity" thesis: that in describing the work of the British Empire, it centers the experience of white men, while neglecting the stories of white and indigenous women.[34] This, in turn, is the result of an imperial and colonial archive that largely contains records of men's deeds and thoughts. It is unclear, for example, whether Price simply abandoned Akarie and her child at Ikoraki in 1848 and/or whether they went back to live with her family in Otago. Very little is known about her life thereafter, except that in 1852 she married another white man, the former whaler William Isaac Haberfield. A family history records that Annie Price, the daughter of Joseph and Akarie, received an expensive Sydney education according to her father's wishes, suggesting that Price sought to bring some colonial respectability to his frontier family.[35] Apart from this, there is no sign that Price regarded his relationship with Akarie as anything other than a marriage of convenience. In the words of Gayatri Chakravorty Spivak, "there is no romance to be found here."[36]

Ngai Tahu Women in the Peraki Log

One of the problems with attempting to reconstruct relationships between Maori women and European men in early New Zealand is that the great majority of the individuals concerned, particularly Maori, are all but invisible in the colonial archive. This is especially true of Maori women, but the Peraki Log, which describes eight years of day-to-day operations at the Peraki station on Banks Peninsula, shows that even the sources that record the personal experiences of European shore whalers are few and problematic. Very few men on the shore stations were able to read or write, and as Harry Morton notes, the letters of those who could were often destroyed before they could reach friends and family, part of a deliberate policy of isolation put in place by station managers and owners "in order to keep any news about the fisheries from reaching competitors in Sydney."[37] Thus, the most one can expect from conventional archival sources is a rough list of the men working at each station, an intermittent series of financial accounts and letters between the station manager in New Zealand and his Sydney backers and in rare cases a journal of comings and goings like the Peraki Log.

As Spivak has shown, colonial archives contain silences and erasures, particularly when one reads them in an attempt to recapture the subjectivity of those in the "shadow of shadows," simultaneously marginalized by both gender and race. Ngai Tahu women who appear in the commercial records of shore whaling companies are no different in this respect. In the Peraki Log, they are nameless, nearly invisible, noted only when they represent a problem, and always appearing after an apostrophe as the belongings of men, whether Maori or European. Like Spivak's example of the Rani of Sirmur, they, too, are "caught" between indigenous patriarchy and British imperialism, although in a very different elaboration of mercantile exploitation and colonial rule.[38] By applying Spivak's methodology of reading the archives to the Peraki Log, we get a glimpse of the role of gender in the everyday operations of shore whaling society, almost as much from the absence of references to Maori women as from their occasional presence. As with Price's memoir, it is possible to detect the unstated importance of Maori women to the establishment and functioning of the shore stations.

Maori men and women were a regular part of shore station life at Peraki from its establishment in March 1837. The earliest entries in the Peraki station log show the whalers' initial reliance on their Ngai Tahu hosts for the simplest of tasks, such as building a shelter and hunting for food. The first reference to a Maori woman comes three weeks later, when the log keeper remarks "This day one of the New-zeland Whooman got young Boay," reminding us that even at this early stage, "half-caste" children were, as Salesa puts it, "part of the icononography of the beach."[39] At the end of the first season of whaling, the schooner *Dublin Packet* sailed for Sydney, "leaving behind Capt. Hempelman and wife and Eight Europeans and one New Zealander." During the summer months, supplies were so short that "every Man must look out for selves for the produce of the Bush and Bay."[40] There is thus at this point no evidence of any sort of strategic alliance or long-term arrangement, or indeed anything comparable to the practice of "wintering over" with First Nations communities in the North American fur trade.

Maori women are not mentioned in the log for the next five years. Revealingly, they reappear in the winter of 1842, at a time when the Peraki station was in dire financial circumstances and the men on several occasions refused to work for want of provisions. It is here that Richards's *wahine* makes her first appearance in the log: "Sunday, 17th May 1842. Wind SW; continual gale. Richards and Mould went to Tumbledown to bring his traps. Maori women bolted. Short of flour. Monday, 18th May. . . . Richards and Mould returned yesterday evening with some traps, his woman, and the Picaninnies [Maori children]."[41] Richards's *wahine* may have been retrieved from wherever she had fled to, but the desertions continued; on July 23, 1842, "Ellis's woman bolted," and this time there is no suggestion she returned. It seems that during times of hardship, these unnamed women were somehow able to escape with their children back to their people, retaining a level of mobility and independence that was in some cases greater than that of Europeans. Nevertheless, we must be careful not to overstate the degree to which Maori women can be shown to have agency. The final pages of the Peraki Log contain a rare admission of domestic violence, in which the log keeper confesses he "was obliged to give Ann a good thrashing today."[42] As Adele Perry notes in her chapter on Salt Spring Island, the use of violence was endemic and commonplace to frontier spaces, however intimate or domestic.

The Peraki Log reveals little about the official stance of shore whaling companies toward relationships between their workers and Maori women. These invisible women became partially visible in the colonial archive only once whalers and other early settlers started taking an interest in land sales, prompting British government agents to begin recording census and other information. When Captain Stanley of the English gunship *Britomart* made a rough survey of early European settlers on Banks Peninsula in August 1840, he reported that William Woods, one of the proprietors of the Oashore whaling stations station, claimed sixty acres of nearby land, "in the behalf of a native woman living with him."[43] Stanley counted a total of seventeen "native women" living among the whalers at Peraki, Ikoraki, and Oashore, the three whaling stations then in operation. His figures seem low, given that the population of shore whalers would have been about one hundred. Although Banks Peninsula shore whaling began at a time when the local Ngai Tahu population was scattered, it is likely that at least fifty of these men formed sexual relationships with Maori women.[44] It is difficult to estimate, since the relationships we know about are those that produced children who survived, and are thus remembered by descendants.

Here it is useful to return to the comparison between shore whaling and the North American fur trade. More than any other factor, it is the nature of the archive that has prevented the emergence of a history of shore whaling to match recent literature on the fur trade and its aftermath. At one level, this stems from obvious disparities in size and scale. The writing of social history requires a minimum amount of personal information, and the mobility of those engaged in short-lived Pacific resource industries means that facts about individuals were less likely to be recorded in detail. Another explanation lies in Sylvia Van Kirk's statement that the fur trade formed "the basis of recorded history in Western Canada."[45] Like the East India Company in British South Asia, fur trade companies such as the Hudson's Bay Company were granted imperial monopolies, creating substantial colonial archives in their own right. Shore whaling companies, on the other hand, were small, speculative, Sydney-based ventures, lacking the bureaucratic power to command imperial attention or engage in the self-conscious production of archives. It is the shape of the shore whaling archive, influenced by the speculative nature of colonial industry and the selective recordings of colonial men, that keeps the intimate details of shore whaling intermarriage tantalizingly out of view.

Conclusion: Intimacy, Empire, Mobility, Agency

Ronald Hyam argues in *Empire and Sexuality* that some indigenous women "were arguably better off by sexual incorporation into the white man's world," a category exemplified by Inuit women married to Canadian fur traders, and one in which he would no doubt also include Maori women who "married" New Zealand shore whalers.[46] By focusing on the memoirs of Joseph Price and his ambiguous relationship with Akarie, this essay has set out to remind scholars of empire that crosscultural sexual encounters such as those that arose out of the shore whaling industry did not always result in the incorporation of indigenous women into the European world, or vice versa. I have sought instead to emphasize the economic function of intimate relationships, comparing the role of Ngai Tahu women vis-à-vis whaling stations to that played by First Nations women in the North American fur trade. As Susan Sleeper-Smith has recently shown, Indian women in the *pays d'en haut* were integral to their husbands' success, constructing elaborate kinship networks between fur trading posts and indigenous communities that allowed greater access to fur pelts and safe transport for other goods.[47] While Ngai Tahu women occupied this role for decades rather than centuries, their unspoken influence was of similar value to European shore whalers, and indeed to their own *iwi*, in an era when the Ngai Tahu dominated coastal transport networks and reestablished itself as a military power and a majority on the land.

The distinction identified in Price's narrative between "sexual hospitality" and unspoken "marriage alliance" is not intended to separate those European men who remained "European" from those who became something different, in the words of one recent writer, "a third kind of New Zealander."[48] Instead, it offers a way of thinking about a group of empire makers who are otherwise very difficult to capture in a single analytical frame, especially when compared to the well-documented archival networks linking the two other rival imperial forces in early New Zealand, namely missionaries and systematic colonizers. The fleeting examples of sexual economy, while illustrating the global patterns of sexual opportunity created by the British Empire, involved European sailors and whalers who had very few ties to New Zealand, even in a commercial sense. Usually they came for fresh provisions or solely for rest and relaxation, before leaving again on a sperm whaling expedition or, like Joseph Price after his flax trading expedition to Kaiapoi, returning to Sydney, the metropole of Australia's expanding Pacific frontier. In contrast, sealers and shore whalers were bound to Maori communities for labor, cooperation, and ongoing supplies. It is these men, and their Ngai Tahu wives, who were responsible for extending the southern maritime frontier to Banks Peninsula, even if, like Joseph Price and Akarie, their relationships did not last long in the new colonial era.

As moving subjects, Price, Akarie, the Peraki whalers, and the unnamed Ngai Tahu *wahine* did not remain fixed in one place long enough to be archived. Ngai Tahu were highly mobile at this time, but it is primarily male movements that were recorded, as when war parties and chiefly delegations traveled the length of the South Island in the aftermath of Te Rauparaha's raids. The Peraki Log examples quoted earlier show some Ngai Tahu women were able to use their kin networks to escape if required. Conversely, many "local" women who fled south of Banks Peninsula as refugees in the 1820s and 1830s made their return once stability returned to the region, some joining pakeha men on the shore whaling stations. Some shore whalers and Ngai Tahu women stayed together after the industry declined in the late 1840s, forming "shagroon" colonies such as that at nearby Okains Bay, where four European ex-whalers lived on the same inaccessible shore, each with their Ngai

Tahu wives and large "half-caste" families.[49] It seems that these men and women felt a common bond, isolated not only from the nearby English settlement of Christchurch but also from their Ngai Tahu cousins, who unlike the Maori wives of whalers had no way of holding onto their land and were thus slowly shuffled off the peninsula onto minuscule Crown reserves.

Richard White observes that in the *pays d'en haut,* male and female remained "master categories that rarely were transcended," even on the middle ground of culture contact, where moments of encounter allowed a degree of "self-fashioning" that often belied fixed ideas of race and cultural difference.[50] Ngai Tahu women, like indigenous women in the fur trade, occupied a unique position as negotiators between existing and incoming social groups, by virtue of both their gender and their "race." While they could not transcend gender expectations in realms such as domesticity and sexual access, they were no doubt able to use their position as cultural mediators to their own advantage. However we have little or no record of this. Following Spivak, this essay has grappled with the adequacy of ethnohistorical method, or whether it is possible to attribute agency to those who did not explain their actions in documents, simply by recreating their cultural context. At times it has been necessary to follow the advice of David A. Chappell, who in trying to describe the shipboard exploitation of Pacific Island women by European sailors, remarked: "if we want to liberate women from androcentric history, we may have to settle at times for portraying their dignity in the face of male oppression."[51] While it is possible to demonstrate the pivotal role played by Ngai Tahu women in early European resource industries, their agency as individual actors, expressing their own subjectivity and looking after their own interests, remains elusively outside the archive.

Notes

The chapter epigraph is in F. A. Anson, ed., *The Piraki Log (E Pirangi Ahau Koe); or Diary of Captain Hempleman* (Oxford, 1910), 142. The material in this essay was originally presented at a seminar on Gender and Empire held at the University of Otago, Dunedin, New Zealand, in October 2004. I am grateful to Tony Ballantyne and Antoinette Burton for encouraging me to develop it into a publication, Leanna Parker and Lesley Haines for their detailed feedback on the final draft, and Ian Smith and the Marsden Fund of New Zealand for funding the research project on which this chapter is based. I would also like to acknowledge my sister Bronwyn, who endured my company through the essay's often painful gestation, and whose cheerful determination in the face of her own adversity inspired its completion.

1. Harry Morton, *The Whale's Wake* (Dunedin, New Zealand, 1982), 281, 217, 262–63. Willard H. Rollings, "Maori People Are Not Indians . . . : Some Aspects of Maori–American Indian Comparative History," *Te Pouhere Korero* 1, 1 (1999): 46–56. For the concept of the "middle ground," see Richard White, *The Middle Ground: Indians, Empires and Republics in the Great Lakes Region, 1650–1815* (Cambridge, 1991).

2. Sylvia Van Kirk, *Many Tender Ties: Women in Fur-Trade Society, 1670–1870* (Winnipeg, 1980). Jennifer S. H. Brown, *Strangers in Blood: Fur Trade Company Families in Indian Country* (Vancouver, 1980).

3. Angela Wanhalla, "Marrying 'In': The Geography of Intermarriage on the Taieri, 1830s–1920s," in Tony Ballantyne and Judith A. Bennett, eds., *Landscape/Community: Perspectives from New Zealand History* (Dunedin, New Zealand, 2005), 73–94. Judith Binney, "In between Lives: Studies from within a Colonial Society," in Tony Ballantyne and Brian Moloughney, eds., *Disputed Histories: Imagining New Zealand's Pasts* (Dunedin, New Zealand, 2006), 93–118.

4. Ann Laura Stoler, "Tense and Tender Ties: The Politics of Comparison in North American History and (Post) Colonial Studies," *Journal of American History* 88, 3 (2001): 829–65.

5. Gayatri Chakravorty Spivak, "The Rani of Sirmur: An Essay in Reading the Archives," *History and Theory* 24, 3 (1985): 247–73.

6. Jim McAloon, "Resource Frontiers, Environment, and Settler Capitalism, 1769–1860," in Tom Brooking and Eric Pawson, eds., *Environmental Histories of New Zealand* (Auckland, New Zealand, 2002), 53–54.

7. Joseph Price, "Reminiscences about Early Days on Banks Peninsula, Whaling," as noted by T. Quealy, 1891, transcript by J. C. Andersen, typescript copy in C. R. Straubel Papers, ARC1900.386, Canterbury Museum, Christchurch, New Zealand.

8. Yvonne Fitzmaurice, *Captain Joseph Price 1809–1901: Mariner, Landowner and Family Man* (Melbourne, Australia, 1984), 1.

9. R. P. Wigglesworth, "The New Zealand Timber and Flax Trade 1769–1840" (Ph.D. diss., Massey University, 1981), 63–65.

10. Price, "Reminiscences," 1–2.

11. *Australian,* May 6, October 21, 1831; *Sydney Herald,* May 6, 1831.

12. Price, "Reminiscences," 3.

13. Dan Sprod, ed., *The Tregurtha Log: Relating the Adventurous Life of Captain Edward Primrose Tregurtha* (Hobart, Australia, 1980), 64, 73.

14. Ronald Hyam, *Empire and Sexuality: The British Experience* (Manchester, England, 1990), 207.

15. Patty O'Brien, *The Pacific Muse: Exotic Femininity and the Colonial Pacific* (Seattle, 2006), 116, 136–38.

16. James Belich, *Making Peoples: A History of the New Zealanders from Polynesian Settlement to the End of the Nineteenth Century* (Auckland, New Zealand, 1996), 152–53.

17. Damen Salesa, "Race Mixing: A Victorian Problem in Britain and New Zealand, 1830s–1870" (D. Phil. diss., Oxford University, 2001),

18. Bruce Biggs, *Maori Marriage: An Essay in Reconstruction* (Wellington, New Zealand, 1960),

19. Rawiri Te Maire Tau, *Nga Pikituroa o Ngai Tahu: The Oral Traditions of Ngai Tahu* (Dunedin, New Zealand, 2003), 195–96.

20. Gayle Rubin, "The Traffic in Women: Notes on the 'Political Economy' of Sex," in Rayna R. Reiter, ed., *Toward an Anthropology of Women* (New York, 1975), 175.

21. Ian Smith, *The New Zealand Sealing Industry: History, Archaeology and Heritage Management* (Wellington, New Zealand, 2003), 29.

22. Atholl Anderson, *The Welcome of Strangers: An Ethnohistory of Southern Maori A.D. 1650–1850* (Dunedin, New Zealand, 1998), 90.

23. Anderson, *Welcome of Strangers*, 224–25.

24. Edward Jerningham Wakefield, *Adventure in New Zealand: With Some Account of the Beginning of the British Colonisation of the Islands*, 2 vols. (London, 1845), 1:233–34.

25. Atholl Anderson, *Race against Time: The Early Maori-Pakeha Families and the Development of the Mixed-Race Population in Southern New Zealand* (Dunedin, New Zealand, 1991), 31. Anderson, *Welcome of Strangers*, 66.

26. Wanhalla, "Marrying 'In,'" 78–79.

27. Price, "Reminiscences," 4.

28. Fitzmaurice, *Captain Joseph Price*, 155.

29. Price, "Reminiscences," 4.

30. Lisa Norling, "'How Frought with Sorrow and Heartpangs': Mariners' Wives and the Ideology of Domesticity in New England, 1790–1880," *New England Quarterly* 65, 3 (1992): 423.

31. C. B. Robinson to Colonial Secretary, June 30, 1843, IA 1 43/1779, Archives New Zealand, Wellington.

32. Price, "Reminiscences," 6–8.

33. Tony Ballantyne and Antoinette Burton, introduction here.

34. Angela Wanhalla, "Transgressing Boundaries: A History of the Mixed Descent Families of Matiapapa, Taieri, 1830–1940" (Ph.D. diss., University of Canterbury, 2004), 6.

35. Fitzmaurice, *Captain Joseph Price*, 155.

36. Spivak, "Rani of Sirmur," 267.

37. Morton, *Whales Wake*, 238.

38. Spivak, "Rani of Sirmur," 265, 267.

39. Anon., "Remarks in New Zealand, March 1837," in Anson, *Piraki Log*, 50–51. Salesa, "Race Mixing," 98.

40. Anon., "Daily Journal of Employment and Remarks at Peracka," in Anson, *Piraki Log*, 58, 64.

41. James Barry, "Remarks, 1842," in ibid., 129, 40.

42. Anon., "Remarks, 1844," in ibid., 145.

43. Stanley to Hobson, September 17, 1840, in Great Britain, *Parliamentary Papers Relating to New Zealand*, 12 vols., 2:311.

44. Anderson, by way of comparison, counts 135 known unions between European men and Ngai Tahu women in Otago and Southland. *Race against Time*, 3.

45. Van Kirk, *Many Tender Ties*, 1.

46. Hyam, *Empire and Sexuality*, 207.

47. Susan Sleeper-Smith, *Indian Women and French Men: Rethinking Cultural Encounter in the Western Great Lakes* (Amherst, Mass., 2001), 4–5.

48. Trevor Bentley, *Pakeha Maori: The Extraordinary Story of the Europeans Who Lived as Maori in Early New Zealand* (Auckland, New Zealand, 1999), 9.

49. See Gordon Ogilvie, *Banks Peninsula: Cradle of Canterbury* (Wellington, New Zealand, 1990), 114–17.

50. Richard White, "'Although I Am Dead, I Am Not Entirely Dead. I Have Left a Second of Myself: Constructing Self and Persons on the Middle Ground of Early America," in Ronald Hoffman, Mechal Sobel, and Fredrika J. Teute, eds., *Through a Glass Darkly: Reflections on Personal Identity in Early America* (Chapel Hill, N.C., 1997), 405.

51. David A. Chappell, "Shipboard Relations between Pacific Island Women and Euroamerican Men, 1767–1887," *Journal of Pacific History* 27, 2 (1992): 131–49.

ELIZABETH VIBERT

3 *Writing "Home"*

SIBLING INTIMACY AND MOBILITY
IN A SCOTTISH COLONIAL MEMOIR

The cold space of empire provides the geographical frame for the mid-nineteenth-century memoir of Murdoch Stewart, a Scottish missionary who emigrated to Cape Breton Island, Nova Scotia, in the 1840s. Cold space—a phrase that conjures both the inhospitable vastness of the North Atlantic and the loneliness of a man pushed from his home by economic need—was a constitutive element of Stewart's adult life. Murdoch Stewart did not simply move across space from one British realm to another. In his memoir he inhabits each place, Cape Breton and Scotland, in terms of the other. In turn, he understands and inhabits each place through the affective ties of family, his responses shaped most powerfully by the bond of affection and loyalty that persisted between himself and his brother Donald, whom he left behind when he emigrated. By recounting and re-presenting that relationship in intimate detail, the memoir seeks to reach across cold space, to mediate between Scottish "home" and colonial strangeness. In this essay I probe Stewart's self-writing with a focus on the strategies he deployed to negotiate the distance between Scotland and Nova Scotia. How did Stewart seek to maintain and reclaim, through writing, the intimate familial connections that so strongly defined his manly identity and sense of place?[1]

It is a deliberate move to define Stewart's family bonds, and particularly the bond with Donald, as "intimate." I wish to unsettle the assumption, common to much of the important recent work on intimacy and empire, that intimacy generally connotes sexual or conjugal relations. While such relations have rightly been shown to be vital to the production and reproduction of imperial relations of rule, surely there could be intimacy—across empire—without sex. As Charlotte Macdonald and Kirsten McKenzie demonstrate in chapters 4 and 13 here, meaningful intimacy could inhere in many other places, including in friendship, in domestic service and other private interactions, and in the veins of colonial political patronage.[2] Perhaps one of the most overlooked realms of the intimate is the sibling relationship, the bond at the center of this narrative.[3]

Murdoch Stewart was born in 1810 into a poor, semirural family in Contin, Ross-shire, on the edge of the northwest Highlands of Scotland. He was the youngest of seven children, all of whom survived to adulthood. His family's social location hovered on the margins of working and lower middle class: his father trained as a tailor but didn't stay with the trade; his parents tried their hands for a time at small-scale farming; and his father ultimately followed his calling and became an itinerant catechist (lay preacher) for the Church of Scotland—the Presbyterian church—in the western Highlands.[4] As I will show, Murdoch's own education and occupation moved him closer to middle class, although he enjoyed few material trappings of that status. Murdoch spent the first thirty-three years of his life in Scotland. He attended parish school in his village and university in Aberdeen before reluctantly emigrating to Nova Scotia to take up a clergy post on the island of Cape Breton. He remained in Cape Breton for the rest of his life, apart from two brief visits to Scotland and a move to his son's home in mainland Nova Scotia for the final two years of his life. He wrote his intensely personal memoir during semiretirement in his sixties and seventies.

Recent work on the value of personal correspondence and self-writing to historians of empire has inspired me in particular ways to unpick the full, fine fabric of colonial domestic lives as represented in writings from the home front.[5] That fabric is comprised, of course, of the intersecting social roles and subjectivities of both women and men. Murdoch Stewart's personal rumination on the making of his own manhood and the meaning of "home" in his life sheds illuminating light on the role of home in the making of the historical subject, and the role of the subject in making history. His meditation on his family of origin provides insight into the making of a colonial man: his becoming a man, alongside the closely studied model of his beloved elder brother Donald; his becoming educated, on a well-trodden Scottish path from poverty to university on scholarships and personal patronage; his becoming actively Christian, through a rather reluctant detour from classical scholarship to theology school; and his becoming exiled, through a very reluctant journey from a supportive family circle to the "wilds" of Cape Breton.[6] The gendered identity Stewart summons in his text is at once personal and national. Less explicit than the voice of the respectable Christian man, but profoundly present, is the imperial voice. Stewart was sent to Cape Breton as a minor player in a larger imperial errand: through immigration, to remake colonial space in the image of the metropole. He was part of the crucial project to convey imperial "regimes of truth" to new colonial domains; his activities and responses are concrete evidence for how these ways of knowing were imposed and contested at the "microsites" of colonial life.[7]

I was drawn to Stewart's memoir because of my interest in how historical ways of knowing reside in the diverse narrative forms produced in the past.[8] As Antoinette Burton has written, all historical narratives are "highly situated knowledge[s]" that remodel as they remember, leaving "the 'original' always in doubt."[9] Historical narratives are fictions of a sort, in that they are socially situated, self-interested, contingent. But they are "fictions that matter" because of the way they clarify the conceptions, concerns, and activities of the cultures from which they spring.[10] My use of the term "fiction" is not meant to discredit historical sources. On the contrary, my point is that a vast array of narratives from the past are potentially valuable social documents.[11] As cultural artifacts, all demand careful interrogation in order to understand their particular systems of logic and representation. The personal records of empire, such as family histories and letters, provide untapped insight into the intimacies of the domestic scene both at home and abroad, and into the larger relations between colony and metropole.

Memory, in this formulation, is the stuff of history. Like Mary Margaret Steedly, I argue that historical experience is validly inscribed in the whole range of rememberings, the whole array of cultural artifacts: "the transcription of historical experience—in names, monuments, genealogies; in collective fantasy and in the regulated social intercourse of everyday life; in law, property, and desire; in stories inhaled with the common air of a shared place or time—is the movement through which subjectivity is produced."[12] Historical production of subjectivity is my interest in this essay. How does a historical actor recall and reconstruct a life? What sorts of insights does that storied memory provide into the social forces at play in a specific time and place—intimate relations of family, gender, and generation, the demands of religion, modernity, race, colonialism, nationalism? More specific to the purposes of this brief essay, how does the writer's relationship to home figure in historical memory? How is the writer's subject status shaped and sustained by the experience of what he or she thinks of as home, and in opposition to spaces that are not home? How does the relationship to home *become* the writer's history, and by extension the history of those of similar social station who did not or could not write? How does home figure in the historical memory of a man whose identity was in so many ways framed by his "public" persona?[13] I am well aware that my own subject position is very much at play in my reading of Stewart's text. I read his text wearing the lenses of a feminist colonial historian whose main research interest is the making of colonial identities and the representation of difference. As with all historians, my scholarly and personal preoccupations frame in a profound way both my reading of Stewart's history and my subsequent *writing* of it.[14]

A particular notion of home is the defining core of Murdoch Stewart's narrative. Some of the details of that notion will be spelled out in the course of this essay. In a limited way home is a physical space: Stewart recalls the "enchantingly beautiful" village where he grew up and the fishing streams and wooded paths of his childhood, although he has little to say about the house.[15] Far more profoundly, home is the social space where Murdoch passed his childhood and learned to be a man. As historian John Gillis has argued, home is both the family we live *in* and the family we live *by*.[16] In Stewart's memoir the family he lived in, his Cape Breton brood, is all but absent. The memoir is crafted for them, in ways I will explore, but they scarcely appear. Home is the family Murdoch lived *by*—the emotional attachments and predispositions that defined his childhood, provided his life models, and formed the site of yearning throughout his adult life.[17] At the center of that family network was Murdoch Stewart's eldest brother, Donald, who long served as mentor and role model to Murdoch. Murdoch's yearning for home was first and foremost a desire to be with Donald again. It was also a desire to be *like* Donald, a desire that in Murdoch's estimation was never quite fulfilled. Donald defined for Murdoch the nature of a good life, well lived: he appears in the pages of the life history as the embodiment of respectable Scottish Christian manhood. Murdoch's yearning, then, is not so much for a house, a region, or a country as for his childhood family, his beloved brother, and the comforting symbols of a particular kind of Scottish middle-class respectability. These desires seemed beyond Murdoch's grasp as he constructed his life story in Cape Breton, thousands of miles from "home."

Literary scholar Kate Teltscher has written that personal letters home from the colonies tend to seek to diminish geographical space, and to reduce the imagined difference between colony and metropole, the strange and the normal.[18] Stewart's memoir does not so much seek to reduce distance as to resist resignation. Despite spending the last forty years of his life in Cape Breton, Stewart was not willing to resign himself to a colonial life. He could not let go of his Scottish home. In this sense, Stewart, like Mary Taylor in Macdonald's essay (chapter 4 here) and Lady Anne Barnard in McKenzie's (chapter 13 here), dwelt in two places at once. He made an apparently full life in Cape Breton as father to ten children and clergyman to a large, dispersed, and grateful congregation. Yet his thoughts in later life, at least as revealed in the memoir, were fixed firmly on the home of his youth.[19] Stewart's writings speak to a conceptualization of place in which localities are not bounded off, enclosed, or contained but are "present in one another."[20] In this notion of place, identities are not defined one against another; on the contrary, specificities of person and place are defined through interrelations. It is at last becoming a commonplace of colonial cultural history that empire and colony were defined in terms of one another. Imperial and colonial spaces have come to be seen as products of "accumulating interconnections within a specific global field," a field characterized by mobility.[21] In Stewart's writing, Scotland and Cape Breton are very much present in one another. His idealized, nostalgic, and highly personal memories of Scotland and his Scottish family are directly conditioned by his memory of alienation in Cape Breton. Cape Breton comes into being in the text mainly as an expression of Stewart's dislocation from Scotland. Stewart's Scotland and Cape Breton imaginaries are constituted through each other.

Murdoch Stewart's memoir is a tale of longing, loss, and displacement—not at all the self-aggrandizing, triumphalist sort of remembering I expected of this patriarch of a noted Nova Scotia family.[22] It is, in the tradition of male memoir, self-focused: Stewart remembers people, places, and events in a manner that references himself in detail. But this is no great man story. Stewart does not appear in the narrative as an autonomous actor charting a path through adversity to self-knowledge and self-actualization.[23] Rather, the text offers a close reading of the intimate social relationships that gave shape to his life. Stewart's narrative begins with brief accounts of the lives of particular ancestors, then moves to his parents, and finally to his siblings. Having established this familial context, the memoir comes to focus on Murdoch himself—or more accurately, on Murdoch in interaction with Donald.[24] Life histories like Stewart's are an important space for "negotiating the irreducible dichotomy of the self-in-society." Stewart's account provides a rich amalgam of articulate individuality and articulation of the self as social being, in particular within the network of other lives that comprised the family.[25] His youth is depicted, at times in quite explicit terms, as a negotiation between a willful yet uncertain young man and a nurturing, sometimes constraining family, represented most powerfully by the elder brother. Within the family and beyond, Stewart's life was patterned through broader social identities—particularly those of gender, religion, class, and nation.

The space of the life history affords the writer the "luxury of reminiscence," a luxury Murdoch's wife Katherine (Kett), mother of their ten children, did not have—whether for obvious practical reasons, or because of the gendered social expectations of memoir writing in the middle class.[26] Unfortunately but not surprisingly, Murdoch sheds little light on the lives of the women in his family. The reader is left to wonder what home life was like in late eighteenth- and early nineteenth-century Ross-shire for his mother, Catherine, as she struggled to raise seven children and make ends meet on a small farming venture and then the paltry income of her itinerant preacher husband. Stewart's memoir recalls his mother fondly, but with tantalizingly few details of the texture of her life. Describing his educational experience prior to age nine, when the family could finally afford to send him to school, Murdoch wrote that he "sometimes got a lesson, but very irregularly, at home."[27] Given that his father was almost always away, and given gender norms of the day, his teacher was his mother: "To keep me awake in the winter evenings my mother, while busily employed in spinning or knitting, would often sing old Gaelic songs to me or tell stories of sufficient interest to draw my attention, after more important subjects—such as committing at least *some* of the Gaelic Questions (Catechism) to memory—had lost the power to keep me awake."[28] Stewart recalled that his mother's Gaelic songs and stories were often told "in praise of either her grandmother or her great-grandmother." He had a "very certain and distinct recollection of her telling repeatedly various particulars in regard especially to her mother's family."[29] These reminiscences point to intriguing elements of Catherine Stewart's life. Particularly poignant is her attempt, through oral storytelling and song, to commemorate—to fix in her child's memory— the lives of other generations of women in her family. Catherine Stewart's project paralleled, although in a different medium, the efforts of her son to memorialize family through memoir. It is a telling commentary on the dilemmas of historical practice that Catherine's diligent memorializing of women in the family is lost to the historian reliant on written texts, while her son's record of the men rests safely in a public archive.[30]

What was life like for Murdoch's elder sisters, who went into domestic service in early adolescence in order to support their parents and enable their three brothers to attend school? How might sister Jessie have recalled home, having spent her life in the houses of other family members, caring first for her brothers and later for her aging parents? Murdoch provides very little insight into these women's positions within the Stewart household. His silence says a good deal about his unquestioning belief in his masculine privilege, and about prevailing cultural norms around girls' and women's gender roles.

Murdoch has rather more to say about his eldest sister, Isabella, who played the role of patron to both Murdoch and Donald. In her early twenties, Isabella came into a well-paying position as housekeeper for two wealthy elderly sisters in Inverness. While Murdoch's father was able to offer no financial assistance to his sons when they went off to university in Aberdeen, Isabella provided reliable support over a period of many years and continued her generosity when, in her thirties, she married a London-based Scottish businessman. Murdoch recalls with gratitude the assistance of "our noble-minded sister Isabella."[31]

As it had been for his mother, the act of fixing in memory his family of origin was profoundly important to Murdoch. Appropriately, it was an event involving his mother's family that set him to writing in the first place. When he took up his pen in the spring of 1872, he had recently read an article in "The Invergordon Times" (Scotland) about the life and death of Scottish geologist Sir Roderick Murchison, a leading Victorian scientist and longtime president of the Royal Geographical Society. The details provided proved to Murdoch that his mother was a close relative of Murchison—perhaps not a first cousin, but a "pretty near" relation.[32] This evidence would have been most welcome to Murdoch as he lived out his life in unwilling exile from Scotland. The familial connection to greatness gave Murdoch purchase on the Scottish national narrative, and the broader British one as well. It enabled him to link his homely personal history with the story of the nation. It was imperative to Murdoch that his own children understand this connection. He was at pains to spell out the relationship, suggesting that he was at pains as well to demonstrate the respectability and national achievement of (at least one of) his forebears. His larger concern, though, was that his children have knowledge of the network of Scottish lives that grounded his history, and that he hoped would ground theirs. The memoir sets out that network in detail.

Murdoch's Cape Breton family might not get much space in the memoir, but it provided him with a passionate motivation for writing. He proclaims his domestic agenda in the opening pages of the narrative. Giving the work the unassuming title "Memoranda," he notes that he is not writing an account of "persons or events of general importance," or a travel narrative. His purpose is conspicuously humble: he seeks to record details of interest to "the circle of my own family," before those details are lost. "I am now growing old; I know not the day of my death. . . . [B]eing in a new country, far from my Native land and relatives, I wish to leave to my dear children some notes that may be of interest to them—regarding their parents and relatives. . . . [I]f I should not write their names it may soon be too late, and they (my children) might find it impossible to ascertain whether they had any relatives on earth or not."[33] Stewart clearly feels a sense of loss on behalf of his children, and a duty to compensate for that loss. Precisely because of the interventions of space, his children have been deprived of relationships with the people who define the family circle. By "writing their names," Murdoch will establish connections between his Scottish family and his children. Names will become relations; their stories will become the children's history. There is a note of urgency to Murdoch's concern that without his writing, the children might be left to wonder whether they had any relatives "on earth." His project in the "Memoranda" is to revisit that family, to re-present their story as history. He seeks to build, if not intimacy, at least a relationship of familiarity between his children and their Scottish ancestors. He seeks to bring to life in memory the family members who for him define home, and to make that memory permanent by passing it on to the next generation.

If Stewart writes out of a sense of paternal duty, at the same time he is clearly aware of his public persona—as head of household, but more particularly as head of a Presbyterian congregation in Cape Breton. Despite his homely reason for writing, the self-introduction in the opening paragraph of the memoir is addressed to a public readership: he defines himself as "The Revd Murdoch Stewart, at present Minister of the Gospel at Whycocomah [sic], Cape Breton, Province of N. Scotia, Dominion of Canada . . . in the Presbyterian Church of the Lower Provinces of British America."[34] The value of the memoir, it seems, is attached to the official, public role of the man. While on the one hand he adopts a self-effacing, modest stance, on the other he seeks validation from his role as a minister of the Scottish church in the Dominion of Canada. On the one hand he writes to fix family history in the minds of his children; on the other he hopes to leave a trace of himself for future generations, to ensure a measure of immortality for his achievements.[35] This dual personality is present throughout the work. While Stewart's life history is perhaps uncommonly domestic in its concerns and uncommonly revealing of personal flaws and private failures, it brims with patriarchal and imperial conviction. Women are marginalized, as noted. The men of the family history, meanwhile, are defined by occupation, their respectability rooted in education, piety, and hard work. Stewart himself and, more clearly, his brother Donald are highly educated, introspective, self-righteous clergymen laboring to save the untutored in the hills—be they Scots Gaelic in the western hills of Aberdeenshire or dislocated Scots in Cape Breton.

Murdoch provides few details about his father. Having described John Stewart's ascent to the post of catechist, he concludes that "[o]f the character of my revered father I need not say anything in addition to what I have said already in connection with the office he held for upwards of 40 years, and what may be gathered from the following short acct of the family he managed to bring up on such an income."[36] It was enough to note that the man occupied a respectable post in the church over many years, and had raised a respectable family: these observations were shorthand for a whole range of desirable character traits.

Murdoch elaborates at length on those traits in his depiction of his beloved Donald. Murdoch's memoir may be self-referencing, but nearly as much detail is provided about this brother. Indeed, it is possible to read the narrative almost entirely as a reflection on this sibling relationship and its importance in the shaping of Murdoch's life.[37] The bond between the brothers was based on mutual affection and a good deal more. Donald, thirteen years Murdoch's senior and childless, acted as surrogate father in many ways. While there seems to have been a loving relationship between the boys and their own father, John Stewart's frequent absence and poverty left Donald to fill the gap.

Murdoch and Donald did not know each other well during Murdoch's early childhood, when Donald was often away at school and later teaching in a parish school or doing farm labor.[38] When Murdoch was eight years old, Donald moved home for two years to study for university entrance. This was a critical period in the formation of the younger boy's gender identity and the time when the bond between the two was cemented. The brothers continued to live together, on and off, until Murdoch finished divinity studies at twenty-eight. The very physical space of home became associated with Donald. Murdoch notes that his home of first resort from mid-adolescence onward was Donald's home in western Aberdeenshire. During this period and for the rest of Murdoch's life, Donald served as mentor, teacher, and moral compass for his younger brother. After Murdoch left Scotland for Nova Scotia, the two remained close correspondents. Donald provided generous financial support to Murdoch's family, particularly the boys. The relationship with Donald was the most profound attachment in Murdoch's childhood and youth, perhaps equaled in adulthood only by his relationship with his wife. This fraternal bond came to define home itself.

Murdoch noted that while Donald was revered by all the family, "I, of all of them, am under the deepest obligations of love and gratitude to him.... [S]ince my 15th year, my eldest Brother acted more than a father's part towards me—boarded, clothed, and taught me."[39] Although at the time of writing Murdoch had not seen his brother in almost twenty-five years, the bond remained powerful: "his kindness and our mutual affection is certainly not less, if not more intense than ever. The time of the departure of both of us cannot be far distant, we do not expect to see each other again on earth; but we do hope to meet in the land that is afar off, but far better and where there shall be no parting."[40] Distance made the heart grow fonder; the bond between the two was perhaps "more intense than ever." Hope of joining Donald in a heavenly home appears to have given Murdoch comfort at a time when he knew he would never see his brother again on earth.

Murdoch's reverence for his brother notwithstanding, his own heart had been set on the life of a scholar. Despite his many academic achievements, Murdoch did not consider himself Donald's equal either in academics or in work ethic. Several sections of the text reflect regretfully on all the time the self-styled feckless young man wasted in salmon fishing, while Donald toiled at his job of schoolmaster and spent every spare moment in study. There is a trace of Donald in many of Murdoch's recollections, a measuring of the self against the model of the brother.[41] Where Murdoch really suffered in comparison to Donald was in Christian dedication. Donald's every move, in Murdoch's rendering, was imbued with Christian meaning. Donald was "known and acknowledged to be the most pious man in the place, I might say in the Parish."[42] He led the family prayers when their father was absent and set a "shining example" for the other young men of the area.[43] Murdoch fully emerges from his brother's shadow only when Donald dies and the Cape Breton segment of the narrative begins. Donald's absence from this portion of the text is a reflection of his absence from this part of Murdoch's life; that absence no doubt contributes to Murdoch's loneliness and melancholy in the Cape Breton narrative.

Even in the adulatory account of the memoir, Murdoch reveals the emotional trials inherent in trying to live up to Donald's example. While Donald's heart had been "set for many years" on a life in the church, Murdoch had not even made this choice by the end of his first degree. The decision was soon made for him—by Donald. As he recounts, "My Brother, to whom I looked up with something of the reverence due to a father, wished me to study Theology but I did not feel very clear on that point."[44] At Donald's urging, Murdoch competed for a full scholarship to the three-year Divinity program at King's. He won the bursary and "I therefore decided on studying Theology."[45] It was neither calling nor drive, but the combination of Donald's wishes and economic need that sent Murdoch to the church. His candor on this point, writing from later life and from the position of the Reverend Murdoch Stewart, is disarming.

Murdoch was clearly embarrassed in later life by the ambivalence he had felt toward a career in the church. His weaknesses and failures are on full display, to the point that he notes his "humiliation" in recounting the course of his life.[46] In some ways this self-effacement is a convention of evangelical life-writing. It is a stance common to such writings in the nineteenth century to bemoan time wasted on this mortal coil, to gesture to the state of spiritual urgency that grew out of the temptations of the corrupt world, and to profess one's sinfulness. It is a stance common to an older tradition of self-writing as well, the Augustinian tradition of confessional writing to an interior God.[47] Murdoch adopts aspects of such conventions in the memoir. Yet as I have argued elsewhere, Murdoch's humiliation does not appear to be before his God, as one might expect of a Presbyterian preacher nearing the end of this life. On the contrary, Murdoch's life is measured and assessed next to that of his brother. Murdoch seems to serve in the text as a foil for the older brother he so reveres.[48] Put another way, Donald's exemplary life is the moral of Murdoch's story: give the heart early to God, be steadfast in devotion and work hard, and life will be well lived. Donald's is an extraordinary life, an almost saintly life in his brother's memory. It serves as a model and a teaching tool both for Murdoch and for the offspring for whom he writes.

Like many young men of poor rural or working-class roots before him, Murdoch left Scotland against his will and for reasons largely economic: there were no positions at home in the Church of Scotland in the early 1840s—or none available to Murdoch, who had "no influence with a proprietor."[49] In other words, he lacked connections to a powerful landowner who might nominate him to a parish. Knowing he had no hope of a regular parish, Murdoch had decided, at Donald's urging, to try for a missionary post in Scotland. This opportunity, too, had vanished. Members of the church's missionary committee informed Murdoch that there were many in line ahead of him for very few posts. The only option the committee left open to him was colonial service. Murdoch balked at the suggestion, having never considered the colonies before and being "pretty certain that my parents would be opposed to it."[50] He was right. It took Murdoch, now thirty-one years old, a number of months to gain his parents' and his brother's consent to his accepting a position abroad. That he felt compelled to ask permission, and that they were not willing to grant it, speaks to the intensity of familial bonds in this family. A series of circumstances, including the dogged persistence of the church's colonial committee and the brewing disruption and splintering of the Church of Scotland, finally convinced Murdoch, Donald, and their parents that "the leadings of Providence" were visible.[51] Murdoch was called to the colonies.

Murdoch left Scotland in the spring of 1843 with a heavy heart. "[I]f I left Scotland," he reasoned, "it wd not matter much to which part of the world I might go."[52] The account of his "long and sad farewell" is touching. After spending several days with his brother in Crathie, he went to Ross-shire to say goodbye to his parents: "On the morning I left, my father accompanied me to the Muir of Ord, where I wd meet the Mail Coach to Inverness. The Coach soon came, we parted. . . . I turned to take, as I thought, the last look of my father. I saw him standing where we parted and looking after me. Then and there, I *mentally* vowed, that if we shd both live another 4 years I would see him! Till that moment I had no thought of ever returning to Scotland."[53]

Murdoch's memoir comes to a temporary halt with his arrival in Cape Breton. At this point, he took an eight-year break from the writing, a hiatus he put down to his preoccupation with church work and failing health. The years of silence may signal his discomfort with this next chapter of his life story, which he presents largely as a story of absence and loss. In the end, it was Donald who sent him back to his writing desk. His first task when he resumed writing in 1880 was to record the loss of the guiding presence in his life—the brother by whose model he lived. He begins with an epitaph to Donald: "Among the noticeable events that have taken place since I ceased writing these notes, the most memorable is the death of my beloved brother Donald, at Aberdeen, on the 24th July 1879, in the 82nd year of his age. [Despite severely failing health] he had long kept on as pastor of his beloved little flock."[54]

The memoir draws to a close with a dismal account of Murdoch's early months in Cape Breton. It might "matter little" where he was headed, but Cape Breton was far from his first choice. "If there was any place to which I was more unwilling to go than another, it was Cape Breton. [L]ittle was known of it in Scotland at that time and that little gave it a bad name."[55] The place figured in the Scottish imagination as wild and lawless, the worst of the western Highlands and worse yet for being thousands of miles remote.[56] Scots had begun emigrating to Cape Breton in significant numbers in 1802, at a time when the Highland economy was convulsed by the effects of land clearances and recession, soon to be followed by the demise of the crofting economy and the kelp market.[57] By the time Murdoch Stewart arrived, the population of the island surpassed forty thousand, more than half of whom were Scots and most of those from the western Highlands and Islands. The indigenous Mi'kmaq people had been systematically pushed off their lands from the time of the British takeover from the French in the 1760s; the colonial government in 1800 ruled the Mi'kmaq an obstruction to "civilization" and gave them no protection from settler encroachment, despite earlier treaties and Mi'kmaq resistance.[58] Some established first-wave Scottish farmers on the island, meanwhile, could boast of a higher standard of living than in Scotland; together with earlier Acadian, British, and Irish settlers, by 1830 they had claimed what little arable land the island had to offer. Many others, particularly those who arrived after the 1820s, were forced onto the rocky and "wretchedly bad" backlands.[59] The region where Murdoch was to minister, in the vicinity of West Bay, Bras d'Or Lake, encompassed many families far too poor to support themselves—and certainly too poor to contribute to the upkeep of the local clergyman.

The predominantly Gaelic-speaking settlers Murdoch had come to serve are clearly excluded from moral equality and respectability in his text. Class rather than race is the principal ground of difference, but the distancing language is of a similar cast.[60] Murdoch was part of a mission to rescue his compatriots from the twin dangers of lack of access to proper religion (Presbyterianism of an evangelical cast) and the degeneration in morals and work habits that threatened life in a remote colony.[61] This imperial aspect of his social identity is too easily overlooked, given that he was sent to Cape Breton to minister to other Scots rather than indigenous people. Yet this project of social uplift and reform was seen as a distinct challenge by those who took it on. The Edinburgh Ladies' Society, which sponsored Stewart's mission, warned that Scottish settlers in the region had not made a promising start. Cape Breton offered "great natural capabilities" to those knowledgeable and industrious enough to make appropriate "improvements." But the people Murdoch was to minister to were "sunk in the most deplorable state": here were settlers "without capital, uneducated, untaught in the art of agriculture, and whose industrial energies had never been called forth by employment in the country which they had left."[62] These folk were styled as idle and dissolute in the west of Scotland, a periphery of empire in itself; the challenge to reform them would be that much greater in the distant colony. Rural Cape Breton, with its few scattered missionaries and widespread poverty, allowed free rein to the "unchecked tendencies of corrupt nature." The Ladies' Society sent a library's worth of "useful and improving reading," from which settlers could learn the arts of agriculture and other "occupations which will qualify them for earning their bread in after life."[63] The language of Christian philanthropy is clearly suffused with economic and class concerns. Not only were Murdoch and his colleagues to rescue the settlers from spiritual destitution; they were to assist in reforming these naturally dissolute folk into orderly, industrious, and, in the end, respectable agents of colonial development.[64] In this project Murdoch Stewart himself, a "small voice" contained in a humble family narrative, becomes an agent—if not always a willing one—in the dissemination and shoring up of imperial categories of difference.[65]

Cape Breton's image was no more favorable in mainland colonial Nova Scotia than it was in Britain. When Murdoch told a fellow steamship traveler—a Glasgow businessman who now lived in Halifax—where he was headed, the man "looked at me amazed and asked what in the world are you going to do there[?]"[66] Murdoch's response to his arrival on the island was strongly informed by such views. Finding his new base near the western shore of Bras d'Or Lake heavily wooded and sparsely inhabited, "my heart sank within like a mass of cold lead."[67] Murdoch repeatedly depicts himself searching for "the settlement."[68] The settlement did not exist, at least not in a form he recognized. Centuries of Mi'kmaq presence go entirely unremarked in his text, a silence of profound political consequence. The landscape offered poignant references to the moors and hills of the Highlands, but far too few familiar signs of human presence.

Murdoch's only positive comments on Cape Breton come in descriptions of the hospitality of select Scots he encountered. In Arichat, his point of entry to Cape Breton, he was invited for tea to the home of a couple from Aberdeenshire and "soon found myself as if at home."[69] A clergy family in Sydney offered "a Scottish—or rather Christian welcome."[70] Surely this is a revealing conflation of terms. On another occasion he rejoiced at the sight of a Scottish host preparing a breakfast of oatmeal porridge. Such reminders offered comfort to a man who found himself "truly lonely" and "very down hearted."[71] What these homes offered, besides a warm welcome and the comfort of familiarity, was Christian respectability of a Scottish variety. The Scots Murdoch identified with were defined by occupation, the best among them clergymen and teachers. Rev. Wilson in Sydney Mines, for instance, was "a most superior specimen of the Lowland Scotch and evangelical ministers."[72] Very likely Murdoch, who came from poorer stock and had struggled to establish a social footing in Scotland, enjoyed the status offered him as an educated and, in this setting, insecurely middle-class Scot. It is clear from the foregoing passages that he worked at maintaining an air of class-based respectability that would distinguish him from the lowlier Scots to whom he ministered. The fact that his own income was chronically insecure had little relevance in Cape Breton, where the material trappings of middle-class identity were few.[73] What mattered was that Murdoch looked, learned, and behaved like the respectable folk he so admired, and whose ranks were so thin on the ground. Fleetingly, Murdoch found himself *almost* at home. Apart from these instances, though, no compensatory account of Cape Breton is ever offered. No hint is given that the place ever became home, ten children and a busy church life notwithstanding. There is no foreshadowing of better things to come on this island, and Murdoch certainly does not use the word "home" in this context. To the end, the memoir's references to home all settle on Scotland and his Scottish family.

Murdoch Stewart lived nearly forty years in Cape Breton and, with his Scottish wife, Kett, raised a family of five boys and five girls. Yet to the end of his life, "home" remained the Scottish family of his youth. Relationships with the male members of his family, his brother in particular, formed the intimate core of a social network that anchored his sense of self and provided his life models throughout adulthood. The intensity of the fraternal bond between Murdoch and Donald, combined with the experience of colonial dislocation—economic exile, as it were, to a colony far from family and personal history—determined the emotional power of Murdoch's recollections. The relationships that he recalls shaping his young life were the attachment points for his memories, their emotional intensity amplified by his experience of removal and loss. Space itself shaped Murdoch's predicament in important ways. His efforts in his narrative to rekindle the bond with his brother, to revisit the family relations of his youth, and to reproduce that family history for his children represent an attempt to bridge the cold space of empire. In the sense that this colonial man came to understand his Scottish home in terms of Cape Breton, and Cape Breton in terms of Scotland, the effort succeeded.

The attempt to retrieve the ever-elusive "home" is, of course, a response shared by many who are removed from home and loved ones. My own interests as a historian and my relationship with the memoir of Murdoch Stewart are shaped in part by my affection for my Nova Scotia "home"; by my maternal Scottish ancestry; and by memories of grandparents who had much in common with characters in Murdoch's text. But I don't wish to take the point too far. Stewart's story is a poignant reminder of the pain and loss that colonial mobility could inflict even on the relatively privileged. Yet his experience of "mobility" and "dislocation" was dramatically different from that of legions of colonized peoples whose territories were seized and homes destroyed, literally or metaphorically. Many commentators have argued that dislocation from home is the defining predicament of modernity. They argue, from a variety of theoretical positions, that as a result of the upheavals of late global capitalism and mass communication, local cultures are fragmenting and people losing a sense of place. It is worth underlining that this predicament is not in any sense new for colonized peoples, the peoples of Africa, Asia, the South Pacific, and the Americas, for whom globalization—in the form of empire—long since destabilized relations to home. For some, colonization removed the very possibility of home as a place where they belonged and that belonged to them, a place to locate identity.[74] Murdoch Stewart had the luxury of such a place, and the luxury of time to reflect on it. He spent many hours in the latter years of his life recalling and reproducing for posterity his Scottish home. The desire to reclaim home, and the family relations at its core, is the central predicament at the heart of Murdoch Stewart's memoir.

Notes

For closer reflections on the nature and production of the text, see the paper out of which this essay grew: "Dwelling in My Brother's Home: Reflections on a Scottish Colonial Memoir," presented in a forum on *Dwelling in the Archive: Women Writing House, Home, and History in Late Colonial India*, by Antoinette Burton (Oxford, 2003), at the annual meeting of the American Historical Association, Seattle, January 2005. I am grateful for comments from Tony Ballantyne, Antoinette Burton, Catherine Hall, Lynne Marks, Adele Perry, Wendy Wickwire, and two anonymous readers.

1. Stewart's narrative is most accurately described as part family history, part memoir. The full text runs to 170 handwritten pages. Roughly the first third reads like an annotated family tree. When Stewart comes to elder brother Donald on the tree, the narrative takes on more of the characteristics of memoir. Rev. Murdoch Stewart, Unpublished Diary, MG 1471 A (hereafter Diary of Murdoch Stewart), Nova Scotia Archives and Records Management, Halifax. (The archival designation of the text is "diary," although it was written retrospectively and does not contain daily entries.)

2. For recent literature on intimacies of empire, see especially Ann Laura Stoler, "Tense and Tender Ties: The Politics of Comparison in North American History and (Post) Colonial Studies," *Journal of American History* 88, 3 (2001): 829–65, and responses in the same issue; Catherine Hall and Sonya O. Rose, eds., *At Home with the Empire: Metropolitan Culture and the Imperial World* (Cambridge, 2007); Philippa Levine, "Sexuality and Empire," in Hall and Rose, *At Home with the Empire.*

3. On historians' neglect of sibling relations, see important interventions by Leonore Davidoff in "Where the Stranger Begins: The Question of Siblings in

Historical Analysis," in her *Worlds Between: Historical Perspectives on Gender and Class* (New York, 1995), and Leonore Davidoff, Megan Doolittle, Janet Fink, and Katherine Holden, *The Family Story: Blood, Contract, and Intimacy, 1830–1960* (London: Longman, 1999). See also Elizabeth Vibert, "Brotherly Love: Making Christian Manhood in a Scottish Colonial Memoir," paper presented at the annual meeting of the Organization of American Historians, New York, March 2008.

4. The lay preacher post may have landed the family on the margins of the ranks of the middle class, but the annual stipend of 15 pounds did not allow for many comforts. I reflect on Murdoch Stewart's own movement into the middle class through university education and ascent to a clergy post in my "Brotherly Love."

5. See, importantly, Burton, *Dwelling in the Archive,* and Kate Teltscher, "Writing Home and Crossing Cultures," in Kathleen Wilson, ed., *A New Imperial History: Culture, Identity and Modernity in Britain and the Empire* (Cambridge, 2004), 281–96. A new collection edited by Angela McCarthy, *A Global Clan: Scottish Migrant Networks and Identities Since the Eighteenth Century* (London, 2006), includes very useful essays on Scots abroad. For related reflections on the importance of Scottish referents to individual colonial identities, see Sarah Katherine Gibson, "Self-Reflection in the Consolidation of Scottish Identity: A Case Study in Family Correspondence," in Phillip Buckner and R. Douglas Francis, eds., *Canada and the British World: Culture, Migration and Identity* (Vancouver, 2006), 29–44.

6. On the making of Murdoch Stewart's manhood, see my "Brotherly Love." On identity as an interactive process of "becoming," see esp. Stuart Hall, "Cultural Identity and Diaspora," in N. Mirzoeff, ed., *Diaspora and Visual Culture* (London, 2000), 21–33.

7. Michel Foucault provides the classic articulation of regimes of truth in his *History of Sexuality,* vol. 1, trans. Robert Hurley (New York, 1980). For useful and comparative reflections on the connections between intimacy and imperial regimes in the "microsites," see Stoler, "Tense and Tender Ties," and responses by Ramón Gutiérrez, Lori Ginzberg, Dirk Hoerder, and others in the same issue.

8. For an earlier foray into such questions and others, see Elizabeth Vibert, *Traders' Tales: Narratives of Cultural Encounter in the Columbia Plateau, 1807–1846* (Norman, Okla., 1997; reprint, 2000).

9. Burton, *Dwelling in the Archive,* 62.

10. Barbara Metcalf, "Narrating Lives: A Mughal Empress, a French Nabob, a Nationalist Muslim Intellectual," *Journal of Asian Studies* 54, 2 (1995): 479. Anthropologist Julie Cruikshank makes a similar point, powerfully, in her work. See, for example, "Negotiating with Narrative: Establishing Cultural Identity at the Yukon Storytelling Festival," *American Anthropologist* 99 (1997): 56–69.

11. Here I concur with Himani Bannerji, who asks, "[cannot] all sources, both subjective and objective, memorial and statistical . . . be turned into resources for writing alternative and reflexive histories through readings from nonpositivist standpoints?" "Methods/Theory," review of *Dwelling in the Archive,* by Antoinette Burton, *American Historical Review* 110, 3 (2005): 5. Unlike Bannerji, I would place quotation marks around "subjective" and "objective."

12. Mary Margaret Steedly, *Hanging without a Rope: Narrative Experience in*

Colonial and Postcolonial Karoland (Princeton, 1993), 22. I was first exposed to Steedly's work through Burton, *Dwelling in the Archive,* chap. 1.

13. For useful reflections on shifting and complex notions of home see Rose-mary Marangoly George, *The Politics of Home: Postcolonial Relocations and Twentieth-Century Fiction* (Cambridge, 1996); Hall and Rose, introduction to *At Home with the Empire,* 1–31. The literature on self-writing is vast. For insight on its value, see Suzanne Morton, "Faire le saut: La biographie peut-elle être de l'histoire sociale?" *Revue d'histoire de l'Amerique française* 54, 1 (2000): 103–10. I do not at all wish to reify the contentious split between "public" and "private/domestic." As the analysis here shows, domestic relationships are a vital part of the intricate social web in which history resides. Yet Murdoch Stewart shows a clear sense of his own "public" role—his social role before the broader community and his church—and very likely made the distinction between his home life and life in the wider world. If Murdoch Stewart's memoir dwells ambiguously in a place both domestic and public, so, it might be said, did the lives of most men in the nineteenth century. As Martin Francis has argued, men traveled back and forth across the "frontier" of domesticity, attracted by the responsibilities and refuge of family life but also by the public validations and autonomy of the public realm: "The Domestication of the Male?" *Historical Journal* 45, 3 (2002): 637–52.

14. Many thanks to Catherine Hall for provocative discussions of such mat-ters.

15. Diary of Murdoch Stewart, e.g., fols. 18, 63, 72–74. He does not reflect on physical space like the women who figure in Burton's *Dwelling,* for instance, for whom memory has a detailed architecture. The differences in emphasis no doubt reflect profound differences in the gendered experience of home.

16. John Gillis, *A World of Their Own Making: Myth, Ritual and the Quest for Family Values* (New York, 1996). Here I switch to referring to Murdoch Stewart by his first name, to distinguish him from the many other Stewarts he writes about.

17. As David Vincent and others have shown, childhood is often a major fo-cus of working-class autobiography: *Bread, Knowledge, and Freedom: A Study of Nineteenth-Century Working-Class Autobiography* (London, 1981). I use the term "predispositions" in the way Bourdieu has used it in his notion of *habitus:* in brief, "the system of predispositions inculcated by the material circumstances of life and family upbringing"; *Outline of a Theory of Practice* (Cambridge, 1977), 72–73, 95; 159–97.

18. Teltscher, "Writing Home and Crossing Cultures," 284–86. For a contrasting view, see David Gerber, "A Network of Two: Personal Friendship and Scottish Identification in the Correspondence of Mary Ann Archbald and Margaret Wod-row, 1807–1840," in McCarthy, *A Global Clan,* 95–126. The relevant literature on identity as interrelational process is vast. See, for instance, Hall, "Cultural Identity and Diaspora."

19. Most unfortunately, I have not yet been able to locate the correspondence between Murdoch and Donald, which family members say was extensive. I am very grateful to Vivian Morrison of Halifax for her insights into family memories of Murdoch and for so generously sharing her personal archive and research.

20. For an illuminating discussion of place in such terms, see Doreen Massey, *Space, Place, and Gender* (Minneapolis, 1994). For Scotland, see Edward Cowan,

"The Myth of the Scotch in Canada," in Marjory Harper and Michael Vance, eds., *Myth, Migration and the Making of Memory: Scotia and Nova Scotia 1700–1990* (Halifax, 1999), 61–62.

21. See the argument by Manu Goswami cited in Burton and Ballantyne's introduction here.

22. Stewart's sons included the first dean of the province's medical school, a doctor of divinity, and a prominent lawyer. A daughter became a mathematician.

23. Stewart's text does not unfold as a story of personal "development," in line with the bildungsroman format so prevalent in novels and life writings from the eighteenth century onward (the "rags to riches" story in popular American form).

24. For thoughtful reflections on the representation of individuals within broader familial and social networks in Indian traditions, for example, see Metcalf, "Narrating Lives," 474–80.

25. See David Arnold and Stuart Blackburn, "Introduction: Life Histories in India," in Arnold and Blackburn, eds., *Telling Lives in India: Biography, Autobiography, and Life History* (Bloomington, 2004), 22. On the importance of family to Victorian middle-class men, see especially John Tosh, *A Man's Place: Masculinity and the Middle-Class Home in Victorian England* (New Haven, 1999).

26. The quotation is from Burton, *Dwelling in the Archive*, 16, borrowing from Janet Frame.

27. Diary of Murdoch Stewart, fol. 72.

28. Ibid., fols. 10–11.

29. Ibid.

30. Family members are not certain how the memoir came to the provincial archives; likely a family member deposited it. The text is filed under "Diaries—1800–1900," suggesting it was considered to be valuable as an account of "pioneer life" in the colonial and early provincial era.

31. Diary of Murdoch Stewart, fol. 44. Among many aspects of sibling relations needing further study, the role of the childless sister in economic support of her siblings is a topic deserving of attention.

32. Diary of Murdoch Stewart, fols. 3–4. See also Gibson, "Self-Reflection in the Consolidation of Scottish Identity," 29, on links made in obituaries between individual accomplishment and Scottish national identity.

33. Ibid., fols. 1–2.

34. Ibid., fol. 1.

35. Arnold and Blackburn make a similar point in "Introduction: Life Histories in India," 12.

36. Diary of Murdoch Stewart, fol. 36.

37. This is the approach I take in my "Brotherly Love." As I argue there, sibling relations have been too long overlooked by gender historians, particularly given their often central role in the formation of gender identities.

38. Murdoch's earliest memories are of his middle brother Thomas, his affectionate playmate in his early years. Imperial mobility defined Thomas's life even more profoundly than Murdoch's. Thomas left the family home for the city in adolescence and died in India in 1834, a soldier with the East India Company. Diary of Murdoch Stewart, fols. 65–67. For insights into Scottish experience in India, see Andrew Mackillop, "Europeans, Britons, and Scots: Scottish Sojourning

Networks and Identities in Asia, c. 1700–1815," in McCarthy, *A Global Clan*, 19–47.

39. Diary of Murdoch Stewart, fol. 61.

40. Ibid., fols. 61–62.

41. Ibid., e.g., fols. 83, 86–88, 112.

42. Ibid., fols. 41–42.

43. Ibid., fols. 41–42.

44. Ibid., fol. 91.

45. Ibid., fol. 94.

46. Ibid., fol. 133.

47. See Norman Vance, *The Sinews of the Spirit: The Ideal of Christian Manliness in Victorian Literature and Religious Thought* (Cambridge, 1985).

48. This passage draws directly on my "Brotherly Love."

49. Diary of Murdoch Stewart, fols. 118–19.

50. Ibid., fols. 120–21. Colonial missions had not long been on the agenda of the Church of Scotland, either. The first foreign missionary society of the kirk, the Glasgow Colonial Society, was founded in 1825 (although the church had earlier supported the London Missionary Society). A revealing account of the establishment of the Cape Breton mission and its private supporters, the Glasgow Colonial Society and the Edinburgh Ladies' Committee, is found in Anon., *A Brief Sketch of the Cape Breton Mission; with a Notice of the Late Mrs Mackay of Rockfield . . .* (Edinburgh, 1851), Dalhousie University Archives and Special Collections. The aim of the kirk's first overseas mission was to provide religious instruction to Scottish immigrants in British North America. The Edinburgh Ladies' Committee, described as an auxiliary to the Glasgow society, began funding its own missionaries to Cape Breton in the 1830s. Stewart was funded by this committee, which became a Free Church auxiliary in 1843. "Inland missions" to Protestantize Roman Catholics in northern and outlying regions of Scotland had commenced in the 1720s with funding under the Royal Bounty scheme of the British Crown. See Elizabeth A. K. McDougall and John S. Moir, introduction to McDougall and Moir, eds., *Selected Correspondence of the Glasgow Colonial Society, 1825–1840* (Toronto, 1994), xi–1. See also Susan Thorne, *Congregational Missions and the Making of an Imperial Culture in Nineteenth-Century England* (Stanford, Calif., 1999), chap. 2.

51. Diary of Murdoch Stewart, fol. 127.

52. Ibid., fol. 125.

53. Ibid., fol. 131. Murdoch kept his word and returned three years later. He stayed nearly a year, during which time he met and married Katherine.

54. Diary of Murdoch Stewart, fol. 133.

55. Ibid., fol. 126.

56. Although writers like Thomas Haliburton and Richard Uniacke had in recent years penned favorable accounts of the island, in large part to attract British immigrants, Stewart no doubt heard much to the contrary. Members of the Edinburgh Ladies' Society and the Glasgow Colonial Society consistently described the material and moral state of Scottish settlers in Cape Breton as "truly deplorable." *A Brief Sketch of the Cape Breton Mission*, 6–7; Eighth Report of the Glasgow Colonial Society (1835), extract in Rev. Alexander Farquharson Papers, MG100, vol. 140, no. 19, Nova Scotia Archives and Records Management. See also the tone of much of the correspondence collected in McDougall and Moir,

The Glasgow Colonial Society, 145–262. For general views in the colonial era, see Brian Tennyson, *Impressions of Cape Breton* (Sydney, 1986).

57. See especially Eric Richards, *A History of the Highland Clearances*, 2 vols. (London, 1982–85); Stephen Hornsby, *Nineteenth-Century Cape Breton: A Historical Geography* (Montreal, 1992). For broader Scottish migration to eastern Canada and beyond, see J. M. Bumsted, *The People's Clearance: Highland Emigration to North America 1770–1815* (Edinburgh, 1982); Marjory Harper, *Adventurers and Exiles: The Great Scottish Exodus* (London, 2003); T. M. Devine, *Scotland's Empire and the Shaping of the Americas, 1600–1815* (Washington, D.C., 2003); Harper and Vance, *Myth, Migration and the Making of Memory.*

58. The Mi'kmaq of Nova Scotia have continuously asserted their aboriginal claim to the land and seacoast, from the time their earliest treaties with the British began to be abrogated in the eighteenth century. For an overview, see Adrian Tanner and Sakej Henderson, "Aboriginal Land Claims in the Atlantic Provinces," in Ken Coates, ed., *Aboriginal Land Claims in Canada* (Toronto, 1992), 131–66. For Mi'kmaq challenges, resistance, and accommodation in the eighteenth and nineteenth centuries see Janet Chute, "Frank G. Speck's Contributions to the Understanding of Mi'kmaq Land Use," *Ethnohistory* 46, 3 (1999): 481–540; Andrew Nurse, "History, Law and the Mi'kmaq of Atlantic Canada," *Acadiensis* 33, 2 (2004): 126–33; Ken Coates, "Breathing New Life into Treaties," *Agricultural History* 77, 2 (2003): 333–54.

59. The best source for this context is Hornsby, *Nineteenth-Century Cape Breton.*

60. Not that class and race are so distinct: in particular historical settings, racializing discourse may draw on class and other cultural signifiers of difference as determinedly as it draws on the body. My understanding of "race" draws heavily on the work of Stuart Hall, whose depiction of race as floating signifier is very illuminating. Among his works see esp. "Race: The Floating Signifier" DVD, Northampton, Mass., 1996; "Cultural Identity and Diaspora"; see also the very useful discussion of the historical specificity of racial understandings in Kathleen Wilson, introduction to *The Island Race: Englishness, Empire and Gender in the Eighteenth Century* (London, 2003), 6–15.

61. The mission in Cape Breton was dominated by Free Church supporters, who followed the evangelical Presbyterian movement that split off from the established Church of Scotland in 1843.

62. *A Brief Sketch of the Cape Breton Mission*, 6–10. At the time this report was written, Mrs. Mackay's mission had five ministers and several catechists in place on the island and was reporting improvements in the spiritual and moral "condition" of the people (11–12). The "deplorable condition" quotation, from 1837, is from one of the missionaries who preceded Stewart, quoted in Hornsby, "Scottish Emigration," 63. See Gibson, "Self-Reflection in the Consolidation of Scottish Identity," for useful observations on the contributions of Enlightenment rationality to such Scottish discourses.

63. *A Brief Sketch of the Cape Breton Mission*, 6–10.

64. Very similar imagery appears in the correspondence of other missionaries in the region. See, for example, a letter from Rev. John Stewart, Murdoch's predecessor, in McDougall and Moir, *Selected Correspondence of the Glasgow Colonial Society*, 252–56.

65. The "small voices" quotation comes from Ann Laura Stoler, "Tense and Tender Ties," 829–65. For such subjectivities in colonial context, see Mary Renda, "'Sentiments of a Private Nature,'" in the round table responses to Stoler, "Tense and Tender Ties," in *Journal of American History* 88, 3 (2001): 882–87; Lori Ginzberg, "Global Goals, Local Acts," in the same issue, 870–73; see also the large literature on subalternity, including Fernando Coronil, "Listening to the Subaltern: The Poetics of Neocolonial States," *Poetics Today* 15, 4 (1994): 643–58.

66. Diary of Murdoch Stewart, fol. 139.

67. Ibid., fols. 152–53.

68. Ibid., e.g., fols. 145, 154.

69. Ibid., fol. 148.

70. Ibid., fols. 160–61.

71. Ibid., fols. 147, 154, 160, 165, 169–70.

72. Ibid., fol. 160.

73. Minutes of the Synod of the Presbyterian Church of the Lower Provinces of British North America, film 3945, Minutes for 1862–1868, Nova Scotia Archives and Records Management. Provision for ministers in Cape Breton had been a concern since the Glasgow Colonial Society began funding missionaries to the island in 1826, precisely because many settlers were too poor (or disinclined) to contribute to clergy stipends.

74. Myriad (post)Marxist and poststructuralist thinkers muse on the experience of disorientation and loss of place attendant on late capitalism in the West. Authors in the Western tradition, from Homer to Carol Shields, have shown the quest for home—as site of family, as place of belonging—to be culturally definitive. Toni Morrison's novel *Beloved* powerfully unsettles the notion that everyone has a place to relate to as home. See thoughtful discussions in Massey, *Space, Place, and Gender*, chap. 7, and in Burton, *Dwelling*, 6–7, 29.

4 Intimacy of the Envelope

FICTION, COMMERCE, AND EMPIRE IN THE
CORRESPONDENCE OF FRIENDS MARY TAYLOR
AND CHARLOTTE BRONTË, C. 1845–55

This story begins at sea, the highway that made empire possible, in the months of October and November 1848. Somewhere on those long sailing routes connecting the ports recently entering the mapped world as Jackson, Chalmers, Nicholson, Lyttelton, and Waitemata[1] to the already-marked ones of Portsmouth, Liverpool, Southampton, Cork, and Gravesend, two ships traveling in opposite directions passed each other. Both were carrying mail, including letters between two friends whose messages, on this occasion, literally crossed at sea. Heading north, or "in," was Mary Taylor's letter of June–July, written in Wellington, New Zealand, to her friend Charlotte Brontë, in Haworth, Yorkshire, England. Heading south, or "out," was Charlotte Brontë's letter to Mary Taylor of September 4. Both letters, and their authors, were to win renown, if in different degrees and in Taylor's case, over a century later.[2] Their exchange was one of innumerable correspondences between family and friends over distance, and in this case, two sides of that strong triangle friendship had formed at Miss Wooler's Roe Head School in Mirfield, Yorkshire, half a lifetime earlier, when Mary, Charlotte, and Ellen Nussey had all met as fourteen-year-olds. In 1848 they were thirty-one, turning thirty-two; Mary had left England three years earlier, in March 1845.

Mary's letter contains a wonderful sequence in which she tells her friend that she has just read *Jane Eyre,* and full of excitement has rushed to the top of Mount Victoria to look for a ship to carry a letter, so full is she of her friend's accomplishment. "I begin to believe in your existence much as I do in Mr Rochester's," Mary tells Charlotte, having just expostulated, with characteristic forthrightness, how she found it "incredible that you had actually written a book. Such events did not happen while I was in England." But the letter is full of much more besides. Well into it Mary takes a breath, moving from the immediate rush of things, and turns over to start a new page and write: "I can hardly explain to you the queer feeling of living as I do in 2 places at once. One world containing books England & all the people with whom I can exchange an idea; the other all that I actually see & hear & speak to. The separation is as complete as between the things in a picture & the things in the room. The puzzle is that both move & act & [I] must say my say as one of each."[3]

The separation imposed by distance did not, as Mary discovered, divide the world neatly into a "here" and a "there." She observed herself simultaneously an actor and imaginary in two worlds. Even more marvelous was the transformation of her friend, from a quiet, reclusive existence as a clergyman's daughter living in a remote parsonage to the forefront of popular attention as the author of the sensation and success that was *Jane Eyre* (first published October 19, 1847, with second and third editions appearing on January 22 and mid-April 1848). While the true identity of "Currer Bell" remained unknown, Charlotte Brontë was living a double life even more dramatically without moving an inch from her home.[4] Charlotte's letter to Mary of September 4, 1848, recounted, in detail, the impulsive journey she and Anne made to London on the night of July 7–8, to prove the separate identities of the "Bells" to publishers George Smith and W. S. Williams, stung by Thomas Newby's misrepresentations. For her friend living at the opposite end of the world, Charlotte Brontë set down the fullest and most vivid account of that remarkable visit.[5] Pages of letters telling news, secrets, and confidences, sealed within envelopes, conveyed the intimacy of friendship from one side of the empire to its extreme at the antipodes. In the materials of ink and paper lay the means to define and transcend imperial space (as Tony Ballantyne and Antoinette Burton suggest in the introduction to this collection).

The story of Mary Taylor and Charlotte Brontë's friendship is not a new one, though it tends to have been told from one side or the other. Taking the correspondence conducted over the years 1845–55, from Mary's departure to New Zealand to Charlotte Brontë's death, the focus here is on the dynamic of exchange between the two—an episode in the culture of empire.[6] In this instance, the intimacy of empire is seen to operate within a relation of friendship, a connection that has drawn relatively little attention to date.[7] As an important place of affective relations, informal and sometimes influential friendships were an intimacy constituting the space of empire (as indicated in the introduction here). They also are an instance of what Ann Laura Stoler has recently described as a source of colonial control: "'structures of feeling'—new habits of heart and mind" that give rise to "categories of difference and subject formation."[8] In particular, the focus is on the ways the mobilities of intimacy, commerce, and imagination acted outside the limits of time and space, allowing Mary and Charlotte to share the new as well as familiar worlds they had come to inhabit, and to narrate known and new identities within these domains. Their new "selves" were not so much part of a status display as they were for Samuel Hudson and the Barnards in the anxious world of the Cape Colony half a century earlier that Kirsten McKenzie describes (chapter 13 here). And as a correspondence—a contemporary exchange— the letters and friendship provide an interesting contrast to the Reverend Murdoch Stewart's memoir, written from Cape Breton, thirty or so years later (though Stewart left Scotland for Nova Scotia just two years before Mary Taylor left Yorkshire for Wellington). As Elizabeth Vibert argues in considering the memoir (chapter 3 here), it is Stewart's relationship with his beloved and revered older brother Donald that forms Stewart's experience of center and "home," as he writes for his children out of paternal duty rather than in expectation of a response. The geography of empire marked the physical poles between which Mary and Charlotte's correspondence flowed, but also the cultural space for what came to be understood as "here and there"; going and staying; ownership, possession, and the silence of dispossession; buying and selling; earning and spending; autonomy and constraint; being and pretending; actual and imaginary; and in the intimacy of the correspondence, "you" and "me."

Charlotte Brontë began her September 4, 1848, letter to Mary with playful indignation: "I write to you a great many more letters than you write to me."[9] Mary is rarely a contrite correspondent, but her letter, then en route to Charlotte, does say that she has come to "exceedingly regret" having burnt Charlotte's letters "in a fit of caution."[10] The surviving correspondence, seven letters in total, all but one from Mary to Charlotte, allows only a partial view of the total exchange. How Mary disposed of Charlotte's subsequent letters remains a mystery. Related correspondence provides a wider context and some indication of the contents of letters between Mary and Charlotte that have not survived.[11] With Mary Taylor, we can only mourn the loss of the originals, and regard the conclusions reached as necessarily provisional, drawn from what remains of an unknowable larger whole.[12]

Well before Mary's departure for New Zealand in March 1845, the world of empire had formed part of the world Mary and Charlotte knew. As early as 1841, Mary considered emigration to New Zealand, specifically the New Zealand Company settlement at Port Nicholson (Wellington). Her father's death at the end of 1840 led quickly to the family's dispersal, as Charlotte Brontë had predicted.[13] Mary was then twenty-four years old, eager to break into new ventures. While her only sister, Martha, was sent to further her education in Brussels, Mary's future was undecided. None of the children was disposed to stay with their mother, the unlikable Anne Taylor, and for a time Mary, together with the youngest in the family, William Waring (known as Waring), contemplated a colonial venture. "Mary has made up her mind she can not and will not be a governess, a teacher, a milliner, a bonnetmaker nor housemaid," Charlotte explained to her sister Emily; she "sees no means of obtaining employment she would like in England, so she is leaving it."[14]

In the end, Mary chose not to leave for New Zealand then, though Waring Taylor did proceed, reaching Port Nicholson in April 1842.[15] Instead, she went to Europe, joining Martha in Brussels at Château de Koekelberg in 1842. Here Mary encouraged Charlotte and Emily Brontë to come to Brussels for what would prove the first of two momentous years for Charlotte Brontë at Pensionnat Heger. Following Martha's sudden death from cholera in October of that year, Mary looked first to Germany for opportunities beyond those she had known, and rejected, in England: poorly paid and subordinate governessing and schoolteaching. In Hagen Mary took music lessons with Friedrich Hallé, and then stepped out of the orthodox by teaching schoolboys algebra.[16] There was novelty in this, but not sufficient sustenance. By October 1844 the New Zealand plan had been revived and Mary determined on it.

Meanwhile, Charlotte had spent a second, more isolated year in Brussels in 1843, and returned home, where she languished in the agonies of unrequited love, and the disconsolate uncertainty of where to apply her own efforts. Passing on the terrible news of Mary's decision to the gentle sympathies of Ellen Nussey, Charlotte mourned, "Mary Taylor is going to leave our hemisphere—To me it is something as if a great planet fell out of the sky."[17] Of strong hearts and heads, all three friends, Charlotte Brontë, Ellen Nussey, and Mary Taylor wrestled with the problem of what direction in which to take their lives. Family duty, the need for a livelihood, marriage proposals, the narrow range of "proper" employment open to young women of the middling classes all imposed limits against which they railed, Mary most vociferously. Going or staying—whether from home, from a position as a governess or schoolmistress, from England, from spinsterhood into marriage—presented uneasy dilemmas. The domain of empire, and in particular, the settler colonies from the 1840s, presented an extended field in which to exercise choice, to resolve the predicament. "Going" was the enactment that defined the colonist—one taken more often by men than women but increasingly presented by groups such as the New Zealand Company as an option for the "anxious" middling classes as well as laboring people. Mary's verve and energy (a product of her upbringing and disposition) was always likely to lead to a more emphatic choice, but her eventual decision to leave the country altogether was an extreme step (she later described it as "a desperate plunge").[18] The distance of her going set an anchoring mark against her friends' staying. For Mary, the world of empire promised scope for what she believed she could not do within the boundaries of the nation: set about earning her own livelihood.

Mary Taylor arrived in July 1845 in Port Nicholson, a town inscribed with the name Wellington—her friend Charlotte Brontë's great idol.[19] The Duke of Wellington, statesman and hero of the Battle of Waterloo, had been the inspiration for Brontë's youthful Angrian tales. The toponymy of the New Zealand Company had originally attached the name "Britannia" to its map of the region, as its surveyors took nominal possession, in parallel with the absolute possession they believed they had secured by exchanging a combination of cash, blankets, and other goods with representatives of the Ngati Toa and Te Ati Awa tribes, the indigenous inhabitants.[20] The directors of the New Zealand Company in London replaced "Britannia" with "Wellington" in May 1840, a decision received in the settlement in November of that year. Small and scattered around a beach front, the town consisted of a collection of modest wooden buildings located between the two principal Maori villages at Pipitea and Te Aro. Sharing a roof with her brother Waring Taylor, Mary wrote letters in 1845–47 that create a picture of vigor, occupation, and novelty lived amid crude physical conditions. In her first three years she put some of her existing, modest capital to work building a house to rent, buying and selling cattle, and working in Waring's trading business. She gave piano lessons and was sought out as a teacher by a few better-off settlers, but was only prepared to do this work at a good rate (she "astonished" some locals by asking 70 pounds a year, and by not marrying her employer, a widower).[21] Charlotte believed Mary to be "in her element—because she has a toilsome task to perform, an important improvement to effect—a weak vessel [Waring] to strengthen."[22] Mary was also weighing plans of a more radical nature.

Mary sought to put Edward Gibbon Wakefield's idea of colonies as radical experiments in "systematic colonization" to the test by putting into practice her belief in women's entitlement to earn an independent livelihood.[23] In this way, Mary shared Samuel Hudson's desire to achieve independence in a colonial setting (see chapter 13 here). In the Cape Colony, Hudson sought freedom from the bounds of domestic servitude; in New Zealand Mary sought freedom from the constraints of respectable femininity.[24] She explained to Ellen Nussey in a letter urging her to come to New Zealand: "There are no means for a woman to live in England but by teaching, sewing or washing. The last is the best. The best paid the least unhealthy & the most free. But it is not paid well enough to live by. Moreover it is impossible for any one not born to this position to take it up afterwards. I don't know why but it is. . . . Why not come here then? & be happy."[25] Ellen Nussey did not respond to her friend's entreaty, but Mary's cousin Ellen Taylor, ten years younger, did, arriving in Wellington in August 1849. Ellen, Mary explained, "has come out with just the same wish to earn her living as I have & just the same objection to sedentary employment."[26] Together the two women were able to command sufficient capital (600–800 pounds) to embark on a business that had prospects of yielding income on a scale beyond merely making ends meet.[27] We "talked for a fortnight before we decided whether we would have a school or a shop, it ended in favour of the shop," Ellen Taylor explained to Charlotte Brontë in a joint letter of August 1850.[28] The shop option Mary had assessed as "decidedly the most healthy, but the most difficult of accomplishment."[29]

As a single woman, highly educated, with some capital of her own, and no (apparent) interest in becoming married, Mary Taylor was a highly unusual member of Wellington society in the late 1840s and early 1850s. Colonies in general attracted fewer women than men; single women were particularly rare; educated single women all the more so; and those with some capital of their own highly exceptional. Mary Taylor resisted the subtext of female emigration, and of organized colonization in general, in which women occupied the sexual, domestic, and reproductive economy and men the productive and commercial economy. Wakefield also highly prized women as culture bearers, guaranteeing cohesion and civility.[30] Mary's robust individuality set her apart. Aware of her status, Mary conveys in her letters a sense that she is enjoying occupying an odd position (as well as poking fun at the quirks of those around her); it was in her nature to stand at an angle to convention. Colonial Wellington offered another place for her to do so. She told Charlotte that her sister-in-law Mary Knox[31] thought her "astonishingly learned but rather wicked."[32]

To Ellen Nussey she wrote: "I pass here for a monkey who has seen the world & people receive me well on that account."[33]

Charlotte Brontë's view of Mary was of her friend sitting "on a wooden stool without a back in a log-house without a carpet" where she was "neither degraded nor thinks herself degraded [by] such poor accommodation."[34] The colonial world Mary constructed for her friends in her letters was one of novelty, improvisation, and unpredictability rather than of fear or danger. Her depictions produce an account of colonies distinct from those purveyed by official sources or in the public discourses of newspapers and magazines. In this way, personal correspondence created "colonial knowledge," in the way Erika Rappaport has suggested for India a decade or so later,[35] and in particular, defined difference, a key part of the cultural work of empire.[36] Unlike the Hudsons and Barnards at the Cape Colony at the beginning of the century, Mary Taylor was aware of but not at all anxious about her status in the small and also, at times, fractious community of colonial Wellington. Departures from conventions that arose from the exigencies of colonial living attracted and delighted her. It was precisely these things that she relished, exaggerating them in her letters to her friends safely ensconced in Yorkshire respectability. And while she was irreverent of social trappings, she was highly attentive to the need and the means by which wealth might be accrued.

While Mary's letters did create "colonies" in the broad sense, both she and Charlotte became increasingly aware that in the exchange of letters between discrete addresses, one in Wellington, one in Yorkshire, both were living at outposts from the metropole—one colonial, one provincial. Charlotte's letter to Mary of 1848 telling of her and Anne's visit to London is infused with Charlotte's sense of the city of London as a distant and foreign place. She emphasizes how strange she and Anne felt in it. A "couple of odd-looking country-women," "insignificant spinsters,"[37] they struggled to find their way around its streets, knew nowhere to stay but the Chapter Coffee House where she and Mary Taylor had spent a night on their way to Brussels in early 1842,[38] and had only odd attire to wear; they were distinctly out of place.

For Charlotte "here" and "there" increasingly became her world and home at Haworth and the other life that opened up as her literary success took her to London, Edinburgh, and other places. Her visits became part of her accounts in letters to Mary Taylor and Ellen Nussey, producing metropolitan knowledge in turn. By the spring of 1852 Mary remarked: "Your life in London is a 'new country' to me which I cannot even picture to myself. . . . I shd like well to have some details of your life but how can I hope for it? I have often tried to give you a picture of mine but I have not the skill I get a heap of details, most paltry in themselves & not enough to give you an idea of the whole."[39] What was at work here was not so much the dichotomy of metropolis and colony, but a recognition of a center from which both Haworth in Yorkshire and Wellington were remote. London, as the imagined and actual metropolis, was the center for both nation and empire, yet it was Haworth and Wellington that were the cultural entrepots. From Haworth came some of the most powerful literary creations of the mid–nineteenth century, and in Wellington was an intimate of their creator who was one of their most discerning readers. Correspondence provided the means of vital interconnectedness between friends at greatly distant locales. The tenor of this friendship was one in which four to six months might elapse between dispatch and receipt of messages, and up to twelve months between message and reply. Yet this elongation of space did not imply a lack of depth or intensity. To Mary Taylor in New Zealand Charlotte Brontë imparted confidences she withheld from her other intimate friend, Ellen Nussey, who lived within a day or two's mail exchange.[40]

The colonial world Mary landed in in 1845 was very much an incomplete colonial project.[41] New Zealand had come into the formal domain of the British Empire only five years earlier, in 1840, when the territory was annexed and a treaty negotiated between representatives of indigenous Maori tribes and William Hobson acting for the British Crown.[42] Undertakings made in the Treaty of Waitangi were quickly undercut by unscrupulous land dealings and by the assertion of British power over local chiefly authority. In various parts of the country, including Wellington, Maori actively challenged the settlers' right to inhabit and occupy the land; Wellington settlers disputed the authority of the governor in the north and shrugged off the attempt to exercise local authority when they were sent a lieutenant governor in the form of the unfortunate Edward Eyre.[43] Economic prospects in the New Zealand Company settlements were risky. Compared with the sharp lines and optimistic plans set out in the company offices in London, the settlement on the ground was slight and flimsy—as were its buildings and even the land itself. A series of earthquakes shook the central part of the country; the worst, in October 1848, brought most of the chimneys and many of the structures tumbling to the ground.[44]

The years of Mary's life there, 1845–59, were the years during which Wellington—initially a settlement perched precariously on the coastal fringe, where wooden houses and schooner anchorages sat interspersed with *raupo whare* (huts made of bulrushes) and *waka* (canoe) landing places—developed into an established site of European dominance and occupation. Initially living in a Maori world, Europeans were, by the early 1850s (if not earlier) setting the terms on which Maori lived in a European world.[45] Where there had been nine villages around the Lambton end of the harbor there were now three; where there had been gardens there were now surveyed sections; where there had been eeling, fishing, or bird trapping areas there were now cattle, sheep, and poultry, and fences to keep stock in, property demarcated, and strangers out. Mary wrote in 1854 of a "mania for emigration to N. Zealand"[46] but advised against just anyone thinking they would prosper by removing themselves from England to the colony.

As in many correspondences from settler colonies, Mary Taylor's letters are almost entirely silent on the subject of the indigenous inhabitants in the territory. The only such mention is in her letter to Ellen Nussey of February 9, 1849, in which she remarks: "The Maories are quiet & we begin to wish for another disturbance for fear the troops should leave the country."[47] Troops had been sent to protect the European settlers in the Port Nicholson area by Governor Grey in February 1846 following an escalation of tension as some local chiefs had resisted the incursion of settlers into areas they considered had not been sold. Forts had been built in several places around the harbor, an armed constabulary raised. In the core colonial relation, between colonizer and colonized, personal correspondence was, in this instance, unforthcoming. Stoler's recent characterization of such contexts as the "haunts" of empire, that which is invisibly occupied, is highly apposite.[48] The assumption that land was available for settlement was unproblematic; that New Zealand was a legitimate place for British settlement was unquestioned. Possession and occupancy, at the heart of the colonial project, exist as silences.

Through the years spanned by their correspondence, Mary and Charlotte both became significant economic agents engaged in buying and selling, earning and spending. While Mary dealt in cattle, house rent, and setting up in business, Charlotte was amassing earnings through writing. Commerce served both as a realm of mobility and as a subject in the intimacy of correspondence. For both women, economic independence was a guarantee of a wider social, emotional, and intellectual autonomy.

Mary embraced empire—colonial space—as a place where she could become a commercial actor in a way that was closed to her in England. She saw herself as an equal actor in the larger field of English and "British" settlement, trade, and endeavor—a small capitalist who could put funds and labor to work in the market for a profit, thereby providing an independent livelihood. Ellen Taylor provided Charlotte Brontë with a portrait of Mary conducting business: "Mary gets as fierce as a dragon &

goes to all the whole sale stores & looks at things, gets, patterns samples &c & asks prices, & then comes home & we talk it over & then she goes again & buys what we want, she says the people are always civil to her."[49] In setting up shop, Mary Taylor risked social position at a time when middle-class femininity was defined by distance and separation from the world of work, industry, and business.[50] Respectability was jeopardized by daily engagement in trade, the menial and sullied work of everyday buying and selling.

Undeterred by these risks, but aware she could only conduct her "experiment" in a colony at great distance from home and neighborhood where she belonged to a social system, Mary was eager to narrate her life as an independent woman in her letters. "As to when I'm coming home," she wrote to Charlotte in August 1850, "you may well ask. I have wished for 15 years to begin to earn my own living, last April I began to try. It is too soon yet to say with what success. I am wofully ignorant terribly wanting in tact & obstinately lazy & almost too old to mend. Luckily there is no other chance for me; so I must work."[51]

Mary and Charlotte's letters (and those to and from Ellen Nussey) contain frequent references to prices, incomes, and earnings. "It's a pity you don't live in this world that I might entertain you about the price of meat," Mary tells Charlotte in the midst of an account of her dealings in stock.[52] Between the three friends there were exchanges of money and goods (and views about these) as well as mail. Mary describes to Charlotte in some detail the amount of capital she has and what her investments might earn over time, as well as the value of railway shares. Mary regarded her shop as an enterprise in which they could all partake, urging Ellen, in particular, to send her things to sell. Mary also asks her friends to purchase things on her behalf. Ellen arranged for a dress and bonnet to be made and sent to Mary's specifications in 1853; on other occasions her friends sent her fashionable collars and cuffs. Of a collar she had received, Mary wrote: the "thick one with lace round I sometimes ride in & tell every one that I have two friends in England wearing the same. I wish I could say I had them here."[53]

Both Mary and Charlotte recognized writing as a means of earning. Mary's letter to Charlotte in 1848 not only contained her wonder at the creation of *Jane Eyre* but also comment on how much Charlotte had been paid for the manuscript. Charlotte Brontë received 500 pounds for the manuscript of *Jane Eyre*, along with contracting with Smith, Elder for a further two titles. Mary considered her friend to have been paid meagerly. Two years later as Mary, having heard the news of Anne Brontë's death, sent her condolences to Charlotte and as Charlotte's second novel,

Shirley, appeared, Mary encouraged her friend to look "for success in writing," to "care as much for that as you do for going to Heaven" and to take satisfaction in the "influence & power" she could derive from her achievements, referring both to public acclaim and wealth.[54]

Jane Eyre (1847), *Shirley* (1849), and *Villette* (1853) were remarkable literary and commercial successes, bringing Charlotte Brontë to the center of mid-Victorian literary circles and vastly expanding her social and corresponding milieux. The name Currer Bell and the books to which it was attached achieved remarkable mobility in the worldwide circulation of print culture. The settler colonies provided a ready domain for the consumption of the print production of the metropolis. Books, magazines, and newspapers that flowed out from England through a multitude of avenues, including the publishing house of Smith, Elder on Cornhill, London, to all corners of the English-speaking world included works of fiction. Distance may have brought some delay in obtaining the latest works, but the culture of empire was easily spanned by print. In her letter to Charlotte of April 1849, Mary recognized that her friend was becoming "a very important personage in this little world."[55] Charlotte received this letter in the same week as the publication of her second and much-anticipated novel *Shirley,* which propelled her to the forefront of public attention. While Charlotte awaited, with apprehension, the critical reception of her new work, the novel illustrated how closely entwined were the worlds of commerce, culture, and friendship.

For all her advice to her friend, Mary Taylor's encounter with *Shirley* in the context of the book as a commodity for sale took her by surprise. Writing at the end of April 1850—in a letter she began by announcing, triumphantly, boldly, "I have set up shop!"—she told Charlotte of her strange experience the previous day: "Du reste—it is very odd—I keep looking at my self with one eye while I'm using the other & I sometimes find myself in very queer positions. Yesterday I went along the shore past two wharves & several warehouses on a St. where I had never been before during all the 5 years I have been in Wellington. I opened the door of a long place filled with packages . . . with [a] passage up the middle & a row of high windows on one side. At the far end of the room a man was writing at a desk beneath . . . 'a' window. I walked all the length of the room very slowly, for . . . what I had come for had completely gone out of my head. Fortunately the man never heard me until I had recollected it. Then he got up & I asked him for some Stone blue, Saltpetre, tea, pickles, salt, &c. He was very civil; I bought some things & asked for a note of them. He went to his desk again & . . . I looked at some newspapers [laid] lying near. On the top was a circular fm Smith & Elder, containing notices of the most important new works. The first & . . . longest was given to *Shirley* a book I had seen mentioned in the Manchester Examiner as written by Currer Bell. I blushed all over; the man got up, folding the note. I pulled it out of his hand & set off to the door."[56]

Amid the barrels, packages, and stores in Bethune and Hunter's Wellington waterfront warehouse was a handbill from Smith and Elder announcing the latest work by "Currer Bell," author of *Jane Eyre.* The worlds of commerce and culture, of business and imagination, jostled side by side. For Mary, her immediate world and identity, as a superior if odd colonist and newly established shopkeeper, were here brought face to face with the distant but equally vivid and intimate world of her friendship with the book's author (still containing the delicious secret of the true identity of the mysterious author). In this moment, Mary was also faced with the prospect of characters in print, open for all to see (and judge), that she knew to be based on herself, her own family, and her former home. Mary was cast into a perplexity and confusion that even her robust nature found difficult to contain. The reach of print, of trade, of promotion, of imagination, of publication was tangible. Here was the commerce of culture; the culture of empire as a commodity—a vivid evocation of the cultural and commercial cosmopolitanism linking the worlds Mary and Charlotte had come to inhabit. The conventions of space as imagined geographical distance did not easily account for the powerful reach of print or the imaginative and affective proximity of the two friends.[57]

In *Shirley* Charlotte Brontë recreated her friend in the character of Rose Yorke, the lively, spirited, intelligent, and attractive daughter of mill owner Hiram Yorke (a close portrait of Joshua Taylor), and the rest of the Yorke family and home bear close resemblance to others of the Taylor family and Red House at Gomersal. A novel "as unromantic as a Monday morning," *Shirley* was set within the class and personal conflicts of the Luddite disturbances in the northern manufacturing districts of 1811–12. At the time Mary wrote to her friend Charlotte, in late April 1850, however, what Mary knew of Charlotte's new novel was limited to brief excerpts she had read in the *Manchester Examiner.*[58] Flush with her own determination to earn a living, and her very latest exuberant realization of it in opening the shop with cousin Ellen Taylor, Mary was wildly indignant. She embarked on a vociferous challenge to her friend, seeing in her depiction of characters Caroline Helstone and Shirley Keeldar a betrayal of the principle that women might work to achieve an economic independence. "You are a coward and a traitor," she accused Charlotte: "A woman who works is by that alone, better than one who does not & a woman who does not happen to be rich & who *still* earns no money

& does not wish to do so, is guilty of a great fault—almost a crime—A dereliction of duty which leads rapidly & almost certainly to all manner of degradation."[59] As if to prove how wrong Charlotte was, Mary fills her letter with detailed description of her own and Ellen's shop work and the deep satisfactions they had gained from it. Mary Taylor and Charlotte Brontë's friendship always had qualities of a combative intimacy.[60]

Only in August 1850 did the mail carrying a copy of the novel *Shirley* reach Mary and Ellen Taylor in Wellington. The mail landed on a Monday, just as the two women were preparing to host a small party the next day. On Wednesday they sat down to read the book.

> I began Shirley & continued in a curious confusion of mind till now principally abt the handsome foreigner who was nursed in our house when I was a little girl.—By the way you've put him in the Servant's bedroom. You make us all talk much as I think we shd. have done if we'd ventured to speak at all—What a little lump of perfection you've made me! There is a strange feeling in reading it of hearing us all talking. I have not seen the matted hall & painted parlour windows so plain these 5 years. But my Father is not like. He hates well enough and perhaps loves too but he is not honest enough. It was from my father I learnt not to marry for money nor to tolerate any one who did & he never wd advise any one to do so or fail to speak with contempt of those who did. Shirley is much more interesting than J. Eyre—who indeed never interests you at all until she has something to suffer. All through this last novel there is so much more life & stir that it leaves you far more to remember than the other.[61]

For Mary, the power of Charlotte Brontë's imagination collapsed time and space. Space was no longer, if it ever had been, a separation between the two friends but formed a relation between them: a relation of multiple strands rather than a continuous surface to cross.[62] "Pretending"—the artifice of fiction—is "more real" to Mary than the world around her. In the intimacy of reading Mary found herself again on the opposite side of the world, in her home in Yorkshire, hearing and seeing members of her family. And Charlotte had given life to her friend in the present as she invited readers to look forward into Rose Yorke's future: she is sitting in a foreign landscape, on the banks of "no European river," the "little, quiet Yorkshire girl is a lonely emigrant, in some region of the southern hemisphere. Will she ever come back?"[63] Imagination had the power to transcend temporal confines. Charlotte Brontë's novel, in its full form, clearly was a source of great delight and rich enjoyment for Mary—in memory, in her friend's achievement, in the story itself, which was more to her liking than *Jane Eyre*. Not all the family agreed. Waring Taylor, Mary reported, had had a letter from "Mama" decrying Miss Brontë's portrait of the family (not surprising, given her own depiction). Borrowing Mary's copy, Waring announced himself unconvinced by the "Yorke" characters and "Briarmains" an inaccurate representation of their home, Red House. Mary believed her brother had "forgotten home altogether."[64]

Responding to *Jane Eyre* in 1848, Mary Taylor was admiring of how her friend had crafted "so perfect a work of art. I expected something more changeable & unfinished." Not only was the work highly polished; Mary Taylor was surprised to discover in her friend's creation a work of such complete imagination. That it was in a novel, the complete creation of plot, characters, scenes, that her friend had made her work. "You are very different from me in having no doctrine to preach. It is impossible. . . . Has the world gone so well with you that you have no protest to make against its absurdities?"[65] Mary may have understated her friend's "protest" in the vibrant and, to some opinions, dangerous character of Jane Eyre and her strong passions. While Charlotte deployed the trans-forming power of fiction, Mary looked to reconfigure the material and social relations in which women lived. Their correspondence maintained a friendship, but also became a place for their changing selves to make contact, to interact.[66]

Imagination was, perhaps, the most powerful form of mobility. If travel writing, emigration propaganda, and the like played a crucial part in creating "the domestic culture of empire,"[67] there was another side in which people in settler colonies consumed works created in the metropole. Mary Taylor provided Charlotte Brontë with vignettes of her colonial readers. About *Jane Eyre* she told Charlotte, "I lend it a good deal because it's a novel & it's *as good as another!* They say 'it makes them cry.' They are not literary enough to give an opinion. If ever I hear one I'll embalm it for you."[68] At the end of the same letter Mary adds, "I have lately met with a wonder a man who thinks Jane Eyre would have done better [to] marry Mr Rivers! he gives no reasons—such people never do."[69] One of Mary's joys in Ellen Taylor's company was that she could discuss books with Mary at the same level and from a perspective similar to Mary's.

The last surviving letter from Mary Taylor's correspondence with Charlotte Brontë is dated "Spring 1852." Its muted tone contrasts with that of the letters of 1850. Ellen Taylor's consumption deteriorated in 1851; she died on December 27. Mary tells Charlotte that she has decided to carry on alone, and of the arrangements whereby she has bought Ellen's share of the business, but it is apparent that the joy of the enterprise faded with the loss of Ellen's company. The "best part of my life" now, she told Charlotte, was "the excitement of arrivals from England. Reading all the news, written & printed, is like living another life quite separate from this one."[70] No letters survive allowing insight into how Mary received Charlotte's third novel, *Villette,* published in January 1853, set closely around their time in Brussels. Mary's last surviving letter from New Zealand to Ellen Nussey expresses her impatience with Ellen's lack of enthusiasm for Charlotte's burgeoning friendship with Arthur Nicholls.[71]

Mary Taylor's puzzle set down in her letter to Charlotte of June–July 1848, her feeling of living in two places at once, in both of which she felt impelled to "move and act" and have her say, was a product of the mobilities of intimacy, commerce, and imagination. These operated to bring distant aspects of the world together rather than keep them apart. Vibert suggests that Reverend Murdoch Stewart, writing in Cape Breton but about his life in Scotland, also "dwelt in two places at once." To Stewart the two poles of his life came to define each other, but the distance was filled by a painful yearning and sense of loss, rather than an animated bond. Mary Taylor and Charlotte Brontë's correspondence maintained a connection (and served to exchange news, ideas, reactions) but was also a place in which the two friends each held up the world she had embraced to show the other. They were showing not only the metropolitan to the colonial world (and vice versa) but also imaginary worlds to the "actual"— their public selves to intimate and familiar selves. Empire, commerce, and imagination acted as paths of transaction, exchange, and connection.[72]

Mary and Charlotte shared the predicament of thousands of their contemporaries whose intimate ties of family and friendship had been sundered by emigration, and the dispersal of empire. Although Mary's departure for New Zealand in 1845 cast the two friends into a great distance from each other, they found, to their surprise, that they had not come to inhabit two separate and distinct places. Wellington and Yorkshire, here and there, metropolis and colony were not separate spaces but two sides of a single entity that defined and created each other, that blurred and entwined, through commerce and culture, the real and the imagined. If we see the "time of empire" as "the time when anatomies of difference were being elaborated,"[73] as Catherine Hall suggests, then we can see in the Mary Taylor–Charlotte Brontë correspondence a rich place where this "work of culture"[74] was occurring. While it is but one set of personal correspondence, one intimacy of the envelope, it provides a telling instance. The intimacy of friendship was a relation of empire that "made both colonizers and colonized";[75] it was also a place where imperial and colonial cultures were shaped.

Notes

I am grateful to Tony Ballantyne and Antoinette Burton for their generous and enlivening stimulus in shaping this essay through the symposium "Gender and Empire," University of Otago, University, Dunedin, New Zealand, October 29, 2004, and for subsequent comments; and to Gill Eastabrook and Martin Staniforth for Yorkshire treads. The Faculty of Humanities and Social Sciences, Victoria University of Wellington, assisted with funds to attend the symposium.

1. Port Jackson, Sydney, Australia. The remaining names are for ports in New Zealand, and all but Waitemata (Auckland) date from European "exploration" and navigation, notably the late eighteenth-century voyages of James Cook. J. C. Beaglehole, *The Journals of Captain James Cook on His Voyages of Discovery*, 4 vols. (Cambridge, 1955–74).

2. Charlotte Brontë, of course, achieved contemporary fame. Mary Taylor (1817–1893) had a modest public profile as the author of articles in the *Victoria Magazine* (1865–70), *The First Duty of Women* (1870), and *Miss Miles, or a Tale of Yorkshire Life 60 Years Ago* (1890). She maintained a small profile as a sideline in the Brontë industry but is not included in the *Dictionary of National Biography* or its supplements. She has become more conspicuous since the publication of Joan Stevens, ed., *Mary Taylor. Friend of Charlotte Brontë: Letters from New Zealand and Elsewhere* (Auckland, New Zealand, and Oxford, 1972), which remains the major work on the friendship and to which this discussion is substantially indebted. See also A. James Hammerton, *Emigrant Gentlewomen: Genteel Poverty and Female Emigration 1830–1914* (London, 1979), 3; Pat Sargison, "Mary Taylor, 1817–1893," in Charlotte Macdonald, Merimeri Penfold, and Bridget Williams, eds, *The Book of New Zealand Women / Ko Kui Ma te Kaupapa* (Wellington, New Zealand, 1991), 657–60; Beryl Hughes, "Taylor, Mary, 1817–1893, Feminist, Music Teacher, Businesswoman, Writer," in *Dictionary of New Zealand Biography*, vol. 1, *1769–1869* (Wellington, New Zealand, 1990), 435–57 (www.dnzb.govt.nz); Jane Stafford, "'Remote Must Be the Shores': Mary Taylor, Charlotte Brontë and the Colonial Experience," *Journal of New Zealand Literature* 10 (1992): 8–15; Juliet Barker, "Taylor, Mary (1817–1893), Advocate of Women's Rights," in *Oxford Dictionary of National Biography* (Oxford, 2004) (www.oxforddnb.com). Jenny Coleman, "'Philosophers in Petticoats': A Feminist Analysis of the Discursive Practices of Mary Taylor, Mary Colclough and Ellen Ellis as Contributors to the Debate on 'The Woman Question' in New Zealand between 1845–1885" (Ph.D. diss., University of Canterbury, 1996); Becki Cardwell, "'Living As I Do in 2 Places at Once': The Inscription of Displacement in the Writing of Mary Taylor," *Journal of New Zealand Literature* 21 (2003): 147–64. Elizabeth Gaskell, *Life of Charlotte Brontë* (London, 1857), was the first of many studies of Brontë, among the most substantial recent ones being Winifred Gérin, *Charlotte Brontë: The Evolution of Genius* (Oxford, 1967), Juliet Barker, *The Brontës* (London, 1994), and with a more iconoclastic slant, Lucasta Miller, *The Brontë Myth* (London, 2001).

3. Mary Taylor to Charlotte Brontë, June-July 1848, in Margaret Smith, ed., *The Letters of Charlotte Brontë* (hereafter *Letters of Charlotte Brontë*), 2:88–89. All references to the correspondence are taken from this definitive edition: vol. 1, *1829–1847*, vol. 2, *1848–1851*, vol. 3, *1852–1855* (Oxford, 1995–2004).

4. Quoting Frances Kemble's 1882 *Records of Later Life*, Smith notes that the

"novel and its mysterious author, Currer Bell, were 'the universal theme of conversation and correspondence'"; introduction to *Letters of Charlotte Brontë*, 2:xvii.

5. Smith describes Charlotte and Anne's London visit as "the most exciting event of the year," ibid. Mary Taylor was the only friend to whom Charlotte Brontë confided anything of the writing or publication of *Jane Eyre*.

6. Catherine Hall, ed., *Cultures of Empire: Colonizers in Britain and the Empire in the Nineteenth and Twentieth Centuries* (Manchester, England, 2000); Kathleen Wilson, ed., *A New Imperial History: Culture, Identity and Modernity in Britain and the Empire, 1660–1840* (Cambridge, 2004).

7. The literature addressing the nature and significance of intimacies of empire is extensive and tends to concentrate on sexual, romantic, and conjugal relations, and the ensuing relations between parents and children produced by liaisons of empire. For an introduction see Clare Midgley, ed., *Gender and Imperialism* (Manchester, England, 1998); Ann Laura Stoler, "Tense and Tender Ties: The Politics of Comparison in North American History and (Post) Colonial Studies," *Journal of American History* 88, 3 (2001): 829–65; Philippa Levine, ed., *Gender and Empire*, Oxford History of the British Empire Companion Series (Oxford, 2004); *Gender and History* 17, 1 (April 2005); Angela Woollacott, *Gender and Empire* (Basingstoke, England, 2006). While studies of personal correspondence "across" or "within" the empire are numerous, they have generally not been framed within the sphere of "intimacy of empire." See, for example, David Fitzpatrick, *Oceans of Consolation: Personal Accounts of Irish Migration to Australia* (Ithaca, N.Y., 1994); Charlotte Erickson, *Invisible Immigrants: The Adaptation of English and Scottish Immigrants in Nineteenth-Century America* (Coral Gables, Fla., 1972); Angela McCarthy, *Irish Migrants in New Zealand, 1840–1937: "The Desired Haven"* (Woodbridge, Suffolk, England, and Rochester, N.Y., 2005).

8. Ann Laura Stoler, "Intimidations of Empire: Predicaments of the Tactile and Unseen," in Stoler, ed., *Haunted by Empire: Geographies of Intimacy in North American History* (Durham, N.C., and London, 2006), 2.

9. Charlotte Brontë to Mary Taylor, September 4, 1848, in *Letters of Charlotte Brontë*, 2:111–17.

10. Mary Taylor to Charlotte Brontë, June-July 1848, in ibid., 2:88.

11. Letters between Charlotte Brontë and Ellen Nussey in particular, but also between Charlotte and Joe Taylor, Amelia Ringrose, and Margaret Wooler, mention other correspondence between Mary Taylor and her Yorkshire friends and family, in ibid.

12. For a larger consideration of this problem see Antoinette Burton, "Archive Stories: Gender in the Making of Imperial and Colonial Histories," in Levine, *Gender and Empire*, 281–93.

13. Charlotte Brontë to Ellen Nussey, January 3, 1841, in *Letters of Charlotte Brontë*, 1:242–43. Charlotte describes the Taylor family as "restless, active spirits" who "will not be restrained always.—Mary alone has more energy and power in her nature than any ten men you can pick out of the united parishes of Birstal and Gomersal. It is vain to limit a character like hers within ordinary boundaries—she will overstep them—I am morally certain Mary will establish her own landmarks."

14. Charlotte Brontë to Emily Brontë, April 2, 1841, in ibid., 1:251.

15. Stevens, *Mary Taylor*, 63. William Waring Taylor's story can be traced through Stevens. See also "Taylor, William Waring, 1819–1903," in G. H. Schole-field, ed., *Dictionary of New Zealand Biography* (Wellington, New Zealand, 1940), 2:376b; B. R. Patterson, "Whatever Happened to Poor Waring Taylor? Insights from the Business Manuscripts," *Turnbull Library Record* 24, 2 (October 1991): 113–31.

16. The unconventionality, and indeed perceived impropriety, of such a position meant that Miss Katherine Wooler, sister of Mary's Roe Head teacher, Miss Margaret Wooler, "cut" Mary. *Letters of Charlotte Brontë*, 1:326 n.

17. Charlotte Brontë to Ellen Nussey, c. October 26, 1844, in ibid., 1:372. The last time the two friends saw each other was in February 1845 when Charlotte spent a week with her friend at Hunsworth Cottage, where Mary was living with two of her brothers.

18. Mary Taylor to Ellen Nussey, February 9, 1849, in ibid., 2:179. See also her letter to Ellen Nussey of September 24, 1842, where she writes: "Going! Going! in to the heart of Germany," "farewell I am going to shut my eyes for a cold plunge—when I come up again I [will] tell you all what its like," in ibid., 1:293. Mary Taylor was brought up in a family radical in political belief and in religious adherence (her father, Joshua Taylor, was a New Connexion Methodist). In *Shirley* Charlotte Brontë models the "Yorke" family on the Taylors, describing them as "racy, peculiar and vigorous."

19. The names by which the harbor and region were known to Maori inhabitants were Te Whanganui-a-Tara, and Te Upoko o Te Ika, with many more names for particular locations and features. Malcolm McKinnon, ed., *Historical Atlas of New Zealand* (Auckland, New Zealand, 1997); Angela Ballara, "Te Whanganui-a-Tara: Phases of Maori Occupation of Wellington Harbour c. 1800–1840," in David Hamer and Roberta Nicholls, eds., *The Making of Wellington 1800–1914* (Wellington, New Zealand, 1990), 9–34. Mary Taylor told Elizabeth Gaskell in 1856 that Charlotte had "worshipped the Duke of Wellington," Stevens, *Mary Taylor*, 159.

20. The terms of the "sale" are currently a matter under investigation and negotiation as part of the settlement of historical claims under the Waitangi Tribunal process (see Wai 145, New Zealand Waitangi Tribunal, *Te Whanganui-a-Tara me ona takiwa: Report on the Wellington District*, 2003). See also Ballara, "Te Whanganui-a-Tara"; Susan Butterworth, *Petone: A History* (Petone, New Zealand, 1988); Alan Ward, *An Unsettled History: Treaty Claims in New Zealand Today* (Wellington, New Zealand, 1999); Alan Ward, *A Show of Justice: Racial "Amalgamation" in Nineteenth-Century New Zealand*, rev. ed. (Auckland, New Zealand, 1995) (originally published 1974).

21. Mary Taylor to Charlotte Brontë, June-July 1848, in *Letters of Charlotte Brontë*, 2:89.

22. Charlotte Brontë to Ellen Nussey, September 13, 1846, in ibid., 1:496–97.

23. See Judith Bassett, "The Pakeha Invasion, 1840–1860," in Judith Bassett, Judith Binney, and Erik Olssen, *The People and the Land: An Illustrated History of New Zealand, 1820–1920* (Wellington, New Zealand, 1990), 39–56; Miles Fairburn, "Wakefield, Edward Gibbon, 1796–1862," in *Dictionary of New Zealand Biography*, vol. 1, *1769–1869* (Wellington, New Zealand, 1990), 572–75; David J. Moss, "Wakefield, Edward Gibbon (1796–1862), Promoter of Colonization," in

Oxford Dictionary of National Biography; Philip Temple, *A Sort of Conscience: The Wakefields* (Auckland, New Zealand, 2002).

24. See chapter 14 here.

25. Mary Taylor to Ellen Nussey, February 9, 1849, in *Letters of Charlotte Brontë*, 2:178–80.

26. Mary Taylor to Charlotte Brontë, April 5, 1850, in ibid., 2:378.

27. Mary told Charlotte she believed that the capital she and Ellen had between them was "as large a capital as probably any in Wellington," Mary Taylor to Charlotte Brontë, April 5, 1850, in ibid., 2:378.

28. Mary Taylor and Ellen Taylor to Charlotte Brontë, August 13, 1850, in ibid., 2:440.

29. Mary Taylor to Charlotte Brontë, April 10, 1849, in ibid., 2:199.

30. Charlotte Macdonald, *A Woman of Good Character: Single Women as Immigrant Settlers in Nineteenth-Century New Zealand* (Wellington, New Zealand, 1990); Hammerton, *Emigrant Gentlewomen*; Raewyn Dalziel, "The Colonial Helpmeet: Women's Role and the Vote in Nineteenth-Century New Zealand," *New Zealand Journal of History* 11, 2 (October 1977): 112–23, and in Barbara Brookes, Charlotte Macdonald, and Margaret Tennant, eds., *Women in History: Essays on European Women in New Zealand* (Wellington, New Zealand, 1986), 55–68; Raewyn Dalziel, "Men, Women and Wakefield," in *Edward Gibbon Wakefield and the Colonial Dream: A Reconsideration* (Wellington, New Zealand, 1997) 77–88.

31. Waring Taylor married Mary Knox in February 1848.

32. Mary Taylor to Charlotte Brontë, June-July 1848, in *Letters of Charlotte Brontë*, 2:88.

33. Mary Taylor to Ellen Nussey, February 9, 1849, in ibid., 2:179.

34. Charlotte Brontë to Ellen Nussey, September 29, 1846, in ibid., 1:501–2.

35. Erika Rappaport, "'The Bombay Debt': Letter Writing, Domestic Economies and Family Conflict in Colonial India," *Gender and History* 16, 2 (August 2004): 233–60. See also Klaus Stierstorfer, gen. ed., *Women Writing Home, 1700–1920: Female Correspondence across the British Empire*, 6 vols. (London, 2006).

36. Hall, introduction to *Cultures of Empire*, 20.

37. Charlotte Brontë to Mary Taylor, September 4, 1848, in *Letters of Charlotte Brontë*, 2:114.

38. Together with Emily Brontë, Patrick Brontë, and Joe Taylor.

39. Mary Taylor to Charlotte Brontë, Spring 1852, in ibid., 3:36.

40. For a useful discussion on the meanings of space see Doreen Massey, *For Space* (London, 2005).

41. See Adele Perry, *On the Edge of Empire: Gender, Race and the Making of British Columbia, 1849–1871* (Toronto, 2001), for exposition of this notion.

42. Claudia Orange, *The Treaty of Waitangi* (Wellington, New Zealand, 1987); G. W. Rice, ed., *Oxford History of New Zealand*, 2nd ed. (Auckland, New Zealand, 1992).

43. Eyre was appointed lieutenant-governor of New Zealand in 1846, arriving in 1847 in the colony, where he served until 1853. Gad Heuman, "Eyre, Edward John (1815–1901), Colonial Governor," in *Oxford Dictionary of National Biography* (Oxford, 2004); Catherine Hall, *Civilising Subjects: Metropole and Colony in the English Imagination 1830–1867* (London and Chicago, 2002).

44. Mary wrote in detail abut the earthquake in her letters and sent an account to Chambers hoping it might be published (it was not); see Mary Taylor to Charlotte Brontë, April 10, 1849, and Charlotte Brontë to Ellen Nussey, c. May 12 and 14, 1849, in *Letters of Charlotte Brontë*, 2:198–99, 208–9. A much stronger earthquake hit Wellington in January 1855; miraculously, there was only one fatality. Rodney Grapes, *Magnitude Eight Plus: New Zealand's Biggest Earthquake* (Wellington, New Zealand, 2000).

45. Rice, *Oxford History of New Zealand*; Michael King, *The Penguin History of New Zealand* (Auckland, New Zealand, 2003), chaps. 9–14; Philippa Mein Smith, *A Concise History of New Zealand* (Melbourne, 2005), chaps. 3–4.

46. Mary Taylor to Ellen Nussey, February 24 to March 3, 1854, in *Letters of Charlotte Brontë*, 3:228.

47. Mary Taylor to Ellen Nussey, 9 February 1849, in ibid., 2:179.

48. Stoler, *Haunted by Empire.*

49. Mary Taylor and Ellen Taylor to Charlotte Brontë, August 13, 1850, in ibid., 2:440.

50. Leonore Davidoff and Catherine Hall, *Family Fortunes: Men and Women of the English Middle Class, 1780–1850* (London, 1987).

51. Mary Taylor and Ellen Taylor to Charlotte Brontë, August 13, 1850, in *Letters of Charlotte Brontë*, 2:439. The shop was a success. By the time Mary left Wellington in 1859 she was able to sell the business profitably with sufficient means to live independently for the rest of her life.

52. Mary Taylor to Charlotte Brontë, June-July 1848, in ibid., 2:89.

53. Mary Taylor to Ellen Nussey, February 9, 1849, in ibid., 2:180.

54. Mary Taylor to Charlotte Brontë, April 5, 1850, in ibid., 2:378.

55. Taylor to Brontë, April 10, 1849, in ibid., 2:198.

56. Taylor to Brontë, c. April 29, 1850, in ibid., 2:391–34.

57. Massey, *For Space.*

58. Excerpts and a review of *Shirley* had appeared in the *Manchester Examiner* of November 7, 1849. Copies reached New Zealand well ahead of the book. Stevens, *Mary Taylor*, 93.

59. Taylor to Brontë, April 29, 1850, in *Letters of Charlotte Brontë*, 2:392.

60. See, for example, the summation offered by Taylor of her friend, Stevens, *Mary Taylor*, 160–61.

61. Mary and Ellen Taylor to Charlotte Brontë, August 13, 1850, in *Letters of Charlotte Brontë*, 2:439.

62. Massey, *For space*, chap. 1.

63. Charlotte Brontë, *Shirley*, chap. 9.

64. Mary Taylor to Ellen Nussey, March 11, 1851, in *Letters of Charlotte Brontë*, 2:586.

65. Mary Taylor to Charlotte Brontë, June-July 1848, in ibid., 2:87.

66. In this way they provide another instance of "bodies in contact"; see Tony Ballantyne and Antoinette Burton, eds., *Bodies in Contact: Rethinking Colonial Encounters in World History* (Durham, N.C., and London, 2005).

67. Hall, introduction to *Cultures of Empire*, 26.

68. Taylor to Brontë, June-July 1848, in *Letters of Charlotte Brontë*, 2:88.

69. Taylor to Brontë, June-July 1848, in ibid., 2:89–90.

70. Taylor to Brontë, Spring 1852, in ibid., 3:36.

71. Mary Taylor to Ellen Nussey, February 24 to March 3, 1854, in ibid., 3:228–30. It is not known when and how Mary Taylor heard the news of her friend Charlotte Brontë's death in March 1855. By the end of that year, however, Mary had received a request from Elizabeth Gaskell for help in the task she had accepted on invitation from Charlotte's father, to write a "Life" of his now famous daughter. To this request Mary Taylor responded fully and quickly. Mary Taylor's greatest literary legacy may, indeed, have been the contributions she made to Gaskell's hugely influential biography of Charlotte Brontë. Beyond this Mary Taylor did not become a keeper of the Charlotte Brontë flame, unlike Ellen Nussey. Mary left Wellington in 1859 and in 1860 was back in England, where she built a house in her old neighborhood of Gomersal, Yorkshire, in which she lived until her death in 1893.

72. The theme and significance of interconnectedness is exemplified in Ballantyne and Burton, *Bodies in Contact.*

73. Hall, introduction to *Cultures of Empire,* 20.

74. Ibid., 20.

75. Ibid., 5.

5 *Suva under Steam*

MOBILE MEN AND A COLONIAL
PORT CAPITAL, 1880S–1910S

On the wharf clusters a crowd of strange figures.
How savage these Fijians look! The hair stiff, erect,
and spreading in a huge mop above the dark faces: the
features flat and negroid: the skin all shades from deep
copper to actual black: the expression untamed and
wild—all these alarm the timid traveller, and he says he
will never go ashore among such savages! For all that, we
are in Suva, the European capital of Fiji, and a populous
and busy town. And the "horrible savages" are merely
the peaceable labourers employed by the Union Steam
Ship Company for cargo work, or else spectators from the
native towns come up to sell coral and shells.

—Beatrice Grimshaw, *Three Wonderful Nations* (1907)

In her narrative of a cruise through the South Pacific, travel
writer Beatrice Grimshaw's initial impressions of Suva echo "first contacts" between indigenous islanders and European explorers. Although
Grimshaw writes from an early twentieth-century vantage point, aboard
a steamship entering a colonial port town, these men staring back are
unknown and, perhaps, forever unknowable. They remain "strange,"
"dark," and "savage." Their appearance conjures up "horrible" visions
of the likely harm that awaits landing. Yet on closer reflection, this is
the European capital of Fiji, a "populous and busy town." Fijian "savages" have become peaceable, nonthreatening wharf laborers and passive
"spectators" through the transformative reach of imperial transportation
and trading networks.

In this chapter I place a specific maritime transport culture at the center of colonial histories of space, mobility, and intimacy in Fiji. A port of call along the routes of various steamship companies, Suva became the regional center of the western Pacific in the late nineteenth century. Steamships facilitated the regular and routine passage of people and goods through this site, while companies' labor demands brought men from diverse racial groups into new forms of contact, exchange, and conflict.[1] To date, scholars have not discussed the maritime dimensions of the late nineteenth century colonial Pacific in any great depth. Epeli Hau'ofa's provocative and influential conceptualization of Oceania as "Our Sea of Islands" counters the marginalization of islands in this ocean as small, dependent, and isolated. He emphasizes long-standing processes of maritime connectivity throughout the Pacific, charting continuity between ancient navigational practices and present-day mobilities. This continuity, he asserts, was fractured by a middle period of colonial rule when Europeans turned their backs on the sea, partitioned islands, and confined indigenous populations to them.[2]

The contraction of indigenous mobility is central to my analysis, yet colonialism was not only about confinement and restriction. Webs of empire, with maritime cultures of their own, drew Oceania into new networks, enlarging land and seascapes in the process. The movement of men to the new port town and the forms of intimate contact, exchange, and conflict between them frame this account of "Suva under steam." The masculine domains of labor on a steamship, at the wharf, and in the branch office depart from those that Ann Stoler privileges in her analysis of race and the intimate in colonial rule. Sexual arrangements in the domestic realm and the relationships between husbands, wives, parents, children, and servants are at the heart of her work.[3] I choose to privilege male bodies in contact, particularly those men who engaged in different ways with the colonial maritime labor market. Many left families behind; these domestic intimacies do figure, though often at a troubling distance. If space is constituted, as Doreen Massey argues, "by the interlocking of 'stretched out' social relations," then Suva was not a static, closed site, but a "particular moment" in these relations.[4] These networks embraced family members in Fijian villages or New Zealand and Australian towns, as well as company colleagues stationed at other port branches and on board steamers throughout the region.

These maritime workers are some of the "active" bodies Ramon A. Gutierrez sees as "sorely missing" in Stoler's analysis: the "bodies that talked back, fought back, and actively resisted the technologies and regimes of their colonial lords."[5] Mary Renda, in looking to other fields of meaning beyond the sexual that fostered racist sentiment, also foregrounds resistance to colonial forms of governance. In response, Stoler cautions against an easy romanticization of resistance, whereby colonizers are collectively grouped as exploiters and the colonized as exploited.[6] The struggles that played out in Suva over different bodies as an economic resource were equally struggles over the regulation of mobility and the control of colonial space.

Historians of crosscultural encounters in the Pacific have employed the metaphor of "the beach" for cultural boundary, an in-between, liminal and ambiguous space rather than a literal site. Greg Dening has been most influential in this respect. He tracks "beach crossings," those moments of encounter with otherness and their implications for individual and collective identities.[7] Encounter histories have, however, tended to privilege "first contacts" between indigenous islanders and Euro-American intruders, and the early decades of mutual engagement with new people, ideas, and technologies. Multiple and diverse histories of passage and exchange in the Pacific in the centuries preceding and following the "discovery" of the Pacific Islands by Europeans are thereby muted.[8]

From the early nineteenth century, communities that sprang up around frequented harbors to service whalers and traders were often known simply as "The Beach." These included Honolulu in Hawai'i, Kororareka in New Zealand, Papeete in Tahiti, Apia in Samoa, and Levuka in Fiji. Beach communities were diverse, peopled by various islanders, foreigners, and mixed-race offspring. Throughout much of the nineteenth century indigenous people with no interest in Europeans or the things and ideas connected to them could avoid these sites by choosing not to go there. In general, as Caroline Ralston concludes, such freedom of choice made for "good" race relations across Pacific port towns.[9] In his work on interracial life in Samoa, Damon Salesa also frames the port as an "optional" space before the late nineteenth century. There was no immediate resettlement of indigenous authority around Apia; the traditional Samoan polity remained paramount and could continue to function without reference to the new port space.[10]

Marginal to both indigenous and the more distant European centers of authority, these ports quickly earned reputations, particularly through the agitation of humanitarian reformers, as lawless, booze-sodden, and vice-ridden places. This in-betweenness spoke of patterns of settlement, economic networks, and forms of political power very different in character from the translational nature of the beach of first contact. With the extension and consolidation of formal colonial rule in the latter part of the century, ports were locked into imperial networks in more durable ways. Episodes of crosscultural encounter and exchange were increasingly multiple, routine, and in many respects familiar, as evidenced by Grimshaw's shift in perspective in the opening vignette.

After decades of informal Euro-American involvement in the Fiji group, a number of chiefs signed the deed of cession to Britain on October 10, 1874. This had geographical ramifications for the island group. The intention to remove the capital from Levuka to Suva was announced in 1877 and took place five years later. On the small island of Ovalau, mountainous terrain hemmed in Levuka along a narrow beach strip. The commanding officer of the Royal Engineers investigated the suitability of the site in 1876 and deplored the "general feeling of *confinement*" and "airlessness."[11] Poor drainage, limited water supply, and the landholding dominance of the Wesleyan church all precluded expansion. Margaret Rodman suggests that colonial administrators preferred the safety afforded by small-island bases in the Pacific, yet by the late 1870s Levuka's "frontier feel" did not project the right image of British colonial power and prestige in Fiji.[12]

Preference for Suva can be traced to Colonel W. T. Smythe's 1860 visit to investigate "King" Cakobau's first offer of cession to the British.[13] This unsuccessful offer included land, twenty-seven thousand acres of which lay in the Suva area. On the southeast of Fiji's largest island, Viti Levu, Suva was better placed to service the needs of white plantation owners and offered ample potential for expansion. In the hope of profitable investment, the Melbourne-based Polynesia Company purchased the land offered by Cakobau in 1868. This was a highly contentious charter, yet settlers were attracted to Fiji, due in part to a depression in the Australasian colonies.[14] James McEwan and Company acquired title to most of the land in the Suva area and allotted the government every alternate block in the late 1870s to encourage the removal of the capital. The government acquired more Suva land through the Native Lands Commission, set up in 1880 to register Fijian titles to land and restore informally alienated land to indigenous owners. The commission upheld settlers' Suva land claims if they could prove occupation and use. Rejected claims remained in government hands; Suva land was not returned to Fijians, as occurred everywhere else in Fiji under the commission. On the relocation of the capital, indigenous Fijians in "Old Suva Village," an area adjacent to the proposed Government House, were relocated across the harbor. This village was named Suvavou (New Suva).[15]

Local and regional politics remained strong beyond Suva, particularly in the interior of Viti Levu, where colonial officials met resistance, and in eastern Fiji, where Tongan influence was marked from the early nineteenth century.[16] People did not simply reorder their lives around the new capital, yet Suva's reach soon extended further than that of the precolonial European center. The colonial state, while upholding the coherence of the "village" as the stronghold of indigeneity, put new emphasis on the "net" of laws and channels of information that would spread across the whole island group. Fiji's first governor, Sir Arthur Hamilton Gordon, encouraged indigenous officials to write to him "at all seasons and at all times."[17] Michelle Moran discusses the colonial intimacy between disease and heightened surveillance in Hawai'i (chapter 15 here). In Fiji the state also increased its surveillance beyond Suva in the name of the "preservation of the race," after an official report was published on the state of indigenous health in 1896.[18]

In charting attempts to reorient life within the Fiji group, Suva's placement within wider imperial networks also demands attention. As the town's "organizing principle," the port influenced its character, structure, and symbolism.[19] Ports are at once both windows to the sea and windows from sea to land. M. N. Pearson critiques a tendency to study port cities in a geographically limited way, straying inland to their supply centers but neglecting the open sea.[20] For some observers, Suva's establishment and growth was a clear narrative of progress, and steam communication with neighboring colonies a distinct marker of this: "We have seen the green knoll where a small wooden church once stood, levelled and rolled out into a pier; the native path along the beach raised to the dignity of Victoria Parade . . . where a few years ago the native canoe alone was seen, or a solitary settler's boat coming up to the solitary store for a few tins of preserved meat and a case of gin, three (if not already four) first-class steamers per month from the Australian Colonies now load and unload cargoes."[21]

The steamship was a defining image of modernity and empire. It both contained and disseminated economic power, political ambition, ideas, and symbolic meanings. It became a matter of both commercial necessity and civic pride to handle large ships efficiently.[22] This drive for efficiency demanded expensive port infrastructure and a sizable workforce ashore and afloat. In the Pacific, the Union Steam Ship Company of New Zealand (USSCo) was a dominant presence. Founded in Dunedin in 1875, by the turn of the century the Southern Octopus—so dubbed by its critics—had a tentacle-like hold over the New Zealand coastal, Tasmanian, trans-Tasman, and Pacific Island shipping trades. Liners traded to Europe, North America, and Southeast Asia, and by the beginning of World War I the USSCo operated a fleet of seventy-five steamers.[23]

New Zealand was initially linked to Fiji in 1873 by an irregular steamer service operating out of Auckland. The USSCo took control of this service in 1881, assumed rights over the Melbourne-Fiji trade the following year, and by the end of the decade had a strong foothold in the Sydney-Fiji trade. The USSCo operated a monthly service between Auckland and Fiji (which connected Fiji to the San Francisco mail service), between Melbourne and Fiji, and between Sydney and Auckland, via Tonga, Samoa, and Fiji. Fiji was thereby routinely linked to the southern settler colonies, and some prominent political and commercial figures viewed the island group as practically a New Zealand outlier.[24] From the perspective of the Fiji government, it was crucial that these steamer routes reinforced Suva's position as the "centre of British trade and influence in the Western Pacific."[25]

On a hierarchy of company routes, the island trades ranked somewhere in the middle, below the trans-Tasman, but above the New Zealand coastal. They were popularly known as "harassing," given the distances traveled, the trying tropical climate, large crowds of passengers, demands of island shippers, the hazards posed by coral reefs, and the threat of hurricanes.[26] The Fiji trade was precarious, irregular, unpredictable, and costly, and ongoing negotiations over concessions with a cash-strapped Fiji government amplified these difficulties. The USSCo appointed a Levuka resident as agent in 1881. Like other mercantile establishments, the company operated agencies out of both Suva and Levuka after the official removal of the capital in 1882. Levuka remained the main commercial base for a number of years, but the USSCo closed its office there in 1888, although an agent remained. In 1899 the Suva agency was upgraded to a branch, its agent a branch manager.[27]

Many employees viewed a posting to Fiji as temporary at best, akin to exile at worst. The first agent resigned in 1884 after investigations into fraudulent trading practices. Ernest Ford, his replacement from New Zealand, had no intention of staying more than a couple of years. He thought "it very doubtful if ever any of our men will take to the country very kindly," yet his successor, Alex Duncan, held the position for nearly twenty years.[28] After Duncan's forced resignation in 1907, Charles Hughes from Sydney was reluctant to undertake the posting and informed company head James Mills that "he feared he might be looked upon as side-tracked and not be available for any more interesting opening that might offer."[29] After a few months George Morgan from New Zealand replaced him. He also committed for a lengthy period, although he believed the position warranted more remuneration.[30]

Management stressed loyalty to "the Service." In the absence of universal telegraph communication between islands or wireless technology on board steamers, letters were central tools in the creation and maintenance of hierarchies of authority. The associated time lag between sending and receiving communications, and the physical distance between men stationed at head office in Dunedin, at various port branches, at wharves, and on ships made letter writing as surveillance technique a fragmented and fraught enterprise. Managerial visits of inspection and the recall of employees to New Zealand branches attest to the power of embodied communication. There was a growing sense that employees afloat "slacked off" in the island trades.[31] Various incidents of misconduct prompted the appointment of an island manager and more regular inspections.

On arrival in Fiji, Ford was instructed that "above all things you should endeavour to attain a good social standing." This involved relinquishing "much of your present free and easy style of manner and dress" and emulating the Australasian United Steam Navigation Company's (AUSNCo) agent, who was "welcome in every household in the Colony."[32] These instructions in gentlemanly business practice sought to counter the challenges embodied by the "bluffing, bouncing crowd" of white shippers and traders in Fiji.[33] "Getting on with the natives" was an admirable trait, yet the ability to hold firm in the face of continual demands from these residents was more prized.[34] Standing aloof was counterproductive, yet overfamiliarity was equally problematic. Ford presented himself in his letters as a steadfast, loyal, and hardworking agent, bent on implementing "systems," yet the agent of the New Zealand Loan and Mercantile Company, Frederick Barkas, witnessed some of his less letter-worthy behavior, which included drunken pranks with other traders about town till the early morning. Barkas ostracized himself from their company: "I'm not built that way nor do I believe that the mystery of conducting 'Good Business' in Fiji is to lie on the edge of one perpetual Spree."[35]

Duncan, Ford's successor, was too intimate with clients. On visiting him at Suva, the company secretary observed that he ran business very informally, with traders walking in and out of his office as if it were their own.[36] In making unauthorized allowances on passages and freight, Duncan undercut the principle of combination in the steamer trade, for the USSCo worked cooperatively rather then competitively with the AUSNCo. His misdemeanors became more serious, and he was finally dismissed in 1907 after threatening the Fiji government with the withdrawal of the Vancouver service if they did not increase company concessions.[37] Duncan's immediate replacement noted within a few weeks, "I find the place terribly dull & the life a lazy one. People here think Suva the hub of the universe and that Fiji is responsible for the Union Coy's proud position today, I am not saying or doing anything to disabuse their minds, but I must say I never have had such extraordinary requests or demands as they make."[38] He also had difficulty keeping business and social life separate: "I know you will pardon my suggesting your not sending a 'jolly good fellow.' Its nothing but cards & liquor in and out of office hours. I haven't touched the former and find it a little difficult to dodge the latter."[39] As Kirsten McKenzie's essay (chapter 13 here) indicates, anxieties over social status exercised colonists across empire; race was thoroughly saturated with class.[40]

I gestured earlier toward a distinction between "settled" colonial port towns and their precolonial forerunners, but Suva, like Levuka, remained in many ways a restless and unstable site. Alongside the establishment of concrete structures of colonial rule, many residents adopted a temporary outlook toward life there. Anxieties about the potential of Suva as a successful commercial base circulated around not only the character of fellow white residents and port town sociality but also the tropical environment. Fiji was widely reputed to be exceptionally healthy for the tropics, particularly given the absence of malaria, yet comments on the health of different individuals and their suitability for life and work there were scattered throughout company letters. Branch staff lamented the impact of climate on domestic life. Frequently ill, Ford's wife returned to New Zealand for recuperation, but died shortly afterward. Duncan rued in 1895, "This place is no great attraction to anyone, the climate is bad and the work is difficult, added to that I have ruined the health of my wife so you can see it would not require much to take me away."[41]

Employees often referred to Fiji as *"Malua* land." *Malua* translated as "no hurry," "plenty of time," "don't fuss," and while many Europeans may have welcomed a more laid-back lifestyle, adherence to timetables and fast turnaround times in ports underpinned company profitability. Ford prided himself on his work ethic, informing Mills that one man "remarked to me the other day he could not make out how I got the work I do out of white men as [he was] sure he could never do it."[42] Despite this, staff could not evade the impact of ill health on daily business or the frequent loss of colleagues who returned to more temperate branches. The weather, as Morgan noted in 1912, "has already found out the weak spots of the staff. J. A. Williams has been away with piles. Watson has had a fortnights bed with mumps and fever while Hodge and Thompson who are just starting their second summer are all to pieces."[43] These "weak spots" were both physical and moral. Dangers of "demoralization, degeneracy, depravity, and debility" exercised colonists across Africa, Asia and Oceania, inflecting debates over the specific form colonialism should and could take in tropical places.[44] Never a formal arrangement, the USSCo did allow their employees breaks in New Zealand and southern parts of Australia during the most oppressive months.

To turn to the company's indigenous employees, colonial rule attempted the transformation and control of native relationships to not only the land, but also the sea. In the translation and distribution of regulations relating to seagoing certificates; unseaworthy vessels; sailing licenses; rule of the road at sea; steering and sailing rules; harbor, quarantine, and customs practices; one Fijian official feared "that the size of this code and the number of subjects dealt with will terrify and confuse the native seamen."[45] These regulations were also a likely offense to indigenous navigation traditions, knowledge, and skills, and a potential threat to the particular models of masculinity privileged in this sphere.[46]

Labor regulations, however, were drafted without seamen in mind. The ambiguous position of labor afloat caused confusion both within government and among Europeans seeking crew. Under the Imperial Merchant and Shipping Act, the only legislation that officially addressed seamen, there appeared to be no restrictions on Fijians as crew on British vessels; they were British subjects and could be hired as such. This freedom of engagement conflicted with local statutes for the "good government of the natives." Some officials feared that the terms set out in this act favored unscrupulous employers, who could potentially tie men for months to work conditions that they were unfamiliar with and might wish to leave after a few days. Moreover, these imperial regulations made no provision for the commutation of native taxes.[47]

Restrictions on Fijian crew for vessels registered in Fiji and trading solely within the island group were of less concern, as they were more immediately within reach of local jurisdiction if abuse occurred. Larger vessels trading within the group generally took out articles (a fixed-term employment contract for work afloat) on which to hire crew. Any Fijian who wished to sign up required a permit of release from his district. For vessels trading beyond Fiji, the ship's master also had to enter into a bond to ensure the crew's safe and timely return. Permits of release and bonds were general regulations that applied to men leaving their districts or the colony for any reason.[48] Native crew from other islands who lived in Fiji, including Tongans, Samoans, and Rotumans and men of mixed European and Fijian ancestry, were not subject to these regulations.[49] Given such restrictions and the increasing trade union pressure in Australasian ports for white crews, indigenous Fijians did not routinely work on board USSCo steamers trading outside of Fiji. From time to time agents did request and receive special leave to ship men, but total numbers were small.[50]

Steamer work at the wharf did not attract routine restriction. Admired for their strong, muscular physique, Fijian men, particularly the young and those of low status in chiefly lineages, were regarded as eminently suitable for heavy manual labor. The majority of waterside workers were drawn from Rewa, the closest province to Suva, and shipping companies came to regard these men as skilled cargo handlers. In surveying labor histories of colonial Africa, Frederick Cooper reflects that "historians emphasize what the workplace brought to African workers rather than the other way around." A linear account of their "making" into a "class" following the classic analysis of the English working class by E. P. Thompson inhibits our understanding of the ways indigenous men and women understood the process, what meanings work had for them, and how they engaged in flexible and mobile ways with new labor demands under colonial rule.[51] I take heed of Cooper's argument, for the opening vignette reveals nothing of these processes. According to Grimshaw "mere" wharf laborers were simply "there," peacefully awaiting the arrival of the next steamer. She seizes on the transformations wrought by the USSCo in the islands, not on the ways indigenous men "went to work" on the company.

Governors Gordon (1875–80) and Sir John Bates Thurston (1888–97) were intent on preserving the imagined "traditional" Fijian way of life. Colonial regulations impeded "unrestrained indigenous proletarianisation" and the related decline of the subsistence village economy. Fijians could still find employment opportunities, and by 1901, it is estimated, up to 15 percent did work away from their homes.[52] To meet the labor demands of plantation owners, Indians and men from other islands in the Pacific, in particular the New Hebrides and the Solomon Islands, were indentured to work in Fiji.[53] Some found employment in town and settled around Suva. Many Tongans, Samoans, and other Polynesians also made their way to Suva, typically aboard USSCo steamers, for a host of reasons related to broader regional patterns of exchange and trade, kinship ties, religion, employment, and adventure. This racial diversity allows us to explore multiple workplace intimacies, yet I focus here specifically on indigenous Fijians, as their economic mobility was of great concern to colonial leaders, both indigenous and European.

Villages sent groups of men to work at the wharf or other labor sites. Their wages were used to purchase commodities or boats and aid in house construction and could replace agricultural produce as tax contributions. Fijians valued wharf employment for its casual nature, in contrast to twelve-month plantation contracts. In this way it may have been regarded as an extension of the cyclical work of gardening and house construction, rather than a rupture in precolonial labor practices. Incorporation rather than disruption was also evident among Melanesian communities participating in indentured labor schemes. This experience could slot into established population mobilities and life cycle patterns, with indigenous "passage masters" mediating between recruiters and recruits.[54] The opportunity to work at Suva also had negative consequences. "Losing" men to the port town (and beyond) meant a loss of vital labor, familial support, and communal contributions; it threatened the social fabric of village life. Yet, as 'Atu Bain argues, although provincial and district chiefs became the "official voice of protest" against overrecruitment and absenteeism, as labor brokers they "showed a persistent ambivalence" to the related questions of bribery, coercion, and labor regulation.[55]

On the expiration of plantation contracts, employers were expected (although many failed) to repatriate men. Steamer work did not carry the same expectation, and many Fijians did not return to their homes on nonsteamer days. Provincial and district chiefs were brought to council meetings and interrogated by government officials as to the state of their villages, yet absentees suffered no such humiliation, as Buli Buresaga (one district chief) protested in 1908: "They defy the chiefs and officials. They have no respect for us or for our customs. They shirk all communal obligations and leave their villages to go to Suva to earn a little money with which they buy collars and neckties and coats! and save 2/—for a fine when they return home. Let them be whipped, then they will listen and take heed of us. If we attempt to assert our position and authority as Chiefs they go to Suva and say we are oppressing them: they lie and scheme and are becoming quite demoralized."[56] Officials saw little available remedy. By law, men could remain absent from their village for up to sixty days without approval from chiefs before being fined. If men were prosecuted and paid their fines, nothing more could be said.[57]

This absenteeism led to an increasing population of "strangers" in Suva. While the colonial government had a duty to provide for its subjects, it feared that erecting housing in town for those who slept in the streets could encourage a more permanent indigenous presence, or what it termed "native vagrancy."[58] Moreover, intimacy with European men in urban places created what was derogatorily termed the "white man's Fijian." Many "low-class" whites, it was felt, "have some native, it may be only one favourite, who lives with them and attaches himself to them." Although chiefs sent for their men, "such natives encouraged and sheltered by Europeans who tell them that every British subject can do as he pleases, resist the messengers and defy the Chiefs."[59] Across the harbor, the native town of Suvavou could not escape Suva's "taint." Its men were "always in Suva picking up ideas from loafing low-class whites."[60] In this respect, the late nineteenth-century port retained objectionable traces of "The Beach"; it was a site of potential corruption and immorality. This history of crosscultural intimacy forged in the context of maritime trade is in stark contrast to the shore whaling stations and patterns of inter-racial marriage David Haines discusses (chapter 2 here).

From the early 1900s, the USSCo met increasing demands for travel-ing and food allowances to and from Suva, and provided housing for men during their employment in town. By 1911 translated newspaper accounts, shipped to Fiji aboard USSCo steamers, detailed maritime labor unrest in colonial ports and prompted Fijian wharf laborers to demand further wage increases.[61] In a report tabled to the Suva Chamber of Commerce, the USSCo held that wage rates at the wharf regulated the price of labor in the rest of the colony. As the independence of men in seeking work was growing, they sought government assistance to replace the casual nature of employment with an indenture scheme and "further consider the question of freeing such men from their communal obligations as an encouragement for them to contract for permanent employment."[62]

After many meetings between the company and Rewa leaders, an agreement was drawn up to recruit 150 men, four or five from every village in the province, for a one-year term. They would be free to re-turn for village duties on nonsteamer days, although a municipal tax would officially free them from communal work and would allow them to spend time planting solely for their families.[63] Some Fijian leaders wanted further wage increases drawn into the contract, "as the work was very hard and dangerous and several men had been disabled." The native commissioner advised them "not to embarrass the shipping coys, and cause them to raise freights which they themselves would have to help to pay through increased prices for the goods they had to buy."[64] Despite the 1911 arrangement, which dispersed recruitment across vil-lages, the Rewa province again registered concerns about absenteeism a few years later. Chiefs requested that the USSCo desist from employing men from their province for a few months while communal work was carried out. The company turned to men from other provinces already in Suva seeking paid employment.[65] This tension between communal and individualist activities impeded earlier maritime economies in Fiji, such as the *beche-de-mer* trade, and continued to hamper successive govern-ments in framing economic policy throughout the twentieth century.[66]

Through dynamic and uneven imperial networks, "mobile men" converged on the new port of Suva from the early 1880s. Located differently across global, regional, and local space, these men made divergent assessments of Suva's significance and their place within it; they occupied different vantage points. Some positioned the capital at the center of Pacific transport and trade; some regarded it as a backwater, distant and isolated from the "real" centers of imperial influence; still others embraced its magnetism, contrasting as it did with life in rural villages. While many Victorians celebrated the industrial transport revolution and its "conquest of distance," time and space collapsed differentially; location still mattered.[67]

The intimacy of the island branch office, particularly as work life spilled into small town social life, confronted some agents sent there from larger branches in New Zealand and Australia. Maintaining some degree of privacy, distance, and separation from all those invested in the affairs of the USSCo proved rather delicate. The tropical experience also proved unsettling. Drunkenness, gambling, boyish pranks, loss of nerves and sickness were common responses to these challenges. Moreover, men frequently understood their time in Suva as temporary and generally lived across space, dividing their time, and their families, between colonies in the tropics and more temperate regions.

Fijian leaders embraced steamer work as a mobile resource, one not entirely at odds with their own cyclical labor practices. They sought to monitor and limit the disruption of new opportunities under colonial rule. When wharf laborers returned to villages on nonsteamer days with wages in hand, ready and willing to perform familial and community duties, mobility was productive and valued as such. For some, the ability to come and go was easily manipulated for ends elsewhere. Mobility in this context was deemed vagrancy or absenteeism. It highlighted struggles over gender, rank, and age in Fijian communities; ties to villages, respect for chiefly control, and domestic relationships became increasingly tenuous and tense.

For its part, the USSCo proved open to negotiation, prepared to periodically fracture and reset its terms of engagement. As was the case with New Zealand shore whaling in an earlier period, interracial cooperation underpinned the success of this maritime industry. These ongoing mediations reinforce Cooper's point that "the nature of work and of conflict were indeterminant. The labor question was a question."[68] They also reinforce for us that colonial space unfolded as interactions between diverse people living across multiple trajectories. These interactions were continuous and unfinished, and did not follow a linear progression to a unitary or stable "modern condition," where men came to identify solely as workers in the service of a maritime industry.[69]

Suva's mobile men were also situated differently within a racialized hierarchy constructed in the context of colonial labor relations. The risk of undue connection between men in the port, whether between "low-class" whites and young Fijian men, or within the contested category white, as seen in Duncan's interactions with traders, was clearly understood to compromise this hierarchy. The management of men at a distance increased such risks. Letters sent from USSCo's head office were easily misinterpreted or ignored, messages sent from village chiefs went unheeded; Suva's mobile men were persistently troublesome to their superiors.

Notes

Research for this chapter was made possible through Australian Research Council funding for the project "Oceanic Encounters: Colonial and Contemporary Transformations of Gender and Sexuality in the Pacific," at the Gender Relations Centre at the Australian National University. I am grateful to Tony Ballantyne, Antoinette Burton, and Margaret Jolly for their comments on earlier drafts.

1. Jerry H. Bentley, "Sea and Ocean Basins as Frameworks for Historical Analysis," *Geographical Review* 89, 2 (1999): 215–24; Karen Wigen, "*AHR* Forum Oceans of History: Introduction," *American Historical Review* 111, 4 (2006): 717–21.

2. Epeli Hau'ofa, "Our Sea of Islands," in Eric Waddell, Vijay Naidu, and Epeli Hau'ofa, eds., *A New Oceania: Rediscovering Our Sea of Islands* (Suva, 1993), 2–16. Land-based rather than oceanic networks were more central for inland populations of the larger Melanesian islands. Their experiences are elided in "Our Sea of Islands."

3. Ann Laura Stoler, "Tense and Tender Ties: The Politics of Comparison in North American History and (Post) Colonial Studies," *Journal of American History* 88, 3 (2001): 829–65. See also Stoler, *Carnal Knowledge and Imperial Power: Race and the Intimate in Colonial Rule* (Berkeley, 2002).

4. Doreen Massey, *Space, Place and Gender* (Cambridge, 1994), 22, 5.

5. Ramon A. Gutierrez, "What's Love Got to Do with It?" *Journal of American History* 88, 3 (2001): 866.

6. Mary A. Renda, "'Sentiments of a Private Nature': A Comment on Ann Laura Stoler's 'Tense and Tender Ties,'" *Journal of American History* 88, 3 (2001): 885–86. Ann Stoler, "Matters of Intimacy as Matters of State: A Response," *Journal of American History* 88, 3 (2001): 895.

7. Greg Dening, *Islands and Beaches: Discourse on a Silent Land, Marquesas 1774–1880* (Honolulu, 1980), 3. See also Dening, *Beach Crossings: Voyages across Times, Cultures and Self* (Carlton, Australia, 2004).

8. Margaret Jolly, "The Sediment of Voyages: Re-membering Quiros, Bougainville and Cook in Vanuatu," in Jolly, Serge Tcherkézoff, and Daryl Tryon, eds., *Oceanic Encounters* (Canberra, Australia, under review).

9. Caroline Ralston, *Grass Huts and Warehouses: Pacific Beach Communities of the Nineteenth Century* (Canberra, Australia, 1977), 188–212.

10. Damon T. Salesa, "'Troublesome Half-Castes': Tales of a Samoan Border-land" (M.A. thesis, University of Auckland, New Zealand, 1997), 58–59.

11. F. E. Pratt (Commanding Officer of Royal Engineers), "Report as to the Site of the Town of Levuka," January 25, 1876, Colonial Secretary's Office (hereafter CSO), 76.138, National Archives of Fiji, (hereafter NAF).

12. Margaret Rodman, *Houses Far from Home: British Colonial Space in the New Hebrides* (Honolulu, 2001), 52, 217 n. 1.

13. Cakobau was the self-styled "king" of Fiji (Tui Viti). He did not exercise authority over all islands in the group or possess all of the land he proposed to cede. He hoped to alleviate a debt of $45,000 to the U.S. government, incurred through damage to American property. See R. A. Derrick, *A History of Fiji* (Suva, 1946), 138–55.

14. Ibid., 177–83.

15. Hirokazu Miyazaki, "Delegating Closure," in Sally Engle Merry and Donald Brenneis, eds., *Law and Empire in the Pacific: Fiji and Hawaii* (Sante Fe, N.M., 2004), 257.

16. Martha Kaplan, "Meaning, Agency, and Colonial History: Navosavakadua and the 'Tuka' Movement in Fiji," *American Ethnologist* 17, 1 (February 1990): 3–22.

17. "Early State Power in Colonial Fiji," *Comparative Studies in Society and History* 32, 1 (January 1990): 152.

18. Ibid., 153–70.

19. "Issues: Ports, Port Cities, and Port-Hinterlands," in Indu Banga, ed., *Ports and Their Hinterlands in India, 1700–1950* (New Delhi, 1992), 26.

20. M. N. Pearson, "Littoral Society: The Case for the Coast," *Great Circle* 7, 1 (April 1985): 1.

21. John Gorrie, "Fiji as It Is," *Proceedings of the Royal Colonial Institute,* March 13, 1883, 160.

22. Josef W. Konvitz, "The Crises of Atlantic Port Cities, 1880 to 1920," *Comparative Studies in Society and History* 36, 2 (April 1994): 301.

23. For a general history of the company, see Gavin McLean, *The Southern Octopus: The Rise of a Shipping Empire* (Wellington, New Zealand, 1990).

24. While not attracting mainstream support, there were two movements for the federation of Fiji with New Zealand, in 1885 and 1900–1902.

25. Colonial Secretary to USSCo agent, March 20, 1889, CSO 89.640, NAF.

26. Henderson to Mills, October 25, 1894, USSCo: Inwards correspondence, AG-292-005-001/034, Hocken Library, Dunedin (hereafter HL); Marine Superintendent to R. G. Hutton, August 26, 1909, USSCo: Masters and Officers Personal Files, H, AF004:4:7, Wellington City Council Archives.

27. February 28, 1888, USSCo: Minutes, AG-292-003-001/005, HL; March 21, 1899, USSCo: Minutes, AG-292-003-001/013, HL.

28. Ford to Mills, March 17, 1886, USSCo: Australia and Fiji, AG-292-005-001/002, HL.

29. Mills to Holdsworth, February 8, 1907, USSCo: Personnel, AG-292-005-001/081, HL.

30. Morgan to Mills, June 26, 1914, USSCo: Australia and Suva, AG-292-005-001/112, HL.

31. E.g., Mills to Holdsworth, April 27, 1908, USSCo: Personnel, AG-292-005-001/086, HL.

32. Houghton to Ford, November 29, 1884, USSCo: Personnel, AG-292-005-001/004, HL.

33. Morgan to Aiken, 24, May 1913, USSCo: Subject File Relating to Staff, AG-292-005-004/120, HL.

34. Irvine to Holdsworth, October 31, 1901, USSCo: N.Z. Branches, AG-292-005-001/056, HL.

35. Barkas to brother, January 9, 1888, Barkas Diaries, vol. 5, Some Memories of a Mediocrity, MS-2491-05, 130, Alexander Turnbull Library, Wellington, (hereafter ATL).

36. Whitson to Mills, September 14, 1898, USSCo: Personnel Head Office and Australia, AG-292-005-001/047, HL.

37. The USSCo also operated the prestigious Canadian Australasian line from 1901. Fiji was a port of call.

38. Hughes to Holdsworth, April 25, 1907, USSCo: Branches, AG-292-005-001/087, HL.

39. Hughes to Holdsworth, May 21, 1907, USSCo: Branches, AG-292-005-001/087, HL.

40. See also Nicholas Thomas and Richard Eves, *Bad Colonists: The South Sea Letters of Vernon Lee Walker and Louis Becke* (Durham, N.C., 1999).

41. Duncan to Mills, August 16, 1895, USSCo: Australia and Fiji, AG-292-005-001/035, HL.

42. Ford to Mills, August 5, 1885, USSCo: Australia and Fiji, AG-292-005-001/002, HL.

43. Morgan to Aiken, October 16, 1912, USSCo: Subject File Relating to Staff, AG-292-005-004/120, HL.

44. David N. Livingstone, "Race, Space, and the Moral Climatology: Notes towards a Genealogy," *Journal of Historical Geography* 28, 2 (2002): 172. See also Richard Eves, "Unsettling Settler Colonialism: Debates over Climate and Colonization in New Guinea, 1875–1914," *Ethnic and Racial Studies* 28, 2 (March 2005): 304–30.

45. Correspondence with Marine Board, December 9, 1886, CSO 86.2360, NAF.

46. I thank Margaret Jolly for pressing this point.

47. Correspondence regarding native crews, June 3, 1893, CSO 93.861, NAF.

48. Correspondence with Levuka Chamber of Commerce, October 12, 1885, CSO 85.2659; Attorney General, May 23, 1893, CSO 93.861, NAF.

49. Correspondence with Levuka Chamber of Commerce, December 16, 1891–January 14, 1892, CSO 91.3885, NAF.

50. The company also operated an interisland steamer within the group, employing Fijian, Melanesian, and Indian labor.

51. Frederick Cooper, "Work, Class, and Empire: An African Historian's Retrospective on E. P. Thompson," *Social History* 20, 2 (1995): 236.

52. 'Atu Bain, "A Protective Labour Policy? An Alternative Interpretation of Early Colonial Labour Policy in Fiji," *Journal of Pacific History* 23, 2 (October 1988): 124, 135. There were shifts in official policy following ongoing conflicts over labor between the government, settlers, and planters.

53. The recruitment of Melanesian laborers from the New Hebrides (present-day Vanuatu) and the Solomon Islands to Fiji and Queensland were marked by incidents of violence and kidnapping until regulations were imposed beginning in the early 1870s. Over sixty thousand Indians were indentured to Fiji between 1879 and 1920; see Brij V. Lal, *Girmitiyas: The Origins of the Fiji Indians* (Canberra, Australia, 1983).

54. Clive Moore, *Kanaka: A History of Melanesian Mackay* (Port Moresby, Papua New Guinea, 1985), 48–81.

55. Bain, "Protective Labour Policy," 125.

56. Buli Buresaga, October 1–2, 1908, Rewa Provincial Council Meetings, vol. 2, 1905–18, NAF. Many Fijians were hired illegally under the Masters and Servants Ordinances rather than the Labour Ordinance. The former imposed more lenient conditions on employers and did not require compulsory repatriation; see Bain, "A Protective Labour Policy," 127.

57. Native Department, November 2, 1910, Rewa Provincial Council Meetings, vol. 2, 1905–18, NAF.

58. Superintendent Police, June 17 and 24, 1882, CSO 82.1495; December 17, 1883, CSO 83.3297, NAF.

59. Memo re Timoce of Rewa, July 14 and 15, 1884, CSO 85.271, NAF.

60. W. A. Scott, Native Officer, January 3, 1901, CSO 01.195, NAF.

61. The 1890 Maritime Strike, which began in Sydney and spread to New Zealand, also found echoes in Fiji. A group of Fijian workers from Suvavou struck for increased pay early in October. This was largely unsuccessful, given that the men failed to combine with other Fijian, Melanesian, and Indian wharf labor, all of whom continued to work the steamers. What knowledge these Suvavou men had of maritime labor unrest in the settler colonies of Australasia is undocumented.

62. Memorandum from Chamber of Commerce to Deputy Governor, November 27, 1911, CSO 11.9051, NAF.

63. Morgan, December 12, 1911, CSO 11.9501, NAF. The colonial archive provides no record of the individual men hired under this scheme. Such archival limitations are also discussed by Haines in chapter 2 here.

64. Native Commissioner, December 19, 1911, CSO 11.9501, NAF.

65. Native Commissioner, March 26, 1914, CSO 14.331; Morgan, April 20, 1914, CSO 14.3603, NAF.

66. R. G. Ward, "The Pacific *Beche-de-Mer* Trade with Special Reference to Fiji," in Ward, ed., *Man in the Pacific Islands: Essays on Geographical Change in the Pacific Islands* (Oxford, 1972), 91–123; Margaret Jolly, "Custom and the Way of the Land: Past and Present in Vanuatu and Fiji," *Oceania* 62 (1992): 331, 339.

67. Richard Knowles, "Transport Shaping Space: Differential Collapse in Time-Space," *Journal of Transport Geography* 14 (2006): 407–25; R. G. Ward, *Widening Worlds, Shrinking Worlds? The Reshaping of Oceania* (Canberra, Australia, 1999).

68. Cooper, "Work, Class, and Empire," 239.

69. Massey reinforces these points throughout her recent work *For Space* (London, 2005). For further critique of linear historical accounts of proletarianization, see William Hamilton Sewell, *Logics of History: Social Theory and Social Transformation* (Chicago, 2005), 271–317, and Frederick Cooper, *On the African Waterfront: Urban Disorder and the Transformation of Work in Colonial Mombasa* (New Haven, 1987).

6 *Performing "Interracial Harmony"*

SETTLER COLONIALISM AT THE 1934 PAN-PACIFIC WOMEN'S CONFERENCE IN HAWAI'I

Writing in her conference diary in 1934, Elsie Andrews noted that the Pan-Pacific Women's Association (PPWA) had celebrated its New Zealand delegation as example to the world. As leader of the delegation, Andrews reported with evident pride that the hit of the Honolulu conference had been the bilingual and bicultural presentation by Maori and pakeha delegates. Their performance had been considered to encapsulate the very kind of harmonious and cooperative race relations that, it was hoped, would facilitate a just and humane future relationship for the peoples of the world. This chapter focuses on Andrews's efforts—through her part in the performance—to constitute herself as a modern settler colonial. Through her account of sharing the international stage with Maori women delegates, particularly with Victoria Bennett, Andrews sought to explain her status as a cosmopolitan and progressive woman of the world. As the introduction to this collection points out, it is in studying affective relations that we locate interconnections between local and long-distance exchanges of empire and colonialism, both within space and time and through the intimacies exchanged therein between embodied subjects. With an international conference in the 1930s as its spatial location, this chapter investigates an account of the interchanges between not one but multiple locals and the larger networks of imperial power, and their supposed transcendence through the formation of an international community of women. Andrews's investment in these exchanges was considerable.

Part travelogue, part conference report, the diary Andrews kept en route as well as during the conference offers at its core a "tell-all" account of her collaboration with Maori delegates, especially Bennett. Mobilizing their exchanges as evidence of her personal growth toward a progressive race consciousness, Andrews proclaimed a friendship with Bennett that spoke not only of her own enlightenment, but of settler colonialism's capacity to lead in the reform of race relations around the world. At the same time, Andrews expressed many anxieties about colonization in her diary. In its pages, she problematized the legitimacy of settler colonialism: her assertion of friendship with Bennett based on a mutual and disinterested exchange (one based on corecognition exceeding the relations of colonial power) required a temporary disavowal of colonization's inherent violence, a disavowal endorsed by the women's international network in which cultural internationalist interests were to facilitate crosscultural friendship. For the PPWA, the staging of the friendship between these two women seemed to confirm settler colonialism's potential to model the cooperative occupation of land and access to resources necessary in the globalizing the twentieth century. In an interview Andrews gave on her return from the conference, she reassured herself and local pakeha that it had been "a surprise and a pleasure for other delegations to know that the Maori and white race were working together . . . in such perfect harmony."[1]

As a staunch New Zealander with British loyalties, Andrews was deeply invested not only in a positive future for settler colonialism but also in its role at the forefront of modernizing empire. Rather than ending colonial control, her aim was to encourage the induction of indigenous leaders into its ranks, women's internationalism offering one site at which to enhance this process of assimilation. That Andrews hoped in this way to secure a just future for relations between the races—with the collaboration of internationally minded Maori women—allowed expression also for her most intimate desire as an internationalist: to be valorized by the Pan-Pacific community as a woman whom indigenous women considered worthy of friendship. While her engagement with the Pan-Pacific ideal may well have been genuine, it was also necessarily strategic and tactical. Such is the ambiguous territory of friendship across the "colonial divide."

Claims to interracial harmony were not new to New Zealand, renowned among international feminist circles for its welfare and maternal health policies, its state education system, and women's suffrage. New Zealand had established a treaty with Maori in the nineteenth century, and then instituted limited Maori representation in parliament, although, as Patricia Grimshaw has shown, claims to exemplary race relations greatly overstated benevolence.[2] Nonetheless, by the interwar years, small but increasing numbers of elite Maori began to be appointed to key policy, church, and social reform positions. According to historian James Bennett, these Maori were appropriated as signs of colonialism's successful assimilation, and were treated as "honorary whites."[3] Several within this elite, including Frederick Augustus Bennett (first Maori bishop, appointed 1928), emerged as social, cultural, and religious leaders with significant political influence across pakeha as well as Maori communities.[4] Numbers of Maori women claimed membership also in the "white tribe."

Already a key figure in the New Zealand Young Women's Christian Association, it was Bishop Bennett's sister-in-law, Victoria Te Amohau Bennett, who joined the New Zealand delegation to the Pan-Pacific Women's Conference in 1934, and who was destined to become the more influential of the two Maori women included among its members. Reflecting their status within the Maori community as well as their familiarity with white women and their organizations, not only did Bennett and her codelegate move confidently among the women of the PPWA, including women from the United States, Canada, Japan, China, Australia, and the Philippines, but they wielded enormous power as cultural translators and high-ranking intermediaries. While their presence worked to confirm the self-asserted status of pakeha women as uniquely placed among other white delegates to progress the issue of "race," they also appeared to confirm the larger aims of the association: to encourage nonwhite women of the region to contribute to women's internationalism, and to enact with their acquiescence a new politics of race based on mutual respect and friendship.

Turn-of-the-last-century transnational political networks provide the historian with a productive location in which to investigate complex exchanges about bodies, space, and their interrelationship. As Antoinette Burton has pointed out, from the late nineteenth century British feminist concerns for Indian women had contributed only one element in a much larger discussion about the definition of feminism circulating within and between both countries.[5] And in her account of transnational networks of abolitionism from the mid–nineteenth and into the early twentieth century, Sandra Stanley Holton notes that as their interactions with a variety of black activists proliferated and white antislavery reformers were confronted by a greater autonomy among leaders of the black rights movement, their ambivalence at these changing conditions frequently was articulated in their letters and personal writings rather than in their public pronouncements.[6] Similar tensions between admiration and self-doubt were expressed by Andrews in her account of her relationship with Bennett, yet the fact of their collaboration points to the political and personal significance of its negotiation for both women.

Not insignificantly, their story took place not in New Zealand but in the heightened surroundings of a women's conference in Hawai'i. In the exotic tourist locale, valorized for its admixture of races and cultures, Andrews and her colleagues found an ideal location in which to proclaim interracial friendship. But the Hawaiian islands were also a settler colony, and while Hawai'i was routinely proclaimed to be the "melting pot" of the Pacific, its indigenous population was widely assumed to be at risk of demise or, at the very least, cultural extinction. As Skwiot shows (chapter 9 here), tourism surged in the interwar years, as haole sought to assert a separate identity from the mainland United States through claiming a particular relationship with indigenous Hawaiian culture. Indigenous Hawaiian women who were taking a leading role in the revitalization of their own culture while conforming to Western gender roles were at the same engaged in the advancement of indigenous culture and rights, their impressive presence as elite women contradicting assumptions of the Hawaiians as a "dying race."

The considered fate of indigenous peoples around the world, if not directly the subject of Andrews's diary, figured nonetheless as a potent backdrop to her concern for the urgent reform of settler colonialism. In this sense, she was a humanitarian who saw beyond the dominant representations of her day concerning the role and place of indigenous peoples. However, she would ultimately distance herself from the vibrant role of Bennett and other Maori women at the conference, deeming instead that it was the responsibility of white people to work toward the preservation of remnant indigenous cultures. This return to white maternalism effectively sutured over her anxieties about colonial rule and acted to resolve, if not in the end allay, the questions about the ethics of modern settler colonialism that her performance of interracial harmony with Bennett had raised.

As became increasingly clear during the conference, although working with pakeha women on the conference performance, the Maori delegates did not consider themselves to be indigenous women under threat of extinction, but modern women in their own right. Furthermore, in Honolulu, they were recognized as elite indigenous women of the Polynesian Pacific and were feted by Hawaiian royalty—Princess Abigail Kawanakoa (featured by Skwiot in chapter 9 here). Their standing was at odds with Andrews's self-appointed role as facilitator of their entry into the world community of women.

At the same time, Pan-Pacific women's internationalism was clearly important to Maori activists. As the editors point out in their introduction, it is important to disprove the assumption that the local remains immobile and that the native or indigenous is passive in relation to intimacy. In contrast, here we see indigenous subjects desiring, strategic, and ambitious in their political and personal aims. Their collaborations with the association, begun in 1934 and extending into the 1950s and beyond, expressed their interest in the potential of women's internationalism in the Pacific region to promote internationally and globally Maori women's concerns for social reform in their own country, particularly in the areas of health and education. Mobile beyond the parameters of the "interracial harmony" or "friendship" imagined by internationalist women like Andrews, their involvement in Andrews's self-proclaimed journey into greater knowledge points to their evident interest in developing the race consciousness of pakeha women more generally.

Writing of women's autobiography and colonialism, Gillian Whitlock notes the significance of mobility to the formation of fluid and contingent ideas about sexual, racial, cultural, and gendered characteristics. Historically produced "in a process of interrelationship between home and away, in a process of transculturation," these ideas take shape in "the intersection and interdependence of identities and identifications between European and colonial women."[7] Andrews's diary figures as such a site of transculturation. While her focus on this "interracial" relationship points to her assumption that the subject of interpersonal intimacy across race would appeal greatly to her readers at home in New Zealand, as well as it evidently fascinated those witnessing its performance during the conference, her self-proclaimed transcendence of racial outlook produced a contradictory effect. The resulting focus in her account on bodies and their proximity directs attention toward rather than away from the forbidden pleasures of interracial relations, pleasures beyond the archetypal imperial trope of the (hetero)sexual white man's desire, here enacted between women. Not least, Andrews was writing primarily for her lifelong woman partner, and enjoyed the frisson of her proximity to Bennett and other women delegates. And yet her more explicitly homosexual gaze was not at odds with the larger erotics of conference participation, especially within the heady environment of crosscultural exchange. Bennett was also a participant in this erotics; her agency within

Andrews's intertwined personal and political agendas belies any simple reading of her as merely an appropriated other, pointing away from colonialism's obsessions with order and fixed identity and toward the "multiplicity of histories, the ground 'in-between' where differences complicate, both across and within individual subjects."[8]

The first Pan-Pacific Women's Conference was organized under the auspices of the Pan-Pacific Union in 1928. The second conference held in 1930 saw the formation of the PPWA itself. The guiding philosophy of the PPWA was the promotion of cultural internationalism, in particular friendship and cooperation between women in the region. Friendly cooperation was to foster humane development in the region, particularly in the protection of women and children, while exchange between women was to safeguard peace. Study groups in the home countries of each delegation prepared information for conferences on various designated topics, including women and industrial work, education and health, and women in politics. These reports were presented at conferences, and recommendations were made. But the PPWA did not see itself primarily as a reform body, and left campaigns to change legislation or policy to women's organizations operating within national borders. Rather, it was in the practice of cultural internationalism during conferences that the PPWA saw its greatest contribution to world peace and cooperation. For Andrews, the pakeha leader of the history-making delegation of 1934, the valorization of her team reiterated the PPWA's cultural internationalist project.

While it is important not to underestimate the significance of the participation of Maori delegates in 1934, in the longer view their remarkable presence in that year tells us less about the association's achievement of interracial harmony than about the legacy of whiteness within its organization. Dominated by white women from the United States, Australia, and New Zealand, the association asserted the importance of "civilized" women—including women from Japan and China—in bringing about progress in the Pacific region. Women of "advanced" countries such as New Zealand assumed that their duty was the uplift of indigenous women, who were not expected to fully represent themselves. Thus Native American women were not among North American delegations to conferences, and Australian delegates, ready to raise the issue of indigenous rights at the 1930 conference, never considered including Aboriginal women among their ranks. Only one indigenous Hawaiian woman became a longtime member of the Hawaiian delegation after World War II. Otherwise, before the war, Pacific Island women were expected to be represented by national delegations of women from Pacific Rim imperial and settler colonial powers. The indigenous people who were present during early conferences were mostly providers of conference entertainment, while non-white women delegates appeared regularly in "traditional" dress at conference events. It was into this contradictory context of "cross-cultural exchange" that the bi-racial New Zealand delegation made its notable entrance.

Recording the conference for loved ones in New Zealand, particularly her longtime woman partner, Andrews kept her unpublished diary in duplicate, sending top copies home as letters. Her behind-the-scenes descriptions of conference events are often wry and acerbic, providing intriguing insight into the work required to create the illusion of interracial harmony performed by her team. At times enthusiastic, at others sardonic, Andrews's diary provides a counternarrative to cultural internationalism's claims of easy crosscultural exchange between delegates.

While Andrews reveled in the promotion of New Zealand as an exemplary interracial community, she was ambivalent concerning the remarkable attention received by the Maori delegates. Her account of their successes veered between proprietorship and admiration. Although the Maori delegates were not afforded voting rights, and often Andrews referred to them as "our" Maori, her exchanges with them were crucial to her increasingly powerful role in the PPWA. At the core of her account of the 1934 conference was the paradoxical task of guiding the Maori women toward their place within the international women's community while she remained dependent on their confirmation of her leadership in the project of interracial cooperation. This paradox inevitably marked her relationships with the Maori delegates, particularly Victoria Bennett.

When she first left for Honolulu as a member of the New Zealand delegation of 1930, Andrews was forty-one. Until then, she had lived and worked for most of her life in New Plymouth. First a schoolteacher, she was the president of the New Zealand Women Teachers' Association and then of the New Zealand National Council of Women, as well as the secretary of the Women's Club of New Plymouth. Funding from the Women Teachers' Association allowed Andrews to attend conferences and to lecture to New Zealand women teachers on her return.[9] She was not an upper-class, independent world traveler as were many of the other conference delegates. A commitment to educational innovation, pacifism, and social reform led her to Pan-Pacific internationalism. Her expertise as a leading New Zealand advocate of the principles of "New Education" resulted in her inclusion in the 1930 delegation.[10] Speaking on "Education for Life" at the conference that year, Andrews had called for children to be taught to be "brothers and sisters in a community."[11] In her unpublished account of her own education in a state school during the late 1900s, she remembered with admiration the Maori children among her classmates.[12] Casting herself as a woman of principle, and laughingly as a "Bolshie," Andrews reported that as a pacifist who considered capitalism and militarism closely interconnected, she was a radical in comparison to most conference delegates.[13]

At the same time that Andrews was at pains to cast herself as a conference leader, she soon found conference social events disconcerting. Applying her ironic style to the PPWA ideal of international exchange, she explained: "I don't think I really have any flair for facile international friendships which is a bit of a handicap at an international conference."[14] Although delegates were supposed to circulate at every mealtime as part of their international practice of making friends, Andrews remonstrated: "My trouble is that I don't want to meet everybody!"[15] At other times, she made fun of conference traditions, while recording nonetheless her own important part in them. She found the presentation of leis by members of the conference welcoming committee, for example, "a very beautiful idea but made me feel like the pet cow of the herd. . . . The weight and scent are almost overpowering." But when it came to the end of the conference, as women of note were plied with leis from their admirers, Andrews was in the thick of it. Proud of the nineteen leis she received from other delegates on her departure, she exclaimed: "By the time the last lei [from a representative of the Women's Christian Temperance Union] was round my neck I [said] I should be a drunkard by way of protest for the rest of my life."[16] (The joke being at the expense of the temperance aims of the union.)

Contrary to conference endorsements of exchange and friendship between diverse cultures and peoples, Andrews remained deeply attached to her New Zealand co-delegates. She expressed through jokes her sense of alienation from non-Western, and specifically "Oriental," delegates. When Chinese delegates invited her and others to lunch during the 1930 conference in Honolulu, she reported that they served "ghastly Chinese tea" and "ghastly looking mixtures." Chinese women remained as types rather than individuals in her accounts of meeting with them. These she kept to a minimum in any case, making a mental note in her diary: "If any more such entertainments are planned I'm going to absent myself."[17] Interactions with Japanese women seem to have been more manageable for her, but again she failed to name these delegates individually, despite both the Chinese and Japanese women taking leading roles in early conference debates, and in the association's hierarchy.[18]

In typically dismissive manner, mixed with barely suppressed oriental-ism, Andrews reduced cultural exchange to a series of misconnections, an idea anathema to Pan-Pacific ideals. "Sneezes are international you will be glad to hear," she wrote. "We can't remember the Japanese names and their English is not always easy to follow, but one sneezed yesterday morning and I understood her instantly."[19] By the end of the conference, Andrews concluded: "It seems odd to do and see and eat more different things in three weeks than in one's previous forty one years. But still I am a wild cat walking on its wild lone and preferring New Zealand above everything and longing for home."[20]

Nor were whiteness and English as a first language sufficient to make Andrews feel at home. She was offended by what she considered the grating accents of the Americans and the Australians. Not only were pakeha her kith and kin, their voices were undulating and delightful to the ear. For the most part, Andrews preferred to make her networks within a small coterie of mostly New Zealanders. "So perhaps even if I am not good at international friendships," she confessed with mock admonition, "I can congratulate myself on some new ones among my own people."[21] (An exception to this rule would be her alliance with Dr. Hildegarde Kneeland, the leader of the U.S. delegation, with whom she wrote a streamlined structure and focus for the PPWA on the last night of the 1930 conference.) Andrews's friendships with pakeha members of the New Zealand delegation were cemented (at least according to Andrews) by mutual admiration.

Of these, only a few, however, were privy to her long-term relation-ship with her ex–assistant teacher. Muriel Kirton had accompanied her to the 1930 conference held by the Pan-Pacific association, and it was to her and a number of close women friends that the top copies from her diary were posted regularly, arriving thus in serial form. Historian of women's internationalism Leila Rupp has shown that same-sex part-nerships were a significant aspect of international women's networks in the late nineteenth and early twentieth centuries.[22] And as New Zealand historian Alison Laurie has argued, Andrews may be located within this larger historical context.[23]

The idea of Maori women joining the New Zealand delegation ap-pears to have become important to Andrews as the result of the confer-ence of 1930. Her journey toward greater inclusiveness began at that conference through questioning her relationship to the British Empire. While attending the movies one evening after a day of debate, she had a crosscultural experience—not between "East" and "West," or black and white, but concerning variations of whiteness and imperialism. In

Hawai'i, a North American colony, she found herself the only one to stand when "God Save the King" was played at the start of a British movie. "It had not struck me before that anywhere in the world 'God Save the King' would not bring people to their feet," she remarked in surprise. "I spose it is the same kind of superiority complex which makes us somehow always visualise God as a white man who speaks English."[24] Such incipient antiimperialism suggested the need for greater self-reflection concerning settler colonialism in New Zealand. She wrote: "We British people seem to have a special devil that needs to be exorcised—the devil which leads to a feeling of superiority and arrogance."[25]

In a classic colonialist move, Andrews sought to distinguish herself from other Anglo delegates through her relationship to things "Maori." Maori culture was the New Zealand she missed while overseas. Performances by Hawaiian musical groups reminded her of Maori songs, and the famous Bishop Museum's display of Maori carvings was one "over which," she wrote, "I hung lovingly."[26] When conference delegates were taken to visit the home of "David," who sang a welcome and then pounded taro, she was reminded of a Maori equivalent.[27] For the Maori delegates, the same moments likely held other significance. We can imagine the shock, perhaps mixed with sorrow or excitement, at seeing these powerful and important traditions on display.

In her 1930 diary, Andrews recorded an important discussion she participated in concerning race relations. On the way to Honolulu on board ship, she had met Australian delegate Constance Ternent Cooke. Cooke, Andrews noted, "is very interested in all matters concerning native races."[28] Cooke had spoken on the subject at the Anti-Slavery and Aborigines' Protection Society in London in 1927, as well as at British Commonwealth League conferences, and had recently been appointed to the Advisory Board on the Aborigines in Adelaide by the South Australian government.[29] For her participation at the Pan-Pacific Women's Conference, Cooke had prepared a scathing report on government policy and Aboriginal conditions in Australia. Although the federal government responded quickly with a denial of her allegations, both would be published later in the official conference report.[30] She and Andrews talked "up on deck" one evening, Andrews reported, "about Australian [A]borigines and [M]aoris. She has made a study of all questions concerning the Australian blacks and is keenly interested in hearing of other native races."[31]

While we do not know how Andrews described Maori conditions to Cooke, she would later question her own attitude on the subject. In a newspaper interview she gave on her return, Andrews declared her rejection of "the absolute pettiness of racial antipathy." She mobilized the trope of women's common experience—the ultimate foundation for women's internationalism—as the source of her revelation concerning the superficiality of racial differences, and of the racism they engendered. The news report continued: "Before she left New Zealand she knew she had that failing and for that reason she had not wanted to go. At the Conference she had felt part of the world's great sisterhood of woman. There are differences between us of course, but how superficial they seemed."[32] Three years later, in a report to the New Plymouth Peace Council, she admitted: "I had always felt a stupid and unworthy shrinking from other races especially when they were of another colour. The conference made me realise once and for all the extreme pettiness of any such feeling."[33] When asked to lead the 1934 delegation, Andrews had already decided that Maori women would be included.

For the two Maori women who joined the delegation, internationalists in their own right,[34] their membership of an international delegation signaled a new opportunity for the promotion their own careers. It also offered an opportunity to promote Maori women's concerns on the international stage. They were Mrs. H. D. Bennett and Mrs. Jean Hammond. Victoria Te Amohau Bennett was a member of an important Maori family. She had been educated privately at Queen Victoria School for Maori girls, one of the exclusive boarding schools for the daughters of wealthy Maori who were expected to make propitious marriage-alliances between elite families. Bennett had hoped to have a career as well. She told Andrews that unfair expulsion from the school had curtailed her ambition to become a nurse.[35] She may have planned to join the emerging group of Maori women health workers who would constitute the basis of the Maori Women's Welfare League in the early 1950s, and who were to be in the forefront of lobbying governments for improved conditions for Maori. Instead, by the early 1930s, she had become a leader within the New Zealand Young Women's Christian Association, and her service was recognized by the governor general in the early 1930s. By 1936, she would be acting president, and would welcome to New Zealand the president of the PPWA, Australian Georgina Sweet, during her tour that year.[36] In a letter appearing in one of the very first issues of the YWCA journal the *New Zealand Girl*, Bennett emphasized the Christian ideals of service and of standing "united and unafraid."[37] In 1934, she was in her early forties, and the mother of three.

Less information appears in the records about Mrs. Hammond. Andrews wrote in her diary that she "looks twenty turns out to be thirty eight and has a daughter of nineteen, also a son at Nelson College, and two younger girls."[38] She noted that Hammond was working on birth control material for the conference.[39] Hammond does not feature in her diaries, or in PPWA reports of the conference. Moreover, of the two women, Bennett, who was awarded honorary life membership in the organization in 1960, is the one who is remembered in the official history of the New Zealand PPWA written in the 1970s.[40]

In Andrews's diary record, Bennett enjoyed a position of considerable power in relation to the New Zealand delegates. According to Andrews, while sailing from Suva to Hawai'i (with, she asserted, nothing but flying fish to distract them), the New Zealand delegates "practiced their native music. Mrs Bennett appears able to take any part, high or low, without the slightest trouble, and the rest simply do as she tells them. We shall be fluent Maori scholars when we come home. Songs and speeches, chants and incantations and war-calls will roll from our lips as fluently as blasphemy."[41] Given Andrews's sardonic sense of humor, the blasphemy she refers to may be that the aggressive tone that the chanting required brought to her mind the act of swearing. But the allusion had more sinister implications, linking indigenous language and culture to the blasphemous and heathen. She and her pakeha co-delegates were in this sense descending into the world of the black arts. Nor could she and the others find the body–mind synergy required by Bennett, as merely going through the motions proved faint substitute for embodied cultural knowledge: "We practised our chant with appropriate gestures. Although Mrs Bennett despairs of us ever acquiring the correct vim."[42] Re-inscribing the notion of the natural sexuality of nonwhite women, the sexualized movements of the dance were represented as inherently difficult for white women to emulate. With her rather hopeless pupils gathered around her, Hammond demonstrated "a most realistic haka like a hula dance and insisted on us endeavouring to imitate her." Andrews invited laughter at her ineptitude, but not too much—after a few halfhearted attempts, she refused to take any further part in singing or learning the *haka*,[43] having "failed miserably."[44] Just as Maori chants became blasphemy in pakeha mouths, so their dance reduced *haka* to burlesque: "Mrs Bennett thinks we can learn to twist and wriggle as Maoris do, but I am convinced that we can't. When she and Mrs Hammond dance all their movements are sheer poetry and beautiful to watch, but the others with the best will in the world, are only a burlesque."[45] Thus the hip swaying of the dance slipped, in Andrews's mind, into the more explicitly (and predominantly white) sexual domain of the music hall.

According to Andrews, her inadequacies cemented a friendship between the two women. In exchange, she claimed to learn something of Bennett's "purple past," although "Without giving away my own," she wrote (no doubt a reference to her relationship). Part of Bennett's purple past, in Andrews's eyes, was her mixed descent: "She is a 3-quarter caste." Later they exchanged Maori stories that pakeha as well as Maori children learned in school, and then they talked about "the entire philosophy of life!"[46] Bennett invited Andrews to visit a Maori *hui* (communal gathering place) as her guest, a gesture formally welcoming Andrews into her extended community. Ever inclined to find the salacious for her diary reader, Andrews remarked on the prospect of spending the night in a communal sleeping hall with this attractive woman. She exclaimed, "Now am I awake or dreaming? I told her my reputation would be gone for ever!!"[47]

Over the next few days, Andrews struggled to memorize the Maori translation of the speech she would present as part of the New Zealand conference presentation. Where official conference reports erase the behind-the-scenes process by which Bennett tutored Andrews for her part in their join presentation, in her diary account Andrews reveals that she knew relatively little Maori and hence was forced to learn the whole speech by rote. "It is going to be a terrible task because it conveys nothing whatever to me," she wrote ironically. "Woe is me that ever my brain conceived the notion of demonstrating the friendliness of our two races."

Although (according to Andrews) she had conceived of the idea of a bilingual performance herself, it would be made possible only through the hard work of her coaches, Bennett and Hammond. This process, of learning a Maori speech, reversed the conference assumption that pakeha were leading Maori into the international fold. It was both a sign of the power that these indigenous women held in relation to the cultural internationalism valorized by the conference, and apparent evidence of Andrews's special relationship with them. Andrews wrote: "I know I should be learning some more Maori. Mrs Bennett and Mrs Hammond are so delighted with the idea of me giving New Zealand's greeting in Maori that I feel I must do it even if the effort bursts a blood vessel." Bennett was to give the same speech in translation but, in contrast with Andrews, her "command of English is really remarkable."[48] Although admiring of Bennett, Andrews betrayed a desire to minimize Bennett's education, her high rank, and her sophistication by implying that her standard of competency in English was unexpected.

Despite her cavalier attitude, Andrews was less aware of the larger politics of language and identity into which she was being recruited. Oratory (*whaikorero*) and speech (*korero*) represented political power. Keeping language alive was central to cultural survival, especially as schools in New Zealand required Maori children to speak only in English. As Maori communities were necessarily bilingual, speeches were often presented in English and then in Maori.[49] Following the same pattern but with a pakeha woman presenting the Maori version was quite a coup for the Maori delegates, one that would undoubtedly be appreciated by Hawaiians in the conference audience.

As the ship docked, the New Zealand delegation had a chance to show off the biculturalism they had rehearsed en route. The *Honolulu Star Bulletin* reported: "when the Royal Hawaiian band finished playing at the docking of their ship, the . . . [the New Zealand delegation] responded from the deck with a Maori song of greeting."[50] This band was important to native Hawaiians, having played at state occasions for Hawaii's royal family, which ruled the country before its "annexation."[51] Following the death of Queen Emma, Hawai'i's royal line continued in symbolic form only. The band still played, but Hawai'i was now a colony, and indigenous Hawaiians had been subjected to colonialism just as had their Maori visitors. It seemed in this moment that an exchange occurred that was not based on conference ideals of interracial exchange but on mutual recognition between two "colonized" peoples. But Andrews's diary account provides a further twist, for it was Bennett's pakeha choir that sang the Maori rejoinder, not the Maori delegates. Andrews wrote that Bennett commanded "'Sing,'" and they had all replied "like obedient school children, with 'Hoki hoki tonu mai.' It sounded beautiful to me and the band applauded to a man."[52]

It was in the Pacific "melting pot" of Hawai'i that Andrews and Hammond were celebrated as "the first of their race to ever attend an international women's conference." Welcomed as "First Maoris for Women's Studies Here," these "two native women" brought with them examples of Maori children's schoolwork as well as their own "native" authority on "Maori lore and customs."[53] In an interview featured alongside their photos several days later, however, Bennett made it clear that she had another assertion to make. She was, she asserted, a woman of the modern world. Like other modern women, she asserted, Maori women were "awakening" to the "international family" without "creeds, of no color or race." Turning the idea of tradition on its head, Bennett called for whites to act on their duty to promote the rights of indigenous peoples within the international family. She concluded: "All around us there comes the special call of the subject races in their struggles, political and economic. Redress may not be specific, but the strong white races have their traditions to live up to, their duties to perform. The care of the weak is by God's will the charge of the strong."[54]

Exciting news spread quickly that Princess Kawananakoa, "last" of the royal Hawaiian line,[55] had announced that she would come to the opening of the conference, but only if she was seated between the two Maori delegates. Abigail Wahikaahuula Campbell Kawananakoa was the daughter of a Hawaiian woman from Maui and James Campbell, a millionaire financier and industrialist who was a powerful figure in Hawai'i at the turn of last century. She married a Hawaiian of noble rank while living in San Francisco, returning to become actively involved in various 'various crossover Hawaiian organizations, including the Daughters of Hawai'i and the Young Women's Christian Association. The elevation of the Maori delegates to quasi-royal status elicited expressions of admiration from Andrews, as well as jealousy, anxiety, and self-doubt. Royalty would not daunt New Zealand's Maori "daughters," she predicted, but yet she wondered whether "They are both going to wear full war paint and we were all bursting to see them."[56] "War paint" is here a double entendre, referring both to the common contemporary term for women's makeup, and for the body painting of "natives." On the night, "Our two Maoris created quite an impression," Andrews continued. Claiming it was too hot for Maori dress (or did she resent the proprietorship of Andrews?), Bennett chose to wear formal evening attire. She "looked absolutely regal in a black lace (backless) dress which she told me she had had made for an investiture at Government House. I was all swollen with pride to be associated with her!"

After the dinner, they traveled back to the conference lodgings with Princess Kawananakoa, who took her lei and put it around Andrews's neck. This was the climax of the night, Andrews wrote, it being "the greatest favour she could show me. . . . [I]t made me one of them so to speak." Andrews achieved her desire to become an honorary elite brown woman. She reported that Bennett was happy to see her kiss the princess's hand at the end of the night. "[Bennett] put it beautifully," she wrote; "'You have won your place. You have opened the way to our hearts.'"[57]

On the last night of the conference, the New Zealand delegation was to make its long-awaited bilingual presentation. Without Andrews, the delegation, led by the Maori women, performed the chants and *haka* they had learned on board ship, to the delight of the audience. Andrews's and Bennett's speech closed the presentation. As noted, their greeting reversed our present-day understanding of crosscultural awareness, with Andrews giving the address in Maori while Bennett responded with the translation in English. In the process she seemed to reiterate Andrews's text: "Maori and pakeha alike send . . . warm greetings to the women of other lands . . . [in] common sisterhood." This sisterhood consisted of three collectivities. First, "our Maoris" bound by "ties of ancient ancestry and tradition" to "our sisters of Hawai'i and other island races."

Second, Westerners tied to "our sisters of the Orient from whose ancient philosophies we have so much to learn." And third, pakeha links to "our sisters of America and of this territory [Hawai'i] and of the Dominions of Canada and Australia who share our Aryan origin and tongue." While British ancestry the English language united settler women, older indigenous connections did not preclude settlers' own attachments to place. Indeed these attachments were the source of a supposedly shared, egalitarian outlook. Addressing her "Aryan" settler sisters, Andrews asserted transnational geographical as well as political connections: "The same blue waters lap our shores as do yours. The same fragrant winds whisper in our valleys and on our mountain peaks. The same pleasant sunshine caresses our fields and pasturelands. And in our hearts glow the same warm desire for the common weal."[58] Thus Andrews represented colonization as a benign force: the settler colonial landscape produced a progressive politics, effectively naturalizing colonial rule.

How did the audience perceive the two women? Again Andrews's desire to celebrate her successes provides us with a glimpse of the work required to perform interracial harmony. Andrews was probably not exaggerating when she asserted that their performance had been a highlight of the conference: "People were interested in our greeting I know, because one can always sense a kind of breathless attention which means more than politeness."[59] But as she was to discover the next day, that breathlessness was not all it seemed. Responses reflected confusion about the New Zealand racial context. Some delegates missed the point of a bilingual and crosscultural presentation entirely, with startling results. "I'm afraid I shall never live down my Maori speech—on Thursday morning I was introduced to an American who looked at me in a bewildered fashion and then said 'So you do speak English?' And someone asked one of our delegates at the dinner—'Does that lady speak any English at all?'"[60]

For others, the dual presentation had been a moving experience beyond even Andrews's expectations. She learned that during their performance Dr. Nadine Kavinoky (a North American specialist in family health) had whispered tearfully to her delegation leader that "'New Zealand has a lesson to teach the world!'" Andrews continued: "But you can never imagine what impressed her most. When we turned to walk back to our chairs I stepped aside to let Mrs Bennett precede me." This was the first time Dr. Kavinoky had seen "deference extended to a 'coloured person.'"[61] In this way, their shared performance was sentimentalized into white benevolence, and an act of politeness (standing to one side) into a startling moment of racial inversion.

Despite the great success of their performance in 1934, in the end, Andrews returned to New Zealand not with interracial harmony in mind, but with the need to "preserve" Maori culture and people. Visiting the grass hut birthplace of the "last" reigning Hawaiian queen, Queen Emma, just before leaving Honolulu, Andrews may have been shown around by indigenous Hawaiian women who were members of the Daughters of Hawai'i (as were conference visitors in 1928).[62] Princess Kawananakoa, who was a member of the organization and a leading campaigner for the protection of cultural sites such as the queen's birthplace, may have personally accompanied Andrews. Whether or not this was the case, Andrews saw evidence of cultural demise rather than the celebration of cultural heritage. She described "a note of tragedy about Hawaiian things which makes me very sad and very determined to learn something of Maori problems in New Zealand so that we can preserve them as an individual race."[63] In the end, despite her various experiences of Maori women's power in Hawai'i, Andrews concluded that the Maori as a people and a culture were to be saved through white protection, their future depending on pakeha guardianship of their traditions and way of life. In Andrews's mind, it seemed the future of the Maori would continue to depend on white people like herself.

Andrews's account of the New Zealand delegation at the 1934 Pan-Pacific Women's Conference in Honolulu provides some remarkable insights into the work required in performing the interracial harmony desired by Pan-Pacific women internationalists. Her letter-book diaries, often flippant and self-effacing, document nonetheless something of the role of Victoria Bennett in making the New Zealand reputation, and of the complex exchange between these two women as a friendship of sorts unfolded between them during the voyage and the ensuing conference. This friendship constituted for Andrews a lens through which to reflect on her pakeha identity to the extent that she was eager for affirmation as an honorable colonialist. Ultimately, Andrews resolved the questions, raised by her friendship with Bennett, concerning the legitimacy of colonial rule in New Zealand. In their place she reinscribed the modern colonial trope of cultural preservation, thereby stripping Bennett of the (worrying) agency she had reasserted as a delegate in Hawai'i, and asserting instead that it was the responsibility of white women to work toward this goal, on the behalf of Maori.

This chapter has been less interested in James Bennett's notion of honorary whiteness than in the desires of pakeha to achieve honorary brownness. The dissonance between their biracial performances on behalf

of the New Zealand delegation and the reality of less-than-ideal race relations in New Zealand itself saw Andrews seeking to constitute herself as
a well-meaning settler colonial, an "honorable" status earned, in her own
mind at least, through her familiarity with the Maori delegates. For her
part, Victoria Bennett asserted her identity not only as a Maori member
of this women's international network but as a Polynesian woman of
high rank. While the two were not necessarily contradictory, their combination exceeded the parameters of Andrews's diary. If the interest of
the Hawaiian royal family in Maori delegates at the conference points to
the importance of a Polynesian internationalism to the history of Maori
activism, the significance Andrews attributed to the kiss she shared with
the princess in the back seat of her chauffeur-driven car reminds us of
the pivotal role that the colonial logics of race, (hetero)sexuality, and
class played in articulating governing subjectivity, even as it made possible the frisson of "forbidden" intimacies exchanged between its mobile
subjects.

Notes

An earlier version of this chapter appeared in *New Zealand Journal of History*
38, 1 (2004): 22–38.

1. Newspaper clipping, Elsie Andrews Papers, MS 312, Puke Ariki (museum),
New Plymouth, New Zealand.
2. Patricia Grimshaw, "Settler Anxieties, Indigenous Peoples, and Women's
Suffrage in the Colonies of Australia, New Zealand and Hawai'i, 1888–1902,"
Pacific Historical Review 69, 4 (2000): 553–72.
3. James Bennett, "Maori as Honorary Members of the White Tribe," *Journal
of Imperial and Commonwealth History* 29, 3 (2001): 33–54.
4. "Bennett, Frederick Augustus, 1871–1950," in *The Dictionary of New Zealand Biography*, vol. 3, *1901–1920*, (Wellington, New Zealand), 49–51.
5. Antoinette Burton, *Burdens of History: British Feminists, Indian Women
and Imperial Culture* (Durham, N.C., 1994).
6. Sandra Stanley Holton, "Segregation, Racism, and White Women Reformers," *Women's History Review* 10, 1 (2001): 5–26.
7. Gillian Whitlock, *The Intimate Empire: Reading Women's Autobiography*
(London, 2000), 14.
8. Ibid., 14 and 5.
9. Agnes J. Shelton, "Elsie Andrews, M.B.E.," Ms 88-19-14/14, Alexander Turnbull Library, Wellington, New Zealand. *History of the New Zealand Branch of the
Pan-Pacific and South-East Asia Women's Association 1928–1978* (n.p., 1978), 33;
"Notes of a Deputation from N. Z. Women Teachers' Association," E2, 1946/27ca,
pt. 1, Res and Remits from NZ Women Teachers Association, State Archives of
New Zealand, Wellington.

10. Elsie Andrews, "Primary School Problems in New Zealand," *Mid-Pacific* 40, 3 (September 1930): 213–17.

11. Diary 1934, Puke Ariki (museum), 116–19.

12. Autobiography, Elsie Andrews Papers.

13. Diary 1934, 94.

14. Ibid., 175.

15. Diary 1930, 60.

16. Diary 1934, 70.

17. Diary 1930, 59.

18. Rumi Yasutake, "Feminism, Nationalism and Internationalism: Japanese Women at the Pan-Pacific Women's Conferences (PPWC), 1928–1940," paper presented at Crossroads Conference, Center for Japanese Studies, University of Hawai'i, Manoa, August 10–12, 2001.

19. Diary 1934, 78.

20. Diary 1930, 97.

21. Ibid., 71.

22. Leila Rupp, "Getting to *Know You,*" in Rupp, *Worlds of Women: The Making of an International Women's Movement* (Princeton, N.J., 1997), 180–204.

23. Alison J. Laurie, "Female Friends or Lesbian Lovers—Elsie Andrews and Muriel Kirton," at the Web site of Victoria University of Wellington, www.vuw .ac.nz/wisc/staff/alison.html.

24. Diary 1930, 93.

25. Diary 1930, 92.

26. Diary 1930, 95.

27. Diary 1934, 51. Such an equivalent, a visit to an "ancient Maori stockade," was regularly advertised in, for example, the *Bulletin of the Pan-Pacific Union* 125 (July 1930): 14. The Pan-Pacific Union was the parent organization of the Pan-Pacific Women's Conferences and published lengthy conference reports.

28. Diary 1930, 5.

29. See Paisley, "'A Brighter Day': Constance Ternent Cooke," in Anna Cole, Victoria Haskins, and Fiona Paisley, eds., *Uncommon Ground: White Women in Aboriginal History* (Canberra, Australia, 2005), 172–96.

30. *Proceedings of the Second Pan-Pacific Women's Conference* (Melbourne, Australia, 1930), 127–45.

31. Diary 1930, 38.

32. Newspaper clipping, no source, Elsie Andrews Papers.

33. Presentation on the Pan-Pacific Conference to New Plymouth Peace Council, December 3, 1934, Elsie Andrews Papers.

34. Maori women were members of New Zealand women's organizations with international networks such as the Young Women's Christian Association and the Woman's Christian Temperance Union. Tania Rei, Geraldine McDonald, and Ngahuia Te Awekotuku, "Nga Ropu Wahine Maori; Maori Women's Organisations," in Anne Else, ed., *Women Together: A History of Women's Organisations in New Zealand; Nga Ropu Wahine o te Motu* (Wellington, New Zealand, 1993), 3–15; Tania Rei, *Maori Women and the Vote* (Wellington, New Zealand, 1993).

35. Diary 1934, 42. Barbara Brookes and Margaret Tennant, "Maori and Pakeha Women: Many Histories, Divergent Pasts?" in Barbara Brookes, Charlotte

Macdonald, and Margaret Tennant, eds., *Women in History: Essays on European Women in New Zealand, vol. 2* (Wellington, New Zealand, 1992), 35.

36. *New Zealand Girl* 1, 3, (March 1936), 4.

37. *New Zealand Girl* 1, 2, (February, 1936), 2.

38. Diary 1934, 20.

39. Ibid., 121.

40. *History of the New Zealand Branch,* 38.

41. Diary 1934, 15.

42. Diary 1934, 29.

43. A women's *haka poi* features swaying movements, fierce expressions, and chants. For an example of pakeha learning *haka poi,* see Alan Armstrong, *Maori Games and Hakas: Instructions, Words and Actions* (Wellington, New Zealand, 1964), 83.

44. Diary 1934, 28.

45. Ibid., 42.

46. Ibid., 42, 50, and 53.

47. Ibid., 102.

48. Ibid., 27 and 17.

49. Armstrong, *Maori Games,* 77.

50. *Honolulu Star Bulletin,* August 3, 1934, 7.

51. Albert Pierce Taylor, *Under Hawai'ian Skies* (Honolulu, 1922), 333–34.

52. Diary 1934, 54.

53. *Honolulu Star Bulletin,* August 3, 1934, 7.

54. *Honolulu Star Bulletin,* August 20, 1934, 3.

55. George F. Nellist, *Women of Hawaii* (Honolulu, 1929), 155–56.

56. Diary 1934, 72 and 78.

57. Ibid., 98, 99, and 101.

58. "Elsie Andrews M.B.E.," 11.

59. Diary 1934, 99.

60. Ibid., 98.

61. Ibid., 178–79.

62. As recorded in a 1928 photograph reproduced in a special report on the first Pan-Pacific Women's Conference. *Mid-Pacific* 36, 6 (December 1928): 432.

63. Diary 1934, 134.

PART 2

"Affective Economies":
Sexuality and the
Uses of Intimacy

MICHAEL A. McDONNELL

7 *"Il a Epousé une Sauvagesse"*

INDIAN AND MÉTIS PERSISTENCE ACROSS
IMPERIAL AND NATIONAL BORDERS

Sometime late in the 1890s, an elderly woman named Angelique told an enthusiastic local historian a tale of her family's journey
from Drummond Island (now in Michigan) to Penetanguishene (now in
southern Ontario) in about 1827, when she was a child. The local historian must have been disappointed with the story, short on colorful details
about the area and the journey itself, but he enthused about Angelique's
"mixed dialect," and transcribed it anyway "almost *verbatim*" because
he thought it so "picturesque and pointed." Suddenly more interested
in capturing an ethnographic moment rather than the story she told, the
local historian was fascinated by Angelique, a self-described "Chippewa
half-breed," whom he described as the "last survivor" of a "somewhat
noted family"—an elderly métis woman who, like the tribes of vanishing
Indians that permeated the popular consciousness in 1900, was on the
verge of extinction in the rapidly anglicizing new province of Ontario,
and new nation of Canada.[1]

Though it was not what the interviewer wanted to hear, in a few
short but revealing sentences the eighty-year-old Angelique pulled back
the curtain on a past and present extended family history spanning at
least a century and a half and crossing multiple imperial, national, and
provincial borders. She told of her grandfather, Charles Langlade, who
came from Montreal, who was a "big, big soldier" in the British Army,
who married an Ojibwe woman, traded furs, and died in Green Bay "ver

rich." She told of mixed-blood uncles, one of whom ended up "way off in Unat Stat" with an Indian tribe, and aunts who ended up in Mackinaw, Montreal, and on Indian reservations at Lac Montaigne, Quebec. She told of her mother, Josephine Ah-quah-dah, who she noted was a "Chippewa squaw, Yankee tribe" and her father Charles, a "French half-breed," born in Mackinac. And she told of brothers who labored and farmed across Ontario, and sisters who journeyed and settled in what are now known as Minnesota, Michigan, and Ontario.[2]

At the heart of the connective sinews of this rich and varied family history was another Angelique—the storyteller's grandmother. The younger Angelique noted that in 1845, at well over a hundred years of age, her grandmother—an Ojibwe woman—slipped along and through numerous borders and traveled up to six hundred miles, probably by canoe, across the Great Lakes from Green Bay, in the new state of Wisconsin, to visit her son, grandchildren, and great-grandchildren across the border in Upper Canada. It may have been on this or other trips that the elder Angelique told tales to her granddaughter of her extended kin and their stories. Literally connecting Angelique with her past and with her distant relations, her grandmother died on this visit to Penetanguishene, giving genealogists and historians some corroborating evidence of her visit, and the younger Angelique a poignant memory of her early years in a new home to pass along to her numerous descendants still living in the Penetanguishene area.[3]

For historians of colonial North America, Angelique's story forces us to confront several important historiographical conventions. Legend has it that when the British forces marched out of Yorktown after their surrender to the Americans in 1781, the band played a popular ditty called the "World Turned Upside Down." Whether true or not, for historians at least, the tune has come to seem appropriate. For the end of the American war for independence—as much as if not more than the end of the Seven Years' War a generation earlier—saw a massive reordering of new political and imperial borders. Historical boundaries were redrawn with a finality that in retrospect seems to have given rise to a historiographical turn away from the early modern era and toward the modern era—away from the old, or first, British Empire, toward the new, or second, British Empire. And as sharply as a different set of imperial historians turned their attention from the Atlantic to the Indian and Pacific oceans, different camps of American historians also use 1781 as a historical and historiographical divide. Narratives of "colonial" America cease, while new narratives of the early republic take life. While Britain and British imperial historians looked eagerly eastward after 1781, America and American national historians looked as eagerly westward—both in search of new empires.[4]

As the new political borders seemed to calcify, and as new historical narratives formed on either side of those borders, one of the old contested centers of imperial North America was cut into pieces and—historiographically at least—left adrift. The *pays d'en haut*, or high country of the Great Lakes region, once the critical commercial heart of the French empire, then a key British holding, was torn in half and divided between the new United States and what was left of British North America. With imaginary political lines drawn through the centers of most of the Great Lakes, this once thriving and interconnected village world of Indians, French, and métis, so richly described by Richard White in *The Middle Ground*, suddenly became a historiographical backwater—a kind of liminal imperial space. Imperial historians with their eyes on the new Cape Colony, India, and the antipodes were uninterested. Canadian historians were not quite sure what to make of the old colonial bits that remained north of the new border and focused most of their attention either on the Loyalist heartland of what would become southern Ontario or wrote histories about employees of the Hudson Bay Company (from their perspective) as they exploited new fur trade networks north and west of the Great Lakes. And of course new national historians of the United States turned their attention fixedly south, following the rush of settlers westward into the more populous states of the lower Midwest and South. At best, the parts of the *pays d'en haut* that remained south of the new border became incorporated into local, state, and regional histories of the Old Northwest.[5] The Great Lakes, once a porous conduit for mobile imperial subjects, became a solid and imposing barrier between new national historiographies—and the new nation-states that those narratives supported.[6]

Yet Angelique's story reminds us that for the Indian, French, and métis peoples who lived in the *pays d'en haut*, the new political boundaries—and the imagined national, cultural, and racial boundaries that historians have subsequently imposed—were less confining than previously imagined and indeed, were often used to facilitate mobility and persistence. Literally and metaphorically, women especially continued to cross borders—much as they had been doing, in a literal and figurative sense, for generations—to create and sustain communities throughout the region. By putting the stories of Angelique, her grandmother, and the mixed offspring of such women in this region at center stage, we can begin to uncover the ways Indian and métis women subtly pursued a gendered strategy of mobility, intermarriage, reproduction, and persistence within and across borders. In doing so, we can also raise important questions not just about intimacy and mobility but also about hybridity, liminality, and our historical subjects. By recentering such stories, too, we can reimagine the ways these women and the intimate relations they cultivated helped create, sustain, and indeed challenge European empires and the conventions of new nations in North America. But to do so, we first need to follow Angelique's cue and recreate a multigenerational family history over the *longue durée*.[7]

It was in fact Angelique's great-great-grandmother, Domitilde, who began the rich tradition of crosscultural marriage and persistence. Domitilde was an Ottawa woman born into a thriving Indian community at the strategic crossroads of Michilimackinac in the early part of the eighteenth century. There, the French had been invited to set up a tiny post alongside as many as two thousand Ottawa on the coast of the straits that controlled the western Great Lakes. With a French post in their midst, the Ottawa took advantage. They grew corn, fished, hunted, and supplied sugar for the garrison, the local *habitants*, the constant stream of traders and explorers who passed through, and the French commanders at the post. The Ottawa also positioned themselves as key players in what was ostensibly an expanding Algonquian-French empire. After the devastating wars with the Iroquois in the seventeenth century, the Ottawa became an important link between the French to the east and the thousands of western Indians of all nations who made the journey to Michilimackinac each spring to trade furs and renew their friendship and alliances with each other, and with the French. Never in a position to coerce the Ottawa, the French were dependent on the hospitality and goodwill of the Ottawa and other powerful nations of the *pays d'en haut*. To facilitate the expansion of the fur trade, the French were forced to make alliances of the diplomatic and intimate kind.[8]

While references to interracial marriages in the region are rare before the 1690s, the sudden (and temporary) withdrawal of the French posts in the *pays d'en haut* corresponded with a sudden rise in the number of reported relationships between French men and Algonquian women at the end of the seventeenth century. Through marriage, French fur traders—*coureurs de bois*—may have been attempting to establish the necessary kin connections with Indians that would allow them to keep trading safely in the area.[9] But if French traders saw advantages to more intimate relationships with native women—and flattered themselves that native women liked "the French better than their own Countrymen"—

they could do so only because their Algonquian trading partners also sought new opportunities.[10]

Among Algonquians, marriage was a social and economic contract between two groups of kin, rather than between individuals. The nuclear family was only one, and the smallest, unit in a series of often overlapping kinship groupings. Native households were often composed of multigenerational or extended kinship groups. Among the Ottawa, entire lineages shared a common dwelling—usually the longhouse or summer cabin. Marriage was "a bridge between lineages and clans, ensuring mutual aid and obligations not only between the partners, but between their respective kin groups." Membership in a patrilineage automatically bestowed membership in a larger kinship unit that cut across band and village lines: the patri-clan, or *nindoodem*.[11]

Moreover, Algonquian daughters and sisters usually married out into other families, away from the country of their birth, and to men of a different nindoodem. Women thus made important connections by marrying men who lived in different communities, sometimes quite considerable distances away. Nindoodemic obligations then meant that travelers could rely on the hospitality of kin as they voyaged through the region. War chiefs could also count on the support of in-laws as allies across a large geographic expanse. In the absence of formal alliances, or a consistent French presence, such relationships were crucial for maintaining and expanding commercial and military ties in a world in flux. They also predated the arrival of the French among many Algonquian-speaking peoples.[12]

Thus, incorporating French fur traders through intermarriage was an extension of a preexisting strategy.[13] And women like Domitilde were vital in creating not just an important role for the Ottawa at Michilimackinac vis-à-vis the French empire but also an important role for the French among the Indian nations. Domitilde, for example, first married Daniel Villeneuve, a prominent trader, with whom she had six children. Of the three sons of this first marriage, at least two were fur traders, one was an interpreter, and two died at the battle of the Plains of Abraham fighting alongside Domitilde's Ottawa kin; though little is known about the third son, he did apparently have two children with Indian women, supposedly slaves. The three daughters from Domitilde's marriage also made productive and close marital alliances that would later serve the Ottawa well, too. Agathe married a commercial explorer; another married three times, and one of her husbands was Pierre le Duc Souligny, who would also work closely with the Ottawa. The third daughter, Louise Therese, married a soldier, Claude Germaine Gautier de Vierville. Their eldest son, Charles Gautier, became a close companion and partner of Domitilde's son by her second marriage, and together they allied themselves closely with the Ottawa for most of their lives.[14]

After Villeneuve died, Domitilde strengthened her alliances further by marrying Augustin Langlade in about 1727–28. Augustin, inheriting neither status nor property, had left his own family near Trois-Rivieres on the St. Lawrence and entered the fur trade at Michilimakinac after a chance journey westward from Quebec. Though not an established trader, Augustin seemed to have prospects—he was involved in a new trade initiative to exploit the fur trade further west, in Sioux country, and his brother's father-in-law had served as an officer in the construction of Forts du Buade and Michilimackinac. After a successful first marriage, Domitilde may have been more interested in a more diplomatic alliance. When Augustin married Domitilde, who was probably at least ten years his senior, he not only married into the fur trading estate and family of Villeneuve but also into an existing Indian kinship network in the thriving Ottawa village at Michilimackinac. One of Domitilde's brothers, "a respected chief," died in the siege of the Sauk and Fox village at Green Bay in 1733 under de Villiers and Repentigny. He was replaced by another of Domitilde's brothers, Nissowaquet, or La Fourche (and variously known as Nosawaguet, Sosawaket, and Fork), who later came to be known by some as the "Great Chief of the Ottawas," and who played a leading role in his village until his death in 1797.[15]

Augustin capitalized on this network to establish himself as a middleman between French suppliers and Indian and French traders at Michilimackinac. By midcentury, Augustin had already opened trading posts at La Baye (Green Bay, Wisconsin) and on the east side of Lake Michigan, at Grand River (now Grand Haven, Michigan). The Langlades continued to trade profitably in this region for years, gaining a monopoly of the trade on the Grand River in 1755, where they continued to trade until 1793. After the British moved in to Michilimackinac in 1763, Augustin moved his family to Green Bay and continued to trade profitably at that site as well, both legally and at times illegally.[16]

But Domitilde's judicious partnerships also helped grease the wheels of an all-important social and diplomatic alliance for the Ottawa at Michilimackinac. Domitilde's relationship with important chiefs in the Ottawa village meant, for example, that a French husband would have an important role to play in maintaining empire, a role of which Domitilde would have been only too well aware. Thus Augustin quickly came to be seen as a strategic intermediary in Michilimackinac between French officials and the Ottawa (along with other western nations), often given clothing, canoes, tobacco, brandy, food, and gunpowder to distribute among the warriors. In 1745 alone, Augustin distributed goods valued at nearly 3,000 livres—mostly goods given by the French to maintain the alliance, but some out of their own pockets to keep the peace. He and then his métis son and relations also attended countless burials and other ceremonies, served as godparents to dozens of Indian Catholic converts at Michilimackinac, and offered goods and gifts to "cover the dead" (as a form of compensation) when necessary. When Augustin took up a lease to trade in Green Bay in the volatile year 1746, he also acted as peacemaker. Within two years of his arrival, one Menominee historian has concluded, the Langlades were able to bring peace to the region through gift giving and arbitration. Peace among the Indians of the *pays d'en haut* meant stability and strength for the French empire.[17]

It also brought stability and strength to the Ottawa. In an important sense, when Domitilde brought Augustin into the Ottawa fold, she gave him access to the Ottawa trade network, in return for taking on a role as a village chief—one who had a special relationship with their nearby French allies. This relationship was further strengthened and in important ways solidified by the birth of their métis son, Charles Langlade, who was a living embodiment of Richard White's "middle ground"— typifying the union of French and Ottawa interests. Not unsurprisingly, Charles took on an even closer relationship with the Ottawa, becoming a kind of village war chief. This role began early, when Domitilde's brother Nissowaquet took ten-year-old Charles on a French-inspired expedition against the Chickasaw to the south. Langlade was later able to utilize his strategic position to achieve promotion in the French armed forces, and to promote the interests of the Ottawa in the imperial alliance. In 1752, for example, he led a force of 250 warriors from the Ottawa and closely allied Ojibwe and Potawatomi villages of the Michilimackinac area against a rebel Miami chief at Picqua, Ohio. Langlade continued to bring scores of warriors to the field throughout the ensuing conflict, earning him a reputation among the French as having "much influence on the minds of the savages," while earning for his Ottawa allies an unsurpassed reputation for loyalty to the French alliance that brought them a privileged position in the fur trade and the French empire, and an abundance of gifts and provisions year after year.[18]

If Domitilde's marriages were vital in securing important trade and diplomatic ties within the French empire, they were also essential in helping the Ottawa navigate *across* imperial boundaries. One of these crucial moments, of course, came with the end of the French regime in North America in 1763. Though the French had surrendered their empire, their allies, and particularly the western Indian nations, were unwilling to simply switch allegiances to the British. After a couple of interim years under the British, it became increasingly clear that good relations with the new imperial power would not bring the same benefits as the old French alliance. Dissatisfaction with the British led to one of the first and largest pan-Indian uprisings in colonial history—the so-called Pontiac's Rebellion of 1763. Across the Great Lakes, Native Americans struck in unison at the recently occupied British forts, including Michilimackinac.[19]

Though there is still some uncertainty as to the course of events at the post, what is clear is that the Ottawa, with the help of Langlade, were able to intercede and save the lives of the British officers garrisoned at the Fort. Snatching them from the hands of allied nations who seemed keen on disposing of them, they took the officers back to the Ottawa village of l'Arbre Croche, where they waited for news of the uprising elsewhere. When it became clearer that assaults on other British garrisons had been less successful, the Ottawa insisted on escorting the British officers back to Montreal.[20] Langlade and Nissowaquet had played their cards right. In Montreal, as the uprising wound down, the Ottawa were greeted with relief, and given copious gifts of gunpowder, rum, and other trade goods. One early report said that "the Officers and Traders can not say enough of the good Behaviour of those Ottawas and Genl. Gage is resolved to use and reward them well for their Behaviour." Nissowaquet was personally rewarded with trade goods and at least one slave, later received a chief's commission and a medal, and was thereafter able to manipulate this alliance effectively, too. The new British commander of Michilimackinac, Robert Rogers, kept the Ottawa in the style to which they had become accustomed under the French, arguing that the chiefs of the Ottawa "take most of their time in serving the English, & keeping peace, among all the Nations." The new alliance paid off: according to one Indian agent, Nissowaquet was "the richest Indian I ever saw."[21]

In the end, every generation of the Langlades served in these important ways, becoming interpreters, cultural brokers, and intermediaries in keeping the fragile bonds of imperial alliances secure.[22] They were able to do so because of their intimate relations with native women. Charles Langlade, for example, formally married a French woman at Michilimackinac, Charlotte Ambrosine Bourassa, daughter of René Bourassa, a prominent fur trader. But before he married Bourassa, Langlade had a relationship and a child with an Indian woman, reported to be a "panis," or slave, in the Ottawa village at Michilimackinac in the late 1740s or early 1750s. Though little is left in the historical record of this woman and her relationship with Langlade, they did have a son, Charles Langlade Jr., who left his mark in the same way as his father. Indeed, the younger Langlade seemed as well integrated with the Ottawa community as his father, and together they fought alongside the Ottawa and other western Indians during the American Revolution, campaigning with Burgoyne in 1777, and in the west against George Rogers Clark in 1779. In 1782, the younger Langlade campaigned with Nissowaquet in Kentucky, where in one of the last skirmishes of the Revolutionary War, they ambushed a group of Kentucky militia led by Daniel Boone, and apparently killed one of his sons.[23]

But of course, though they successfully managed to switch imperial alliances, the Langlades and the Ottawa—like many western Native nations—ended up on the "losing" side of the American war for independence, and the Langlades seem to have been unable to help the Ottawa negotiate their way across imperial borders into the novel terrain of new national borders. As the western Indians' own revolution wound up in the 1790s, Langlade and his son offered their services to the British to raise warriors to fight against Anthony Wayne in 1794. But they were too late. Wayne managed to smash the remnants of the forces opposing him, and break up another pan-Indian confederacy. Faced with an emerging aggressive new nation on their eastern flanks and a vacillating and reduced British imperial presence on their northern flanks, the writing seemed to be on the walls of the newly drawn national borders that the options were narrowing for the peoples of the *pays d'en haut*. Though Indian hopes of a resurrection of British imperial scheming were temporarily buoyed by continued skirmishes, culminating in the War of 1812, there were fewer and fewer opportunities to play off competing powers. Without those opportunities, vital cultural intermediaries like the Langlades also lost their power.[24]

And so began the disintegration of the ties that seemed to bind. And on the surface at least, the Langlades' story at this point becomes increasingly bounded by the larger historical and historiographical barriers noted earlier. The elder Charles Langlade apparently severed most of his former official and informal ties with the Ottawa in Michigan when he retired to Green Bay, where he died in 1801. Perhaps ironically, in death the memory of Langlade quickly became anglicized—a county was named after him, and regional historians were keen to claim him as an important founder. Incredibly, he and his father, Augustin, are today perhaps best known in the state of Wisconsin for their role as "Fathers of Wisconsin"—as the first so-called permanent (and presumably "European") settlers in the state.[25]

In this seemingly disintegrating world, the younger Langlade, like several prominent Indian groups, tied his fortunes to the British, and moved into British North America, where he served as an Indian interpreter in the new century, briefly reviving his old role as warrior chief during the War of 1812 when a combined Canadian–First Nations expedition recaptured and occupied the United States–held Fort Michilimackinac for most of that conflict. But here his story ends, too—and with much less fanfare than his father's. Little is actually known of the younger Langlade in his later years. Indeed, public memory of the younger Langlade has only succeeded in confusing him with his son. For years, most local historians have assumed that it was the younger Langlade who ended up in Penetanguishene, in what is now southern Ontario.

Left without their cultural intermediaries, and without the competing interests of different imperial powers from which to draw sustenance, the Ottawa seemed to spiral into an all too familiar pattern of decline, dispossession, and removal in the face of American advance. Nissowaquet died in 1797. Even by 1799, a priest visiting the once thriving Ottawa village noted how appalled he was by its rundown condition, and believed the children were poorly cared for while once mighty warriors lay drunk in the street. By 1836, the Ottawa had lost their land.[26] Reflecting the larger history of Native Americans in the once vital *pays d'en haut,* the Ottawa's once mighty influence in the region—indeed, in the history of the empires that clashed over the area—seems to come to a crashing end, either in 1794, or in 1815. Thereafter, if treated at all, they are treated within the confines of those new national narratives and borders. In these stories, the Ottawa become a mere footnote to a larger tale of Indian dispossession and removal, mainly focused on states to the south.[27]

Thus, with the elder Langlade in Green Bay, the younger Langlade in Upper Canada, and the Ottawa bereft between the two in the new state of Michigan, the Langlades and their Ottawa kin became a divided family in the dividing histories of new nations and states at the turn of the new century. Their stories—told and retold by nineteenth- and twentieth-century historians—have traditionally come to an end at this point. We lose sight of all of them in the nineteenth century.

———

Until Angelique told her tale. The narrative of the younger Angelique, and the journey of the elderly Angelique from Green Bay to Penetanguishene in 1845, almost lost to the written record, helps change that picture, and forces us to think across those new borders. In part, it does so by focusing us on the women in the Langlade genealogy, forcing us to reconsider what more traditional narratives of fur trade economies and battlefield exploits tell us, too. Perhaps most appropriate, Angelique's narrative helps resurrect what has been, for years, a missing generation that straddled this momentous period. Most genealogists, local historians, and early chroniclers of the exploits of Charles Langlade Sr. have assumed that the Charles Langlade she speaks of as her father was Charles Langlade Jr., and thus Angelique her grandmother was the Indian woman her *grandfather* (Charles Langlade Sr.,) had had a relationship with all those years ago. But close reading of Angelique's short narrative compelled a second look at the birth and marriage records of both Michilimackinac and Penetanguishene. And there, in the local genealogists' notebooks, was another Charles Langlade listed as born in Mackinac in 1771, which was confirmed by the Mackinac register of baptisms (though amended there to 1786), when Father Payet recorded the baptism of "Charles, about fifteen months old, natural son of Sieur danglade, the younger, and of a savage mother." The "savage mother" was Angelique the grandmother, and the newborn was "Charlie," Angelique's father. And this was the start of a whole new mixed-blood generation—a generation completely missed by nineteenth-century memoirists, early twentieth-century antiquarians, and late twentieth-century historians.[28]

Further investigation revealed that Charles Langlade the younger may have had as many as three sons and three daughters with Angelique. Though the details are unclear, these may have included Louis Langlade, who became a lieutenant in the British service, was stationed at Toronto, and ended up at Oka, an Indian mission near Montreal. Of the daughters, one was married to Abram Le Brun, and when last heard from was residing at the Lake of Two Mountains, a prominent Indian community near Montreal. Another daughter may also have ended up in Montreal—certainly Angelique the younger believed she had numerous relations in that city, including her great-aunt. The last daughter was reputedly still living at Mackinaw with her husband, Francis Luzienias, as late as 1857. Angelique also spoke about two other great-uncles—Alixe (who she said had been made a "big chief way, way off in Unat Stat"), and Napoleon (who she recalls leaving a long time ago and never coming back, and who most people spoke of as being dead a long time).[29]

Finally, as noted, in 1786 Angelique and Charles Jr. also produced another son named Charles—Angelique's father—who ended up in Penetanguishene. This Charles married Josephine Ah-quah-dah, an Ojibwe woman probably from near Mackinac as well. They apparently lived for a time with the British at Drummond Island, where they had removed when the Americans took over Mackinac. After the War of 1812, the boundary line was again redrawn, and Drummond Island was also found to be in American territory. Thus it was that in the 1820s, the British garrison, together with most of the French, English, métis, and Indian community, evacuated the settlement at Drummond Island and established a new naval base, fur trading community, and settlement at Penetanguishene. Charles and Josephine brought ten métis children with them—including the younger Angelique—and had another daughter after moving. Together with the other large and mixed families that moved from Drummond Island, the Langlades helped firmly establish a previously overlooked new community of métis in southern Ontario. Preliminary evidence indicates, too, that borders posed few barriers for this family as well—with at least four of the children and grandchildren ending up in far-flung Great lakes locations such as Duluth, Minnesota, and Marquette, Michigan.[30]

Moreover, the elder Angelique's journey reminds us of the continued *connections* between these far-flung groups and between families on both sides of those supposedly calcifying borders—connections made possible by mobile bodies. Angelique's grandmother had likely stayed in Mackinac after the British, and her family, left. One memoirist states that her husband, Charles Jr., returned to Mackinac, where he lived with Angelique's kin until his death. Angelique may then have returned to Green Bay, where she lived among her extended family.[31]

There were more than a few among whom to choose hospitable living quarters. As noted, after Langlade the elder and his Indian wife had their son Charles, Langlade married a French woman, Charlotte Bourassa, with whom they had two daughters. Though little is known of the elder Langlade's daughter Charlotte Catherine, we do know that his youngest daughter, Louise Domitelle, born at Michilimackinac on January 30, 1759, became the second wife of Pierre Grignon, a well-known fur trader. Grignon's first wife was a Menominee woman, and Charlotte Catherine ended up fostering three children from that first marriage, along with having nine of her own with Grignon. Amazingly, of the nine children of Grignon and Louise Domitelle (who are considered by some as the "dominant force in Wisconsin" during the first quarter of the nineteenth century), we know that at least six married Native American (three Menominee and one Ottawa) and/or métis women. In addition, a son from Pierre Grignon's first marriage married a Winnebago woman. Moreover, incomplete records indicate that a not inconsiderable number of the grandchildren (at least twenty-seven at last count) followed these marriage patterns. So, not only was it a large family, but it was also very much a métis family. And though we don't often associate Green Bay with métis peoples, there was, at least for several generations, a thriving métis community of which the Langlade-Grignons were only a part.[32]

And all of this helps explain some significant statistics that are generally overlooked. As Jacqueline Peterson pointed out long ago, the métis population of the northern Great Lakes was probably on the *rise* in the late eighteenth and early nineteenth centuries. At Michilimackinac, for example, between 1698 and 1765 about 55 percent of marriages were between Europeans and Indians, or between métis peoples and Indians or Europeans. Between 1765 and 1838, this proportion rose to about 75 percent. As Peterson urged, rather than assume that the products of these mixed marriages were Europeanized and assimilated, we need to examine them more closely not only for their ties to the reemergence of the native population of the old Northwest states in the twentieth century but also for their ties to communities across the border in the Red River region and in Ontario. The younger Angelique's "mixed dialect" and broken English in telling her tale—as late as 1900—points to the intriguing persistence of cultural and linguistic continuities.[33]

Moreover, we also need to reexamine the role of these mixed-bloods in easing conflict between natives and newcomers well into the nineteenth century in places such as Michigan. As Langlade and others like him had done for almost three-quarters of a century, these métis may have helped in delaying or even allaying what Peterson called the "direct or directed cultural annihilation of the northern Great Lakes and western Canadian tribes."[34] How much such peoples helped the Ottawa village and community into which Langlade was born in coping with new challenges in the postrevolutionary period is not yet clear, but the Ottawa continued to maintain peaceful relations with both the nearby American garrison at Michilimackinac and the British at Drummond Island right through the tumultuous period of the War of 1812. Though the Ottawa sided with the British during that conflict, and continued to travel across borders to receive annual annuities and presents from the British, they also managed to negotiate their way to more or less peaceful relations with the Americans.[35]

In the end, the Ottawa eventually lost their original land base in Michigan, but they successfully evaded Removal, and most ended up staying in the region, where they continued to trade furs, raise crops, and fish—activities they had engaged in for centuries. They also continued to make frequent journeys across now international borders to pick up British annuities and to trade with kin in Ontario at least as late as 1870.[36] Though limited, evidence of this nature suggests that the Ottawa remained staunchly independent through the early nineteenth century.

And in the end, as Helen Hornbeck Tanner has shown so graphically, the Ottawa—like many Indian populations in the northern parts of the Great Lakes—had achieved a stable pattern of distribution and growth by 1810, patterns that would persist throughout the nineteenth century. While Indian peoples were almost completely swept out of what we might call the main line of westward white emigration and settlement through Ohio, Indiana, and Illinois, they sustained a significant presence in the less-populated northern country of the Great Lakes—where in 1980, New York, Michigan, Wisconsin, and Minnesota had a combined Indian population of about 150,000, with perhaps another 90,000 living in adjacent sections of Ontario.[37]

In the end, Angelique's story forces us to confront multiple historiographic frontiers. In the first place, Angelique compels us to rethink the role of intimacy and mobility in the construction of empires and new nations. For utilizing Doreen Massey's idea of space as a meeting place of histories, not just a space that Europeans crossed, we need to recognize that imperial intimacies, too, need to be understood on indigenous terms (as in the incorporation of newcomers, and the construction of kinship alliances). Sometimes European empires created new intimacies by (often literally) connecting new peoples—creating, for example, the métis phenomenon. But empires often used, as it were, older spaces—the French then British empires in northern North America in particular were hung on the framework of existing Native spaces, mobilities, and intimacies within that space. Europeans created posts around native villages, and utilized existing trade networks. Michilimackinac was at the crossroads of preexisting native trade networks and became one of the centers of empire in North America. Europeans were sometimes readily, even eagerly, incorporated into existing indigenous intimacies. Given this, can we be sure that "colonial intimacies," as Stoler puts it, were always "first and foremost sites of intrusive interventions"?[38]

Bodies may have been sites "through which imperial and colonial power was imagined and exercised," but they could also be sites on which empires were initially constructed and maintained, too. Once we understand this, we can see that those intimacies and those spaces—and the mobilities enabled by them both—also continued to exist independent of those empires, subverting new national boundaries. In an important sense, because of this engagement with indigenous space, when new national boundaries dissected those so-called imperial boundaries, they would never be able to entirely dismantle the framework on which they had always rested. Thus Angelique and her family were living testimony to the dynamic connection and tension between European and Native worlds and the key roles that métis people (most explicitly products of the new imperial intimacies) played in mediating between the two.[39]

A multigenerational study, then, compels us to focus on transnational continuities rather than on discontinuities created by new imperial and national borders. It also forces us to rethink the historiographic conventions that we have brought with us from the older imperial and national narratives, and that tend to dominate our new transnational and comparative endeavors. One of these, for example, is our tendency to see the relationship between intimacy and the rise of racism as a linear development—always narrowing. In North American historiography, crosscultural intimate connections are generally seen as diminishing toward the end of the eighteenth century, replaced with hardening attitudes about race, nation, and intermarriage. Catherine Hall, summarizing Adele Perry's work on British Columbia, narrates a familiar tale: the increased mobility of the mid–nineteenth century, improved communications, and the move from trading posts to settlements with missionaries and teachers all brought the once isolated world of the fur trader into closer proximity with the metropole, threatening family affections among mixed-bloods and bringing increasingly hostile attitudes toward miscegenation.[40] And as Kerry Wynn, Christine Skwiot, and Katherine Ellinghaus show (chapters 8, 9, and 10 here), such developments coincided in the nineteenth and early twentieth centuries with an increased concern over such relationships on the part of colonial regimes.

Angelique the younger's proud assertion of her mixed-blood heritage, the continued and increasing intermarriages between people of Indian, French, and mixed heritage that she reveals, the persistence of the Ottawa and other groups in the region, and the connections between them all exposed by her grandmother's travels all point to a less certain outcome, even as late as 1900.[41] Of course, such a different outcome may have been facilitated by the very mobility that had always marked the Ottawa's seasonal subsistence strategy, their historic migrations around the Great Lakes, and their intermarriages among new communities. The "borderlessness" of the Ottawa may have meant that there were fewer borders that colonial officials could penetrate or tear down, in contrast to the Cherokee studied by Wynn. But this "borderlessness" may also have been facilitated by the same processes and historical developments that rendered the Great Lakes a liminal space by the mid–nineteenth century. That very liminality may have helped the Langlades and others like them to avoid the colonial gaze, to avoid scrutiny and regulation. It certainly delayed the "swamping" of the local population by an increasing settler population.[42] It may have helped Angelique's grandmother slip unnoticed back and forth across now international borders.

But this marginalization came at a price. Following the course of empires and new nations, and the inevitable paper trail necessary to the historical project, we tend to focus on moments of conflict rather than continuity. As Burton and Ballantyne note in the introduction, we focus on clashes between the moving and the "immobilized" rather than the "accumulating interconnections" of the mobile.[43] And when we do study these interconnections, we tend to focus on the "successful" subjects—more "prominent" intercultural mediators such as Charles Langlade, for example. They have, after all, left the best and most records. But in studies of hybridity, intercultural adaptation, and intimacy, "success"—at least as measured as "prominence"—almost inevitably proves the undoing of our subjects, as they invariably come into increasing contact with the colonizer, become whitened (literally, or figuratively), and become "disaffected" from their native cultures. Yet, as studies of Native Americans on the east coast of America in the nineteenth century have shown, the less "successful" simply fall out of the colonizer's, hence our, view. As the chance meeting with Angelique demonstrates, such people persisted and still flourish. And while their very mobility and liminality may have worked in their favor, our current historical narratives yet obscure them.[44]

Notes

1. The narrative of Angelique can be found in A. C. Osborne, "The Migration of Voyageurs from Drummond Island to Penetanguishene in 1828," *Ontario Historical Society Papers and Records* 3 (1901): 147–48.

2. Ibid.

3. For a list and introduction to the families that moved to Penetanguishene that contains an intriguing but untraceable photographic image of one "Minnie 'Longalde' Marvin" with her daughter Charlotte, a descendant of the original Drummond Islanders, see Bryan Gidley and Gwen Patterson, comps., *The Penetanguishene List of the Drummond Islanders 1815–1828* (Penetanguishene, Ontario, 1991). For their nineteenth- and twentieth-century descendants, including many Langlades, see Denise Ladouceur, transcriber, *St. Ann's Church (Roman Catholic) Penetanguishene, Ontario: Baptism Registers and Confirmations, 1835–1910* (Privately published, Midland, Ontario, 2004), National Library and Archives, Ottawa, 365–71, 647–58, and Hubert A. Houle, comp., *Répertoire des Mariages de Lafontaine, Penetanguishene, Perkinsfield* (Vanier, Ontario, 1976), esp. 94–95, 206.

4. The idea that the loss of the American colonies was a marker for the division

between the end of the "First British Empire" and the beginning of the "Second British Empire" was in circulation long before the first volume of the *Cambridge History of the British Empire* labeled it *The Old Empire from the Beginnings to 1783* in 1929. Indeed, as P. J. Marshall points out, the idea was in circulation as far back as the first half of the nineteenth century and continues in the minds of more recent commentators with the publication of works such as Frederick Madden with David Fieldhouse, eds., *Select Documents on the Constitutional History of the British Empire and Commonwealth*, vol. 2, *The Classical Period of the First British Empire, 1689 to 1783: The Foundations of a Colonial System of Government* (Westport, Conn., 1985). See also P. J. Marshall, "The First British Empire," in Robin W. Winks, ed., *The Oxford History of the British Empire*, vol. 5, *Historiography* (Oxford, 1999), 43–53.

5. While we've learned a great deal of late about the roles of cultural brokers in general and specifically women as intimate cultural mediators, and "negotiators of change," for example, most treatments divide along modern national boundaries even while they hint at continued crossborder relations. Even Richard White's masterful study begins to come to an end with the American Revolution, and we lose sight of his subjects in both the new republic and early Canada. Richard White, *The Middle Ground: Indians, Empires, and Republics in the Great Lakes Region, 1650–1815* (Cambridge, 1991). And while White's critical insights about the "middle ground" have been adopted and widely used by scholars in this and many other fields and disciplines, few historians have revisited the Great Lakes region since his book came out, and most have remained on safer footing in the Anglo-American world south of the Great Lakes. See also Susan Sleeper-Smith, *Indian Women and French Men: Rethinking Cultural Encounter in the Western Great Lakes* (Amherst, Mass., 2001), 2–3, 116–17, who discusses the limits of White's work, but whose own rich and evocative study stays firmly focused on the southern Great Lakes and what would become states in the new republic. So, too, does the fascinating work of Lucy Eldersveld Murphy (see "Public Mothers: Native American and Métis Women as Creole Mediators in the Nineteenth-Century Midwest," *Journal of Women's History* 14, 4 (Winter 2003): 142–66, *A Gathering of Rivers: Indians, Métis, and Mining in the Western Great Lakes, 1737–1832* (Lincoln, Neb., 2000), and "Autonomy and the Economic Roles of Indian Women of the Fox-Wisconsin Riverway Region, 1763–1832," in Nancy Shoemaker, ed., *Negotiators of Change: Historical Perspectives on Native American Women* (New York, 1995), 72–89. Jennifer S. H. Brown, in her pathbreaking *Strangers in Blood: Fur Trade Company Families in Indian Country* (Vancouver, British Columbia: University of British Columbia Press, 1980), mainly focuses on areas north of the Great Lakes and principally under the British in the nineteenth century. The need to look at southern Ontario and its links with métis and Indian communities across the Great Lakes more closely has also been recently stressed by Gwen Reimer and Jean-Philippe Chartrand, "Documenting Historic Métis in Ontario," *Ethnohistory* 51, 3 (Summer 2004); 567–607. See John E. Foster, "Some Questions and Perspectives on the Problem of Métis Roots," and John S. Long, "Treaty No. 9 and Fur Trade Company Families: Northeastern Ontario's Halfbreeds, Indians, Petitioners and Métis," both in Jacqueline Peterson and Jennifer S. H. Brown, eds., *Being and Becoming Métis in North America* (Winnipeg, 1985), 73–94, 137–62, for questions about the existence of other local communities of métis. Studies

of the rise of the Red River community in Manitoba also note the need to look at continuities between the Great Lakes and the later more well-known métis community to the northwest. Jacqueline Peterson's work is a notable exception to this nationally based historiography (see, for example, "The People in Between: Indian-White Marriage and the Genesis of a Métis Society and Culture in the Great Lakes Region, 1680–1830" (Ph.D. diss., University of Illinois, Chicago, 1981), as well as the collected essays in Peterson and Brown, *Being and Becoming Métis in North America.* On the potential for such studies to challenge nation-bound histories, see Dirk Hoerder, "How the Intimate Lives of Subaltern Men, Women, and Children Confound the Nation's Master Narratives," *Journal of American History* 88, 3 (2001): 874–81.

6. After the loss of the American colonies, most imperial history textbooks turn their attention eastward, after only a brief look at the influx of Loyalists into British North America. The continuing fur trade, of course, is often discussed but the narrative mostly focuses on the activities and rivalry of the North-West and Hudson Bay Companies as they competed further north, and west, of the Great Lakes. If Britain's North American holdings are discussed again, it is usually only in the context of far western expansion. See, for example, T. O. Lloyd, *The British Empire, 1558–1983* (Oxford, 1984). The *pays d'en haut* rarely makes an appearance as a coherent region after 1812. Indeed, since at least the 1950s, when Vincent T. Harlow published *Discovery and Revolution,* vol. 1 of *The Founding of the Second British Empire, 1763–1793* (London, 1952), the Great Lakes region, or the "Middle West" as he called it, has been used, if at all, as a model testing ground for the Second British Empire and the shift in emphasis from "trade" to "dominion." The "Middle West" as in Harlow's own work, however, then hardly gets another look as historians follow the construction of the "empire of Oriental trade" (*Founding,* 1:5–6). For a vivid sense of the liminality of the Great Lakes in imperial thinking, note the absence of any discussion of the area in any of the historiographical essays in Winks, *Oxford History of the British Empire,* vol. 5. And see especially the essays in that volume by C. A. Bayly, "The Second British Empire," 54–72, and D. R. Owram, "Canada and the Empire," 146–62. For a recent assertion of the historical shifts that legitimate this historiographical emphasis, see Jeremy Adelman and Stephen Aaron, "From Borderlands to Borders: Empires, Nation-States, and the Peoples in Between in North American History," *American Historical Review* 104, 3 (June 1999): 817–23.

7. As early as 1983, Jennifer S. H. Brown, in "Woman as Centre and Symbol in the Emergence of Metis Communities," *Canadian Journal of Native Studies* 3 (1983): 39–46, called for multigenerational studies of métis communities specifically focused on women in order to understand dynamism and expansion of métis communities in eighteenth- and nineteenth-century North America (45). For one short but intriguing study along these lines, see Theresa M. Schenck, "The Cadottes: Five Generations of Fur Traders on Lake Superior," in Jennifer S. H. Brown, W. J. Eccles, and Donald P. Heldman, eds., *The Fur Trade Revisited: Selected Papers of the Sixth North American Fur Trade Conference, Mackinac Island, Michigan, 1991* (East Lansing, Mich., 1994), 189–98. Though Schenck stays firmly focused on the male line of Cadottes, she provides ample evidence of their intergenerational marriages to Indian women. Jacqueline Peterson, "Prelude to Red River: A Social Portrait of the Great Lakes Metis," *Ethnohistory* 25,

1 (Winter 1978): 41–67, provides an important exception and illuminating guide to the possibilities inherent in a transnational intergenerational study focused on families. She also discusses the scholarly neglect of this area in the Canadian and American historiography (45).

8. For Michilimackinac, see White, *Middle Ground*, 42–45; "Relation of Sieur de Lamothe Cadillac . . ." (1718), *Wisconsin Historical Society Collections* 16 (1902): 350 (hereafter *WHC*); Helen Hornbeck Tanner, *Atlas of Great Lakes Indian History* (Norman, Okla., 1987), 31; *The Jesuit Relations and Allied Documents: Travels and Explorations of the Jesuit Missionaries in New France, 1610–1791*, edited by Reuben Gold Thwaites (New York: Pageant Book, 1959), 73 vols. (hereafter *Jesuit Relations*), 55: 135–67. There may have been as many as six thousand to seven thousand Ottawa, Huron, and Ojibwa peoples living within a pistol shot of the straits in the early eighteenth century (see Peterson, "People in Between," 38). The Ottawa at Michilimackinac were in turn divided among themselves. For a very recent interpretation of these divisions, see Heidi Bohaker, "*Nindoodemag:* The Significance of Algonquian Kinship Networks in the Eastern Great Lakes Region, 1600–1701," *William and Mary Quarterly* 63, 1 (January 2006): 23–52. Contemporary Ottawa often use the term Odawa, and the group descended from the Michilimackinac Ottawa refer to themselves as the Waganawkezee Odawa, or Waganakasi, meaning "it is bent," or "crooked tree," which refers to the area around an old pine tree that leaned over a cliff into Little Traverse Bay, and served as a landmark for the Ottawa village after they moved from Michilimackinac in 1741. Historically, the new village was known to Europeans as l'Arbre Croche, or Crooked Tree. James M. McClurken, "Augustin Hamlin, Jr.: Ottawa Identity and the Politics of Persistence," in James A. Clifton, ed., *Being and Becoming Indian: Biographical Studies of North American Frontiers* (Chicago, 1989), 83, and the Little Traverse Bay Band of Odawa Indians' website history, at www .victories-casino.com/tribal_history.html. For an indigenous perspective on the history of the Ottawa in Michigan, see Andrew J. Blackbird, *History of the Ottawa and Chippewa Indians of Michigan; A Grammar of Their Language, and Personal and Family History of the Author* (Ypsilanti, Mich., 1887).

9. Richard White speculates that the sudden rise of marriages may have been a reaction to formal French attempts to force *coureurs de bois* out of the *pays d'en haut*, culminating in abandonment of western posts in the late 1690s.

10. Peterson, "People in Between," 59–60.

11. Bohaker, "*Nindoodemag,*" 47.

12. Ibid., 47–48.

13. The western Great Lakes fur trade in particular, Susan Sleeper-Smith has written, "encouraged intermarriage, both marriage in the manner of the country' as well as marriage sacramentally sanctioned by missionary priests." See Sleeper-Smith, "English Governance in the Great Lakes, 1760–1780," International Seminar on the History of the Atlantic World, working paper no. 97–17, summer 1997, 3. See Sleeper-Smith, *Indian Women and French Men;* Sylvia Van Kirk, *Many Tender Ties: Women in Fur Trade Society, 1679–1870* (Norman, Okla., 1983); Sylvia Van Kirk, "The Custom of the Country: An Examination of Fur Trade Practices," in Lewis H. Thomas, ed., *Essays on Western History* (Edmonton, 1976), 49–68; Sylvia Van Kirk, "The Role of Native Women in the Fur Trade Society of Western Canada, 1670–1830," *Frontiers* 7, 3 (1984): 76–80; Sylvia Van Kirk,

"'Women in Between': Indian Women in Fur Trade Society in Western Canada," in Robin Fisher and Kenneth Coates, eds., *Out of the Background: Readings on Canadian Native History* (Toronto, 1988), 150–66; Brown, *Strangers in Blood.*

14. Much of this essay is based on research in progress on the Langlades, the Ottawa, and the new métis communities of the Great Lakes. The genealogical and biographical data on the Langlade family that I employ throughout this essay has been taken from numerous sources. But my starting points include nineteenth-century memoirs left by members of Langlade's family and other Wisconsin antiquarians, which usually focus on Charles Langlade (Domitilde and Augustin's son), including the influential biographical sketch by his grandson, Augustin Grignon, "Recollections," printed in the *WHC* 3 (1857): 197–295; together with an account by Joseph Tassé in *WHC* 7 (1876): 123–88 (expanded in his chapter on Langlade in his book *Les Canadiens de l'Ouest* (Montreal, 1878), 1–103; and another short account in *WHC* 18 (1908): 130–32. See also Montgomery E. McIntosh, "Charles Langlade: First Settler of Wisconsin," *Parkman Club Papers* 8 (September 1896): 205–23, and Benjamin Sulte, "Origines de Langlade," manuscript, Wisconsin State Historical Society, Madison, Wis. By far, the best single contemporary source on Langlade's full and varied life is the short account given by Paul Trap, "Charles-Michel Mouet de Langlade," in *Dictionary of Canadian Biography* (hereafter *DCB;* www.biographi.ca/EN/index.html). Trap has also written an unpublished manuscript on the life of Charles Langlade that he has generously shared with me and has been an invaluable source of information and leads to resources: "Charles Langlade Manuscript" (undated). See also Michael A. McDonnell, "Charles-Michel Mouet de Langlade: Warrior, Soldier and Intercultural 'Window' on the Sixty Years' War for the Great Lakes," in David C. Skaggs and Larry Nelson, eds., *The Sixty Years' War for the Great Lakes, 1754–1816* (East Lansing: Mich., 2001), 79–104; Peterson, "Prelude to Red River," 57–59.

15. Peter L. Scanlon, *Prarie du Chien: French, British, American* (Menasha, Wis., 1937), 25–26; "Narrative of de Boucherville," no author, 1728–1729, *WHC* 17 (1906): 36–38; Trap, "Charles Langlade Manuscript," chap. 1, pp.18–19, 28–29, chap. 3, pp. 1, 4, 14; David A. Armour "Nissowaquet," in *DCB.* This alliance may have been a product of—at least as much as, if not more than, Augustin's fur trading ambitions—the Ottawa's desire to create a reciprocal social and economic tie that would bind the village even more closely with the nearby trading post of Michilimakinac. For examples of this practice, see Van Kirk, "Role of Native Women," 76, 77. Though patrilineal, Cadillac noted, the Ottawa "were not jealous of their wives . . . and they are absolute mistresses, so that the men do hardly anything without their consent"; "Relation of Sieur de Lamothe Cadillac," 359.

16. Trap, "Langlade," *DCB;* McDonnell, "Charles-Michel Mouet de Langlade," 79–104.

17. Felix M. Keesing, *The Menomini Indians of Wisconsin: A Study of Three Centuries of Cultural Contact and Change* (Madison, Wis., 1987), 71–72; Trap, "Charles Langlade Manuscript," chap. 2, p. 9. For the Langlades' numerous and intimate connections with other families, traders, and Native Americans at Michilimackinac, see "Register of Marriages in the Parish of Michilimackinac, 1725–1821," *WHC* 18 (1908): 469–513, and "Register of Baptisms of the Mission of St. Ignace de Michilimakinak, 1695–1821," *WHC* 19 (1910): 1–149.

18. See Trap, "Charles Langlade Manuscript," chap. 3; McDonnell, "Charles Langlade."

19. This episode has been discussed by numerous commentators, but the best and most recent account is Gregory Evans Down, *War under Heaven: Pontiac, the Indian Nations, and the British Empire* (Baltimore, 2002).

20. David A. Armour and Dirk Gringhuis, eds., *Attack at Michilimackinac* (Mackinaw Island State Park, Mich., 1971), 49–70; Trap, "Charles Langlade Manuscript," chap. 7.

21. Armour, "Nissowaquet"; "Journal of Lieutenant James Gorrell, 1761–1763," *WHC* 1 (1855): 36–48; Trap, "Charles Langlade Manuscript," chap. 7, pp. 7–21; Capt. Daniel Claus to Sir William Johnson, Montreal, August 6, 1763, *WHC* 18 (1908): 257.

22. The literature on cultural brokers, mediators, and boundaries is growing, but significantly, French and métis brokers do not figure large in most of these biographical accounts. See, for example, Margaret Connell Szasz, *Between Indian and White Worlds: The Cultural Broker* (Norman, Okla., 1994), and William S. Penn, ed., *As We Are Now: Mixblood Essays on Race and Identity* (Berkeley, 1997). For the most recent review of brokerage studies, see Eric Hinderaker, "Translation and Cultural Brokerage," in Philip J. Deloria and Neal Salisbury, eds., *A Companion to American Indian History* (Oxford, 2004), 357–76.

23. The relationship was noted by no less than Governor Duquesne of New France in 1752 when he praised Charles Langlade for his leading role in the attack on La Demoiselle and the rebellious Miami. Duquesne wrote to his superiors in Paris that Langlade should be rewarded, but since he was not officially in the service, and "has married a Savage woman" ("qu'il a Epousé une Sauvagesse"), that a pension of 2001 livres should be sufficient. Duquesne to the French minister, October 25, 1752, *WHC* 18 (1908): 128–31, original in MG 1, Fonds des Colonies, série C11A, Corresp. gén. Canada, C11A, vol. 98, fols. 27–28, Archives Coloniales, Paris.

24. See White, *Middle Ground;* for the Langlades' offer of service during Wayne's campaign, see J. G. Simcoe to R. G. England, August 12, 1794, and J. G. Simcoe to Alexander Mckee, August 13, [1794], in E. A. Cruikshank, ed., *The Correspondence of Lieut. Governor John Graves Simcoe, with Allied Documents Relating to His Administration of the Government of Upper Canada,* 5 vols. (Toronto, 1923–31), 2:367–68 and 5:103.

25. See Trap, "Langlade," *DCB;* McIntosh, "Charles Langlade," 205–23.

26. Father Gabriel Richard to Carrell, 1799, in J. A. Girardin, "Life and Times of Rev. Gabriel Richard," in *Michigan Pioneer Historical Collections,* 39 vols. (Lansing, Mich., 1874–1915), vol. 1 (1874), pp. 481–95; and Armour, "Nissowaquet."

27. For a recent interpretation along these lines, see Adelman and Aaron, "From Borderlands to Borders," esp. 839–41. The apparent end of this story also seems to confirm a historiographical trajectory cultivated among colonial American historians about racial attitudes, too—one that begins hopeful, and ends with the hardening of increasingly racialized atittudes in the late eighteenth century. See, for example, Jane Merritt, *At the Crossroads: Indians and Empires on a Mid-Atlantic Frontier, 1700–1763* (Chapel Hill, N.C., 2003).

28. See Trap, "Charles Langlade Manuscript," app. B, and Grignon, "Recollections," for nineteenth- and twentieth-century genealogies; "Register of Baptisms," 82. Trap was familiar with the Register, but like me, may have been puzzled at that date of the birth because he took his cue from Grignon, a direct descendant of Langlade and therefore an apparently authoritative figure. But by the time he wrote his memoir, Grignon may have been only too happy to have erased a more recent instance of mixed-marriage in the family. My thanks to Gwen Patterson for helping me to sort out this seeming anomaly and for guiding me through the local records.

29. Either Charles Langlade Jr. or possibly his father may have had another daughter, Mararette Okemauk, with a woman named Nonnoganah, who may also have been a slave of the Ottawa. Nonnoganah subsequently had as many as four husbands, all Ottawas except the last, who was a Menominee, and had children by them all (Grignon, "Recollections," 203).

30. Identifying métis communities outside the well-known Red River Colony region has been a difficult task. Hence the community at Penetanguishene, and the possibility of finding other related communities throughout the Great Lakes, is intriguing. See especially Reimer and Chartrand, "Documenting Historic Métis in Ontario," 567–607.

31. Grignon, "Recollections," 199.

32. See Trap, "Charles Langlade Manuscript," app. B, 1–7; Peterson, "Prelude to Red River," 58.

33. Osborne, "Migration of Voyageurs," 147–48. See Peterson, "Social Portrait," 55. See also Keith R. Widder, *Battle for the Soul: Metis Children Encounter Evangelical Protestants at Mackinaw Mission, 1823–1837* (Lansing, Mich., 1999), 3–4. Peterson notes that by the late 1820s, a population of ten thousand to fifteen thousand residents of métis communities south and west of Lakes Superior and Huron alone "seems a plausible estimate" (see Peterson, "Many Roads to Red River," 63). For the continued persistence of the idea that the métis peoples disappeared from this area, see R. David Edmunds, "'Unacquainted with the Laws of the Civilized World': American Attitudes toward the Métis Communities in the Old Northwest," in Jacqueline Peterson and Jennifer S. H. Brown, eds., *The New Peoples: Being and Becoming Métis in North America* (Winnipeg, 1985), 185–94. For a more recent look at the importance of métis communities more generally, see Jennifer Brown and Theresa Schenck's review of recent literature on métis peoples in "Métis, Mestizo, and Mixed-Blood," in *Companion to Indian History,* 323–38. Mixed-bloods were important enough to the Ottawa that they secured specific provisions for their welfare in the 1836 treaty in which they ceded their lands (see Charles J. Kappler, ed., *Indian Affairs: Laws and Treaties,* vol. 2, *Treaties* (Washington, D.C., 1904), 450–56).

34. See Peterson, "Many Roads to Red River," 55.

35. On this point, see McClurken, "Augustin Hamlin," esp. 106–8.

36. Ibid., 108; "Letter of Mr. Slater, dated Ottawa Colony, Richland, June 10, 1839," *Baptist Missionary,* (1836–49), September 1839, 225; Tanner, *Atlas,* 130, 166, 175. See also Blackbird, *History of the Ottawa and Chippewa Indians,* chap. 12. The Ottawa and other tribes continued to receive annual presents from British posts on Lake Huron until at least 1837, when the British made the presents

contingent on residency within British North America. The formal annual trips to Drummond Island, and then Penetanguishene after the British move there, almost certainly kept the Ottawa in crucial touch with the French and métis populations there, including the Langlades. Tanner, *Atlas*, 126, 130, 132–33. On land loss, see "Treaty with the Ottawa, etc., 1836," in Kappler, *Indian Affairs*, 2:450–56. Significantly, article 6 of the Treaty of 1836 set aside $150,000 for "half-breeds," and a roll dating from September 4, 1836 identifies 584 individuals, with their names, ages, residences, fractions of blood, and tribes. See James L. Hansen, "'Half-Breed' Rolls and Fur Trade Families in the Great Lakes Region: An Introduction and Bibliography," in Brown, Eccles, and Heldman, *Fur Trade Revisited*, 165.

37. Tanner, *Atlas*, 12, 96, 100, 175–79.

38. Doreen Massey, *For Space* (London, 2005), 4, 5; Ann Laura Stoler, "Intimidations of Empire: Predicaments of the Tactile and Unseen," in Stoler, ed., *Haunted by Empire: Geographies of Intimacy in North American History* (Durham, N.C., 2006), 4. See also Ballantyne and Burton, *Bodies in Contact*, 6; Adelman and Aaron, "From Borderlands to Borders," 819.

39. Massey, *For Space*, 13.

40. Catherine Hall, "Commentary," in Stoler, *Haunted by Empire*, 458–59. See also Stoler, "Intimidations of Empire," 3–4.

41. Many questions, of course, remain to be answered. And there do seem to have been differences across the borders. For example, see Peterson's introduction to "People in Between," wherein she notes an attempt in Green Bay by new American settlers to force older French and Metis settlers to solemnize their marriages with Native Americans. See also Susan Sleeper-Smith, "'[A]n Unpleasant Transaction on This Frontier': Challenging Female Autonomy and Authority at Michilimackinac," *Journal of the Early Republic* 25 (Fall 2005): 417–43; and Virginia Glenn Crane, "History and Family Values, a Good Wife's Take: Mary Elizabeth Meade Grignon of Kaukauna, 1837–1898," *Wisconsin Magazine of History* 80, 3 (Spring 1997): 179–200. And the meaning of these mixed marriages through time has to be investigated further. On this point, see Sylvia Van Kirk, "From 'Marrying-In' to 'Marrying-Out': Changing Patterns of Aboriginal/Non-Aboriginal Marriage in Colonial Canada," *Frontiers* 23, 3 (2002): 1–11. McClurken, in "Augustin Hamlin," 108, suggests that though racial tensions may have risen in Michigan during the peak white settlement period in the middle decades of the nineteenth century, the experience of métis Augustin Hamlin suggest that racial boundaries in the region may again have become permeable after this period.

42. On these points, see the introduction to this volume.

43. See the introduction to this volume.

44. Stoler, "Intimidations of Empire," 3. For studies of the "invisible" poor of New England, see "On Events and Nonevents: 'Vanishing' Indians in Nineteenth-Century New England," in Sergei Kan and Pauline Turner Strong, eds., *Native Peoples of North America: Cultures, Histories, and Representations*, (Lincoln, Neb., 2005), and "'They Are so Frequently Shifting Their Place of Residence': Land and the Construction of Social Place of Indians in Colonial Massachusetts," in Rick Halpern and M. J. Daunton, eds., *Empire and Others: British Encounter with Indigenous Peoples, 1600–1850* (London, 1999).

KERRY WYNN

8 "Miss Indian Territory" and "Mr. Oklahoma Territory"

MARRIAGE, SETTLEMENT, AND CITIZENSHIP
IN THE CHEROKEE NATION AND THE
UNITED STATES

When Oklahoma became a U.S. state in 1907, organizers of the first Oklahoma statehood day celebration at the new state capital planned a series of extravagant events to entertain and reward the men and women who had lobbied for statehood. Perhaps the most striking event took place immediately after the reading of the declaration of statehood, when the two territories joined in the new state, Indian Territory and Oklahoma Territory, were united as one political entity. Once the proclamation had been read, "Mr. Oklahoma Territory," an American businessman, took the stage and proposed marriage to "Miss Indian Territory," portrayed by Anna Bennett, a citizen of the Cherokee Nation. Newspapers reporting on statehood day events recorded an elaborate proposal and acceptance, culminating in a marriage ceremony officiated by a Christian minister. The centrality of the mock wedding on statehood day reflects the importance of affective relationships to the imagination of territorial acquisition, settlement, and the U.S. empire. Indian Territory was the domain of sovereign American Indian nations—nations that consistently resisted incorporation into the United States. In the face of competing claims to territorial sovereignty, the spectacle of the statehood day wedding cast the union of the two territories as voluntary and even desired by Indian Territory nations themselves.

The focus of this essay on marriage is not intended to reinstate conjugality as the fundamental domain of intimacy, for as several scholars in this collection note, "the intimate" includes myriad forms of affection and violence. Marriage served as one of many intimate relations constituting an affective terrain of negotiation between Indian Territory nations and the United States, but the visibility of its figurative and legal forms in the debates between these nations indicates the utility of marriage for representing competing claims to sovereignty. The wedding of "Miss Indian Territory" and "Mr. Oklahoma Territory" drew on a prolonged debate over marriage that threaded through negotiations between the nations of Indian Territory and the United States. Debates about marriage assumed great significance for defining the borders of nations, attributing meaning to individual migration, and narrating the relationship of nations to each other. If, as Tony Ballantyne and Antoinette Burton write (in the introduction), we conceive of "empire as the ground of consistently territorialized mobility," we can delineate the ways competing visions and embodiments of Indian Territory served as claims to render heterogeneous constructions of space untenable.

This essay focuses on the relationship between the United States and the Cherokee Nation, one of the five nations governing parts of Indian Territory, in order to understand the ways individuals mobilized marriage for both colonialist and anticolonialist purposes. Many Cherokees used marriage to defend their sovereign right to control Cherokee population and resources by restricting American immigration to and citizenship in the Cherokee Nation. In the Cherokee Nation, as well as in the United States, legislation and custom linked marriage, citizenship, and property, so that marriage served as both a powerful regulatory tool and a persuasive language. Throughout the late nineteenth and early twentieth centuries, Cherokees and Americans fought to locate marriages of Cherokee women and American men in paradigms of Cherokee sovereignty and "civilization" or American naturalization of colonial invasion.

This specific debate regarding marriage is embedded in both the affective basis of empire and its particular manifestations in the history of U.S. imperialism. The image of "Miss Indian Territory" points to the common imperial deployment of female figures to represent indigenous lands, found in the context of European travel narratives, political debates over the acquisition of territory, and legitimizing narratives of conquest.[1] The gender ideologies upholding these representations also fostered the creation of legal categories of race in marriage legislation crafted by colonial powers seeking to create a colonial order, and by American legislators drafting domestic policies that established the power of white men.[2] In the United States at the turn of the twentieth century, politicians used images of marriage to articulate a subordinate relationship for proposed colonies and to communicate the perceived danger of extending the U.S. empire into territories where white Americans defined the indigenous population as nonwhite.[3] The American celebration of a contemporary marriage between a white American man and an American Indian woman necessitates contextualization in the changing discourse of U.S. imperialism, a discourse that included not only Americans but also the citizens of American Indian nations.

An examination of the use of marriage to protect or subvert American Indian sovereignty at the turn of the twentieth century refocuses attention on U.S. colonialism on the North American continent contemporaneous with the U.S. search for overseas empire. Scholars of U.S. imperialism have questioned artificial distinctions between national culture and the imperial project, connected conquest overseas to colonization on the North American continent, and interrogated the multiple antecedents of U.S. imperial policy in racial segregation and immigration policy.[4] However, in examinations of U.S. empire, the continuing twentieth-century struggle of American Indian nations to protect their sovereignty against the U.S. government is often ignored in the discussion. Thus, this essay addresses the substantial literature on American Indian sovereignty and continuing struggles against the effects of colonialism on American Indian nations and institutions in the twentieth century, bringing these topics to bear on the narratives of empire told about the United States.[5] If scholarship in American Indian history is divorced from current scholarship on American empire, we risk perpetuating the very myth the U.S. government sought to create—the myth of disappearing nations.

In order to understand the full importance of the marriage of "Miss Indian Territory" and "Mr. Oklahoma Territory" for the foundations of the U.S. empire, we must view the ceremony in light of the history of interaction between the nations of Indian Territory and the United States. Indian Territory was ruled by five sovereign American Indian nations—the Cherokee, Choctaw, Chickasaw, Creek, and Seminole nations—often referred to at the time as the "Five Civilized Tribes." These nations had been forcibly relocated from the Southeast in the 1830s, in spite of the U.S. Supreme Court's affirmation of their sovereignty as a status predating the founding of the United States, and a quality that could not be taken from them without explicit consent. From the 1830s to 1907, citizens of the Five Tribes and Americans crossed the boundaries between their nations for numerous reasons—to engage in trade, seek education and adventure, secure an emotional attachment, and conduct diplomacy. As individuals traveled and settled, they created multiple imaginary geographies, choosing to configure their environments as part of a particular nation or outside of the operation of laws. In the late nineteenth century, as the United States increasingly exerted its influence in Indian Territory, Americans began to settle illegally there in large numbers. In the early years of the twentieth century, the United States pressured the Five Tribes into signing treaties that provided for the allotment of their communally held lands, the dissolution of their sovereign governments, and the integration of their citizens into the United States.

Americans sought to cast these developments as natural and inevitable, but the prolonged conflict between the nations of Indian Territory and the United States ensured the instability of that narrative. The very existence of American Indian control over thirty-one thousand square miles of land, located in the middle of the continent in the late nineteenth century, disrupted the U.S. narrative of continental expansion. This narrative cast "the colonization of the Great West" as a part of the American past, a completed task that gave the United States a unique history and national character.[6] The symbolic deemphasis and attempted erasure of American Indian sovereignty through a language of marriage served the purpose of maintaining the core fiction of American empire in the West as linear and complete. The Cherokee use of marriage, however, demanded attention to the sovereignty American legislators sought to erase. Cherokees asserted their right to govern throughout this period, and in the era after Oklahoma statehood, as elite Cherokees moved to establish themselves as the foundation for the new state, distinct Cherokee communities persisted and eventually fostered the reestablishment of a full Cherokee national government in the middle of the twentieth century.

In the late nineteenth century, as illegal settlement overshadowed fluid mobility across boundaries, concern for territorial integrity invested discourses on marriage with new meaning. The land tenure system of the Cherokee Nation differed markedly from that of the United States. As the United States colonized territory throughout the western portions of North America, surveyors established grids for American settlement, dividing land into individual parcels—town sites and rural lots for quick sale and integration into the imagination of the American nation. In the Cherokee Nation, citizens owned the land collectively. While individuals claimed the right to improvements—such as barns, houses, and crops—

they placed on the land, they did not hold title to the land itself. Land could only be sold by the nation, and the benefits of sale were distributed to all of its members. The Cherokee government guarded its membership to control its own population and to limit access to this communal property. The clash between Cherokee and American systems of land tenure intensified in the late nineteenth century, as the United States began its allotment program. To encourage the assimilation of American Indian lands and populations into the United States, federal officials followed a policy of dividing the communally held lands of American Indian nations into individual parcels to be distributed to members of those nations. Cherokees and many other American Indian groups resisted allotment, as it struck at the heart of beliefs about communal land tenure and often led to the alienation of tribal property.

Throughout the nineteenth century, Cherokee legislators used marriage regulations as a means to define their national population. Community recognition of intimate relationships had long been a means to control integration into Cherokee society, which was composed of the members of seven matrilineal clans. Women played an essential role in the creation and structure of Cherokee society, as they passed their clan affiliation to children. Through intimate relationships, Cherokee women gave outsiders (including Africans, Europeans, and American Indians of other tribes) a place in Cherokee society, and the children of Cherokee women and non-Cherokee men became members of clans, considered fully Cherokee by other tribal members.[7] With the Cherokee Constitution of 1827, Cherokee legislators made citizenship the official category of belonging to the nation, and included the children of both Cherokee men and women.

In subsequent years, restrictions placed on citizenship and marriage in the Cherokee Nation, as in many other indigenous nations, reflected both the gendered foundations of Cherokee clans and the legacy of chattel slavery and racism. Cherokee legislators passed laws against the marriage of Cherokees to slaves or free black persons, exempting those men and women with both African and Cherokee ancestors, who were entitled to Cherokee citizenship.[8] Laws regulating marriage in the Cherokee Nation reinforced conceptions of unions between white men and Cherokee women as a normative model.[9] Marriage regulations specifically required white men to meet increasing requirements throughout the nineteenth century, including paying a fee, obtaining a license, and swearing an oath of loyalty to the Cherokee Nation.[10] The gender-specific structure of the legislation may have arisen from the greater frequency with which American men married into the Cherokee Nation in comparison to American women, but it pointed to several specific domestic and international concerns that marriage legislation addressed. Cherokee women, as the keepers of clans, had the power to integrate new members in ways Cherokee men did not. On the other hand, white men were accorded the right to vote in the Cherokee Nation, a privilege women (Cherokee or American) did not share. Taking into account the benefits men could attain on their citizenship and the desire to prevent the alienation of Cherokee resources, legally documenting the status of American males who became citizens of the Cherokee Nation was particularly important.

In keeping with both the status of the Cherokee Nation as a sovereign entity and the long Cherokee history of women's importance to the structure of society, Cherokee women expected to maintain their citizenship on marriage to an outsider, regardless of their husbands' decisions to join the Cherokee Nation or remain U.S. citizens. The movement of American men into the Cherokee Nation alone did not impart to them rights to property, rights that citizens enjoyed. Cherokee women's citizenship not only articulated their belonging to the Nation but also provided protection of their personal property. For example, in 1883, Mrs. Wade, a Cherokee woman, asked Judge L. W. Shirley, of Tahlequah, to recover property from her ex-husband. The woman's citizenship and her husband's refusal to obtain Cherokee citizenship played a large role in her plea to Shirley to correct a miscarriage of justice. Wade wrote, "He has never married in accordance with the laws of the Cherokee Nation and has never taken the oath of allegiance to the Cherokee Government. He is therefore, for all intents and purposes, an intruder." She asked that Shirley not allow her husband to hold any of her property "until he proves that he is a citizen of the Cherokee Nation and that he has any just claim to any property I now hold."[11] Wade cast herself as an insider who needed protection from an outsider who had no right to lay claims to her property. Her husband's settlement in the territory was not a protection of his rights, as he failed to acquiesce to the sovereign government of the Cherokee Nation. By labeling her husband an "intruder," the term used for illegal squatters in the Cherokee Nation, Wade cast even his movement into the Nation as suspect.

In the United States, as Katherine Ellinghaus notes (chapter 10 here), politicians and reformers infused debates on marriage policy for U.S. citizens and American Indians with a colonialist discourse centered on concepts of "civilization." At the turn of the twentieth century, many U.S. states prohibited marriage between citizens defined as white and those defined as nonwhite, categories that varied by state and region, and in a dozen states included American Indians as nonwhite.[12] In national venues, however, self-proclaimed reformers often affirmed marriages between European Americans and American Indians to encourage the integration of the latter into the American body politic. This point of view met with significant opposition from Americans who envisioned a stigmatized category of "mixed-breeds," imagined to be dangerous to indigenous nations and the United States. Although divided on their position regarding intermarriage, both supported the policy of claiming American Indian lands for the United States, and used a discourse of racialization to do so. Ellinghaus explores the connections and dissonances between assimilationist paradigms in the United States and Australia, noting the importance of tribal landholding to U.S. policy. Debates on assimilationist marriage legislation also included the voices of citizens of American Indian nations, such as those individuals in the Cherokee Nation who protested the laws that assimilationists lauded.

The U.S. discussion of marriage between Cherokees and Americans assumed different contours from debate on other regions and tribes due to the visibility in the states of elite Cherokee women. The image of these women—English-language-educated, expensively attired, many with both Cherokee and white American ancestors—had long been associated with the development of the Cherokee state, particularly in the realm of education. As the American government allotted the lands of American Indian tribes directly west of the Five Nations and sold "surplus" lands to Americans in order to create Oklahoma Territory for U.S. citizens, some Cherokees and others of the Five Tribes who sought to defend their sovereignty in the American public sphere asserted fundamental similarities with elite white Americans. Images and descriptions of Cherokee women became important to this discourse, in part because the Cherokee Female Seminary, a boarding school established by the Cherokee national government in 1851 on the model of Mount Holyoke, could easily be cast as similar to schools for elite women in the United States. The Female Seminary drew great criticism within the Cherokee Nation from Cherokees who disapproved of the solely English education offered there and admissions policies and tuition that limited students to those among the economic upper class.[13] However, those Cherokees most likely to communicate frequently with Americans in positions of political and economic power were of the upper class, and as discussions of sovereignty in Indian Territory appeared more frequently in an American context, the image of the refined Cherokee woman provided a symbol with which to argue against the American assertion of the cultural superiority of the United States.

In 1888, a U.S. marriage bill ignited a protest in Indian Territory newspapers that demonstrated the connection between images of refined Cherokee womanhood and the defense of the sovereignty of the Cherokee Nation. This bill originally proposed to prevent white men married to American Indian women from becoming tribal citizens and sharing in tribal assets, to make American Indian women married to U.S. citizens into citizens of the United States, and to strip American Indian women of their tribal membership. The categorization of the husbands as "white men" in some cases and "citizens" in others existed in the wording of the original bill. The bill was later amended to guarantee the retention of women's tribal citizenship and to exempt the Five Tribes. The marriage bill ignited controversy in the Cherokee Nation on the part of those who rejected the inclusion of the Cherokee Nation in its provisions and, after their exemption, those who suspected that the precedent it would set might be used against the Cherokee Nation in the future. The application of the bill to the Cherokee Nation would disenfranchise intermarried white citizens of the Cherokee Nation, prevent them from sharing in tribal land, and—more important for many who wrote to Indian Territory newspapers protesting the bill—strip the indigenous citizenship rights from the significant numbers of women of the Five Tribes who married U.S. citizens. As a sovereign entity, the Cherokee Nation assumed the right to determine its own population, and those who protested the bill defended the Cherokee Nation as sovereign territory, in opposition to U.S. assumptions.

Protests in Indian Territory newspapers noted the implications of the marriage bill with regard to sovereignty and land tenure, placing the proposed legislation in the context of the U.S. desire to colonize Cherokee land. With U.S. threats to citizens and territory at the fore, contributors to the Cherokee Nation newspaper, the *Cherokee Advocate,* cast arguments against the bill as a defense of Cherokee womanhood and Cherokee women's rights against the ignorance of American officials. Cherokees held Henry Dawes, the chairman of the Senate Committee on Indian Affairs, personally responsible for the bill, so much of the commentary focused on Dawes and reminded readers of his desire to divide commonly held American Indian lands into individual parcels, making them more susceptible to sale outside of the tribes and dramatically decreasing the amount of land held by American Indian nations. The marriage bill was referred to in Congress and the press as the "Squaw man" bill, a derogatory reference to American men who married American Indian women. Contributors to the *Advocate* reacted violently against the characterization of Cherokee women as squaws, a term that cast American Indian women as drudges, and instead posited Cherokee women as the source of civilization.[14]

Submissions to the *Cherokee Advocate* that characterized the marriage bill as a threat to Cherokee sovereignty warned of American desires to allot the lands of the Cherokee Nation, a policy that undermined the character of Cherokee land tenure and governance. One writer, who placed the bill in the context of robbing women of their rights, went on to accuse Dawes of encouraging "land grabbers" and viewed the marriage bill as an attempt to attack the sovereignty of the Cherokee Nation.[15] Another writer turned the discourse of civilization against Senator Dawes, arguing that his proposal to "sever the Nation" with the marriage bill revealed Dawes's nature as "a pure savage," and warned Cherokees that "the battle is now at hand which will require the Nations of this Territory to put forth their utmost strength."[16] A Cherokee woman wrote to the newspaper of the hypocrisy at the heart of the marriage bill, which was portrayed by Americans as protecting American Indian tribal assets but struck at the heart of national sovereignty by dividing American Indian populations: "Their plan is that the Indians should entirely run out. In other words, they want our land, and if they succeed in getting it they would care little or nothing of what becomes of us."[17] Cherokees pierced the facade of the "reformist" nature of the legislation, noting its desire to separate individuals from the societies they and their spouses had chosen to live within.

Defenses of Cherokee womanhood also filled the pages of the *Advocate* in the immediate aftermath of the bill's proposal, as contributors brought together responses to Dawes and concerns about the future of Cherokee sovereignty. One lengthy article reminded Dawes that Cherokee women who married whites would "compare favorably, in point of education and good manners, with his own wife and daughters," and ended with a blessing for Cherokee women, "the noble women of this Nation, who have done much assisting in educating its people. They have helped prepare them to bravely and successfully resist attacks on their rights, property, and nation."[18] Noting the importance of Cherokee women in preparing Cherokees to defend their rights and property recalled attention to the preservation of Cherokee sovereignty. This tied Cherokee women's rights to the defense of the nation and its territory, a battle that appeared even more critical in the face of the ignorance of legislators and American citizens about Indian Territory and the treaties the Five Tribes had negotiated with the United States. The editor of the *Advocate* characterized Dawes's influence over other senators as "the blind leading the blind," and voiced the frustration of many Cherokees when he reprinted errors of fact reported by the St. Louis *Globe-Democrat*, asking, "When the Chairman of the Senate Committee and the foremost of newspapers don't know what they are talking about how will other Senators and the mass of the people get posted unless our authorities people and delegates spend a great deal of time and patience informing those who ought to know?"[19]

What many Cherokees believed legislators and prominent Americans "ought to know" was the "civilized" state of the Cherokee Nation. Since the early nineteenth century, Americans had referred to the Cherokees, Choctaws, Chickasaws, Creeks, and Seminoles as the "Five Civilized Tribes," noting the adoption of Christianity, slavery, and the English language by some Cherokees. This discourse of civilization was always a double-edged sword, usable by American Indian nations or the United States, but unable to be controlled by either. While Cherokees asserted "civilization" in the name of sovereignty, Americans used the same term to argue for Cherokees' integration into the United States. Rather than using images of elite Cherokee women to defend Cherokee sovereignty, Americans who sought Indian Territory land proposed these women as marriage partners for white American men, bringing with them land, stipends, and the sexual intimacy implied by the marriage contract.

The American discourse on the Cherokee Nation with regard to marriage often focused on the European ancestry of many elite Cherokee women. On the topic of Cherokee politics and communal landholding, American politicians and businessmen searching for arguments to support allotment accused unscrupulous "half-breeds" and "mixed-bloods" of plundering the resources of the Cherokee Nation.[20] Discussions of Cherokee women with Cherokee and white ancestors, however, often exoticized the women because of their ancestry. The same was true for American descriptions of women from all of the Five Tribes. For example, an 1897 report on the Five Tribes printed in the *Kansas City Star* opined, "The admixture of white and Indian blood in the women gives them a grace and beauty that is surprising."[21] The report went on to describe in detail "Indian characteristics" and how women's appearances changed as "the Indian blood becomes more and more attenuated."[22] In detailing a visit to a theater in Indian Territory, the author exclaimed, "Women predominated—and such women."[23] The discourse on marriage in the United States incorporated these depictions and conflated characterizations of race, class, and behavior.

In the late nineteenth century, American stories of marriage to Indian Territory women as a way to wealth became increasingly popular. American newspapers featured stories that asserted that women of the

Five Tribes sought white American husbands, never failing to mention the land that the women held, which their husbands would be able to access. Whether the articles provided laudatory or derogatory portrayals of the women involved, they still advertised the taking of a wife from the Five Tribes as a way to gain land and fortune for American men. For example, an October 1900 article in the *Chicago Daily Tribune* included photographs of women from the Cherokee, Chickasaw, and Choctaw Nations and opined on the beneficial and denigrating effects intermarriage had brought to the nations. Casting the women of the Five Tribes as "highly civilized" yet with "vile tempers," the author emphasized the women's "inborn desire to marry palefaces," and clearly gave the impression that an attractive white man could easily find a landed wife.[24] The same newspaper ran an article in 1907 titled "Looking for Indian Wife? Chickasaw Maidens, with Plenty of Land, Say They Want White Men for Husbands."[25] The marketing of Indian Territory women by booster magazines and mainstream American periodicals mobilized the imagery of "the princess" and "the squaw," twinned images of American Indian women in American folklore described by Rayna Green.[26] Women of the Five Tribes were portrayed in American newspapers as beautiful and desirable, or volatile and undesirable, but both sets of images were used by Americans to support the colonial project.

The story of women of the Five Tribes seeking husbands and imparting land rights through marriage provided a convenient narrative for Americans seeking to explain the continuing conquest of Indian Territory. This narrative shifted the story of colonization from the international negotiations between governments and a wave of American intruders on sovereign foreign lands to the tale of land willingly given from wife to husband. Illegal settlers in Indian Territory vastly outnumbered intermarried citizens who came from the United States. In their refocusing of the narrative to the point of distorting the character of American movement to Indian Territory, the stories of Five Tribes women inviting white men into the territory are reminiscent of the symbolic move made by Buffalo Bill's Wild West and other narratives of the American frontier story that "turned conquerors into victims."[27] Historian Richard White has described the story of colonization offered by Buffalo Bill and others at the turn of the century as "an account of Indian aggression and white defense" that validated U.S. conquest of American Indian nations as the story of "valiant white victims overpowered by numerous savage assailants."[28] Stories of violence and marriage both cast Americans as simply responding to the actions of American Indians, whose actions invited revenge or intimacy. At the turn of the twentieth century, for a U.S.

audience, the narrative of violence characterized the past, and marriage presented the current incarnation of American expansion.

Citizens of Indian Territory nations voiced exasperation with the narratives of wholesale intermarriage, and publications from Indian Territory asserted repeatedly that women of the Five Tribes were not interested in men who only cared for their financial resources. Cherokees applauded stories that debunked the American marital narrative line. In 1901, the *Tahlequah Arrow* carried two pieces from other newspapers that focused on the scheme of two Seminole women who had scammed men by promising a Seminole wife to every man who sent a request and included a $5 payment. The *Dallas News* congratulated these women for cheating "suckers . . . under the impression that they could cheat a female Lo out of her money and probably then go back among the whites to spend it."[29] Men who appeared to be searching solely for land or money and dismissing the intelligence or desirability of Indian Territory women gained the ire of the Cherokee Nation as well. While they opened the door to men who married into the Cherokee Nation and participated in its social life, the Cherokee government repeatedly requested the removal of "intruders" who lived in the Cherokee Nation without the permission of the government, including those who had relationships with Cherokee women other than marriages legally contracted in the Cherokee Nation.

Stories of women of the Five Tribes seeking white American husbands reveal the political pitfalls of the way the upper classes of the Cherokee Nation articulated their vision of citizenship and sovereignty. The image of the elite Cherokee woman was captured and deployed in two ways that damaged the unity of the Cherokee Nation in this period. First, the use of the image in the service of proving that Cherokees and other members of the Five Tribes had created governments and societies not only equal to but also similar to the United States limited the vision of the exemplary Cherokee citizen that appeared to the American public. The defense of sovereignty through elite images that was to liberate Cherokees from American racism merely shifted the burden of racism and colonialism to Cherokees with more adherence to Cherokee traditions or with fewer economic resources. Second, the American insinuation that scores of Cherokee women were available for marriage to American men, bringing with them dowries of land and government payments, twisted a previously Cherokee icon into an American tool for usurping the power of the Cherokee Nation.

The implications of the narrative line provided by this marriage imagery allowed it to overshadow other intimate connections between Cherokees and Americans at key moments. Innumerable intimate relations tied Cherokees and Americans in unique ways. Cherokee citizens also demonstrated their connection to nation and land through genealogies, and, as in the cases Christine Skwiot describes in Hawai'i (chapter 9 here), white Americans attempted to insert themselves in these genealogies to gain citizenship or symbolic power. Cherokee families shared bonds of intimacy that discounted national boundaries, similar to the networks of the Langlade family Michael McDonnell recounts (chapter 7 here). Marriage, however, provided the most spectacular representation of the connections between mobile subjects.

The 1907 statehood celebration at the Oklahoma state capital in Guthrie played on the American image of an elite Cherokee woman as the wife for a white American man and reified the division of tribal citizens through its use of the mock wedding. Organizers played on the elite status and Anglo-Cherokee background of Anna Bennett to shore up the power relations in the new state. By symbolically uniting a white man and a Cherokee woman in a mock wedding, organizers of statehood day provided a subtle way of articulating the relationship they hoped the constituencies of the new state would have. The metaphor of marriage was malleable, and more palatable certainly to members of the Five Tribes than other metaphors of conquering and integration. Still, the casting of Indian Territory as the female partner symbolized a lower status being offered to Indian Territory in the joining of the two territories into one state. The strategic erasure of the male heads of state of the Five Tribes, as well as the privileging of marriage partners and a Christian ceremony, presaged the splitting of the Cherokee population after statehood. While elite Cherokees participated in the planning and government of the new state, Cherokees with fewer economic resources and more Cherokee ancestors became subject to the guardianship of the American federal government, and faced the alienation of their lands and homes.

The statehood day imagery of marriage between a white American man and a Cherokee woman drew on the stories of Indian Territory women seeking white husbands but turned those tales into a grand narrative to imagine the creation of the new state. According to the model, as the property of American women passed to their husbands on their marriage, so would the land of Indian Territory pass to the new state and the American government. The conjugal story of an American Indian woman and white American man turned the attention away from the boosters, railroad officials, corporations, and profit-seekers who had already attempted to breach the boundaries of Indian Territory and would now flood the area, seeking to swindle individual parcels from members of the Five Tribes who had resisted allotment in the first place. In this narrative, the nationalizing and gendering of the wedding participants was necessary to achieve the simultaneous recognition and erasure of indigenous sovereignty, as it was necessary to communicating the power relationships that the organizers expected to see in the new state.

The mock wedding between "Miss Indian Territory" and "Mr. Oklahoma Territory" followed the declaration of statehood, when C. G. Jones, an Oklahoma City businessman and politician, proposed marriage to Anna Trainor Bennett, a descendant of prominent Cherokees and Massachusetts blue bloods, a graduate of elite Indian Territory schools, and the wife of an American physician, newspaper owner, and U.S. marshal. A reporter for the *Oklahoma State Capital* provided an account of the wedding that included a series of elaborate speeches, characterizing the Oklahoma and Indian Territories as individuals who embodied particular attributes and experiences. According to the *State Capital*, "Mr. Oklahoma Territory" was the assertive partner, confessing that he had "grown tired of being alone, though he was fully capable of taking care of himself."[30] Jones described Oklahoma as a youthful and commanding man, and Indian Territory as a spinster, yearning for a permanent and "harmonious union."[31] Dismissing the political claims of Indian Territory through references to spinsterhood, Jones used the imagery of marriage and the subsuming of the wife's political identity into the husband's to mirror the dynamic of earlier tales of U.S.-Cherokee marriage relations, assuming the alienation of land through supposedly consensual means.

Before the minister could perform the mock wedding, it was up to "Miss Indian Territory" to accept Jones's proposal. While the "bride" waited offstage, William A. Durant, a Choctaw politician who had served as the sergeant-at-arms for the state constitutional convention, accepted the proposal. Painting the principal chiefs of the Five Tribes out of the picture, the organizers had turned to this younger man who had participated in the formation of the new state. Durant's portrayal of Indian Territory deemphasized the sovereign governments of Indian Territory, by characterizing "Miss Indian Territory" as "a political orphan, tutored by federal office holders, and controlled by an indifferent guardian residing 1,000 miles from her habitation."[32] This caricature symbolically erased the sovereign control the Five Tribes exercised in Indian Territory and insinuated that Indian Territory needed Oklahoma Territory in order to secure a closer source of support and guidance. "Mr. Oklahoma Territory" would not go unrewarded, however, as he gained a natural and tragic beauty—"a face intended by nature to give back only the warm smiles of God's pure sunshine," "a beauteous maiden," "the last descendant of the proudest race that ever trod foot on American soil; a race whose sons have never bowed their neck to the feet of an oppressor; the original occupants of the American continent."[33] Positioning "Miss Indian Territory" as the "last descendant" romanticized the dismantling of the governments of the Five Tribes and completely ignored the continued existence of indigenous nations throughout the United States.

In the bonds of matrimony, "Miss Indian Territory" was to be forever subsumed within the identity of her husband. The portrayal of marriage that appeared in the pages of the *State Capital* was certainly an American depiction, with power to grant citizenship and make decisions granted to the husband, who was "entrusted the care of this princely estate" to be managed for the good of the state. The majority of the mock wedding had been conducted entirely by men. "Miss Indian Territory" was only needed to give her consent to the union. Wearing the latest in Western fashion, a lavender dress made for her in Kansas City and an elaborate hat, Anna Bennett stepped to the fore to become (with "Mr. Oklahoma Territory") the symbol of the new state.

By using Bennett to represent Indian Territory, the organizers symbolically erased the participation and political agendas of the men and women who had fought against statehood and for American Indian nations' sovereign control over the land of Indian Territory. Although Cherokees had long used marriage to assert the sovereignty of their nation, the wedding on statehood day served the erasure of that sovereignty. The portrayal of sovereign nations as individuals entering into a marriage contract gestured to the goal of U.S. policy toward American Indians—to weaken American Indian nations by assimilating individuals into the United States. The mock wedding, intended to symbolize the union of the two territories, demonstrated the integration of those in agreement about statehood and the symbolic erasure of others who protested the formation of the new state and the blow it dealt to American Indian sovereignty.

As the representation of Oklahoma's statehood, the mock wedding privileged a narrative intended to erase American responsibility for violating the sovereignty of the Cherokee Nation and the other nations of the Five Tribes. Orchestrating the "deterritorialization and subsequent reterritorialization," as Ballantyne and Burton put it (in the introduction), of Indian Territory through embodied representatives, the wedding modeled a consensual transfer of territory, excusing illegal American settlement and graft through affective ties. This conception of history and space supported an American narrative of expansion and settlement that simultaneously consolidated and elided the existence of the U.S. empire.

The malleability of the marriage metaphor ultimately ensured that the wedding of "Miss Indian Territory" and "Mr. Oklahoma Territory" could be reworked in many forms. In subsequent decades, reenactments of the mock wedding served as the final scenes in multiple pageants of Oklahoma history performed by schools and chambers of commerce, and at numerous anniversaries of statehood day. The wedding has been portrayed variously as the culmination of a centuries-long history of American Indian, Spanish, and U.S. settlement in Oklahoma, a story of the unique place Oklahoma holds in the American nation, and a celebration of Oklahoma's multicultural origins. At the time of the ceremony, as well, the wedding must have held multiple meanings for participants and the audience, some of whom could interpret the ceremony in the light of partnership, rather than domination. This could be the case for the citizens of Indian Territory nations who participated in the ceremony, along with others who founded the Oklahoma state government and society, and worked to empower an American Indian political presence in the new state.

The celebratory expression of the joining of the territories as marriage, however, ultimately distracted attention from what one author has called the "orgy of exploitation" that followed Oklahoma's entrance into statehood, as corrupt grafters swindled members of the Five Tribes out of their allotted lands.[34] In spite of its changing meanings, the origins of the wedding of "Miss Indian Territory" and "Mr. Oklahoma Territory" are directly rooted in this history of illegal American commandeering of American Indian lands. For decades, Cherokees sought to use marriage to distinguish between legal and illegal American immigration and to assert their rights as a nation sovereign and separate from the United States. Americans twisted that discourse into something useful to the obscuring narrative of U.S. imperialism—the familiar portrayal of American colonization as justified and even invited. Even after the alienation of Cherokee land, however, the sovereign status of the Cherokee Nation remained. While sovereignty could be obfuscated by the imagery of statehood, and had to be continually asserted in relation to U.S. policy, it remains a fundamental attribute of the Cherokee Nation the United States could not erase.

Notes

1. See Jennifer Morgan, "Male Travelers, Female Bodies, and the Gendering of Racial Ideology, 1550–1770," in Tony Ballantyne and Antoinette Burton, eds., *Bodies in Contact: Rethinking Colonial Encounters in World History* (Durham, N.C., 2005); Anne McClintock, *Imperial Leather: Race, Gender, and Sexuality in the Colonial Context* (London, 1995); Rayna Green, "The Pocahontas Perplex:

The Image of Indian Women in American Culture," *Massachusetts Review* 16 (1975): 698–714.

2. See Ann Laura Stoler, *Carnal Knowledge and Imperial Power: Race and the Intimate in Colonial Rule* (Berkeley, 2002); Ann Laura Stoler, ed., *Haunted by Empire: Geographies of Intimacy in North American History* (Durham, N.C., 2006); Peggy Pascoe, "Miscegenation Law, Court Cases, and Ideologies of 'Race' in Twentieth-Century America," *Journal of American History* 83, 1 (1996): 44–69.

3. Kristen Hoganson, *Fighting for American Manhood: How Gender Politics Provoked the Spanish-American and Philippine-American Wars* (New Haven, Conn., 1998), 137–38.

4. See Amy Kaplan, *The Anarchy of Empire in the Making of U.S. Culture* (Cambridge, 2002); Richard Slotkin, *Gunfighter Nation: The Myth of the Frontier in Twentieth-Century America* (New York, 1992); Mathew Frye Jacobson, *Barbarian Virtues: The United States Encounters Foreign Peoples at Home and Abroad, 1876–1917* (New York, 2000).

5. David E. Wilkins and K. Tsianina Lomawaima, *Uneven Ground: American Indian Sovereignty and Federal Law* (Norman, Okla., 2002); Luana Ross, *Inventing the Savage: The Social Construction of Native American Criminality* (Austin, Tex., 1998).

6. Frederick Jackson Turner, "The Significance of the Frontier in American History," in Richard W. Etulain, ed., *Does the Frontier Experience Make America Exceptional?* (Boston, 1999), 19.

7. Theda Perdue, *"Mixed Blood" Indians: Racial Construction in the Early South* (Athens, Ga., 2003).

8. Tiya Miles, *Ties That Bind: The Story of an Afro-Cherokee Family in Slavery and Freedom* (Berkeley, 2005), 166–68.

9. The Cherokee Supreme Court later clarified that white women marrying into the Cherokee Nation were entitled to the same rights as white men.

10. Nancy Hope Sober, *The Intruders: The Illegal Residents of the Cherokee Nation, 1866–1907* (Ponca City, Okla., 1991), 30.

11. Mrs. B. W. Wade to Hon L. W. Shirley, October 23, 1883, folder 83, box 2, D. W. Bushyhead Collection, Western Historical Collections, University of Oklahoma Libraries.

12. Pascoe, "Miscegenation Law," 49.

13. Martin Blackwood, interviewed by W. J. B. Bigby, June 22, 1937, Indian Pioneer History Collection, Oklahoma Historical Society.

14. For more on the creation and effects of the "squaw" image, see Green, "Pocahontas Perplex."

15. Thompson, letter to the editor, *Cherokee Advocate*, January 18, 1888, 2.

16. "Communicated," *Cherokee Advocate*, January 18, 1888, 2.

17. Letter to the editor, *Cherokee Advocate*, February 1, 1888, 1.

18. Ibid.

19. "He Don't Know Although He Ought to Know," *Cherokee Advocate*, 18, January 1888, 2; "How Senator Daws' Indian Marriage Bill Affects the Cherokees," *Cherokee Advocate*, January 18, 1888, 2.

20. Andrew Denson, *Demanding the Cherokee Nation: Indian Autonomy and American Culture, 1830–1900* (Lincoln, Neb., 2004), 197–8.

21. "Report on the Five Civilized Tribes," *Kansas City Star,* February 7, 1897, reprinted in *Chronicles of Oklahoma* 48, 4 (1970): 416–30, quotation from 428.

22. Ibid.

23. Ibid.

24. "More Indian Girls Marry White Fortune Hunters," *Chicago Daily Tribune,* October 28, 1900, 54.

25. "Looking for Indian Wife? Chickasaw Maidens, with Plenty of Land, Say They Want White Men for Husbands," *Chicago Daily Tribune,* May 28, 1907, 1. The same article appeared in the *New York Times:* "Indians Seek Husbands. Chickasaw Girls Want Only White Men—Students Write to Them," *New York Times,* May 28, 1907, 1.

26. Green, "Pocahontas Perplex."

27. Richard White, "When Frederick Jackson Turner and Buffalo Bill Cody Both Played in Chicago in 1893," in Etulain, *Does the Frontier Experience Make America Exceptional?* 53.

28. Ibid.

29. "Matrimonial Bureau," *Tahlequah Arrow,* August 10, 1901, 1.

30. "The Wedding Consumated," *Oklahoma State Capital,* November 17, 1907, 1.

31. Ibid., 2.

32. Ibid.

33. Ibid.

34. Angie Debo, *And Still the Waters Run* (1940; reprint, New York, 1966), viii.

CHRISTINE M. SKWIOT

9 *Genealogies and Histories in Collision*

TOURISM AND COLONIAL CONTESTATIONS
IN HAWAI'I, 1900–1930

Mrs. Emma Metcalf Nakuina springs from bloodlines
which touch Plymouth Rock, as well as midseas islands.
High priests, statesmen, and warriors join hands in their
descendents with pilgrims, lawmakers, and jurists.

—*Hawaii, Its People, Their Legends* (1904)

In the preface to Emma Metcalf Nakuina's *Hawaii, Its People, Their Legends*, the Hawaii Promotion Committee (HPC) asserted that marriages between elite haole men and *ali'i* women[1] had anchored haole in Hawai'i, bound Hawai'i to the United States, and resulted in U.S. annexation in 1898 "at Hawaii's own request."[2] After the United States made Hawai'i a formal colony in 1900, members of the former annexationist leadership helped organize the HPC. While charged with increasing Anglo-Saxon tourism and settlement, haole insisted that the HPC was "not a tourist bureau" but an agency devoted to "advanc[ing] the best interests of Hawaii."[3] To advance the paramount haole interests of the time—legitimizing and naturalizing colonial rule—the HPC mobilized discourses of the genealogies of Nakuina and Princess Abigail Kawananakoa, both daughters of high-ranking *ali'i* wives and haole sugarplanter husbands. Haole travel writers appropriated Hawaiian genealogies to recast colonial rule as the consensual outcome of a long history of crosscultural marriage and governance. They sought to erase the fact that leading *ali'i* women married to haole men, like Kawananakoa's mother, had led the nationalist associations that organized the vast majority of Hawaiians who opposed annexation to protest it.[4] Contestations over genealogy and history, belonging and identity, roots and routedness complicated the consolidation of haole governance.[5]

Tourism was an arena where political and cultural production converged in "the making of intimacy *with* the colonizing state and the making of intimacy *for* the colonizing state," as Warwick Anderson puts it so well in a very different material but similar ideological context.[6] This essay examines two moments when collisions between Hawaiian and Anglo-American histories and genealogies played out in travel narratives. Hawaiian resistance to the imposition of formal colonial rule in 1900 marked the first moment. For a decade after its founding in 1903, haole used the HPC as a forum for staking genealogical and historical claims to Hawai'i. Nakuina critiqued these claims in her collection of "legends" published by the HPC in 1904. Although intended for a reading public of white settlers and tourists, Nakuina's *mo'olelo* (histories, stories) also addressed Hawaiians and offered them strategies for surviving the devastations of colonialism. The second moment began in 1920 when Hawaiian legislators and Japanese and Filipino workers, respectively, threatened haole's access to cheap land and cheap labor. These challenges to haole governance prompted U.S. officials to call for the imposition of military rule. As part of a broader effort to reassert their authority, haole engaged Princess Kawananakoa to direct the opening ceremony of the Royal Hawaiian Hotel in 1927. It simulated a coronation that transferred Hawaiian monarchical power and privilege to an imagined aristocracy of white residents and tourists. At once social and political, the ceremony erased challenges to haole governance and recast its leaders as enlightened aristocrats committed to preparing Hawaiians and Asians for eventual self-government from above.

Nakuina and Kawananakoa followed a long line of Hawaiian women married to haole men (most famously Queen Lili'uokalani) who worked within adapted frameworks of Western civilization to defend the *lahui* (Hawaiian nation and people) from the effects of imported diseases, land alienation, and all manner of colonial incursions. Both women opposed the illegal overthrow of the queen and kingdom in 1893 and forcible U.S. annexation in 1898. Both continued to resist colonial rule as *ali'i* whose mana (spiritual-political power) emanated from their genealogies and ability to promote the well-being of Hawaiians. While performing prescribed Euro-American gender roles in the private sphere, Nakuina and Kawananakoa carved out spaces that enabled them to exercise customary and hybrid forms of indigenous female power in the public sphere. Rejecting haole discourses of Hawaiians as a "dying race" doomed to extinction, they worked to advance indigenous rights, revitalize Hawaiians and their culture, and embody resistance to oppression.[7] Their conformist resistance suggests that haole hegemony was neither as complete nor secure as many white contemporaries and historians proclaimed.[8]

By 1900, haole had institutionalized bourgeois marriages in Hawai'i, and the HPC promoted those between haole men and *ali'i* women as a founding fiction of the new colonial state. Women like Nakuina and Kawananakoa challenged haole efforts to translate the power of patriarchal husbands over domesticated *ali'i* wives into haole's rule over a dependent Hawaiian "race."[9] Hawaiians contested the classification of Polynesians as part of the Aryan race, a claim haole used to assert that governance must be limited to male members of that race's ostensibly superior branch of Anglo-Saxons.[10] Intimacies, here figured through cross-cultural marriages and genealogies, were contested, hybrid resources that were mobilized by haole to consolidate and Hawaiians to negotiate colonial rule.[11] Although the "management of intimacy" proved pivotal to the legitimation of colonial rule, haole did not characterize marriages between white men and Native women as affective.[12] They cast them as "consensual," a legalistic term that presented state-sanctioned marriages as constitutive of haole national belonging and colonial governance. Haole tourism promoters limited discussions of crosscultural marriages to the minority of them that were between haole men and *ali'i* women, ones they believed would legitimate their claims to Hawai'i and transform *hapa-haole* (part-white) Hawaiians into Americans. They elided discussion of other "mixed" marriages, particularly the majority of those involving Asians, that haole believed threatened political and racial order and Anglo-Saxon civilization.[13]

Genealogies represent a form of historical articulation and, like historical narratives, are bound up with struggles over power. Marriage and genealogy offered haole a way to narrate the inevitability of white colonialism while effacing historical contingencies. Haole sought to impose Anglo-American genealogies on Hawaiians to demonstrate the desire of both parties to translate marital unions into a political one between Hawai'i and the United States. As Kerry Wynn compellingly argues (chapter 8 here), white U.S. colonists employed the imagery of marriage to paper over native anticolonial resistance, by casting the political union of territories as a voluntary and mutually desirable one in which indigenous wives and feminized nations agreed to forever subsume their political identities to white U.S. husbands and their masculine nation.

Nakuina and Kawananakoa contested haole efforts to write themselves into Hawaiian genealogies in order to lay claim to Hawai'i, erase colonial conquest, and naturalize white rule. They reasserted Hawaiian conceptions of ancestral relationships and the ways they structured political authority. Far more than diagrams of who begat whom used to confer individual entitlements, Hawaiian genealogies trace Hawaiian origins to the land and the sea; they "connect people to one another, to place, and to landscape: they are about relatedness."[14] They are also "the Hawaiian concept of time," binding people and place, present and past: Hawaiians look "forward" to the known past and "back" to the unknowable future.[15] Their genealogies constitute temporal and spatial relationships that establish multiple and extended identities, loyalties, and obligations. In appropriating Hawaiian genealogies, haole sought to acquire rights without accepting responsibilities, violating the mores that governed acculturation into Hawaiian society, identification as Hawaiian, and the legitimation of power.

Protesting Pilgrims' Progress

In 1900, a U.S. federal government official declared "without question" that "Hawaii would be governed by a 'ruling class' of 4,000 Americans and other Anglo-Saxons who were to have dominion over the remaining 145,000 residents of the Islands."[16] Proclaiming haole dominion proved easier than asserting white rule, as the continued authority of the deposed queen and a key decision made by U.S. colonial architects indicate. On the eve of annexation, Lili'uokalani challenged haole's claims that they were "Hawaiians by birth" or "Hawaiians of American descent." She asserted the primacy of Hawaiian genealogical traditions: "They are not and never were Hawaiians." Hawaiians are "the children of the soil— the native inhabitants of the Hawaiian islands and their descendants."[17] Despite efforts to deny U.S. citizenship to Hawaiians on racial grounds, recognition of them as the indigenous people and citizens of a once sovereign kingdom acknowledged as such by the world family of nations in this instance overrode U.S. legal equations of citizenship and whiteness. The metropole made Hawai'i a U.S. territory and granted U.S. citizenship to Hawaiians and the vote to Hawaiian men.[18]

Hawaiian voters did not have the power to prevent the consolidation of haole governance, but they did delay and set some limits on it. In the territory's first elections in 1900, Robert Wilcox, the Hawaiian leader of an 1895 countercoup against the annexationist government, led the Home Rule Party.[19] Its candidates swept elections and blocked haole legislative action for three years. Then, haole backed Prince Jonah Kuhio Kalaniana'ole as delegate to U.S. Congress. Kuhio Kalaniana'ole split the Hawaiian vote, enabling the haole-dominated Republican Party to take control of the legislature. His victory compelled haole to govern more according to the wishes of Hawaiians than they would have otherwise.[20] The election of an *ali'i* imprisoned for participating in the 1895 revolt and venerated for helping defeat an 1897 annexation treaty inscribed Hawaiian persistence and resistance into the colonial state. After the election of Kuhio Kalaniana'ole, haole renewed efforts to stake genealogical and historical claims to Hawai'i.[21]

Acknowledging the authority of the queen, haole abandoned efforts to lay claim to Hawai'i by virtue of birthplace. They instead wrote themselves into Hawaiian genealogies. The ideas of Thomas Jefferson proved valuable to this quest. Jefferson had argued that marriages between white colonials and Native Americans would legitimate the white colonials' ties to the land and forge the "bonds of affection and love," in the words of Jefferson historian Peter Onuf, needed to render conquest a consensual process. For Native Americans devastated by disease and dispossession, such marriages would effect "the moment of their restoration" and "rebirth as Americans."[22] In merging Jeffersonian and Hawaiian genealogical traditions, haole sought to claim rights to Hawai'i and transform Hawaiians into Americans, a process that entailed racially reconstructing them as white.[23]

Haole argued that crosscultural marriages between haole and Hawaiians resulted in the "dilution" of their offspring's Hawaiianness, the distillation of their Americanness, and their incorporation into a U.S. citizenry and body politic rooted in whiteness. As the historian J. Kehaulani Kauanui argues, "because the enfranchisement of Hawaiians entailed the domestication of a previously recognized sovereign entity (the Kingdom of Hawai'i), the project of erasing the Hawaiian people through discourses of deracialization and deracination became essential to the politics of assimilation."[24] Continued intermarriage with haole would eventually whiten Hawaiians into Americans worthy of the full rights and responsibilities of self-government. Katherine Ellinghaus shows that state practices and popular notions of intermarriage diverged across space and nation (chapter 10 here). Whereas in Australia whites conceived of marriage between whites and Natives as a force "diluting" and "absorbing" native blood, in the United States such marriages were seen as a way to elevate indigenous people and prepare them for self-government. In Hawai'i, these discourses converged. Haole asserted that marriages between haole and Hawaiians "diluted" the blood and identities of these partners' offspring, thereby working to "absorb" them into the American body politic and elevate their political and racial status and hence claims of belonging in the U.S. nation. Haole insisted that the "thinning" of Hawaiian blood, identities, and loyalties resulted in the "thickening" of their American ones.

In his one-page preface to Emma Metcalf Nakuina's *Hawaii, Its People, Their Legends,* an unnamed haole asserted that her "bloodlines" linked "Plymouth Rock" to "midseas islands," genealogically and geographically connecting haole to Hawai'i and Hawaiians to the United States. Operating on the assumption that Hawaiians were Aryans, Nakuina's biographer contended that her Hawaiian ancestry of "high priests, statesmen, and warriors" and Anglo-American ancestry of "pilgrims, lawmakers, and jurists" had sociopolitical ties to an imaginary England, specifically late nineteenth-century discourses of England as both a feudal and modern monarchy presided over by king, church, and martial aristocracy.[25] In 1620, the Pilgrims had fled this imaginary England to escape post-Norman corruptions of "true" Anglo-Saxon culture, faith, and governance.[26] They alighted in Massachusetts on or near Plymouth Rock, although they paid it little mind. But on the bicentennial of their landing, Daniel Webster consecrated this broken granite boulder as the birthplace of a regenerated Anglo-Saxon people destined to spread their uncorrupted liberties to others.[27] The same year, New England missionaries landed in a Hawai'i that had made remarkable progress toward modernity, a process aided by the fact that the state of Hawaii's civilizational status and political relationships, according to the HPC, was "not more than four hundred years behind that of England when the islands were discovered." Variously dating this moment to the arrival of Captain Cook in the eighteenth century or the Spaniards in the sixteenth, the haole argued that on the broad eve of Western contact, Hawai'i resembled the imaginary England the New England missionaries' Pilgrim ancestors had fled.[28] Time and space collapsed and destiny and history converged when the rulers of the newly centralized nation of Hawai'i welcomed a procession of New Englanders some of whom married Hawaiians and most of whom labored to Christianize, civilize, domesticate, and otherwise bring Hawai'i into an Anglo-Saxon civilization that the Pilgrims and their descendants had purged of Old World corruptions in the process of relocating it to the New Worlds of the Atlantic and Pacific.

A similar elision of time and space took place in the haole's representations of Nakuina's heritage and presentation of her as a domesticated and disenfranchised U.S. citizen who ostensibly renounced her Hawaiian identity and *ali'i* women's rights of governance. In a colonialist act of erasure, the haole did not name her *ali'i* ancestors but only her haole ones and attributed her character and loyalties to them. "Broadly and liberally educated under the immediate care of her father," Theophilus Metcalf, "a Harvard man [and] nephew of the late Chief Justice Metcalf of Massachusetts," Nakuina, a classically educated descendant of a minor U.S. founder, was as "fitted to present" the legends of "her people," the "Hawaiian Race," to white tourists and settlers as she apparently was content to leave affairs of state to haole men.[29]

This preface served to make a bridge between numerous tourist tracts written by haole and published by the HPC (all with the title *Hawaii*) beginning in 1903 and Nakuina's collection of "legends," the sole HPC narrative written by a Native, published in 1904. Each haole-authored version of *Hawaii* asserted that Hawaiians were "well fitted to appreciate civilization when it came." After Cook's fatal visit, "the influence of white races rapidly altered native customs." In one HPC narrative Kamehameha, "counseled by white men and with the aid of gunpowder, . . . united the islands into one kingdom."[30] In another, after Kamehameha subdued Maui, Moloka'i, and O'ahu, "the latter rebelled." He returned to O'ahu "with a few white men incorporated into his army." They triumphed in the Battle of Nu'uanu, "when the remnants of the Oahu forces were forced over the great cliffs to their death." Unification "marked" the beginning of "progress" in Hawai'i "from this time forward." King Kamehameha and Queen Ka'ahumanu "built up the empire along modern lines." According to the HPC, "in rapid succession, political rights were granted, the lands . . . were subdivided, the constitution was framed."[31]

Although haole credited Kamehameha and Ka'ahumanu with "administrative genius" for promulgating these measures, they simultaneously altered time to assert that the same features of "permanent civilization followed the arrival of the American missionaries in 1820."[32] Haole deemed the New England missionaries and lawyers as the personages most "fitted to undertake the rehabilitation of the aboriginal kingdom." They worked with *ali'i* to make the kingdom into a modern constitutional monarchy comprised of literate, law-abiding, Christian citizens: "And so as the missionaries had laid the foundations for character, the lawyers and instructors built up [sic] good government and intelligent citizenship."[33] Telescoping to the then future, haole tourist tracts presented the anticipated annexation "at Hawaii's own request" as the outcome of a process of collaborative governance by and consensual marriages between haole and *ali'i*. They asserted that Hawaiian women on embracing civilization voluntarily removed themselves from the public sphere, exemplified by Princess Bernice Pauahi Bishop, "a daughter of

the Kamehamehas who preferred domesticity to the throne." The same
was true for the hapa-haole Hawaiians, who formed "almost a separate
race," one that "brings to American citizenship [a] grasp of public affairs,
much capacity for development, and charming graces of hospitality."[34]
Their feminization and domestication into educated yet immature citizens and gracious hosts affirmed that governance resided in the bodies
of Anglo-American men.

Yet for women like Bishop and Nakuina, domesticity did not translate
into their withdrawal from the political sphere, acquiescence to colonial
rule, or renunciation of their Hawaiian identities and loyalties. They rejected the notion that membership in Anglo-Saxon civilization and haole
high society hinged, in the words of Ann Laura Stoler, on "a demonstrated
disaffection for one's native culture and native mother."[35] In *Hawaii, Its
People, Their Legends,* Nakuina proffered lessons of Hawaiian resistance,
persistence, and adaptation to colonial conquest and civilizing projects
aimed at cultural and political erasure. She did not merely write about "her
people" for white settlers and visitors.[36] She wrote to and for them. She
preserved select *mo'olelo* by translating them into English shortly after
haole had banned the Hawaiian language as a medium of instruction and
public discourse. Far from timeless legends, Nakuina constructed "proper"
mo'olelo, ones that, Jonathan Kamakawiwo'ole Osorio argues, offered
"lessons from the past . . . intended to guide" behavior in the present.[37] In
challenging haole genealogies and histories, Nakuina created usable pasts
for Hawaiian survival and strategies for maintaining indigenous identities and asserting Native rights in presents rerouted but not eradicated
by mass death and colonialism, conversion and domesticity.[38]

Nakuina began by reflecting on whether Native Hawaiians "had
descended from the great Aryan race" or "the lost tribes of Israel." She
proposed that Hawaiians more closely resembled "the Israelites," who
clung "to their beliefs in the face of persecutions." In her narrative, Euro-
American explorers seem less to have discovered the Hawaiian Islands
than gravitated to their magnetic people once they had "increased in
numbers and waxed rich." Like the Israelites, Hawaiians became the
"objects of envy to the people around them," people "who would in
time either expel them or attempt their destruction." Marriages between
Hawaiians and haole resulted from the Hawaiians' loyalty to the *ali'i*
who authorized some "unusually beautiful Sarahs or Rebekas"—and also
"Josephs"—to be "taken in marriage by the powerful and rich among
whom they sojourned" to formalize ties between sovereign nations. She
rejected haole claims that these marriages were consensual yet unequal
ones that placed the kingdom on a teleological path to annexation and

resulted in the voluntary subordination of the Hawaiian people and nation of their persons and property to the United States. For haole paeans on the civilizing mission she substituted *mo'olelo* of adaptation to a host of conquering strangers, whose arrival her Hawaiian ancestors had prophesied and from whom, like the Israelites, they had been promised deliverance.[39]

Haole narratives of the progressive advance of "civilization" met their match in Nakuina's account of the destructive forces unleashed by its wake. She critiqued the haole belief in the progressive influence of Western law. Prior to the arrival of the New Englanders, Hawaiians maintained "stringent laws and regulations of the taking of fish, looking toward their preservation." But then "the white man, with his alleged superior knowledge, prevailed on chief and commoners to throw down their wholesome restrictions." New laws rooted in a liberal faith in the inexhaustible supply of natural resources replaced old ones, with "the result that fishes are very scarce in Hawaiian waters and getting more and more so every year." Nakuina spoke with authority. She had served the kingdom as commissioner of water rights and ways for eighteen years, earning the reputation of "judge of the water court."[40] The decimation of the environment and people went hand in hand in the Hawaiian cultural imagination. Nakuina challenged haole's use of Hawaiian genealogies to legitimate their authority without accepting the responsibilities of Hawaiian ancestry, which obligated those in power to manage the land and its resources for the benefit of the governed as well as the governing.

Nakuina continued her critique by reclaiming her Hawaiian ancestors and reinterpreting postcontact history. Her history of Kamehameha's conquest of O'ahu and founding of the *lahui* featured no white men, unlike haole narratives that exaggerated their importance and ignored their acculturation into Hawaiian society.[41] She mobilized Hawaiian genealogies to highlight adaptation to usurping strangers. "A young chiefess, the daughter of the high priest Kanaloauoo, whose residence was on Punchbowl crater, and who was connected with the Hawaii chiefs by the father's side, but whose mother was one of the *tabu* (high-ranking) princesses of Kukaniloko, the famous cradle of Oahuan royalty," she recounted, "was compelled to be married to one of his [Kamehameha's] generals, Nahili, whom he appointed to govern the conquered island." The chiefess accepted this marriage "with unquestioning obedience." But she "displayed her fidelity to her slaughtered kindred and people by calling her first born Kaheananui," that is, "the great heap of the slain" for those who died in the Battle of Nu'uanu. Kamehameha could have put her to death for this transgression. But "on hearing of this covert act of feminine defiance,

[he] only smiled indulgently and approved of her fidelity to the memories of the dead." Nakuina expressed gratitude for this dispensation, for the chiefess Kalanikupaulakea was her great-grandmother.[42] War represented a customary path to power in Hawai'i, but the legitimation of rule conferred on the conqueror obligations to the conquered.[43]

Nakuina embodied "the sanctity of home, obedience to superiors and full justice" but not just in the manner presumed by her haole biographer. She pledged allegiance not solely to the authority of haole fathers and statesmen but also to the male and female Hawaiian ancestors to whom the land had given birth and who had empowered women like her great- and great-great-grandmothers to govern and care for the land and people. Nakuina's great-grandmother accepted marriage to Nahili because it enabled her to continue to protect the interests and well-being of her conquered kin. Her great-grandmother's act of honoring the dead by naming the first-born son of this marriage in their memory testified to Hawaiian endurance amid the ruptures of conquest and colonialism. Rejecting haole views of Hawaiian legends as the static tales of a dying people, Nakuina plumbed a dynamic past to present contemporary lessons for persistence that, as Julia Clancy-Smith argues in a similar context, "permitted the survival of her cultural patrimony in a society literally and figuratively under siege."[44]

Nakuina showed that Hawaiian survival depended on a mixture of conformity and resistance. On the one hand, she accepted haole as the latest in a series of usurping strangers who had brought "four changes of government or rather the personnel of the governing people," as she defiantly put it. On the other hand, Nakuina asserted that the failure of this most recent wave of usurping strangers to accept the obligations and loyalties conferred by Hawaiian ancestry undermined their legitimacy and right to governance. She decried the fact that "most of the stone" of Kamehameha's residence "had been carted away, evidently for the making of piers or buttresses for the wharf that extends from and parallel to what was the entrance and altar to the temple."[45] Through the desecration of the seat of the *lahui* and the ancient temple on which it sat, haole demonstrated that they revered their ancestors who were "pilgrims, lawmakers, and jurists" but not those who were "high priests, statesmen, and warriors." Their loyalties lay solely with their New England ancestors and their version of Pilgrims' progress. Nakuina contrasted the legitimation of power by Kamehameha at the turn of the nineteenth century with the failure of haole to do likewise at the turn of the twentieth.

While Kamehameha apparently accepted Nakuina's great-grandmother's "covert act of feminine defiance," Nakuina's haole contemporaries did not do the same for her. Typically, the HPC reprinted its publications or adapted their text for use in new ones. But it never reprinted *Hawaii, Its People, Their Legends* in whole or part. The HPC and its next two successor agencies never again published a narrative authored by a Hawaiian or any other narrative that contested prevailing haole interpretations of genealogy and history. Haole recognized the threat of performative resistance in Nakuina's writing. Perhaps this explains the tight script imposed on Princess Abigail Kawananakoa at the grand opening of the Royal Hawaiian Hotel in 1927. Yet her lineage, wealth, and performances as Hawaii's most legendary hostess compelled haole to accept her authority and exercise of power in the political arena. They enabled her, as Michelle Moran argues (chapter 15 here), to continue the ongoing negotiations between colonizer and colonized that entered a new phase upon the imposition of formal colonial rule in Hawai'i at the turn of the twentieth century.

Resisting the Royal Resort

By World War I, Hawaii's haole ruling class felt confident of its hegemony. But a year after that war ended, Hawaiian legislators and Japanese and Filipino workers, respectively, threatened haole's access to cheap land and cheap labor. Haole successfully disputed Hawaiian land claims and put down striking workers. Yet the metropole responded these challenges from below by threatening to place Hawai'i under U.S. military rule. Haole again turned to tourism to reassert their authority. The Hawaii Tourist Bureau, which replaced the HPC in 1919, committed to the production of new narratives of white supremacy as consensual colonialism. Haole invested in the cultural production of Hawai'i as home to an imagined aristocracy of white tourists and settlers that had inherited their power and privilege from the Hawaiian monarchy.

In 1920, a Hawaiian legislator introduced in the U.S. Congress a bill designed to "return" Hawaiians to the land. In 1894, the annexationist government had seized title to 1.75 million acres of Crown lands; it ceded them to the United States on annexation. Although haole presented these transfers of land and title as consensual acts, most Hawaiians regarded them as illegal. Debates on the bill initially focused on whether the kingdom had held Crown lands in trust for Hawaiian commoners. Haole convinced enough U.S. congressmen that Hawaiians had neither right nor title to former Crown lands. They then moved to limit the number of Hawaiian beneficiaries eligible for "rehabilitation." Congressmen supported defining Hawaiians either as the subjects and descendants of King

Kamehameha III or by a blood quantum criterion of one thirty-second. Haole protested that such an inclusive definition threatened the "white race" and its access to "valuable public lands." Haole prevailed. The 1920 Hawaiian Homes Commission Act defined Hawaiians by a blood quantum criterion of 50 percent. So an act initially proposed to return Hawaiians to the land instead protected the leases of the haole and their ancestors who had alienated Hawaiians from the land. As Kauanui argues, "Hawaiianness was racially institutionalized within the context of subordination to white identity and whiteness as property." Haole restricted land entitlements available in theory (but rarely practice) to a fraction of "deserving natives" of a "dying race" but denied them to the Hawaiians haole cast as "diluted" Americans or "degenerated" Asians. According to this racial legal logic, Hawaiians would cease to exist in the near future.[46]

As Hawaiians challenged haole claims to cheap land, Asian workers threatened their access to cheap labor. A long and determined strike by Japanese and Filipino cane workers for better wages, conditions, and the right to be treated as American settlers rather than alien immigrants shook the foundations of haole rule. Alarmed metropolitan officials called for placing Hawai'i under U.S. military rule. Challenges from below and above threatened the haole ruling class, whose wealth and power depended on local governance without interference from the metropole. Haole succeeded in repressing laborers and staving off military governance before moving to present themselves as the rightful heirs of the Hawaiian monarchy and its royal "playground" at Waikiki.[47]

The decision in 1919 to organize the Hawaii Tourist Bureau to sell Hawai'i as a destination of royalty and romance also dovetailed with changes in the international tourism industry at the end of World War I. Hawaii's promoters joined others around the Mediterranean, the Caribbean, and the Pacific in constructing a host of "royal resorts." They sold their destinations as ideal combinations of the aristocratic and the democratic, the feudal and the modern, and the foreign and the familiar. Developers erected resorts fit for kings and queens, while travel writers merged history and fantasy to cast tourists as aristocrats whose status gave them license to indulge in pleasures created just for them.[48]

In devising a tourism identity unique to Hawai'i, promoters offered U.S. white elites a temptation that many found as irresistible as they did intriguing: acceptance into an accredited "American" aristocracy. New York City may have emerged from World War I as the symbol of the United States as a global cultural and financial capital, but the U.S. Territory of Hawai'i boasted the nation's only real palace, once home to actual kings and queens. Hawai'i catered to wealthy whites who realized that they could no longer imagine the United States as the racially and culturally homogenous republic it had never been, especially in a period characterized by the class, labor, and racial strife that animated white nativist anticommunist, antiimmigrant, and antiworker movements. In place of this shattered republican myth, haole offered tourists the privilege and deference they believed was due their race, class, and station. Responding to the dual opportunities to exploit a promising market and reconstitute their contested authority, haole mobilized the financial and cultural capital that was used to build the Royal Hawaiian Hotel and to write narratives of Hawai'i as a royal resort presided over by an enlightened modern aristocracy. For haole, the grand opening of the Royal Hawaiian at Waikiki Beach in 1927 was the social event of the decade. The twelve hundred invited guests represented the *crème de la crème* of haole society: prominent planters and businessmen, the governor, high-ranking U.S. military officers, the society page editors, and wealthy tourists. Few *ali'i* received invitations.[49]

Haole produced entwined genealogies for the property of the Royal Hawaiian and the person of Princess Abigail Kawananakoa. The haole genealogists who created the royal lineage for the hotel noted that it occupied land that Princess Bernice Pauahi Bishop inherited from the Kamehameha dynasty. They traced the use of Helumoa, an "ancient cocoanut grove" in the "immediate vicinity" of the hotel, as the seat of royal residences from the "big grass house of Kalanikapule, King of Oahu" to the "grass hut" of Kamehameha I to the coral house of King Kamehameha V, where Hawaiian royalty hosted a luau for the duke of Edinburgh in 1869. Kalakaua, the last king, maintained residence at Waikiki, where he hosted Robert Louis Stevenson at the most celebrated luau in haole memory. Kawananakoa sometimes stayed at Lili'uokalani's beach house, evidence of a continued Native royal presence at Waikiki.[50]

The Royal's opening staged the merging of the worlds of Hawaiian royalty and Anglo-Saxon capital and civilization. Simulating a coronation, it choreographed the end of an era of native monarchs and the beginning of an era of wealthy white aristocrats.[51] Representing the Hawaiian monarchy and directing the transfer of royal power and privilege was Princess Kawananakoa. She was a daughter of James Campbell, a Scotch-Irish settler who became one of Hawaii's wealthiest landowners, planters, and financiers, and Abigail Kuaihelani Maipinepine Bright, a member of a prominent Anglo-Hawaiian family of Maui and descendant of Hawaii's ruling chiefs. The princess, whom boosters proclaimed "could have been Hawaii's queen if the monarchy had survived," was the widow of Prince David Kalakaua Kawananakoa, a nephew of King Kalakaua's consort, Queen Kapi'olani. A number of identities and genealogies merged in the body of the princess. She represented the product of unions between Hawaiian nobility and Anglo-Saxon wealth. Her ancestors included premonarchical chiefs and Hawaii's first and last kings. A titled descendant of the *ali'i* and haole who brought Anglo-Saxon civilization and the modern nation-state to Hawai'i, Kawananakoa possessed the authority to designate an imagined white aristocracy the rightful heirs to the Hawaiian monarchy.[52]

After a haute cuisine dinner at which the soup and fish courses bore the names of the first Hawaiian king, "Green Turtle Soup *Kamehameha*," and the last direct male heir of that line, "Supreme of Mullet *Albert*," Princess Kawananakoa led the guests to the beach for a ceremony she "arranged and directed." According to the *Honolulu Star-Bulletin*, "the curtain of time was drawn back" in a re-creation of Kamehameha's landing on Waikiki on completion of his "conquering tour." Five "princesses" greeted actors dressed as Kamehameha and his warriors, oarsmen, *kahili* (feather standard) bearers, and *tabu* bearers when they alighted at "the site of Royal Hawaiian." Taking the throne, the "king," his retinue, and guests enjoyed an hour of hula and *mele* (chant), likely including the Royal's *mele inoa* (name chant suitable for royalty).[53] The "strains of a foxtrot" issuing from the ballroom marked the end of the historical pageant. "The curtain dropped back in place" as "Kamehameha" and his retinue descended from the throne and faded into the dark. Princess Kawananakoa, the first guest to register at the Royal, did not stay the night. Haole returned from beach to ballroom, from re-created past to recreational present, from Hawaiian kingdom to U.S. territory. The next day, the *Honolulu Advertiser* elevated the tourist industry to the same status the opening ceremony conferred on whites: "If Sugar is 'King' and Pineapple 'Queen' of Hawaii," then the "Tourist Trade is Surely the 'Prince Royal.'"[54]

The Royal Hawaiian's opening ceremony naturalized haole hegemony as the outcome of an unbroken history of consensual marriage and collaborative governance in which *ali'i* and haole cooperated first to civilize Hawai'i and domesticate Hawaiians and then to subordinate their property and persons to haole men and the U.S. nation in marital and political unions allegedly desired and consented to by both parties. It offered a lesson in lineage, succession, and state-building that made it appear that haole had not illegally overthrown the sovereign monarch of an independent kingdom politically and militarily but had properly ascended to the royal court culturally and socially. Narratives of Waikiki as a "royal playground," once for Hawaiian *ali'i* but now for rich whites, masked the slow appropriation of land, power, and wealth by haole over the nineteenth century and the determination of Hawaiians to maintain the sovereignty of the Kingdom of Hawai'i.[55] These narratives erased the brutality of U.S. imperialism and did further violence by appropriating Hawaiians' genealogical ties *with* the land to legitimize haole acquisitions *of* land in the form of property through marriage, purchase, and conquest. They effaced the opposition of most Hawaiians to the sudden overthrow of Queen Lili'uokalani and the Hawaiian kingdom in 1893 and Hawaii's forcible annexation to the United States in 1898. They elided the fact that Kawananakoa's mother, her then future husband, and his brother, Prince Kuhio Kalaniana'ole, had led the anticolonial nationalist movement to restore queen and kingdom. Indeed in 1893, Kawananakoa's parents named her newborn sibling Royalist, a resistant act of naming that recalled that of Nakuina's great grandmother.[56]

Princess Kawananakoa commanded the respect of haole for her service as high society's most renowned hostess. Her public performances as a titled aristocrat compelled haole to accept her political work on behalf of Hawaiians. For haole, she served as a symbol of royalty. For Hawaiians, she also served as an *ali'i* and a symbol of the *lahui* and its persistence. She demanded the respect due her station and signed her correspondence and answered her telephone with the single word Princess. After her brother-in-law and ten-time territorial delegate to U.S. Congress, Prince Kuhio Kalaniana'ole, died in 1922, Kawananakoa became the principal leader of the Hawaiian community and engaged more actively in politics. She continued his work advocating for Hawaiians in Hawai'i and the United States. She promoted women's rights and welfare legislation for women and children and helped register voters and get out them out for territorial elections. She served as the Republican national committeewoman for Hawai'i from 1924 through 1936. From 1935 to 1940, she was a member of a reorganized Hawaiian Homes Commission. She put the agency on sound financial footing, initiated a new "rehabilitation" project, and struggled to make the agency take seriously its mandate to return Hawaiians to the land.[57]

Concluding Thoughts

Antoinette Burton and Tony Ballantyne note that the essays in this part of this collection move beyond "accommodationist" and "anxiety" analyses of crosscultural and interracial marriage to consider how much these apparently antithetical models and modes of apprehension share in common. In Hawai'i, discourses of crosscultural and interracial marriages were especially strategies of reterritorialization that were not necessarily associated with a particular stage or phase of colonialism. Unlike the colonialists in many other colonies, haole did not initially sanction and pursue miscegenation as a strategy for acquiring land, power, and status only to reject and seek to proscribe it after securing sufficient measures of them.[58] Rather, in different ways and under various circumstances from 1900 to 1930, as in this essay, and from the mid–nineteenth to the mid–twentieth century, more broadly, haole mobilized and deployed discourses of interracial marriage in efforts to legitimize and naturalize white colonial rule, erase ongoing indigenous resistance, contest Native sovereignty and authority, and assert haole power and authority over unruly female and feminized subjects who refused to equate their civilization and domestication with their subordination to or immobilization under haole governance. Henry Yu recently reflected on various historical moments of openness toward miscegenation in the United States. His argument that such moments have seldom proved progressive and antiracist and more often have been "associated with the reorganization of white supremacy and the ways that it produced racial hierarchy" certainly fits the case of colonial Hawai'i.[59]

Haole sought to present mixing and hybridity as a one-way process through which American blood, histories, identities, and loyalties replaced and ultimately would erase Hawaiian ones. Haole men asserted that in wedding *ali'i* women, they married into Hawaiian society, thereby acquiring what Euro-Americans regarded as entitlements to indigenous property, power, and privilege. By contrast, haole asserted that in the same matrimonies, Native women married out of Hawaiian and into Anglo-American society and civilization, in effect divorcing themselves from Hawaiian culture, heritage, and claims to culture, land, and sovereignty. Again, haole conceived "marrying in" and "marrying out" less in terms of the temporal than the spatial, as part of an ongoing and contested project to deterritorialize Hawai'i as Hawaiian and reterritorialize it as American.[60] Yet however much haole wished that mixing and hybridity constituted a one-way street on which Hawaiians progressed steadily closer toward America and Americanness and away from Hawai'i and Hawaiianness, haole acutely felt their need to lay claims to indigeneity and indigenous affiliations and affections in order to render colonialism as consensual. Moreover, because securing Hawaii's incorporation into the republic as a U.S. territory legally—at least in the rhetorical arena—obligated haole to commit to preparing all of Hawaii's present and future U.S. citizens for eventual democracy, an eventuality many hoped lay in the most distant and unforeseeable future, haole also wrote themselves

into Hawaiian genealogies and histories to justify their decidedly an-
tidemocratic, even authoritarian rule to those in the U.S. metropole.
Haole's desire and need to lay claim to "royal" Hawaiian ancestry and
authority helped enable Nakuina and Kawananakoa to continue to exercise a measure of customary and hybrid *ali'i* authority, embody resistance
to the colonial state, and adapt Hawaiian genealogies and histories for
innovative uses in resisting and adapting to formal colonial rule.

Notes

I am deeply indebted to Duane Corpis, Jared Poley, Joe Perry, Alecia Long, and
Pedro A. Cabán for their incisive and insightful comments on various drafts of
this essay. I presented an earlier version of part of this essay at the annual meeting
of the American Historical Association, Philadelphia, January 5–8, 2006; I thank
the panel chair, Philippa Levine, copanelists John Carroll, Julia Clancy-Smith,
and Durba Ghosh, and members of the audience for their excellent comments and
suggestions. I thank Ian Christopher Fletcher for introducing me to this wonderful group of scholars. Mahalo nui loa to J. Kehaulani Kauanui, who generously
shared her important and provocative work with me. All errors, omissions, and
oversights are mine.

1. "Haole" originally meant "stranger"; after the mid–nineteenth century, it referred specifically to Anglo-Saxon strangers and settlers. *Ali'i* customarily referred
to ruling chiefs and chiefesses; after the mid–nineteenth century, it also referred
to the Hawaiian kings and queens of a Westernized constitutional monarchy.

2. Emma Metcalf Nakuina, *Hawaii, Its People, Their Legends* (Honolulu, 1904),
preface; Hawaii Promotion Committee, *Hawaii* (Honolulu, 1903) (hereafter HPC
Hawaii 1903a), microfilm, Bancroft Library, University of California, Berkeley, 8;
Tom Coffman dates narratives on annexation as resulting from Hawai'i's request
to 1898 in his *Nation Within: The Story of America's Annexation of the Nation
of Hawai'i* (Kane'ohe, 1998), xi.

3. Will J. Cooper, "Promotion Committee Progress," *Paradise of the Pacific,*
December 1908, 24.

4. Noenoe K. Silva, *Aloha Betrayed: Native Hawaiian Resistance to American
Colonialism* (Durham, N.C., 2004).

5. Vicente M. Diaz and J. Kehaulani Kauanui, "Native Pacific Cultural Studies
on the Edge," *Contemporary Pacific* 13, 2 (2001): 315–42; James Clifford, "Indigenous Articulations," *Contemporary Pacific* 13, 2 (2001): 468–90.

6. Warwick Anderson, "States of Hygiene: Race 'Improvement' and Biomedical Citizenship in Australia and the Colonial Philippines," in Ann Laura Stoler,
ed., *Haunted by Empire: Geographies of Intimacy in North American History*
(Durham, N.C., 2006), 98.

7. Cristina Bacchilega, "Media Translation in the Production of Legendary
Hawai'i," *Indian Folklife* 4, 1 (2005): 5–8, www.indianfolklore.org/pdf/newsletter/
ifl_18.pdf; Richard A. Hawkins, "Princess Abigail Kawananakoa: The Forgotten
Territorial Native Hawaiian Leader," *Hawaiian Journal of History* 37 (2003):
163–77.

8. See, for example, Noel Kent, *Hawaii: Islands under the Influence* (Honolulu, 1983); Gavan Daws, *Shoal of Time: A History of the Hawaiian Islands* (Honolulu, 1968); Lawrence H. Fuchs, *Hawaii Pono: An Ethnic and Political History* (Honolulu, 1961); Ralph S. Kuydendahl and Gavan Daws, *Hawaii: A History from Polynesian Kingdom to American Commonwealth* (New York, 1948).

9. Sally Engle Merry, *Colonizing Hawai'i: The Cultural Power of Law* (Princeton, 2000), esp. 263.

10. Tony Ballantyne, *Orientalism and Race: Aryanism in the British Empire* (New York, 2002); Elizabeth A. Povinelli, "Notes on Gridlock: Genealogy, Intimacy, Sexuality," *Public Culture* 14, 1 (2002): 215–38; Anne McClintock, *Imperial Leather: Race, Gender, and Sexuality in the Colonial Contest* (New York, 1995).

11. Antoinette Burton and Tony Ballantyne, eds., *Bodies in Contact: Rethinking Colonial Encounters in World History* (Durham, N.C., 2005); Ann Laura Stoler, *Carnal Knowledge and Imperial Power: Race and the Intimate in Colonial Rule* (Berkeley, 2002).

12. Ann Laura Stoler, "Tense and Tender Ties: A Politics of Comparison in North American History and (Post) Colonial Studies," and reply by Ramón A. Gutiérrez, "What's Love Got to Do with It?" *Journal of American History* 88, 3 (2001): 829–69.

13. J. Kehaulani Kauanui, "'A Blood Mixture Which Experience Has Shown Furnishes the Very Highest Grade of Citizen-Material': Selective Assimilation on a Polynesian Case of Naturalization to U.S. Citizenship," *American Studies* 45, 3 (Fall 2004): 33–48; on marriage as an Americanization project in colonial Puerto Rico, see Eileen J. Findlay, *Imposing Decency: The Politics of Sexuality and Race in Puerto Rico, 1870–1920* (Durham, N.C., 1999), esp. chap. 2.

14. Diaz and Kauanui, "Native Pacific Cultural Studies on the Edge," 317–20; J. Kēhaulani Kauanui, "Rehabilitating the Native: Hawaiian Blood Quantum and the Politics of Race, Citizenship, and Entitlement" (Ph.D. diss., University of California, Santa Cruz, 2000), 16.

15. Lilikala Kame'eleihiwa, *Native Land and Foreign Desires: Pehea La E Pono Ai? How Shall We Live in Harmony?* (Honolulu, 1992), 19–22; J. Kehaulani Kauanui, "A Fraction of National Belonging: 'Hybrid Hawaiians,' Blood Quantum, and the Ongoing Search for Purity," in Neferti X. M. Tandiar and Angela Y. Davis, eds., *Beyond the Frame: Women of Color and Visual Representation* (New York, 2005): 153–70.

16. Cited by Gary Y. Okihiro, *Cane Fires: The Anti-Japanese Movement in Hawaii, 1865–1945* (Philadelphia, 1991), 13.

17. Jonathan Kay Kamakawiwo'ole Osorio, *Dismembering Lahui: A History of the Hawaiian Nation to 1887* (Honolulu, 2002), 237; Lydia Kaulapai, "The Queen Writes Back: Lili'uokalani's *Hawaii's Story by Hawaii's Queen*," *Studies in American Indian Literatures* 17, 2 (2005): 32–62, quotations from 55, 56. As Kaulapai points out, the queen's definition was used to identify those to whom the United States apologized for this illegal overthrow of the Kingdom of Hawai'i in 1993 on the occasion of its centennial.

18. Lauren L. Basson, "Fit for Annexation but Unfit to Vote? Debating Hawaiian Suffrage Qualifications at the Turn of the Twentieth Century," *Social Science History* 29, 4 (2005): 575–98; Kauanui, "'Blood Mixture.'"

19. Ernest Andrade Jr., *Unconquerable Rebel: Robert W. Wilcox and Hawaiian Politics, 1880–1903* (Niwot, Colo., 1996).

20. Kent, *Islands under the Influence*, 68; Daws, *Shoal of Time*, 294–95; Fuchs, *Hawaii Pono*, 156–60.

21. Silva, *Aloha Betrayed*, 139, 189–90.

22. Peter S. Onuf, *Jefferson's Empire: The Legacy of American Nationhood* (Charlottesville, Va., 2000), 51, 52, 191.

23. On Americanization and whiteness as entwined and mutually sustaining discourses, see David R. Roediger, *Working toward Whiteness: How America's Immigrants Become White, The Strange Journey from Ellis Island to the Suburbs* (New York, 2005), esp. 9.

24. Kauanui, "'Blood Mixture,'" 40; Povinelli, "Notes on Gridlock."

25. Emma Metcalf Nakuina, *Hawaii, Its People, Their Legends* (Honolulu, 1904), preface.

26. Reginald Horsman, *Race and Manifest Destiny: The Origins of American Racial Anglo-Saxonism* (Cambridge, Mass., 1981); Stephanie Barczewski, *Myth and National Identity in Nineteenth-Century Britain: The Legends of King Arthur and Robin Hood* (New York, 2000).

27. Sargent Bush Jr., "America's Origin Myth: Remembering Plymouth Rock," *American Literary History* 12, 4 (2000): 745–56.

28. Hawaii Promotion Committee, *Hawaii* (Honolulu, 1903) (hereafter HPC *Hawaii* 1903b; different work from HPC *Hawaii* 1903a cited in note 2), Hawaiian Collection, Special Collections, Hamilton Library, University of Hawai'i at Manoa, 10.

29. Nakuina, *Hawaii, Its People, Their Legends*, preface.

30. HPC *Hawaii* 1903a, 7.

31. HPC *Hawaii* (Honolulu, 1904) (hereafter HPC *Hawaii* 1904), Hawaiian Collection, Special Collections, Hamilton Library, University of Hawai'i at Manoa, n.p.

32. HPC *Hawaii* 1903a, 7.

33. HPC *Hawaii* 1904, n.p.

34. HPC *Hawaii* 1903b, 7, 10

35. Ann Laura Stoler, "Intimidations of Empire: Predicaments of the Tactile and Unseen," in Stoler, *Haunted by Empire*, 3.

36. Nakuina, *Hawaii, Its People, Their Legends*, preface; Bacchilega, "Media Translation in the Production of Legendary Hawai'i."

37. Osorio, "'What Kine Hawaiian Are You?' A Mo'olelo about Nationhood, Race, History, and the Contemporary Sovereignty Movement in Hawai'i," *Contemporary Pacific* 13, 2 (2001): 371.

38. Clifford, "Indigenous Articulations."

39. Nakuina, *Hawaii, Its People, Their Legends*, 7, 8; Ballantyne, *Orientalism and Race*, 164–167.

40. Nakuina, *Hawaii, Its People, Their Legends*, 11; Barbara Bennett Pearson, ed., *Notable Women of Hawaii* (Honolulu, 1984), 281.

41. K. R. Howe, *Where the Waves Fall: A New South Seas History from First Settlement to Colonial Rule* (Honolulu, 1996), 154–58.

42. Nakuina, *Hawaii, Its People, Their Legends*, 20–21; Kame'eleihiwa, *Native Land and Foreign Desires*, 80.

43. Kame'eleihiwa, *Native Land and Foreign Desires*, 153–54; Greg Dening, "Sharks That Walk on the Land," in Dening, *Performances* (Chicago, 1992), 64–78.

44. Julia Clancy-Smith, "Saint or Rebel?: Resistance in French North Africa," in Alice L. Conklin and Ian Christopher Fletcher, eds., *European Imperialism, 1830–1930* (New York, 1999), 197. This idea is more fully developed in the larger work from which it is drawn; see *Rebel and Saint: Muslim Notables, Populist Protest, Colonial Encounters, Algeria and Tunisia, 1800–1904* (Berkeley, 1994), esp. 251–53.

45. Nakuina, *Hawaii, Its People, Their Legends*, 54, 62; Dening, "Sharks That Walk on the Land."

46. J. Kehaulani Kauanui, "'For Get' Hawaiian Entitlement: Configurations of Land, 'Blood,' and Americanization in the Hawaiian Homes Commission Act of 1920," *Social Text* 17, 2 (1999): 123–41, quotations from 134, 136, 137; see also Susan Y. Najita, "History, Trauma, and the Discursive Construction of 'Race' in John Dominis Holt's *Waimea Summer*," *Cultural Critique* 47 (2001): 167–214.

47. Okihiro, *Cane Fires*; Edward D. Beechert, *Working in Hawaii: A Labor History* (Honolulu, 1985); Ronald Takaki, *Pau Hana: Plantation Life and Labor in Hawaii, 1835–1920* (Honolulu, 1983).

48. Orvar Löfgren, *On Holiday: A History of Vacationing* (Berkeley, 1999); Cleveland Amory, *The Last Resorts* (New York, 1952).

49. *Thrum's Hawaiian Almanac and Annual for 1928* (Honolulu, 1927), Hawaiian Collection, Special Collections, Hamilton Library, University of Hawai'i at Manoa, 32; Stan Cohen, *The Pink Palace: The Royal Hawaiian Hotel, A Sheraton Hotel in Hawaii* (Missoula, Mont., 1986), 41–50; *Honolulu Star Bulletin*, January 31, 1927.

50. Elsie Kuhn Brown, "Hawaii—Where Romance Is Enthroned," *Paradise of the Pacific*, December 1926, 31; "Royal Hawaiian Hotel Souvenir Edition," *Keeler's Hotel Weekly*, August 26, 1927, 7, 47; "The Opening of the Royal," *Paradise of the Pacific*, February 1927, 25; Thomas Kemper Hitch and Mary Ishii Kuramoto, *Waialae Country Club: The First Half Century* (Honolulu, 1981), 34, 38, 145, 146; Richard Walter Coller, "Waikiki: A Study of Invasion and Succession as Applied to a Tourist Area" (M.A. thesis, University of Hawaii, 1952), 67.

51. On narratives of Waikiki, see Houston Wood, *Displacing Natives: The Rhetorical Production of Hawai'i* (Lanham, Md., 1999); George S. Kanahele, *Waikiki, 100 b.c. to 1900 a.d.: An Untold Story* (Honolulu, 1985); Don Hibbard and David Franzen, *The View from Diamond Head: Royal Residence to Urban Resort* (Honolulu, 1986).

52. Hawkins, "Princess Abigail Kawananakoa"; John S. Whitehead, "The Antistatehood Movement and the Legacy of Alice Kamiokila Campbell," *Hawaiian Journal of History* 27 (1993): 43–64. Alice Kamiokila Campbell was a sister of Abigail Kawananakoa.

53. "Ancient Pageantry, Music, and Dancing to Feature Opening," *Honolulu Star-Bulletin*, January 31, 1927; "Royal Hawaiian Hotel Souvenir Edition," 47; "Perfection in Every Detail," *Honolulu Star Bulletin*, February 2, 1927; Jane C. Desmond, *Staging Tourism: Bodies on Display from Waikiki to Sea World* (Chicago, 1999), 89–91; *Paradise of the Pacific* (February 1927), 25; Rob Wilson,

Reimagining the American Pacific: From South Pacific to Bamboo Ridge and Beyond (Durham, N.C., 2000), xiv.

54. Desmond, *Staging Tourism*, 91; "All the Glamour and Glory of Old Hawaii Remain," *Honolulu Star Bulletin*, January 31, 1927; *Honolulu Advertiser*, February 1, 1927; Helen Geracimos Chapin, *Shaping History: The Role of Newspapers in Hawai'i* (Honolulu, 1996), 148.

55. Wood, *Displacing Natives*; Silva, *Aloha Betrayed*; Merry, *Colonizing Hawai'i*; Osorio, *Dismembering Lahui*.

56. Matt K. Matsuda, *Empire of Love: Histories of France and the Pacific* (New York, 2005), 110–12; Silva, *Aloha Betrayed*, 189–90; Coffman, *Nation Within*, 315; Peterson, *Notable Women of Hawaii*, 209.

57. Hawkins, "Princess Abigail Kawananakoa;" Peterson, *Notable Women of Hawaii*, 209–11.

58. As Durba Ghosh argues, although over time the "grammars of racial categories shifted from vague notions of 'cultural competence' . . . to scientific and biological notions of racial difference," they did not do so in either a "linear or progressive" manner. Durba Ghosh, "Who Counts as 'Native?': Gender, Race, and Subjectivity in Colonial India," *Journal of Colonialism and Colonial History* 6, 3 (2005), http://muse.jhu.edu/login?uri=/journals/journal_of_colonialism_and_colonial_history/v006/6.3ghosh.html.

59. Henry Yu, "Tiger Woods Is Not the End of History: or, Why Sex across the Color Line Won't Save Us All," *American Historical Review* 108 (December 2003): 1406–14, quotation from 1408.

60. Sylvia van Kirk, "From 'Marrying-In' to 'Marrying-Out': Changing Patterns of Aboriginal/Non-Aboriginal Marriage in Colonial Canada," *Frontiers* 23, 2 (2002): 1–11. This article "argues that over the course of the colonial period, from the early seventeenth to the late nineteenth centuries, the practice of Aboriginal/non-Aboriginal marriage shifts from 'marrying-in' to 'marrying-out.'"

KATHERINE ELLINGHAUS

10 *Intimate Assimilation*

COMPARING WHITE-INDIGENOUS
INTERMARRIAGE IN THE UNITED STATES
AND AUSTRALIA, 1880S–1930S

In the late nineteenth and early twentieth centuries, settler
nations such as Australia and the United States envisioned the transformation, even the disappearance, of indigenous identity. Their ideas were
shaped by a social evolutionary theory that proposed that indigenous
people could be pulled up the evolutionary ladder from "savagery" to
"civilization" through education and Christianity. Governments hopeful of removing the financial obligation they owed to indigenous peoples
also had a powerful part to play in colonial societies' plans for their future. Utilizing a comparative methodology, this chapter investigates a
third phenomenon that profoundly shaped ideas about assimilation in
the United States and Australia—the occurrence of intimate, sexual relationships between white and indigenous people.

In the United States, where black-white relationships have dominated
the historical imagination, historians have often understood the dominant discourse about interracial relationships as being, as Stephen Small
has argued, "invariably hostile."[1] Scholars have traced how, through the
early colonial period, in slave states and on the frontier, legislatures introduced laws to prohibit "amalgamation" and, later, "miscegenation."
They have examined how scientists and medical doctors produced evidence that racial mixing "contaminated" the white race, how literature
and film reflected the titillation and disgust with which interracial rela-

tionships were viewed, and how interracial relationships were cited as a reason why civil rights and equalities could not be awarded to nonwhites. This essay moves beyond this framework of hostility to explore how certain kinds of interracial relationships were understood, by contrast, in terms of assimilation and absorption. David Hollinger points out that the story of Indian-white interracial mixing was not part of the discourse of taboo surrounding miscegenation between black and white, nor that of assimilation surrounding the immigrant "melting pot."[2] Laws prohibiting miscegenation were applied only inconsistently to Indians—hinting that part of this story is about acceptance rather than prevention, about turning a blind eye rather than taboo, and about incorporation and absorption rather than racial purity or integrity. Few scholars, however, have explored this aspect of interracial relationships in the United States.[3]

In Australia, on the other hand, historians have focused on assimilation policies that clearly went beyond a hostile reaction to miscegenation and saw interracial relationships between white and Aboriginal people as a means of biological absorption.[4] While not openly encouraging the sexual exploitation of Aboriginal women by white men, some Australian politicians saw these relationships and the children they produced as conduits of whiteness. People of mixed descent in some states were declared white, part-Aboriginal children across the country were removed from their communities to be "absorbed" into the mainstream, and young Aboriginal women were put to work for white families as domestic servants, resulting in high rates of unregulated illegitimate pregnancies. Some government officials were accused of openly advocating relationships between white men and Aboriginal women. In recent scholarship, Australian histories of assimilation include these stories alongside discussions of government policies, schools, missions, and other methods of acculturation.[5]

These historiographical differences reflect, in part, the contrasting policies of assimilation in each nation. In the United States, assimilation was most often couched in terms of social mobility. Indians were to be "elevated" to citizenship, and a "spirit of personal independence and manhood . . . a desire for possessing property, and a knowledge of its advantages and rights" was to be inspired in them. Then they could partake of the opportunities provided by the great American nation, in which an individual's social status was determined by his or her hard work and abilities. Only then would the "last great chapter in the solution of the Indian problem . . . be written."[6] After the General Allotment Act (which translated assimilation policies into legislation) was passed in 1887, a period ensued in which the government provided significant funding for the establishment of Native American schools. Education was seen as the passport to at least the bottom rung of American society. "Indian children taken from a life which represents Anglo-Saxon barbarism of more than a thousand years ago may," commissioner of Indian affairs Thomas Morgan wrote in 1891, "if placed at an early age in proper relations with modern civilization, enter very largely into participation of the best results of nineteenth century life."[7] Once given this opportunity, innate ability would see some Indians rise up the ladder of success, while others would be left behind, just like white Americans. Although industrial training and underfunded institutions characterized Native Americans' education throughout this period, these ideas persisted. In 1919 Cato Sells wrote of his aim to "speedily sift the Indian who should stand on his own merits, pay taxes, discharge the service and exercise the freedom of citizenship, from those who will require the protection of the Government for some time before taking on such responsibilities."[8] Thus implicit in the discourse of assimilation was the assumption that some Native American people could ascend not just the Darwinian ladder but also the social one. In some cases they did so. Educated, acculturated Native Americans became writers, doctors, lawyers, and businesspeople, and while they were certainly not immune from the disadvantages of their racial identity, they were also able to acquire some middle-class trappings.[9]

By contrast, although Australian commentators often talked about the necessity to "civilize" Aborigines in the late nineteenth and early twentieth centuries, and various missionaries operated as a Christianizing influence, there was no concerted government effort to create educational institutions or to allocate land to Aborigines on which they might become self-sufficient farmers, as occurred in the United States under the General Allotment Act. Government officials, philanthropists, and educators who spoke about cultural assimilation were certainly not envisioning Aboriginal people as "ascending" to their own social status. As Henry Reynolds has argued, "despite the fine words about civilisation and Christianity the reality was that all Europeans offered to the Aborigines was the life of the poor and powerless at the bottom of the 'scale of graduated classes' with virtually no chance of social mobility or of the 'improvement' which well-meaning whites talked so much about."[10] Thus Australian Aborigines had little opportunity to do more than provide itinerant, low-paid labor to white employers, or live a segregated life on reserves receiving minimal government support.

This essay utilizes a comparative methodology to relate these separate national stories, attempting to do justice to both the emotional history of interracial relationships and state attempts to control them.

Focusing on intermarriage as an important part of assimilation throws light on vast national differences but also some important similarities and connections. A common set of discourses on social mobility, cultural assimilation, education, Christianization, segregation, antimiscegenation, and absorption were all present in assimilationist thinking in Australia and the United States, albeit in different measures at different times. These commonalities, along with recent scholarly developments in global, transnational, and comparative analysis, mean that it is no longer appropriate to analyze these societies as only distinct and disconnected. In each, colonization created a shared and contested space defined by complex power relations and blurred ethnic boundaries. As Antoinette Burton and Tony Ballantyne argue in the introduction, intimate relationships were the product of that shared space and contributed to the cultural confusion and compromised power that colonizers in both nations tried so hard to ignore, control, and suppress. Thus, the arena of the intimate is particularly informative of how seemingly incommensurate nations such as the United States and Australia are actually comparable in important ways. Indeed, as Ann Stoler has suggested, it is in the realm of the intimate that we are most likely to see the United States, a nation often out of touch with its settler origins, as "colonial."[11]

Taking up the broader argument of this collection about the ways mobilities in the intimate sphere underlay imperial power, this essay begins by exploring how marriages between white and indigenous people were affected by the different assimilation policies of each country, and moves on to take account of the extraordinary complexity of the discourses that impacted on these relationships. This comparison of two disparate places, each with its own vocabulary of colonialism, points to connections and similarities that gave shape to broader aspects of the global imperial project. Colonial attitudes to indigenous-white intermarriage drew on a mixture of often fanciful, transnational, cultural beliefs about gendered and raced identities and simultaneously a pragmatic, financially based, all-too-common view about the potential of assimilation policy. Discernable here is a conflict—between popular ideas about people of indigenous descent and government policy—that partially explains complex attitudes to intermarriage. But nor were the two separate. Indeed, to understand assimilation policies we must see them as a statement of an ideal, an imagined solution far removed from the reality of individual experiences or what was set out in government records.[12] Part of that reality was numerous crosscultural relationships, of all kinds, that slipped under and over the radar of public scrutiny and acceptance. Whenever one of these relationships was formed, racial segregation was undermined, crosscultural communication took place, lives became entangled, and the boundaries of white and indigenous became blurred.

My focus on marriage is meant to contribute one suggestion to the project of exploring what exactly historians mean when they invoke the realm of the "intimate."[13] Marriage, as opposed to casual liaison, clearly reveals the leakage of the intimate into the public realm. As Kerry Wynn and Christine M. Skwiot argue (chapters 8 and 9 here), indigenous/white marriage was an important symbolic tool that could be used to imagine empire, define national borders, or even evoke the founding fictions of new colonial states. In addition, as Nancy Cott has shown, the act of marriage itself is public as well as a private, and the social status of an individual has significant impact on the status of his or her spouse.[14] This impact was tempered by gender and race. As Ann Stoler has argued, "European men were assured that their 'invisible bonds' of nationality remained intact regardless of their legal partner. European women, on the other hand, were summarily (but temporarily) disenfranchised from their national community on the basis of conjugal choice alone."[15] Intermarriages as well as casual relationships between white and indigenous peoples raised a variety of gendered questions and concerns about economic ownership, special rights, citizenship, nationality, and social mobility. Reactions differed radically according to the gender of the white spouse. The gendered response to white/indigenous relationships reveals that a broad project of gradually reducing the meager special benefits allocated to indigenous people was, despite national differences, unarguably the motivation of government policies in both Australia and the United States throughout the late nineteenth and twentieth centuries, despite rhetoric to the contrary. Underlying government reactions to interracial marriages between white and indigenous people, therefore, was a base concern about the transmission of property, as well as other social, cultural, and political concerns inevitably raised by relationships that brought together two cultures as well as two people.

Also determining responses to marriages between indigenous and white people were particular assumptions about what it meant for a spouse to be "Indian" or "Aboriginal." Romanticized, idealized as the "noble savage," and expected to "vanish" or "die out," indigenous people were hardly a sexual threat to the purity of the white nation (as were African Americans). Although they were coded as profoundly "nonwhite," in both nations ideas of assimilation, acculturation, and absorption sometimes allowed them to be seen as close to acceptable spouses for white people, or at least as the procreative conduits of whiteness that would see the "Indian" and "Aboriginal problem" disappear forever. Gender had a part to play here, too. Common to Australia, the United States, and the imperial world were ideas about white women as symbols of racial purity whose sullying by the touch of nonwhite men augured badly for the state of the empire, and white men whose conquest of land often included the conquest of native women's bodies. That versions of these beliefs were shared by more than one colonial site suggests crossovers and connections between Australia and the United States that are explored briefly in the final section of the chapter.

I begin my comparison in the United States, where in 1888 Congress approved an Act aimed at thwarting what they saw as the selfish, capitalist impulses that prompted white men to marry Native American women. The Act, called the Act in Relation to Marriage Between White Men and Indian Women, prevented these men from becoming entitled to "any tribal property, privilege, or interest," and forced every Native American woman who married a white man, except those belonging to the so-called Five Civilized Tribes, to become an American citizen on her marriage.[16] The Act can be understood better when seen as part of the project of reducing the numbers of Indians who lived in traditional ways on reservations. Men who married Native American women and took advantage of their property were not crossing the racial boundary in the right direction. By living with their wives' communities, they were inhibiting the gradual absorption of Indian lands and identity into the white body politic. They were also taking advantage of the special grants of land meant only for Indians—a significant component of the 1887 General Allotment Act was the division of reservations into individual allotments meant to provide Indians with the means of self-sufficiency while simultaneously releasing the United States from its treaty promises. E. P. Briscoe, the agent at the Crow Agency in Montana, also writing in 1888, wanted all such white men married to Indian women to be "ordered off the reservation. With their superior advantage of civilization and education," he said, "they have selected the choicest places of location, and without the consent of the agent [and] have [claimed on behalf of their children] the most fertile agricultural valleys. . . . One . . . claims the right, by virtue of his wife and children, to pasture 20,000 sheep on the reservation."[17]

At the same time, white men who married Indian women could also be seen as a means of assimilation, serving, as president-to-be Theodore Roosevelt wrote, "as connecting links between [Indians] and civilization, and rendering the road upward very much easier for them."[18] Indeed, for acculturated native women, white men might in fact be a good choice of spouse. A report from a member of the Indian Rights Association (perhaps the most influential nongovernment organization promoting assimilation in this period) of his trip around Alaska expressed this view while being unusually open about immorality in mining towns such as Juneau. "Among the [women] leading a life of prostitution, it is sad to relate that many have been scholars at the . . . school," he wrote: "While at the school they were under good moral influences, but only for two or three years at the most. On leaving, they have no occupation to engage in. . . . They are clean, attractive, and know their own worth. To go back to a life of dirt, ignorance and superstition in the native village is loathsome to them . . . girls who have married white men or elevated Indians . . . have made excellent wives and good mothers."[19] Tellingly, the position assimilationists took on such marriages often focused on husbands' potential for economic self-sufficiency. Marriages between white men and Indian women, if they followed the correct rules of gender, were based on property descending from the father, were no drain on government resources, and could hasten both absorption and assimilation.

If we turn to case studies of white women who married Indian men, it becomes apparent that interracial relationships between Indians and whites were caught up in the specific ideas about citizenship that applied to white women. "Throughout the history of the United States," Linda Kerber says, "virtually all married women's identities as citizens were filtered through their husband's legal identities."[20] Until the mid-1930s, American women who married "foreign" husbands almost always lost their citizenship, and in 1907 an Act of Congress mandated that they did so (meanwhile, in almost every state it was illegal for a white woman and an African American man to marry). The converse applied when American men married foreign wives. In 1855, Congress passed a statute declaring that any woman "who might lawfully be naturalized under existing laws" who had married or would marry an American man gained American citizenship in doing so. As Nancy Cott has argued, this "act was remarkable in its gender specificity" and understood "male headship of the marital couple as a *civic* and *political* norm."[21]

Intermarriage was supposed to be a means of assimilation into the dominant society, not the other way around. When the white partner was a man, this made perfect sense. But women, seen traditionally as following their husbands' nationalities and status, were a more complicated prospect. For white women who married Indian men who were still "unassimilated," their legal status was often a source of confusion and anxiety. Concerns about the legal status of his daughter motivated the Reverend Arthur M. Wood to write to the Office of Indian Affairs in 1935. In his first stiff and formal letter, Wood bombarded the Office with a series of questions. Would a white woman who married an Indian lose her citizenship if the couple lived on a reservation? What about the children of this marriage? Would they receive money from the government to "keep them from starvation"? Would the children be educated? Would the couple have to pay taxes? If they were given a farm, would they also be given farming implements and stock? Whose laws should the couple obey—those of the reservation or those of the nation?[22] John Collier, the commissioner of Indian affairs, replied sympathetically, referring the case to the agent in charge of the reservation where the couple lived, who in turn responded with a long letter describing Wood's new son-in-law, the reservation itself, and the economic opportunities available there.[23] Three years later Wood wrote the Office again to ask for news. His query was again passed on to the agent, from whom he received a detailed reply, which described the couple's property, including which buildings were not yet completed, the breed of their cows, their children, and even Wood's daughter's last confinement.[24] In this marriage that put the rules of gender and assimilation into conflict (the transformation of "Indian" to "white"; the greater influence of husband over wife) and that potentially did not have a competent, breadwinning husband, this father's concerns were allayed not with humanitarian rhetoric about the equality of Native Americans (which John Collier, author of the "Indian New Deal," was no stranger to) but with information about property, self-sufficiency, and financial well-being.

As I have argued elsewhere, however, when Indian men appeared to be more assimilated, their marriages to white women could make sense according to prevailing ideas about the civilizing and domesticating potential of middle-class white femininity. Elaine Goodale Eastman's marriage to Dakota Charles Eastman, for example, was seen by many as connected to her career as a reformer, author, and educator interested in the plight of Native Americans. And because Charles was one of the most well-known acculturated Indian spokespersons of his time, a doctor, author, and public speaker, the couple was seen by many as a living symbol of the potential for assimilation.[25] Indian men who were chosen by women such as Elaine Goodale Eastman were well on their way to becoming citizens, if they were not already. (The 1887 General Allotment Act allowed heads of households to be awarded citizenship rights if they demonstrated sufficient acculturation.) A white wife was sometimes seen as one of the few options for these men, who lived lifestyles and moved in circles very different from those of the average Indian woman of the time, circles in which a white wife might even be seen as a reward for their assimilation. Most important, these marriages, almost by definition, required acculturated Native American husbands to take on the white role of breadwinner; thus these couples and their children ostensibly no longer required the benefits of Indian status.

In the United States, the tendency to see interracial relationships between white and Indian partners in the context of assimilation is brought sharply into focus when contrasted with views about relationships with African Americans. As Werner Sollors has argued, "the black-white divide [is] the deepest and historically most pervasive of all American color lines."[26] Only twelve states legislated against white–Native American marriages, and Native Americans were actually one of the groups least often included in antimiscegenation laws—laws that always included African Americans.[27] Interracial relationships involving whites and Indians were more acceptable than those involving African Americans. "Indians are possessed of noble traits not shared by their African brethren," Phillip C. Garrett argued in support of fusing the Native population with the white one in 1886.[28] Nor did African Americans have any financial benefits tied to their racial status—no treaties entitled them to lands or compensation from the government. On the whole, by comparison, marriage with an Indian had far more to recommend it than that with an African American.

In Australia, it was not until the late nineteenth and early twentieth centuries that white-Aboriginal relationships became a cause for public concern. The so-called protection legislation passed by nearly all colonies, states, and territories to control their indigenous populations authorized enough surveillance and control to allow some states to regulate Aboriginal women's, and more rarely men's, marriages, and there is evidence that others did so without formal authority by law.[29] Some protection legislation also contained clauses designed to limit white men's sexual access to Aboriginal women. Aboriginal people had few property rights that white men might gain by marrying an Aboriginal woman. Perhaps it was no coincidence that the most common interracial relationships were the fleeting and exploitative ones that took place between white men and Aboriginal women on the frontier.

By the 1920s and 1930s the growing number of people of mixed descent was beginning to be read as a threat to the nation's whiteness. In 1937 the chief administrators of Aboriginal policy from each state gathered to discuss "Aboriginal welfare" and debated whether the mixed descent population was, in fact, a solution to the Aboriginal problem. Influenced by eugenics, politicians and commentators believed that those of full descent would expire, while those of mixed descent, through constant interracial mixing, would eventually be absorbed into the white Australian population. It was not until the post–World War II period that assimilation policies prepared Aborigines for citizenship at all.[30] White men and women who married or were involved in long-term relationships with Aboriginal people were mostly marginalized, seen as somehow outside the bounds of acceptable society.

In contrast to the United States, then, marriage to an Aborigine was not a way for white Australians to gain access to tribal property, or to contribute to a project of assimilation. The foundation of the Australian nation on the doctrine of *terra nullius* gave no legal recognition to Aboriginal ownership of land at the time of settlement, and therefore removed the obligation of white Australians to compensate Aborigines for the loss of their resources. Aboriginal communities were not recognized as legal entities and were simply gathered on small parcels of land to which they had a dubious claim at best. The only recompense offered them by the Australian colonial governments was rations, and the meager financial contributions required to run the stations and reserves on which they lived. From the government's perspective this was not only enough, it was something that ought to be reduced further and removed from as many Aborigines as possible.

In some states it was one of the basic criteria of Aboriginal identity that the individual be "habitually associating and living with aboriginals," as stated by the 1869 Victorian *Act to Provide for the Protection and Management of the Aboriginal Natives*, the first piece of legislation aimed directly at the Aboriginal population. A liaison with a white person was more than enough to prompt the Victorian Board for the Protection of Aborigines to force the couple to live off the station, with no government support.[31] The New South Wales Aborigines' Welfare Board was also hesitant to provide government support for Aboriginal men married to European women, even when they were in considerable hardship.[32]

State governments, particularly in the southeast, also maintained a certain amount of control over whom Aboriginal people could marry, with a financial bottom line firmly in mind. Marjorie Steadson's letter to a board inspector informing him and the board that she was marrying a white man and thus wished to take possession of the wages the board had withheld from her when she was a ward prompted a flurry of correspondence. The board began making enquiries about the young couple, mostly directed at whether or not they would be self-supporting and independent. The local police at Nyngan not only inspected Marjorie but also made enquiries about her husband. The police report stated that he was a good worker, was honest, had no "Aboriginal blood," and had "steady temperate habits." Marjorie was described as a "good worker, clean and tidy, and of good character." In light of this favorable report, which augured well for the couple's self-sufficiency, the board decided, "no obstacle should be placed in the way of the proposed marriage."[33]

Because of the lack of emphasis on social mobility in Australian assimilation policies, there was less possibility, as John Maynard has argued, that for Aboriginal men "having the bravery to step across the race divide [would] open doors of acceptance."[34] Thomas Braham, who married Agnes Smith, a white woman, in Warrnambool in 1876 and who wrote an eloquent letter to the Victorian Board for the Protection of Aborigines arguing that his marriage should be seen as indicative of his acculturation (as it might have been in the United States), could not convince Australian officials that he should be given land to become self-sufficient.[35] Meanwhile, white Australians engaged in public debates about whether even people of mixed descent would ever be equal citizens. "Can the mixed-bloods be made full members of our social, economic, and political system?" asked well-known anthropologist A. P. Elkin in an article printed in the *Morpeth Review* in 1932: "Are these folk of mixed blood capable of sustained attention and effort . . . or is there in them an inherited call of the bush which from time to time makes them listless, and tends to make them find their real interest in a nomadic camp life? In other words, are they really biologically capable of playing an average part in civilized society?"[36]

In an inversion of the American concern that white men were unfairly gaining tribal benefits through their marriages to Indian women, Australian officials were worried that nonwhite, nonindigenous men, such as men from Indonesia, the Pacific Islands, or elsewhere in Asia (all subsumed under the category "Asiatics" in official discourse), could gain some form of Australian citizenship through a marriage with an Aboriginal woman. When in 1939 the bishop of Carpentaria proposed giving permission to indentured seamen at Thursday Island who had married local Aboriginal women to remain in Australia under exemptions in the Immigration Act, the Australian government greeted this suggestion with hostility. "If the Bishop's request were approved," the prime minister wrote to the premier of Queensland, "it would probably mean an increase in the number of such marriages and this of course would have a serious effect on the 'White Australia' policy."[37]

With no connection between marriage to white partners and the assimilation project, the white Australian public sometimes saw the issue of casual relationships between white men and Aboriginal women as almost preferable to marriage, despite their immorality. Australian politicians certainly spoke of white men who had sexual relationships with Aboriginal women with a mixture of repugnance and empathy. White men who "consorted" with Aboriginal women were portrayed as having "lost all sense of decency and of public morals" and as belonging "to the coarser and more unrefined members of the higher races."[38] Still there was some expression of a more understanding attitude. Speaking in the Western Australian Legislative Council in 1936, the Hon. J. Nicholson argued against legislation that made casual liaisons with an Aboriginal woman a criminal offense. "This may occur to the son of any hon. member here or to my son," Nicholson pointed out. "The young fellow may commit an offence that amounts merely to obeying a natural law or impulse and for doing so he will be branded as a criminal." Nicholson reserved his wrath for the white man who "cohabits, or habitually lives, with a black woman. . . . Such a man should suffer the punishment he deserves. When the offence is of a casual nature, it is different."[39] "The best type of white man," wrote J. W. Bleakley in his report to the federal government in 1929 on conditions in the Northern Territory, "is not anxious to outcast himself" by marrying "superior half-caste[s] or quadroons." Instead, the man of better character apparently preferred "to satisfy his lust with casual lubras (female Aboriginal Australians) until able to return to white society."[40] Whatever the rhetoric accompanying them, laws were far more likely to punish white men who had long-term, visible sexual relationships with Aboriginal women than those who engaged in the more fleeting variety.

Nor were white women who married Aboriginal men understood in terms of the assimilation project. While the discourse of the "civilizing angel" provided a way for white Americans to understand the marriage of an educated, middle-class, humanitarian-minded woman to an acculturated Native American man, this trope was very rarely to be found in the Antipodes. Few examples of middle-class women marrying Aborigines exist, and when they did so, they were greeted with little understanding.[41] Indeed, an audible concern among government officials was an anxiety about single women missionaries alone and in contact with Aboriginal communities, presumably because of the potential for interracial relationships to develop. The minute books of the New South Wales Aborigines' Welfare Board through the 1910s and 1920s show the determined application of a policy to prevent "lady missionaries" from residing on reserves. Unmarried female missionaries were refused appointments, the policy was made known to private missionary bodies such as the Australian Aborigines Mission and the Aborigines Inland Mission, and police and managers were asked to report on the presence of unmarried female missionaries or teachers working alone on reserves. In 1918, the board occupied itself at length with the "marriage of [a] white female missionary with [a] ½ caste" in a rural New South Wales region.[42] White authorities did not take kindly to the idea that white women placed in an official position of power over Aboriginal people should in any way compromise their social distance from their charges.

This was also unfortunately true of the antipodean feminist response to such issues. In the United Kingdom, feminist groups lobbied through the 1920s and 1930s to change the laws that said that they lost their nationality on marriage to an "alien." It was not until 1948 that the legislation was changed.[43] The Australian feminist campaign firmly located white Australian women inside the British Commonwealth, bemoaning their flimsy hold on citizenship. The issue of marriages to Aboriginal men was not raised.[44] As Angela Woollacott has argued, white Australian women's articulations of whiteness leaned firmly on identification with the British Empire and the racist power structures within it.[45]

Thus, how white people understood marriages between whites and Indians and Aborigines in settler societies such as the United States and Australia depended not just on how they imagined the assimilation or even the eventual absorption of indigenous people into the body politic but also on gendered rules about the transfer of property and status. Interracial relationships involving white men could be understood as a conduit for assimilation, but with different degrees of benefit attached to indigenous identity in each country. In the United States, such relationships were sometimes seen as a legitimate means for Indian people and their children to become acculturated, as long as the law did not allow them to become a means for white people to take advantage of special rights and statuses accorded to Indians. In Australia, where there was less focus on long-term, marriage-like relationships, these unions were seen more often as useful for hastening the process of biological absorption. Taking place on the fringes of society, they could not be seen as a means of social mobility.

But beyond assimilation policies and concern about property and budgets, broader forces were at work in dictating how white-indigenous marriage was viewed. We might speculate that the African American population altered the saliency of Indian-white marriages for white Americans. Indians seemed more easily assimilable and were perhaps even further up the evolutionary scale than black Americans. Australian Aborigines were firmly placed below both Native Americans and African Americans in these constructed racial hierarchies, and their diminishing numbers made extinction through absorption such a tantalizing possibility that interracial marriages seemed hardly a serious problem.[46] They were certainly not a phenomenon occurring enough to warrant understanding them in terms of assimilation and social mobility as occurred in the United States.

With no equivalent-sized nonwhite population, white Australians could quite happily imagine themselves as a "White Australia," as their 1901 Immigration Act was unofficially titled. America on the other hand had to deal in more hands-on ways with its "crucible of race."[47]

Nor were these completely separate national stories. Indeed, historian Marilyn Lake has argued that the Australian "idea of the 'white man's country'" was in fact "a global project forged in response to white colonial apprehension at the emergence of a post-colonial world." There are direct links, Lake has found, between the ideas of the Australian "federal founders" and the American literature on the failure of Reconstruction that they read.[48] There is also some evidence that popular white Australian understandings of "blackness" were drawn from knowledge of the United States. There were small numbers of African Americans in Australia from very early years of settlement, but transnational ideologies about threatening nonwhites were far more influential, as were racial hierarchies that placed Australian Aborigines firmly at the bottom. White Australians saw the United States as having dealt with "racial problems" of a far greater magnitude, and for far longer, than Australia. "They not only have the North American Indians to deal with," a member of the Queensland Parliament marveled in 1897, "but the descendants of the African blacks and it is about the biggest problem the United States or any other country in the world has to deal with."[49] Comparatively with the United States, then, the numerically smaller, more manageable "Aboriginal problem" was easily swept aside. The United States was often raised as an example when individuals wished to argue for the dangers of "developing a coloured race which would be a menace to the white population," an oversight in North America—claimed Cecil Cook, who held the government office of "chief protector" of Aborigines in the Northern Territory—that caused a civil war, lynchings, and vigilantism.[50] The United States example was drawn on by politicians to point out that the sexual exploitation of nonwhite women was hardly unique to Australia, and that, like "Red Indians," the Aborigines were not alone in their powerlessness "to resist the undermining influences" of civilization, to which they would "succumb readily."[51] When Jimmy Governor, an Aboriginal man, went on a killing spree among the rural settlements of New South Wales in 1901, leaving behind his white wife and mixed-descent baby, stereotypes about sexually threatening non-white men were resonant because of the American example. "It is rather hard to get the subject of the black men off one's mind at present, and it crops up this time in the memory of the great racial question which affects America," the *Mudgee Guardian* wrote in 1900 in a report on the Governor case. "Statistics show that [African Americans] are most horribly criminal, deeds of blood and lust being of terrible frequency. In some of the Southern States their power is so great . . . it is realised that the whites will soon be unable to live there."[52]

I have argued in this essay that the particularities of assimilation policies in each nation affected how white-indigenous marriages were viewed, but also that transnational ideas about gender, race, assimilation, and crossracial sexual relationships can be seen to have influenced their reception. We must not forget, however, the contribution of the character and efforts of the spouses themselves, who often negotiated this minefield of policy and prejudice with no little courage and temerity. Wynn and Skwiot tell compelling stories of how indigenous people in Oklahoma and Hawai'i were able to use intermarriage to negotiate power for themselves and their communities (chapters 8 and 9 here). Nor should we fail to recognize that these unions were based on real human emotions, which are often hard to find in the historical record. In every letter Carlos and Marie Montezuma, an Apache man and his Romanian-born wife, wrote to each other during their separation in 1921 they professed their love and longing for each other. Marie sent "love and kisses" with many of her letters, and Montezuma signed himself in each one "Your loving husband, Wassaja." When Montezuma died only a little over a year later, Marie was devastated. She wrote only a few days later that "his sickness and dea[th] came so fast that I can[']t believe he is dead[.] I cannot tell you my deep sorrow of loving him at this time[,] it is hard for me to bear it."[53] Carlos and Marie's intimate relationship put them at the mercy of local racists, national policies and laws, and even ideologies about race and colonialism that crossed oceans, but their love for each other existed despite these external pressures. In the end, racial and cultural boundaries are never totally secure; and the ability of people to test them is correspondingly, and inspiringly, boundless.

Notes

1. Stephen Small, "Colour, Culture, and Class: Interrogating Interracial Marriage and People of Mixed Racial Descent in the USA," in David Parker and Miri Song, eds., *Rethinking Mixed Race* (London, 2001), 120.

2. David A. Hollinger, "Amalgamation and Hypodescent: The Question of Ethnoracial Mixture in the History of the United States," *American Historical Review* 108, 5 (2003): 1367.

3. Exceptions are Patrick Wolfe, "Land, Labor, and Difference: Elementary Structures of Race," *American Historical Review* 106, 3 (June 2001): 866–905, and David D. Smits, "'Squaw Men,' 'Half-Breeds,' and Amalgamators: Late Nine-

teenth-Century Anglo-American Attitudes toward Indian-White Race-Mixing," *American Indian Culture and Research Journal* 15, 3 (1991): 29–61.

4. See Warwick Anderson, *The Cultivation of Whiteness: Science, Health, and Racial Destiny in Australia* (Melbourne, Australia, 2002), 216–43; Russell McGregor, *Imagined Destinies: Aboriginal Australians and the Doomed Race Theory, 1880–1935* (Melbourne, Australia, 1997), chap. 4; Wolfe, "Land, Labor, and Difference"; Robert Manne, "The Stolen Generations," in Manne, *The Way We Live Now: Controversies of the Nineties* (Melbourne, Australia, 1998), 15–41.

5. See, for example, Anna Haebich, *Broken Circles: Fragmenting Indigenous Families, 1800–2000* (Fremantle, 2000).

6. Report of Commissioner of Indian Affairs J. D. C. Atkins, October 5, 1885, in Wilcomb E. Washburn, ed., *The American Indian and the United States: A Documentary History*, vol. 1 (New York, 1973), 357, 359.

7. Report of Commissioner of Indian Affairs T. J. Morgan, October 1, 1891, in ibid., 528.

8. Report of Commissioner of Indian Affairs Cato Sells, September 30, 1919, in ibid., 889.

9. See Katherine Ellinghaus, *Taking Assimilation to Heart: Marriages of White Women and Indigenous Men in the United States and Australia, 1887–1937* (Lincoln, Neb., 2006), chaps. 3 and 4.

10. Henry Reynolds, *With the White People: The Crucial Role of Aborigines in the Exploration and Development of Australia* (Ringwood, Victoria, 1990), 99–109.

11. Ann Laura Stoler, "Tense and Tender Ties: The Politics of Comparison in North American History and (Post) Colonial Studies," in Stoler, ed., *Haunted by Empire: Geographies of Intimacy in North American History* (Durham, N.C., 2006), 32–39.

12. Anna Haebich, "Imagining Assimilation," *Australian Historical Studies* 33, 118 (2002): 62.

13. Ann Laura Stoler, "Intimidations of Empire: Predictions of the Tactile and Unseen," in Stoler, *Haunted by Empire*, 12.

14. Nancy Cott, *Public Vows: A History of Marriage and the Nation* (Cambridge, Mass., 2000).

15. Ann Laura Stoler, "Sexual Affronts and Racial Frontiers: European Identities and Cultural Politics of Exclusion in Colonial Southeast Asia," in Frederick Cooper and Ann Laura Stoler, eds., *Tensions of Empire: Colonial Cultures in a Bourgeois World* (Berkeley, 1997), 221.

16. U.S. Congress, House, *Annual Report of the Commissioner of Indian Affairs*, 50th Cong., 2d sess., 1888, 340.

17. Ibid., 154.

18. Theodore Roosevelt, *Report of Hon. Theodore Roosevelt Made to the United States Civil Service Commission, upon a Visit to Certain Indian Reservations and Indian Schools in South Dakota, Nebraska, and Kansas* (Philadelphia, 1893), 8.

19. *Eighth Annual Report of the Indian Rights Association, 1890* (Philadelphia, 1891), 61.

20. Linda K. Kerber, "The Meanings of Citizenship," *Journal of American History* 84, 3 (December 1997): 839.

21. Nancy F. Cott, "Marriage and Women's Citizenship in the United States,

1830–1934," *American Historical Review* 103, 5 (December 1998): 1456. Cott's emphasis.

22. Rev. Arthur M. Wood, Cazenovia, N.Y., to Office of Indian Affairs, September 1, 1935, 1829–1935, file. no. 742, Record Group 75, Central Classified Files 1907–39, National Archive and Record Administration, Washington, D.C. (hereafter NARA).

23. Ralph Fredenberg, Superintendent of Keshena Indian Agency to Rev. Arthur M. Wood, February 26, 1935, file. no. 742, Record Group 75, Central Classified Files 1907–39, NARA.

24. Ralph Fredenberg, Supt. Keshena Indian Agency, Wisconsin, to Arthur M. Wood, Cazenovia, N.Y., October 26, 1938; F. H. Daiker, Asst. Commissioner, to Ralph Fredenberg, October 22, 1938; Arthur M. Wood to Indian Affairs, October 10, 1938, Keshena 63641–1938–742, Record Group 75, Central Classified Files 1907–39, NARA.

25. Margaret Jacobs, "The Eastmans and the Luhans: Interracial Marriage between White Women and Native American Men, 1875–1935," *Frontiers* 23, 3 (2002): 29–54; Valerie Sherer Mathes, "Nineteenth-Century Women and Reform: The Women's National Indian Association," *American Indian Quarterly* 24, 1 (Winter 1990): 1–18, and Ellinghaus, *Taking Assimilation to Heart*, 81–104.

26. Werner Sollors, *Interracialism: Black-White Intermarriage in American History, Literature, and Law* (New York, 2000), 3–4.

27. Pascoe, "Race, Gender, and Intercultural Relations: The Case of Interracial Marriage," *Frontiers* 23, 1 (1991): 7.

28. *Proceedings of the Fourth Annual Meeting of the Lake Mohonk Conference, 1886* (Philadelphia, 1886), 9.

29. Katherine Ellinghaus, "Regulating Koori Marriages: The 1886 Victorian 'Aborigines Protection Act,'" *Journal of Australian Studies* 67 (2001): 22–29.

30. See John Chesterman and Brian Galligan, *Citizens without Rights: Aborigines and Australian Citizenship* (Melbourne, Australia, 1997).

31. Ellinghaus, "Regulating Koori Marriages."

32. Aborigines' Welfare Board, Minute Books 1890–96, 4/7108-7111, August 31, 1893, Archives Office of New South Wales, Sydney.

33. Dianne Decker, *Long Time Coming Home: As Recalled by Marjorie Woodrow* (Lake Haven, New South Wales, 2001), 58–66.

34. Victoria Haskins and John Maynard, "Sex, Race and Power: Aboriginal Men and White Women in Australian History," *Australian Historical Studies* 36, 126 (2005): 214.

35. Minutes of Meeting of the BPA [Board for the Protection of Aborigines], July 20, 1877, item 3, B314, National Archives of Australia, Melbourne location.

36. A. P. Elkin, "Cultural and Racial Clash in Australia," *Morpeth Review* 21 (September 1932): 25, 42, 44.

37. J. A. Perkins, Prime Minister, to Premier of Queensland, September 22, 1939, file labeled "Asiatics engaged in pearling industry, Western Australia—Marriage with aboriginal women," D349/3/4, A461, National Archives of Australia, Canberra location·

38. *Queensland Parliamentary Debates* 165 (1934): 1555; "Preliminary Report on the Aboriginals of the Northern Territory by Professor W. Baldwin Spencer, 1913," *Commonwealth Parliamentary Papers* 3 (1912): 47.

39. *Western Australian Parliamentary Debates* 98 (1936): 1068, 1197.

40. "The Aboriginals and Half-Castes of Central Australia and North Australia. Report by J. W. Bleakley," *Commonwealth Parliamentary Papers* 2, 21 (1928); 28.

41. Haskins and Maynard, "Sex, Race and Power," 198–200; Ellinghaus, *Taking Assimilation to Heart,* 149–66.

42. Aborigines' Welfare Board, Minute Books 1890–96, 4/7108-7111, July 22, 1911; October 12, 1911; November 30, 1911; January 18, 1912; February 8, 1912; March 21, 1918; April 3, 1918; July 13, 1921, and circular no. 68, April 10, 1915, Aborigines' Welfare Board, Copies of letters sent 1914–27, 4/7128, Archives Office of New South Wales.

43. M. Page Baldwin, "Subject to Empire: Married Women and the British Nationality and Status of Aliens Act," *Journal of British Studies* 40, 4 (October 2001): 522–56.

44. See, for example, Australian Federation of Women Voters, *The Nationality of Married Women* (Sydney, [193–?]), pamphlet, in Australian Collection, National Library of Australia, Canberra.

45. Angela Woollacott, "'All This Is the Empire, I Told Myself': Australian Women's Voyages 'Home' and the Articulation of Colonial Whiteness," *American Historical Review* 102, 4 (October 1997): 1003–29.

46. Gillian Cowlishaw, "Colour, Culture and the Aboriginalists," *Man* 22, 2 (June 1987): 221.

47. Gary Gerstle, *American Crucible: Race and Nation in the Twentieth Century* (Princeton, 2001).

48. Marilyn Lake, "White Man's Country: The Trans-national History of a National Project," *Australian Historical Studies* 24, 122 (2003): 352.

49. *Queensland Parliamentary Debates* 68 (1897): 1542.

50. Commonwealth of Australia, *Aboriginal Welfare: Initial Conference of Commonwealth and State Aboriginal Authorities Held at Canberra, 21st to 23rd April, 1937* (Canberra, Australia, 1937), 34.

51. *Western Australian Parliamentary Debates* 28 (1905): 424.

52. *Mudgee Guardian,* August 9, 1900, 3.

53. Maria Montezuma to Mr. L. V. McWhorter, c. February 4–14, 1923, in John William Larner, ed., *Papers of Carlos Montezuma* (Wilmington, Del., 1984), microfilm.

PART 3

Bodies on the Move:
Scandals of Imperial Space

ADRIAN CARTON

11 "Faire and Well-Formed"

PORTUGUESE EURASIAN WOMEN
AND SYMBOLIC WHITENESS IN
EARLY COLONIAL INDIA

> The task is not to figure out who was colonizer and who
> was colonized, nor to ask what the difference between
> metropolitan and colonial policy was; rather, it is to ask
> what political rationalities had made these distinctions
> and categories viable, enduring, and relevant.
>
> —Ann Laura Stoler, "Tense and Tender Ties:
>   The Politics of Comparison in North American
>   History and (Post) Colonial Societies," *Journal
>   of American History* (2001)

In the *Lusiad*, published in Lisbon in 1572 and regarded by
some scholars as the national epic of Portugal, Luis de Camoens describes
how the Greek gods helped the Portuguese to acquire their Indian possessions in a spectacular narrative of myth, legend, and maritime travel
account. The so-named age of discovery at the end of the fifteenth century
and the repositioning of Europe from its marginal position on the far western fringes of Afro-Eurasia to a central position in the world economy was
part of a broader exchange of ideas and bodies across both vast and more
easily accessible distances, where European colonies became sites for the
reproduction and transformation of new social distinctions. While the
macro level of this transition has been charted by world historians from
a "bird's-eye" view, the local nodes by which crosscultural exchange was
experienced as a lived material reality are only beginning to emerge in
the new postcolonial global histories.[1] In particular, Ann Laura Stoler has

urged a more sustained politics of comparison on a global scale whereby "connections between the broadscale dynamics of rule and the intimate domains of implementation" in different colonial settings may help us to rethink how to frame the relationship between changes in the world system and the contested politics of the intimate.[2]

After the completion of the first circumnavigation of the globe by Magellan in 1521, the cultural gaze of Europeans was widened through the notion of "discoverie,"[3] and the interconnectedness of the new capitalist world-system saw the Portuguese become the first European presence in a global web linking Portugal with Africa, the Americas, and Asia.[4] The largely male encounter with the "other" inevitably led to the proliferation of travel narratives that attempted to make sense of the place of interracial intimacy as part of the discourse of a new world system. In the *Lusiad,* the offspring of Portuguese men and Indian women emerge as the corporeal metaphors of the imagined anxiety felt in the early modern European mind toward sex across the racial divide. This manifested itself in de Camoens's deployment of the symbol of the monster to shape the perception that reaching beyond the racial contours of the European cosmos was tantamount to transgressing the biological border of the human species. In chapter 12 this description appears of the quasi-horror of intercorporeal amalgamation: "An Indian Woman married to a Portuguese was delivered at Bardes of a Monster with Two Heads and Teeth, the Ears Like a Monkey, on the forehead an Excrescency of Flesh like a Horn, the Legs sojoyned they looked like one, leaping out of the Midwife's hands, it seized a Black [*sic*] and bit out a piece of her flesh."[5]

In reality, however, such fantastic and semidemonic images of Eurasian children were more likely to be literary devices to tantalize and to entertain rather than windows through which to gauge the social acceptance of miscegenation in new colonial contexts, where interracial intimacy was not spectacular and extraordinary but absorbed into the politics of everyday life. The imperial canon in numerous global contexts provides us with ample evidence to suggest that the European male encounter with the sensual and exotic "other" was often translated as a sexual encounter with indigenous women in which the project of commercial conquest and the acquisition of female bodies were symbolically intertwined with each other. This merging of transcontinental mobility with crosscultural sexuality was encouraged as the social corollary of economic conquest, since marriage with "native women" necessitated the important objective of Catholic conversion. Hence gender and religion were important frames by which "mixedness" gained political currency, and they were often the crucial hinges on which the Portuguese colonial project gained its legitimacy in the sixteenth and seventeenth centuries.

In India, as in Brazil and places such as Mozambique, Angola, and other parts of Africa, interracial unions were sanctioned by both the Portuguese state and church in the early period of imperial conquest, since commercial sustainability and social survival relied heavily on forming local alliances with those who could act as intermediaries, interpreters, and cultural brokers.[6] The sexual politics of interracial liaison building in the private sphere were, therefore, as politically important as the military and economic maneuvering in the public sphere. Echoing the North American context, where the sites of interracial sexual intimacy were strategically important levers for the consolidation of colonial governance, this hybrid landscape of Portuguese India was, in effect, far from strange, subhuman, and monstrous. Historians such as Michael Pearson and Sanjay Subrahmanyam have emphasized that marriages between Portuguese settlers and Indian women were actively promoted as a tool of colonization from the earliest days of the vice-royalty of Goa, where a distinctive *mestiço* culture developed to consolidate permanent settlement on the subcontinent. Their work suggests that the hybrid worlds of the Portuguese colonies placed interracial sexuality at the heart of the strategic tactics of imperial expansion.[7]

As Ann Stoler has argued, the politics of métissage and the social categorization of mixed-race children constituted a social and political space where the colonial state sought to enforce categories of rule.[8] Different colonial environments in the modern era, from British India to French West Africa to the Dutch East Indies, illuminate the global relevance of this relationship between the classification of mixed-race subjects and the colonial state. To be sure, Charles Boxer has demonstrated that racial categories operated in much the same way in Portuguese India, where political power was indexed quite clearly with skin color and gradations of whiteness, and where the colonial state had a vested interest in the maintenance of white privilege.[9] However, as Stoler points out, "mixedness itself was a moving and strategic category,"[10] and (as Katherine Ellinghaus and David Haines also illuminate in chapters 2 and 10 here) different imperial projects produced a range of contested responses to métissage across time, space, and location.[11]

This essay also addresses this valuable point from two different angles in view of the fact that there has been surprisingly little attention to the moving category of whiteness in the context of early colonial India. On the one hand, India was a place where multiple imperial projects were in contestation with each other, inevitably producing complex and divergent framings of racial mixing at the same point in time. On the other hand, there may need to be more acknowledgment of the historical specificities of time and place in the framing of cultural difference in an era where both skin color and emerging notions of "race" were often ambiguously fused with other markers of social distinction. For example, colonial policy in Portuguese India was deeply implicated in the ecclesiastical imperatives of the Catholic Church, in ways that enable us to engage with the insights of Stoler on the subject-constituting practices of the colonial state from the perspective of the religious filter through which such racial categories were imagined. The children of Portuguese fathers and local women were treated as Catholic subjects, given quasi-European status, and in most cases were given Portuguese citizenship. In this essay, I suggest that both gender and religion were important "political rationalities" that shaped the contours and meaning of whiteness in the discursive space of colonial India in different ways in the sixteenth and seventeenth centuries. By focusing on the cultural dialogue between English and Portuguese colonialisms, I wish to chart how the role of Catholic Portuguese Eurasian women can illuminate these rationalities through the lens of intimate relationships that were deeply implicated in the politics of colonial knowledge.

Britishness, Interracial Intimacy, and Colonial Knowledge

Drawing from both feminist and postcolonial critiques of the epistemology of imperialism, scholars such as Lynn Zastoupil argue that interracial intimacies in imperial arenas played a fundamental part in the construction of colonial knowledge.[12] Applying Zastoupil's reflections to the legacies of métissage in Portuguese India, there seems to be an important correlation between Portuguese constructions of racial mixing and the emergence of British colonial knowledge. The very words employed to name and describe individuals of mixed Indian and European origin entered the English language through the legacy of Portuguese etymology. According to Hobson-Jobson, the term *mestizo* is first known to have been used in English in 1588, to describe an individual who was "halfe an Indian, and halfe a Portugall."[13] In fact, the early English and French appellations for Portuguese Eurasians retained the Portuguese derivation of these terms, with *mestezaies* noted by Foster in the late 1630s,[14] and the Portuguese Eurasians of St. Thomé were referred to as "these ill-nurtered *musteezes* or mungrells of St Thomé"[15] in 1647. This essay suggests that the dominant paradigm of British imperial history has forgotten an earlier landscape of hybridity in Portuguese India, where religious distinctions framed the political currency of racial mixing.

That the historiography of interracial intimacy has been concerned with the British experience is hardly surprising, since the most significant insights dealing with relationships across the colonial divide have been framed in this context, but in perhaps three broad and divergent ways. The first is the study of the Anglo-Indian community as the ontological product of interracial intimacy. This historical trajectory is concerned with the emergence of a distinctive British Eurasian community in the early nineteenth century, as illustrated by the study by Christopher Hawes, and the ways British patriarchal descent framed the subsequent political development of a "mixed-race" community in India.[16] Other studies turn toward an earlier era when relationships across the racial divide between British men and Indian women were common. Set in a romantic mode, these are mostly studies of interracial relationships in the upper levels of both British and Indian society in which shared notions of elite status are perceived to have largely outweighed the concern with racial difference. With celebratory nostalgia, white male colonizers who "go native" tend to emerge in this vision as benevolent protectors of Indian tradition and promoters of interfaith cosmopolitanism.[17] The third approach sees the important feminist and postcolonial interventions of scholars such as Indrani Chatterjee and Durba Ghosh who argue in different ways against this image of the interracial couple as an example of idyllic social relations. Grounded in a decidedly unromantic mode, Chatterjee charts the ways much interracial sexuality between British men and Indian women in the eighteenth and nineteenth centuries was not intimate but exploitative and repressive, leaving "native women" as passive victims of both capitalist and colonial power relations.[18] On the other hand, Ghosh calls into question the effaced status of the voiceless "native woman" in relationships with British men in the eighteenth century by arguing that they were active agents in the constitution of hybrid identity and colonial relations. In this sense, she resurrects the "native" partners of white men as central to the constitution of colonial knowledge.[19]

Building on the important insights of Ghosh in relation to "bringing indigenous women back into the story" of racial hybridity in early colonial India,[20] this essay maps another possible route. Whereas these three approaches have concentrated on the relationships between British men and Indian women from the late eighteenth century and revealed the emergence of "mixed-race" identity in the nineteenth and twentieth centuries, recent scholarship has rarely delved into the sixteenth and seventeenth centuries—the period of the earliest Portuguese colonial encounters in India—or indeed charted the impact of that legacy on the articulation of racial hybridity. Moreover, while these three approaches draw on the ways class and gender relations mediate the "interracial" experience between "British men" and "native women," little is known of how the Protestant-Catholic divide within European communities may have undone or reworked transgressions based on color. Prefiguring the arrival of British men in India, what effect does our knowledge of the role of Catholic Portuguese Eurasian women in the construction of whiteness do to our understanding of colonial categories and, indeed, to our conception of hybridity in an Anglo-Indian frame?

Moving "Portuguese" Subjects

The establishment of permanent colonies in India by Portuguese men and the general absence of European women meant that sexual relationships with Indian women were commonplace. Portuguese women tended to be discouraged from accompanying men to India, due to the length of the voyage, the high mortality rates in transit, the subsequent danger of disease, and the harshness of the climate after arrival. In a far-off colonial outpost where warfare was continuous in order to consolidate Portuguese power, all the way to the end of the eighteenth century, few white Portuguese women went out to India compared to men.[21] There were habitual attempts by the Portuguese authorities to provide assisted passages for female orphans and other single Portuguese women to address the imbalanced gender ratio in Goa and other Indo-Portuguese settlements throughout the sixteenth and seventeenth centuries, but the overall numbers have been the subject of much scholarly debate. The research conducted by the historian Germano Correia in the 1940s and 1950s claims that more white women left Portugal for the Indian colonies than has previously been acknowledged, but his population estimates, taken from the Goan censuses, are generally race blind and they assume that all Portuguese females were originally from Portugal or were the offspring of white Portuguese women.[22] It is far more likely that the number of white Portuguese women who came to India directly from Portugal in this period was never more than a few thousand, even with the support of assisted passages.[23]

What is more certain from the sources is that the decision to populate Goa with white women from Portugal came only after a long and sustained policy of promoting interracial marriage that resulted in the formation of a large, racially mixed, Portuguese-speaking, Catholic com-

munity that reconstructed the contours of whiteness. The earliest population censuses for Goa in 1540 show the inclusion of *mestiço* children as
members of the European community.[24] Under the direction of the Portuguese colonial governor, Alfonso de Albuquerque, marriages between
Portuguese men and Indian women in Goa were encouraged as a mechanism both to regulate the high incidence of casual interracial sexuality
outside the confines of a morally acceptable union and to increase the
numbers of Christians through the process of conversion. These arrangements were not always voluntary but could be coercive and exploitative,
as revealed in the diaries of Albuquerque himself. Writing in 1512, he
refers to corrupt ecclesiastical practices, bribery, and a desire to prosely-
tize as the general contexts for "conversion marriages" through which
Indian women could very well become sexual slaves who were transferred
from one man to another: "I married in Goa an honest woman and good
looking to a Joao Cerveira, a good man: the latter died and she married
again. . . . Another man who is now dead fell in love with this woman,
he bribed the friar, and he severed the marriage, and had her placed in
the house of a man where the deceased used to do what he liked with her.
As that man died, the friar at once married her to another man."[25]

Furthermore, the seventeenth century Portuguese historian Faria y
Sousa comments that the official encouragement of these marriages by Albuquerque did not assume that the European men knew or recognized the
women who were to be their wives, even on the wedding night itself:

> He married some Portugueses [*sic*] to Women of the Country, giving
> them in Portion, Lands, Houses, or Employment, the better to secure
> his Colony. One Night that some of these Weddings were celebrated,
> the Brides were so mixt and confounded together among the People, that
> some of the Bridegrooms went to Bed to those that belonged to others,
> and next morning, finding the Mistake, they changed them, each taking
> his own, and all equal as to point of honour. This gave the more occasion
> to some Gentlemen to ridicule the care of Albuquerque.[26]

According to Charles Boxer, most of the women who entered into
early unions with the Portuguese in Goa were drawn from marginal
groups or they were widows or dancers, and these were also more likely
to have converted to Catholicism as a means of improving their social
status.[27] Hence the evidence seems to suggest that the essential difference between Christians and "heathens" was the primordial social distinction that moderated the social acceptance of intercultural marriages
in Portuguese India in the early modern period, rather than notions of
"race" or skin color per se. The symbolic anointing of Indian women as

Catholic subjects was an essential marker of cultural conversion, making an interracial marriage acceptable within the established boundaries of the Portuguese cultural universe.

The way mixed-race children of Portuguese men and Indian women were perceived and categorized in the sixteenth and seventeenth centuries is ambiguous. On the one hand they are represented in population censuses as Catholic Portuguese subjects, and as Europeans, and on the other they are marked out for special attention due to their physical appearance.[28] There is increasing emphasis on the importance of the body and the significance of color in corporeal descriptions of Portuguese Eurasians by the late sixteenth century. The writings of Dutch traveler Jan Huygen van Linschoten confirm that by 1586 the subject of racial mixing was important enough to warrant a separate chapter in his *Discours of Voyages*. The twenty-ninth chapter of this work, entitled "Of the Customes of the Portingales, and such as issued from them, called Mestiços, or half-countrimen, as well of Goa, as of all the Oriental Countries," provides the contemporary reader with a fascinating account of the ways Eurasians were represented and categorized under the European male gaze. Unlike colonial representations of the eighteenth and nineteenth centuries that emphasized the enduring difference between the Europeans and Eurasians, van Linschoten emphasizes their intrinsic similarity. He talks of the ways everyday Eurasian life in Goa was very similar to European life in Europe, describing the clothes they wore, their prayers before meals, their strict observance of Catholic ritual, and their houses in the European quarters of the white town.

Written into an imperial trope of mimicry, Portuguese Eurasian women are singled out from *mestiço* men in van Linschoten's representation for their sexual attractiveness and pleasing demeanor to European men: "The Portingales in India are many of them marryed with the naturall borne women of the countrie, and the children proceeding of them are called Mestiços, that is half-countrimen. These Mestiços are commonlie of yellowish colour, not withstanding there are manie women among them who are faire and well-formed."[29] The descriptions "faire" and "well-formed" seem to indicate that "Portuguese" women were represented in this text as exoticized spectacles for male sexual consumption, their "yellowish colour" conferring upon them a virtue that was not incompatible with a status as European wives and mothers; and their bodies are textually inserted into sexual circulation for a white male readership. The fact that European men perceived the attractiveness of Eurasian women through their fairness meant that they were accorded a cultural status that made them both sexually available and sexually desirable in the cosmology of Portuguese notions of beauty.[30] Compared to *mestiço* men, who are not sexualized in this travel account, Eurasian women emerge as the bearers of a colonial whiteness that is at once similar to that of European women but also reconstituted as essentially different.[31]

However, by the seventeenth century it is clear that those who appeared more like the "natural-born" people of the country in skin color and habits, despite some Portuguese origin, were situated on the fringes of the reinvented category "Portuguese," whereas white men born in Portugal were the most esteemed and were placed above those born in the colonial environment, who, as *castiri*, were of a lesser whiteness. Kirsten McKenzie notes how social status and class anxieties shaped notions of symbolic whiteness in the Cape of Good Hope, where both upward and downward mobility was possible, depending on one's relative distance to the trappings of colonial power (chapter 13 here). There is some convergence between this case and the fluid transplantation of whiteness in Portuguese India in an earlier era. The journals of François Pyrard de Laval, a French traveler to Goa, offer a window into these taxonomies of social status. The second part of the 1619 edition to Pyrard's voyage memoirs, for example, contains an illuminating description of internal hierarchies of whiteness operating within the category "Portuguese": "But for the Portuguese, there is a great difference of honour between them: because the most esteemed are those who have come from Portugal, who are called Portuguese of Portugal, then there are those born in India of a Portuguese father and mother, and are called Castiri, that is to say of their caste and stock, the least esteemed are those bred of a Portuguese father or mother and Indians, who are called Metices, that is to say Métifs."[32] Despite the increasing influence of color in these emerging racial representations, it is also clear from Laval's observations that *mestiços* were nevertheless considered to be integral members of the European, rather than of the Indian, community, due to the fact that they were Catholic, possessed Portuguese names, and lived within the social and cultural landscape of the European settlements. In the absence of significant numbers of white women, the cultural notion of being "Portuguese" was far more culturally elastic than it was in Portugal. Being "Christian" in an early modern context mediated perceptions of cultural otherness, but it also shaped new understandings of the colonial self in relation to a perceived alien and hostile heathen environment. As a consequence, Portuguese Eurasian women were highly valued by European men of all nationalities for their symbolic whiteness and as acceptable Christian mothers of European children.

However, the term "Portuguese" remains ambiguous and elusive in colonial discourses. The French explorer François Bernier, traveling through Bengal around the same time as Thomas Bowrey, noted in his diary of encountering dark-skinned people dressed in European clothes who called themselves "Portuguese" but were either "Natives or Mesticks."[33] Likewise, the seventeenth-century French traveler to India Jean-Baptiste Tavernier claimed that he saw many "Portuguese" working in the hospitals of the Mughal court but that these were mixed-race descendants rather than white settlers from Portugal.[34] Furthermore, early English sources, including the diaries of Streynsham Master in the 1670s, indicate that the term *Portuguez* could refer to any individual with a Portuguese name and was used by the English to describe the existing Europeanized population, whether "white," Eurasian, or Indian, who identified with Portuguese culture and had recognizable Portuguese names. On the other hand, the prefix "black" could also be added to refer to the *topas* community, that is, the community of Portuguese-speaking Catholics who were predominantly of South Asian origin. Master uses the term "black Portuguez" in his diaries to refer to the indigenous Christian converts, originally lower-caste Hindus and Muslims, who spoke Portuguese, wore European dress, and bore Portuguese names.

In an entry dated December 15, 1676, for instance, he refers to "Nicola De Parteca, a black Portuguez, farming the Salt trade of this place"[35] when describing the impact of Portuguese trade on the economy of Bengal. However, it continues to remain unclear whether the individual concerned was an indigenous Christian or a *mestiço,* as the distinction is not made. This sense of ambiguity continued to be an intrinsic quality of early English appellations to describe the Portuguese well into the eighteenth century. European Portuguese, Portuguese Eurasians, and Indian Christians with Portuguese names were all employed by the armies of the East India Company in the capacity of soldiers, sentinels, and drummers. An abstract of the East India Company's garrison at Fort William for 1746, for example, reveals that there were 426 personnel, including 259 Europeans and 41 "black Portuguez."[36] In the muster rolls for 1745, names such as Fereza, Fernandes, Gomez, da Costa, Rodrigues, and de Rozario are found in the list under the heading "European," and names such as de Rozario, de Cruz, Cardoza, and Fernandes are found under the heading "black Portuguez."[37] My point is that although there was a clear racial demarcation between the Portuguese personnel who were considered European and those who were Indian Christians, those who were *mestiço* were not identified separately and could have ostensibly straddled both groups and been included in either. This seems to illustrate well the contention of Stoler that "métissage operated on the frayed edges of taxonomies that were at the core of colonialism's inconsistent racial politics."[38]

What becomes clear is the lack of a consistent and concrete historical category by which *mestiços* existed as a racially hybrid group. Although terms such as *musteez, mustee,* and *mustezas* were used by the early English settlers to describe Portuguese Eurasians, they appear to be largely descriptions of the European imagination and had no discernible historical meaning for the subjects themselves. While representations of *mestiços* under the European traveler's gaze spoke of racial stratification, Eurasians continued to be very ambiguously classified in early modern accounts but were commonly included in a broad category, "Portuguese," that included Europeans, Eurasians, and many Europeanized Indian groups in a cosmopolitan and multiracial sense. The term continued to be racially ambiguous well into the nineteenth century, when it included Eurasians of all European nationalities. The evangelical missionary William Carey, writing in 1801, claimed that the children of "English, French, Dutch and Danes, by native women, are all called Portuguese."[39] The point, however, is that despite its ambiguous multiracial and multinational dimensions, the term "Portuguese" was a cultural metaphor for a wider Christian constituency.

English Intimacies and Catholic Threats

An important factor in the association of early colonial European men with "Portuguese" women was the latter's ability not only to act as intermediaries between Indians and Europeans but to speak Portuguese, which was the lingua franca of all European commerce and Christian practices in the early modern period. For example, Protestant ministers sent out from England in 1710 were equipped with Portuguese versions of the Bible in order to further their chances of proselytization among the "heathens" and Catholic Eurasians.[40] By 1712, the East India Company in London instructed that every religious minister sent out to Bengal should learn both the "native language" and Portuguese within a year of arrival to "enable them to instruct the Gentoos that shall be servants or slaves of the Company's, or Agents in the Protestant Religion."[41] Furthermore, Portuguese was still the preferred language of commercial exchange in India at the beginning of the eighteenth century.[42] In the early colonial Indian context, it was the language that transcended national and racial distinctions to become a vehicle of common discourse. Early Dutch traders, for example, were as likely to converse in Portuguese as were Portuguese Eurasians or Indians who had either converted to Catholicism or lived in areas of significant Portuguese influence.[43]

The emergence of Portuguese Eurasian communities that were Portuguese-speaking, Christian, and encoded as symbolically "white" was not only a significant legacy of sixteenth- and seventeenth-century colonial Goa. Portuguese settlements across India (most notably in Gujarat, the south of India and Bengal) were precursors to later European settlements in the seventeenth and eighteenth centuries.[44] The establishment of Dutch, French, English, and Danish trading companies saw the entry of more single European men, who found that women who spoke Portuguese and professed the Christian religion were very much a part of the Indian landscape. Thomas Bowrey's geographical account of Bengal in the 1670s refers to the feminine nouns "Portuguezas and Mustezas,"[45] acknowledging the existence of Portuguese Eurasian women in the old Portuguese settlements of Hughli and Chittagong in Bengal whom, the author thought, would make suitable wives for the early English traders in the absence of white women from England.

Many of the early English factors at Fort St. George in the 1660s found wives among the Catholic Portuguese Eurasian women whose families had originally come from the nearby settlement of St. Thome. The common practice of Protestant Englishmen taking Catholic women as wives and sexual partners at this time became the cause of great alarm, due to the fact that the children of these unions were being baptized as Catholics. A protest letter from William Isaacson, a Protestant minister, seems to sum up much of the threat represented by these women to the maintenance of the boundaries of Protestant Englishness when he accuses two French Catholic friars of baptizing the children of Englishmen and Portuguese Eurasian women as Catholics. In this revelatory letter, he accuses the Catholic friars of "likewise in the night gone to Englishmen's houses, when they have bin upon their duty in the Fort, whose wives are newly delivered, to Baptize young infants, pretending them to be very weake."[46]

The practice of having the children of English Protestant men and Portuguese Eurasian women baptized as Catholics seems to strike at the heart of this anxiety. Sectarian distinctions held greater cultural currency than those of skin color per se in a colonial world where the Catholic threat to English identity was expressed as abhorrence for interfaith marriages. The threat that the religion of Portuguese Eurasian women posed to Protestant identity become such a source of concern that Englishmen in Fort St. George were discouraged from forming relationships with Eurasian women not on account of their racial background, but on account of their religious persuasion. In a letter to the commander at

Fort St. George dated August 31, 1660, in response to English requests to have the two French Catholic friars expelled from the settlement, the decision is made to act on this, but to also identify "Portuguese" women (or "mustezas") resident in English settlements as potential threats to English commerce, peace, and security. While tolerating their presence as the wives of Englishmen, if they converted to Protestantism, the East India Company advised that if the security of the settlement was under threat from French attack, that they should also be expelled from the settlement and their church converted to a Protestant place of worship: "If you cannot live without the *mustezas* (for Portugalls [sic] there are none, as we are informed, or few at the least), there must be a submission at present: but if the Honourable Company's trade may be there drove, and the Fort and government secured without them, we absolutely conclude they are, upon receipt of these, to be dismissed [from the] the town and their church converted into a place for more true worship."[47]

The question of the threat posed by "Portuguese" Catholic women to the perceived boundaries of Englishness has often been an overlooked feature in the construction of hybrid knowledge in the imperial canon in India. In fact, the most often quoted piece of evidence employed in Anglo-Indian histories to demonstrate the early English encouragement of interracial marriages with "native women" obscures the religious assumptions for the enactment. Known as the *Despatch of the Court of Directors to the President of Madras*, dated April 8, 1687, the edict promotes marriages between Englishmen and "native women" and encourages a financial reward to be paid to the mother if the child of such a union is baptized in the Protestant religion: "The marriage of our soldiers to the native women of Fort St George formerly recommended to you is a matter of such consequence to posterity, that we shall be content to encourage it, with some expence, and have been thinking for the future to appoint a Pagoda to be paid to the mother of any Child, that shall be hereafter be born, of any such future marriages, upon the day the Child is Christened, if you think this small encouragement will increase the number of such marriages."[48]

Hence this early English "encouragement" of interracial marriage is a response to the threat that the relationships between Protestant Englishmen and Catholic Portuguese Eurasian women were seen to pose to the future course of Protestant identity in a late seventeenth-century context. Hence, while marriages to Portuguese Eurasian Catholic women were discouraged for fear of the spread of the "Popish threat," marriages to Indian women were encouraged if the woman in question and her children converted to Protestantism. This, of course, creates a plethora of seeming historical contradictions in the contemporary context, since a "mixed marriage" was therefore one negotiated between a Protestant and Catholic, such as between a Protestant Englishman and a Catholic Portuguese Eurasian woman, and not one negotiated between a Protestant Englishman and a converted Protestant Indian woman.[49] Despite the marking of Protestant boundaries and the financial inducements offered to women to have their children baptized in the "orthodox church" in the seventeenth century, English authorities continued to regard Catholic Portuguese Eurasian women with fear and suspicion well into the eighteenth century. The fear of Catholicism was more than a cultural fear concerning the future shape of English identity in India. It was symptomatic of the cultural relevance of religious distinctions in the making of colonial whiteness, where the political fear of potential disloyalty to a Protestant nation engulfed by the "Catholic menace" in Europe was transported to the Indian context, where the Portuguese Eurasian woman became the corporeal site where global interactions found localized meaning.

By the Battle of Plassey, the Catholicism of Portuguese Eurasian women was perceived by English authorities to be a significant political threat to the East India Company's power in Bengal. During the siege of Calcutta in 1757, for instance, when many Portuguese Eurasian women found refuge in Fort William, the Company protested to the Court of Directors in London that due to their Catholicism, these women did not deserve English military and commercial protection, since they would be natural political allies of the French in the prospect of an Anglo-French war. Hence their integrity as prospective loyal English subjects was questioned. In a letter to London in 1757, officials in Calcutta reported:

> The inconvenience we experienced from the siege of Calcutta from the prodigious number of Portuguese women who were admitted for Security into the Fort, the very little or no service which that Race of People are to the Settlement, added to the Prospect we had of a War with France, in which case We had reason to suppose they would refuse to take up Arms against an Enemy of their Own Religion, should we be attacked, Induced us upon our Return to interdict the publick Exercise of the Roman Catholick religion, and to forbid the Residence of Their Priests in Our Bounds.[50]

The threat that "Portuguese" women were seen to pose to the security of early colonial English settlements in India was therefore metaphorically translated as a sexual threat to the Protestant male body.[51] In a wider international context, this seemed at odds with the general tolerance of Portuguese Catholics by the English, who conferred the protection of the English Crown to them under a treaty made with Portugal in 1661 when Bombay was transferred to British control. This agreement stipulated that the Portuguese inhabitants in India "be permitted to stay there freely to exercise Roman Catholic Religion in the Same Manner as They Do."[52] The continuing and friendly relations between the British and the Portuguese, including British protection of the Portuguese settlements in India, meant that Catholic missionaries were tolerated and Catholic subjects were entitled to legal protection. Despite the national affiliations between the English and Portuguese nations that provided the framework for toleration, the tension remained in regard to primordial loyalties and whether Catholic subjects (regardless of their nationality) could, in fact, ever be trusted as English subjects with the ever-present threat of Portuguese religious commonality with the French.

In 1787, for example, the Catholic presence in Madras was a matter of great anxiety to British authorities for precisely these reasons:

> The Roman Catholics form a considerable part of the population of this Coast and it is said amount in the whole to about 100,000 souls. Of these we have nearly 17,000 within the Walls and about the environs of Madras. It must therefore be of great consequence to this Government to attach such a considerable body of people to our Interest by every tie by which society is held together, but unfortunately for us some difficulties occur in forming the strongest of all ties, that of Interest and Religion. The former, however, under the prosperity of . . . our Government may be certainly secured to them and the latter is also in our power to grant by leaving them free exercise of their own faith and affording them every protection and support which good and faithful subjects deserve. By an early attention to these circumstances, it is to be hoped our rivals will not possess superior influence over them on account of their being in the same communion.[53]

If "being in the same communion" as the Catholic French made "Portuguese" women a political threat to English identity by virtue of their Catholicism, then their position as the mothers of "white" English children in India was more favorably secured by their conversion to Protestantism.

Conclusion

By venturing beyond conventional Anglo-Indian interpretations, this essay has sought to demonstrate the significance of female agency in the construction of colonial knowledge by emphasizing the role of Portuguese Eurasian women in sixteenth and seventeenth-century India.[54] By looking at the politics of racial mixing along a Catholic versus Protestant axis, we might have a broader and more complex view of the cosmos in which Portuguese Eurasian women were active agents in the making of white subjectivity.[55] Their role as Catholic subjects and as agents of cultural change in this earlier era also offers an alternative narrative with which to view the construction of colonial knowledge according to an engagement with the politics of religious location.[56]

By the last quarter of the eighteenth century, the syntax of whiteness entered a more pronounced racial constellation, with the consolidation of British imperialism and the emergence of skin color as a more visible grammar by which the difference between colonizer and colonized was articulated. As racial mixing became intertwined with the politics of British colonial knowledge, some insights might have been forgotten in retelling the story of interracial contact in India. First, the "grids of intelligibility" underwriting the meaning of "mixedness" in a different time and place were originally concerned with the politics of religious affiliation.[57] Hence the relationship between métissage and colonial knowledge might need to reclaim the significance of religion sectarianism in a protoracial grammar to reveal more complex categories of cultural difference. What it meant to be "white" in the early modern period of European expansion and exploration was a highly problematic and contested category often articulated through invisible markers not associated wholly with skin color. Second, this "whiteness" begs to be historicized according to global context and the cultural genealogies by which racial subjectivity in early colonial India was reproduced. The religious dialogue between Portuguese and English colonialisms might shed new light on the politics of cultural amnesia operating within the articulation of colonial knowledge itself. Third, the rush to celebrate interracial unions through the cosmopolitan filter of the British patriarchal experience, as Chatterjee and Ghosh have argued, may erase the agency of those who were important bearers of a symbolic whiteness in their role as mothers to future generations of European children. However, those women were not necessarily "native" but already hybridized, Christianized, and bearers of a politically threatening Catholic disposition.

The reconstruction of colonial categories through interracial relationships was the work not only of white men from the "top down" or the work of voiceless "native women" from the "bottom up" but also of women who challenged Protestant male authority by embodying their whiteness with a very different political rationality.

Notes

Versions of this essay were presented at the symposium "Gender and Empire" Otago University, Dunedin, New Zealand, October 29, 2004, and at the "Old Worlds, New Worlds" conference, University of Auckland, New Zealand, February 3, 2005. Sincere thanks to Antoinette Burton, Tony Ballantyne, and the anonymous peer reviewers for their helpful and generous comments.

1. For the "bird's-eye" view of global processes in human history, see J. R. McNeill and William H. McNeill, *The Human Web: A Bird's Eye View of World History* (New York, 2004), 3, 8. On the need for the term "global" to encompass historical particularity and cultural specificity, see Felicity Nussbaum, ed., *The Global Eighteenth Century* (Baltimore, 2003), 2. For a rigorous methodological discussion, see Tony Ballantyne and Antoinette Burton, eds., *Bodies in Contact: Rethinking Colonial Encounters in World History* (Durham, N.C., 2005), 406.

2. Ann Laura Stoler, "Tense and Tender Ties: The Politics of Comparison in North American History and (Post) Colonial Studies," *Journal of American History* 88, 3 (2001): 831.

3. Wilcomb E. Washburn, "The Meaning of 'Discovery' in the Fifteenth and Sixteenth Centuries," in Ursula Lamb, ed., *An Expanding World: The European Impact on World History, 1450–1800* (Aldershot, England, 1995), 49–69.

4. On the global reach of the Portuguese in the new capitalist modern world-system, see Michael N. Pearson, "The Modern World-System and European Expansion in Asia to 1750," in Pearson, *Before Colonialism: Theories on Asian-European Relations, 1500–1750* (Delhi, 1988), 32–50.

5. Quoted in the English translator's 1778 introduction to Luis de Camoens, *The Lusiad; Or the Discovery of India, An Epic Poem,* trans. W. J. Mickle (Oxford, 1778), pt. 4, chap. 12, 412.

6. Charles R. Boxer, *Race Relations in the Portuguese Colonial Empire, 1415–1825* (Oxford, 1963), 9.

7. See Sanjay Subrahmanayam, *The Portuguese Empire in Asia, 1500–1700* (London, 1993), 219, 220, 230, and Michael N. Pearson, *The Portuguese in India* (New York, 1987), 102.

8. Ann Laura Stoler, *Race and the Education of Desire: Foucault's "History of Sexuality" and the Colonial Order of Things* (Durham, N.C., 1995), 46–47.

9. Charles Boxer, "The Colour Question in the Portuguese Empire, 1415–1825," Raleigh Lecture on History, February 15, 1961, in *Proceedings of the British Academy 1961* (London, 1962), 113–38.

10. Stoler, "Tense and Tender Ties," 836.

11. See Katherine Ellinghaus, *Taking Assimilation to Heart: Marriages of White Women and Indigenous Men in the United States and Australia, 1887–1937* (Lincoln, Neb., 2006).

12. Lynn Zastoupil, "Intimacy and Colonial Knowledge," in *Journal of Colonialism and Colonial History* 3, 2 (2002): 1. The important ways same-sex intimacies (whether interracial or between white colonizers) provide a "counternarrative" to hegemonic notions of intimacy have been less understood in colonial contexts and given far less attention due to the emphasis on the relationship between racial transgression and the production of hybrid subjects. Few studies have dealt with

the subject of same-sex intimacies in imperial exchanges. For an exception, see Robert Aldrich, *Colonialism and Homosexuality* (London, 2003), 1. The role of female same-sex intimacies in the construction of colonial knowledge remains remarkably rare (whether interracial or between white women).

13. H. Yule and A. C. Burnell, *Hobson-Jobson: Being a Glossary of Anglo-Indian Colloquial Words and Phrases of Kindred Terms* (London, 1903), 605. This term is also cited as being used by the English in reference to Portuguese Eurasians in 1644. See W. Foster, *The English Factories in India, 1642–1645* (Oxford, 1908), 166.

14. Foster, *The English Factories in India*, 71.

15. Ibid., 70.

16. Christopher Hawes, *Poor Relations: The Making of a Eurasian Community in British India, 1773–1833* (London, 1996).

17. The idea that racial distinctions were more fluid in early modern India before the consolidation of the British colonial state has been an enduring theme in the imperial historiography of interracial sexuality. See Thomas George Percival Spear, *The Nabobs: A Study of the Social Life of the English in Eighteenth-Century India* (Oxford, 1932), and William Dalrymple, *White Mughals: Love and Betrayal in Eighteenth-Century India* (New York, 2003).

18. Indrani Chatterjee, *Gender, Slavery and Law in Colonial India* (Delhi, 1999).

19. Durba Ghosh, *Sex and the Family in Colonial India: The Making of Empire* (Cambridge, 2006).

20. Ibid., 251.

21. Boxer, *Race Relations in the Portuguese Colonial Empire*, 58.

22. The claim that there were substantial numbers of white Portuguese women in India is made by A. C. Germano da Silva Correia, *História da colonização portuguesa na India*, 6 vols. (Lisboa, 1943–58), who states that up to eighty thousand women may have emigrated from Portugal to India during the period 1500–1700. This is disputed by Boxer, *Race Relations in the Portuguese Colonial Empire*, 59, who notes the race-blindness of these population figures and finds the figure eight thousand, or one-tenth of Correia's estimate, "very generous." Some scholars have accepted Germano da Silva Correia's interpretation of the sources, but have also disputed the overall numbers. See L. A. Rodrigues, "Portuguese Feminine Emigration for Colonization of India," *Journal of Indian History* 58 (1980): 57.

23. Geneviève Bouchon, "Les femmes dans la société coloniale ibérique," in Bouchon, *L'Asie du Sud à l'époque des Grandes Découvertes* (London, 1987), 207.

24. See Pearson, *Portuguese in India*, 92.

25. Letter 9, April 1, 1512, "Letters of Albuquerque," I/3/fol. 162, India Office Records, British Library, London (hereafter IOR).

26. Manuelde Faria y Sousa, *The Portuguese Asia: Or, The History of the Discovery and Conquest of India By The Portuguese*, trans. J. Stevens (London, 1695), pt. 2, chap. 5, 173.

27. Charles R. Boxer, "Fidalgos Portugueses e Bailhadeiras Indianas. (Séculos XVII e XVIII)," in *Separata da Revista de Historia*, no. 45 (São Paulo, 1961), 83–105.

28. Mrinalini Sinha, "Signs Taken for Wonders? The Stakes for Imperial Studies," *Journal of Colonialism and Colonial History* 3, 1 (2002): 4.

29. Jan Huygen van Linschoten, *His Discours of Voyages into Ye Easte and West Indies,* trans. W. Phillip (London, 1598), chap. 24, 53.

30. In the sixteenth-century Japanese context, Gary Leupp notes that Portuguese and Italian observers often commented on the "whiteness" of Japanese women and the correlation of paleness with beauty. See Gary P. Leupp, *Interracial Intimacy in Japan: Western Men and Japanese Women, 1543–1900* (London, 2003), 23–25.

31. For the role of gender in the reconstitution of whiteness in the metropole vis-à-vis the colonies in other global contexts, see Angela Woollacott, "'All This Is Empire I Told Myself': Australian Women's Voyages 'Home' and the Articulation of Colonial Whiteness," *American Historical Review* 102, 4 (1997): 1003–29, and Alison Blunt, *Domicile and Diaspora: Anglo-Indian Women and the Spatial Politics of Home* (Oxford, 2005), 139–74.

32. François Pyrard de Laval, *Du Voyage de François Pyrard de Laval, Depuis l'arrivée à Goa, jusques à son retour en France* (Paris, 1619), chap. 2, 39.

33. F. Bernier, *The History of the Late Revolution of the Empire of the Great Mogol, Together With the Most Considerable Passages for Five Years Following that Empire* (London, 1676), 134.

34. *Travels in India by Jean-Baptiste Tavernier, Baron of Aubonne, translated by* V. Ball (London, 1925), 160, 313.

35. "A Diary Kept by Streynsham Master in His Inspection of the Factorys of Metchlepatam and the Bay of Bengale, and Regulating the Same," G/40/14/fol. 317, IOR.

36. "An Abstract of the East India Company's garrison at Fort William for 1746," L/MIL/10/130/fol. 64, IOR.

37. "An Abstract of the East India Company's garrison at Fort William for 1745," L/MIL/10/130/fol. 60, IOR.

38. Ann Laura Stoler, *Carnal Knowledge and Imperial Power: Race and the Intimate in Colonial Rule* (Berkeley, 2002), 208.

39. W. Carey, "Miscellaneous Communication," *Periodical Accounts Relative to the Baptist Missionary Society* 2, 8 (1801): 189. This appears to be confirmed in relation to Bengal, where Campos confirms that "Portuguese" was a metaphorical term to describe all individuals of "mixed race" regardless of nationality. See J. J. A. Campos, *History of the Portuguese in Bengal* (London, 1919), 188.

40. See Josiah Wedgewood to Protestant ministers, November 21, 1710, on the need for the New Testament to be translated into the Portuguese language to increase the chances of converting the "heathen" in India, H/MISC/59/10/ fol. 191, IOR.

41. "Extract of a General Letter," February 2, 1712, H/MISC/59/10/fols. 196–97, IOR.

42. See Friar Achilles Meersman, *Annual Reports of the Portuguese Franciscans in India, 1713–1833* (Lisboa, 1972), 18–19.

43. See "The Portuguese in North India," *Calcutta Review* 4, 10 (June 1846): 284.

44. See Campos, *History of the Portuguese in Bengal,* and Michael N. Pearson, "Early Relations between the Portuguese and Gujarat: A New Overview," *Indica* 35, 2 (September 1998): 81–96.

45. Thomas Bowrey, *A Geographical Account of the Countries Round the Bay of Bengal, 1669 to 1679,* ed. R. C. Temple (Cambridge, 1905), 3 n. 5.

46. The original petition that gathered eyewitness accounts (including that of William Isaacson) of the activities of the two French Catholic friars in Madras who were accused of attempting to forcibly convert the children of Protestant men and "Portuguese" women to Catholicism is entitled "Copies of Attestations Concerning Two French Padres"; January 24, 1660, E/3/26/fol. 2840, IOR. What is most striking about the "accusation" is that the children of such a union are perceived to be the property of their English Protestant fathers, not of their Eurasian Catholic mothers.

47. The official response to the "interfaith" marriage crisis and the East India Company's reaction to the presence of Portuguese Eurasian Catholic women in English settlements is articulated in a letter entitled "To Agent Trevisa-Bengala, To Agent Chamber at Fort St George," August 31, 1660, G/36/fol. 85, IOR.

48. This is quoted from the original resolution, which is subtitled "Encouragement for Soldiers to Marry Native Women," April 8, 1687, in East India Company's Despatch Books, 1626–1753, E/3/91/fol. 290, IOR. Known as the *Despatch of the Court of Directors to the President of Madras,* this order is often cited as the edict confirming early English encouragement of "mixed-race" marriages among the military of the East India Company. Most commentators, however, have omitted the important concerns of gender and religious sectarianism that would have shaped the meaning of this encouragement in historical context. See, for example, Evelyn Abel, *The Anglo-Indian Community: Survival in India* (Delhi, 1988), 12, and Cedric Dover, *Half-Caste* (London, 1937), 117–18. I have discussed this edict as part of a theoretical discussion on the diverse meanings of "hybridity," in "Historicising Hybridity and the Politics of Location: Three Early Colonial Indian Narratives," *Journal of Intercultural Studies* 28, 1 (February 2007): 146–48.

49. The idea that a "mixed marriage" was essentially a contract between a Protestant and a Catholic held social currency in India well into the nineteenth century among the European and Eurasian Christian communities. See "A Mixed Marriage: How the Promise Is Kept by the Protestant," *Bengal Catholic Herald,* November 19, 1842, 290, and S. Riordan, *The Directory for the Use of the Clergy and Laity, of the Apostolic Vicariate of Western Bengal for 1856* (Calcutta, 1856), 206–9.

50. Letter to the Court of Directors, January 31, 1757, E/4/23/292/, para. 14, IOR.

51. As Dana Rabin demonstrates in her essay in this volume, this appears to be a mutually constitutive process. She explores how metropolitan notions of cultural difference were also deeply inflected by gendered threats to the national body. In her discussion of the Canning case in eighteenth century Britain, Rabin shows how women who were perceived as outsiders to the nation were represented through the lens and language of xenophobia.

52. "Treaty between Portugal and Great Britain," June 29, 1661, H/MISC/60/1/fol. 1, IOR.

53. "Extract Fort St George Consultations," October 30, 1787, H/MISC/59/9/fol. 36, IOR.

54. Lynn Zastoupil notes that a "growing body of scholarship on inter-racial intimacy and hybrid families in colonial societies indicates the need for more expansive notions of the role of agency and symbiotic relationships in the construc-

tion of colonial knowledge." See Zastoupil, "Intimacy and Colonial Knowledge," 2. For gendered notions of indigenous agency, see Antoinette Burton, "South Asian Women, Gender, and Transnationalism," in *Journal of Women's History* 14, 4 (Winter 2003): 196–201; Indrani Chatterjee, "Colouring Subalternity: Slaves, Concubines and Social Orphans under the East India Company," in Gautam Bhadra, Gyan Prakash, and Susie Tharu, eds., *Subaltern Studies* 10 (Delhi, 1999), 49–97; Michael Fisher, "Becoming and Making 'Family' in Hindusthan," in Indrani Chatterjee, ed., *Unfamiliar Relations: Family and History in South Asia* (New Brunswick, N.J., 2004), 95–121; and Durba Ghosh, "Decoding the Nameless: Gender, Subjectivity, and Historical Methodologies in Reading the Archives of Colonial India," in Kathleen Wilson, ed., *A New Imperial History: Culture, Identity and Modernity in Britain and the Empire, 1660–1840* (Cambridge, 2004), 297–316.

55. On the need to "historicize" hybridity in colonial discourses, see Avtar Brah and Annie E. Coombes, introduction to Brah and Coombes, eds., *Hybridity and Its Discontents: Politics, Science, Culture* (London, 2000), 2; Adrian Carton, "Historicising Hybridity and the Politics of Location: Three Early Colonial Indian Narratives," *Journal of Intercultural Studies* 28, 1 (2007): 143–55; Dane Kennedy, "Imperial History and Postcolonial Theory," *Journal of Imperial and Commonwealth History* 24 (May 1996): 345–63; Ania Loomba, *Colonialism/Postcolonialism* (London, 1998), 178–79; Nikos Papastergiadis, *The Turbulence of Migration* (Cambridge, 2000), 195; and Pnina Werbner and Tariq Modood, *Debating Cultural Hybridity: Multicultural Identities and the Politics of Anti-Racism* (London, 1997).

56. Himani Bannerji, "Politics and the Writing of History," in Ruth Roach Pierson and Nupur Chaudhuri, eds., *Nation, Empire, Colony: Historicizing Gender and Race* (Bloomington, Ind., 1998), 290.

57. Ann Laura Stoler, "Racial Histories and Their Regimes of Truth," in *Political Power and Social Theory* 11 (1997): 183.

12 The Sorceress, the Servant, and the Stays

SEXUALITY AND RACE IN
EIGHTEENTH-CENTURY BRITAIN

On New Year's Day 1753 Elizabeth Canning (1734–73), an
eighteen-year-old servant maid, disappeared from London's East End, apparently a victim of kidnapping. When she returned to her mother's home
a month later, she explained her disappearance by accusing a woman, later
identified as Mary Squires, "gypsy," of arranging her abduction, attempting to lure her into a life of prostitution, and keeping her a prisoner on
bread and water for twenty-eight days in a house in Enfield twelve miles
north of the city of London. In addition to her allegations against Mary
Squires, Canning implicated Susannah Wells, a reputed brothel keeper. A
young prostitute, memorably named Virtue Hall, who had been arrested
along with Squires and Wells, testified that she was living at Wells's
house in January and had witnessed Canning's capture. On the basis of
this evidence, the two older women were arrested and accused of assaulting Canning and stealing her belongings: Squires was sentenced to death
and Wells to six months in jail. But contradictory evidence presented at
the trial raised doubts about the facts of the case. An investigation by Sir
Crisp Gascoyne (1700–1761), lord mayor of London, resulted in Virtue
Hall recanting her testimony, and on May 21, 1753, Squires was granted
a full pardon. Elizabeth Canning was brought to trial for perjury in April
1754; she was found guilty and transported to the American colonies.

The case immediately became a "trial of the century." "The conversation of every alehouse within the bills of mortality,"[1] the case generated an unprecedented amount of published material, including broadsides, ballads, pamphlets, and prints. Questions about the young woman's true whereabouts for the first twenty-eight days of January 1753 continue to frame the Canning case. Although we may never know what really happened, the case points to the preoccupations and anxieties of English society in the mid–eighteenth century.[2]

This essay will explore the nexus of race and sexuality in the narratives of three of the single women involved: Elizabeth Canning, Mary Squires, and Virtue Hall. The explicit disputes about these women concerned their whereabouts, their physical integrity, and their moral character. Embedded in these discussions was a debate about the implications of Britain's imperial expansion, specifically the reality of a religiously, racially, and ethnically diverse London populated by Jews, gypsies, Asians, Africans, Scots, Irish, Catholics, and nonconforming Protestants, for definitions of Englishness as a cultural tradition and England as a nation.[3] The written record left by the case exposed an unwieldy female autonomy that made a lie of conventions regarding English femininity, domesticity, chastity, and virtue and collapsed imagined spatial divisions within the metropole. Ultimately what propelled the Canning case into the headlines and the alehouses were discomforts associated with empire and the moral and social threat it posed through its multiplicity of sites and the mobile bodies that moved in its shadows and hidden spaces.[4]

I suggest that although a prurient interest in sex may have spurred initial attention, an examination of the intersection of sexuality and race in the case reveals the story's repercussions for definitions of belonging that gave the scandal its wide appeal. With its exaggerated images of Mary Squires as a gypsy defined as "a member of a wandering race (by themselves called Romany)," who first arrived in England at the beginning of the sixteenth century, "believed to have come from Egypt," the story foregrounded long-held anxieties about vagrancy and concerns about insiders, outsiders, and interlopers, as it revealed the reality of geographic mobility that shattered early modern notions of continuity, place, and community, considered the most trustworthy means of measuring character and credibility.[5] Each site in the accounts mapped a specific cultural meaning, each place imagined as distinct and separate. Mention of Aldermanbury Postern, Elizabeth's home, confirmed negative associations of London's East End with working-class poverty and crime, while Dorchester, where Squires claimed to be on the night of the crime, and its proximity to the coast summoned images of smuggling. As the site of Susannah Wells's brothel, Enfield Wash contaminated country respectability. The appearance of all three locations in the same story destabilized a geographical imagination that relied on the strict division of place as an authentic constant and space as a signifier of contact and interrelationships.[6]

Proponents on each side, whether Canningites or Egyptians, read their "evidence" about who belonged "to a civilized Nation"[7] and who posed "the greatest danger to the safety of all his majesty's good subjects"[8] on the bodies of Elizabeth Canning, Mary Squires, and Virtue Hall supporting their case with a set of "facts" they claimed as authoritative and definitive.[9] Each reading proved the impossibility of knowing the truth with which to substantiate a worldview.

Attention to the legal setting must foreground any discussion of the Canning story. Such an examination sheds new light on the intersection of English law and British imperial aspiration in the eighteenth century. Despite Henry Fielding's claim that "there is nothing more admirable, nor indeed more amable, in the Law of England, than the extreme Tenderness with which it proceeds against Persons accused of capital Crimes," Squires's conviction and death sentence reflected a cultural consensus about the inherent criminality of gypsies. Her trial and subsequent pardon along with Canning's perjury trial a year later became a test of the ideology of fairness and equality before the criminal law so often praised as uniquely English and cited as proof of English superiority and the very reason for imperial expansion.[10] The representations of Canning as the virtuous white woman, Hall as the white prostitute, and Squires as the foreign procuress luring Englishwomen into an immoral livelihood determined the definition of the crime and the credibility assigned to each witness. The adversarial process created evidence to validate Canning's accusations and to substantiate her story despite its myriad inconsistencies.

The First Story

On Wednesday January 31, three days after Canning's reappearance, the *London Daily Advertiser* reported her return to Aldermanbury Postern. In the "extraordinary account" attributed to Elizabeth herself, Canning described her visit with her aunt and uncle, Alice and Thomas Colley, on New Year's Day at Saltpetre Bank. After dinner, Mr. and Mrs. Colley walked her half of the way home, leaving her at Houndsditch. She continued to Moorfields by Bethlehem-wall, where "two fellows . . . pulled off her hat and gown, cut off her apron, then gagged her, and threatened her with bitter imprecations if she cried out to cut her throat."[11] They carried Elizabeth to the house of "one Mother Wells" in Enfield, where they arrived at four in the morning. According to Elizabeth, the two men left her there, and "the woman of the house immediately cut off her stays . . . and with horridest execrations forced her into a room, where she was kept upon bread and water."[12]

The story of the crime abruptly shifts to Elizabeth's escape, when she "broke her way through a window almost naked, and in that wretched condition came home," leaving "several unhappy young women in the house, whose misfortune she has providentially escaped."[13] The threat of sexual transgression shapes this account. Mary Squires does not appear in this version of the story; instead, the article implies that the owner of the house, Susannah Wells, had cut off Elizabeth's stays.

The first pamphlet about the case appeared following the arrests of Squires and Wells on February 1. It still referred to the occupants of the house as "an old woman and two young ones," adding an alleged promise from the old woman that Elizabeth would "want for nothing" "if she would do as they did, (which was whoring and thieving)."[14] The pamphlet ascribed ownership of the house to "that notorious woman . . . mother Wells" and later referred to her as "that monster of a woman." It appealed to "public-spirited people, and every one who has any regard for the safety of their own children and relations" for "compassion and charitable contributions" and called for immediate action to detect and prevent "the same inhuman and cruel usage" from "such a nest of villains . . . the greatest danger to the safety of all his majesty's good subjects."[15]

Alternate narratives expressed doubts about Elizabeth's story. Detractors called it "absurd, incredible, and most ridiculous."[16] They questioned how she could have been dragged ten to twelve miles from central London to Enfield Wash without a single witness reporting it, and they wondered how she had survived for twenty-eight days on only a "quartern loaf" of bread and a jug of water, and how she had disciplined herself to apportion the food so exactly. They inquired about her claim that she had passed no stool in the month she was gone, and they asked why she had not come home earlier, seeing as she was able to escape as soon as she decided to do so.[17] Several of her earliest supporters dropped away after she was taken to Susannah Wells's home on February 1. Elizabeth could not find the stairs that led to the room where she was kept, and her description of the attic as dark with bare floors was belied by two windows and a "Quantity of Hay."[18] Most glaring was the dramatic change in her story: during the visit to Wells's home, Canning first saw and identified Mary Squires as the woman who cut her stays. Until then only Susannah Wells had been implicated, and there had been no mention of the gypsy.

Canning's detractors accused her of sexual transgression and its results: venereal disease, abortion, childbirth, and infanticide. They explained her disappearance with references to a lover, a lying in, a miscarriage, or a salivation (treatment for syphilis).[19] These counternarratives may have found their source in the missing person advertisements placed by Elizabeth's mother suggesting that "she was forcibly taken away by some evil-disposed Person." They were followed by the assertions of the midwife Mrs. Canning summoned immediately on Elizabeth's return that Elizabeth had not borne a child.[20] More evidence of sexual misconduct came from Canning's supporter Dr. James Dodd, who revealed that for five months before her disappearance she "had had the Common female benefit [menses] totally obstructed."[21] Dodd argued that such an obstruction, combined with Canning's "naturally costive" nature, explained how she survived on so little food. Daniel Cox, another of Canning's defenders, discussed the relative cleanliness of her shift and concluded that the lack of stains on it meant that Canning had had no sexual relations during her absence.[22] Canningites and Egyptians alike showed no inhibitions about discussing the most intimate physical details of Canning's bodily functions and secretions. The obsessive (re)iteration of these details confirms Christina Straub's observation that "anxieties about English identity are channeled through anxieties about women's sexuality . . . [which] both threatens and constitutes that which is English."[23]

The Gypsy Becomes a Witch

In light of the "absurdities, inconsistencies and improbabilities" that riddled Canning's story, questions of race, ethnicity, and nation were magnified and put at the center of the definition of the crime and its investigation. The first version of the story made no mention of the gypsy; instead the story's tellers dichotomized familiar representations of Canning, the virtuous servant, chaste and domesticated, and Wells, the lewd, fallen woman, scolding and promiscuous, to construct a coherent narrative out of the conflicting details. By the time of the trial three weeks later, however, the image of Mary Squires—gypsy, criminal, and procuress—had emerged making the story a shocking, troubling scandal. These narratives relied on portrayals of gypsies as "vagrants, paupers, and nomads," the "worst face of an uncivilized and unacceptable society."[24] Movement, mobility, and migration were critical to this representation.

The first mention of "an old Gipsey Woman" appeared in newspaper stories on February 3 relating the arrests of Susannah Wells and Mary Squires.[25] Canning described Squires as a gypsy when she was deposed by

Henry Fielding on February 7.[26] In a story published on February 17 the *London Evening Post* reported that during her examination by Fielding on February 15, Squires "behaved as a Person traditionally and hereditarily versed in the antient Egyptian Cunning, making the most religious Protestations of her Innocence; though she was afterwards heard to say, 'Damn the young Bitch!'"[27] The story praised the "Public-Spirited and humane Gentlemen" who had supported the "poor, injured innocent Girl, and done such singular service to their country, by their Endeavours to eradicate from his Majesty's subjects a Gang of desperate and cruel Villains, of the greatest Danger to a civilized Nation."[28] The words "civilized Nation," absent from the earlier account identifying Wells as the perpetrator, appeared for the first time. While the earlier warnings had described threats facing "his Majesty's subjects," the new wording suggests a focus on national boundaries with Mary Squires, gypsy, someone clearly identified as an outsider, taking a prominent place in the narrative.[29]

At the February 21 Old Bailey trial of Mary Squires and Susannah Wells, Squires was accused of assaulting Elizabeth Canning, "putting her in corporal fear and danger of her life," and stealing "one pair of stays, value 10s the property of the said Elizabeth."[30] Wells was tried as her accomplice. The trial narrative prominently featured Mary Squires, gypsy, and stereotypes about gypsies played a central role in the recitation of the crime and its subsidiary details. These descriptions corroborated unflattering, threatening expectations of this ethnic group: an association with criminality, an itinerant lifestyle, a livelihood in sales, distinctive dress, a familiarity with magic, and an association with promiscuous sexuality.[31]

According to her trial testimony, the first thing Elizabeth saw when she entered the house was "the gypsey woman Squires," who "took me by the hand, asked me if I chose to go their way, saying if I did, I should have fine cloaths." Canning refused, and in response Mary Squires took a knife out of the dresser drawer and "cut the lace off my stays, and took them from me." Canning told the court that she thought "she [Squires] was going to cut my throat, when I saw her take the knife." Squires then gave Canning "a slap on the face," pushed her upstairs into a hayloft, and said that "if ever she heard me stir or move, or any such thing, she'd cut my throat."[32]

Mary Squires spoke up several times during the recitation of the evidence against her to deny any knowledge of Canning and to declare "I am as innocent as the child unborn." Perhaps strategically, she did not speak in her own defense. Instead, several English (i.e., not Romany/gypsy) witnesses appeared on her behalf. Their testimony referred to and at times emphasized the negative characteristics associated with the group labeled the gypsies. John Giben said he had known Squires for three years and provided her an alibi. He testified that between January 1 and 9, 1753, Squires and her children had stayed at his inn, the Old-Ship, in Abbotsbury, six miles from Dorchester and about 130 miles southwest of London. William Clark corroborated this account saying that he had seen Squires at Giben's inn when he went to "have a pot of liquor" on New Year's Day. Clark explained that the last time he saw Squires was on January 10, 1753: "I met with them on the road, we went some way together, we parted at Crudeway-foot, four miles from Abbotsbury and three from Dorchester." Thomas Grevil testified that he had seen Squires and her children when they stopped in Coombe (near Salisbury) on January 14. All three men cited the itinerant nature of Squires's lifestyle to support their contention that she had not been in London on the night of Elizabeth Canning's abduction.[33]

The testimony of her alibi witnesses connected the constant travel associated with Squires and with gypsies to their engagement in commerce. When asked how long he had known the defendant, Clark told the court that he had seen Squires and her son and daughter "three years ago come March, at Abbotsbury, they came with handkerchiefs, lawns, and muslins to sell."[34] Giben said the same, adding that Squires and her children "offered them to sell to me, and others, my wife bought two cheque aprons."[35] This image of gypsies as rootless, shifty vagrants engaged in some sort of commerce was reinforced when Clark added that he "saw them going about the town in the time, to sell things."[36]

Several witnesses were asked about the clothes worn by Squires and her children. Canning described Squires "sitting in her gown with a handkerchief about her head." Asked what the children were wearing, Clark said that "the son [was] in a blue coat and a red waistcoat and had a great coat with him" while the daughter was "in a camblet gown." These questions point to images of gypsies dressed in colorful garb, characterized by one author as "od and phantasticke," and intersected with the specifics of this case: Squires's commerce in "handkerchiefs, lawns, and muslins," her supposed promise to Canning that in return for a life of prostitution, she "should have fine clothes," and the allegation that she cut and stole Canning's stays.[37] Taken individually these details lacked any inherent criminality; considered together they worked as a condemnation of women's vanity, attributing to gypsies in particular a proclivity for drawing attention to themselves as potent sexual beings managing their sexual image and destiny. These references associated Squires in the minds of jurors and readers alike with depictions of gypsy women said to be trained for sensuality and lacking in shame.

In its rebuttal of Squires's alibi, the prosecution skillfully inserted a reference to magic, the black arts, and the supernatural so often associated with gypsies. John Inister said that he had spotted Squires "several times every day up and down before she was taken." He implied that he had seen her in Enfield when she claimed to be in Dorchester, and he added that "she walked into people's houses pretending to tell fortunes. She told mine once."[38]

Allan Ramsay (1713–84) noted in his pamphlet written in June 1753 after Squires's pardon that he "could not help being surprised to find upon what slight grounds [Fielding] and many other sensible men, had founded their belief in her [Canning's] veracity; and that they should be satisfied with evidence that seems to be in no manner adequate to the nature of the facts meant to be proved by it."[39] Given Ramsay's observation, and my examination of the trial, I want to suggest that Mary Squires's otherness and foreignness were absolutely necessary in order to make Canning's story at all believable. Squires's conviction reflected a belief that gypsies were inherently dishonest, promiscuous, cunning criminals. Ramsay said as much when he explained that Canning's accomplices remained silent for "their own preservation" or because "their friendship for her makes them prefer her safety and character to the life of an old gipsey."[40] Ramsay seems to be looking for an explanation for the failure of the English legal system, which in the absence of a paid police force depended so heavily on information provided by members of the community. He attributed the inaction of those who may have known something about the incident to their perception that their responsibility to testify was nullified by the gypsy's status as an aged outsider who did not belong to the local or national community.

The visual representations of the Canning case vividly map the categories of difference onto the bodies of the women involved. Figure 12.1, a print that was widely circulated and often reproduced, shows the two protagonists, Canning and Squires, side by side; the sharp distinction between them leaves no question as to what the viewer is to think about their respective innocence and guilt. Canning stares at the viewer with a modest but forthright look that captures the incapacity for deceit, the "Goodness, as well as Childishness and Simplicity of her Character" that Fielding attributed to her when he said she was "a child in years and yet more so in understanding."[41] Her face, framed by a bonnet, is completely unobstructed. Although she wears a cape, it is drawn aside to reveal a

Figure 12.1. "Elizabeth Canning and Mary Squires the Gypsy" (Copyright Trustees of the British Museum)

tightly laced bodice that seems to encase her honor and her virtue. In contrast, Squires looks away from the viewer, her hat and closed cloak suggesting an effort to conceal and obfuscate. The image of Canning is bright, her skin excessively white in comparison to the darkness that enshrouds the portrait of Squires. The young woman epitomizes passivity and docility, while the old woman suggests an active agent of threat and deceit.

The prints present Mary Squires, depicted as a crone, a witch, and "the sovereign of the Lapland race," as a deceitful interloper, performer of black magic, unwelcome, and constantly on the move. Figure 12.2 produces a visual form of John Hill's written portrait of Squires's face: "like that of no human Creature. The lower Part of it affected most remarkably by the Evil: the under Lip of an enormous Thickness; and the nose such as never before stood in a mortal Countenance." Another image, entitled "the Dame, whose chiromantic Pow'r, Foretells the' auspicious, or th' unlucky hour and warns the world, what wonders may befall, To Hell, to Virtue or to Justice Hall," articulates the physical and moral dangers Squires posed.[42] By her very presence she destabilized English values, institutions, and identities.

"The Gypsy's instantanious Flight from Enfield to Abbotsbury and back again" (fig. 12.3) portrays her menacing mobility and geographical autonomy. Quoting MacBeth (act. 1, sc. 1) as she rides on her broomstick through billows of smoke, Squires shouts to those watching from below "Fair is foul and foul is fair I fly through fog and filthy air." The onlookers accuse her of luring "maids" to prostitution, colluding with the devil, and flying to hell. The references to pollution and "infected" air confirm the anxiety about perceived trespasses and the gypsy's seemingly limitless ability to move through space unbounded by gravity or the laws of physics. Her mastery of the air contrasts strikingly with the earthbound impotence of those gazing at her. From this perspective her pardon on May 21 was a

Figure 12.2. "Mary Squires the Gypsy" (Courtesy of the Lewis Walpole Library, Yale University)

Figure 12.3. "*Gypsy's Instantanious Flight from Enfield to Abbotsbury and back again*" (Prints and Photographs Division, Library of Congress)

license to elude English law, making her and those influences she represented seem that much more invincible. While some reasoned that this proved English justice was blind, others feared that the pardon rendered the English criminal legal system, with its ideology of "equality before the law," powerless to protect "his Majesty's subjects [from] a Gang of desperate and cruel Villains, of the greatest Danger to a civilized Nation."[43] In contrast to the reactive portraits of the colonized as set out by Ann Stoler in *Haunted by Empire*, these imperial subjects are dynamic and on the move, feared for their agency, changeability, and uncontainability.[44]

Virtue Coerc'd

The prosecution's only corroborating witness was Virtue Hall, a young woman who said that she went to the home of Susannah Wells "as a lodger, but I was forced to do as they would have me," implying that she, unlike Canning, was successfully forced into prostitution.[45] Hall's report that John Squires, "the gypsie man said, 'mother, I have brought you a girl, do you take her?'" echoed stories and warnings about abductions and networks of prostitution run by gypsies whose reputed lack of moral shame contributed to their supposedly voracious and deviant sexual behavior.[46] Hall said that Mary Squires "ripped the lace off [Canning's] stays and pulled them off, and hung them on the back of a chair in the kitchen" before pushing Canning up into the room, saying "damn you go up there then, if you please." Then, according to Hall, John Squires "took the stays off the chair and went out with them." This vivid image of Canning's ripped stays captured the violence of the scene and encapsulated for Canning's supporters the loss of innocence, virginity, and purity.[47]

Skeptics questioned how Hall's testimony came to support Canning's story so exactly. More specifically, how did Henry Fielding (who did not preside in Enfield or Aldermanbury) come to hear the case and obtain this version of events, recorded in Hall's deposition dated February 7 and recounted by her at the Old Bailey on February 21?

On February 10, 1753, the *Publick Advertiser* printed the following: "On Thursday Evening a Girl who lived in the house . . . was brought before [Mr. Justice Fielding], and was under Examination from Six 'till Twelve at night." This six-hour interrogation featured "many hard Struggles and stout Denials of the Truth" before Hall "at length, confessed the Whole."[48] Elizabeth Canning and her supporters had originally come to the Guildhall, where Alderman Thomas Chitty had issued a warrant for the arrest of Susannah Wells. On February 1 Canning identified Wells and Squires in front of Merry Tyshmaker, a justice of the peace for the county of Middlesex, who interviewed Canning, Squires, Wells, and Hall.[49] Despite the protestations of the women of Enfield Wash that they had never seen Canning before—including Hall's declaration that "Elizabeth Canning had never been in Wells' house, to her Knowledge, till that Day, nor had she ever seen her Face before"—Tyshmaker committed Squires to New Prison in Clerkenwell and Wells to the adjoining bridewell.[50] Five days later, on February 6, Canning's solicitor, Samuel Salt, brought her to see Henry Fielding, seeking advice on how to move forward with the case.[51] According to Fielding, he agreed to hear the case, despite reservations about overriding Tyshmaker's authority.[52]

Fielding deposed Canning on February 7 and immediately issued a warrant for anyone left at Wells's house. The warrant yielded Hall, who appeared before the justice "in Tears" and "a trembling Condition."[53] Fielding promised her that if she told "the whole Truth of this Affair, I give you my Word and Honour, as far as it is in my Power, to protect you; you shall come to no Manner of Harm." When she agreed to cooperate, Fielding offered her a chair and began to examine her "in the softest Language and kindest Manner I was able, for a considerable Time."[54]

In the face of what he termed "so many Prevarications and Contradictions," Fielding's "kindest manner" dissipated, and he promised to "commit [Hall] to Prison, and leave her to stand or fall by the Evidence against her."[55] Fielding framed the stakes explicitly, advising Mr. Salt within Hall's earshot "to prosecute her as a Felon together with the Gipsy Woman."[56] Hall understood the dire consequences of this threat to intertwine her fate with that of Squires and responded accordingly. She "begged I would hear her once more, and said that she would tell the whole Truth." With the words attributed to her by Fielding she distinguished herself from the sinister otherness of Squires. Hall situated herself as another victim of Mary Squires and explained her initial reticence as a result of "Fears of the Gipsy Woman and Wells."[57]

With her compliance assured, Fielding "asked her a few Questions, which she answered with more Appearance of Truth than she had done before." He then directed Canning's lawyer "to go with her and take her Information in Writing; and at her parting from me, I bid her to be a good Girl, and be sure to say neither more nor less than the whole Truth."[58] Salt and Hall emerged two hours later with a deposition that corroborated even the smallest details in Canning's story. Hall repeated the same information in front of "several Noble Lords" a week later.[59]

Acting on his doubts about the case, Sir Crisp Gascoyne, lord mayor and one of the presiding judges at Mary Squires's trial, ordered the investigation of the gypsy's alibi on February 24, three days after her conviction. The corroborating evidence arrived on March 5. The next day, Gascoyne heard from John Hill (1714–75) that Virtue Hall was in the Gatehouse prison in Westminster, where she was supported by Canning's friends, who wanted to ensure her presence and cooperation as a witness in case George Squires returned. According to Hill, Hall showed "great signs of uneasiness, and a willingness to declare the truth."[60] When Hall appeared before Gascoyne, she came escorted by Canning's supporters. Although she refused to speak in front of them, "no sooner had we retired with her, but she instantly burst into a flood of tears, and confessed that all she had sworn was false."[61] Hall's recantation combined with the affidavits from Abbotsbury led to the collapse of the prosecution's case and Canning's eventual trial for perjury almost a year later in April 1754.

In reconstructing Hall's role in the case, mobility and intimacy again resurface as important themes. Her sequestration at the Gatehouse contrasts with the mobility, autonomy, and masculinity represented by George Squires. Furthermore, the key moments in the relation of Hall's narratives took place "off stage," each in an intimate setting, whether alone with Salt or with Sir Crisp. Such private moments were not allowed a woman whose virtue and honor were intact; their transgressive choreography drew attention to the sexual threats posed to English womanhood by foreign influence.

The visual images suggest that the lengths to which Gascoyne went to defend Mary Squires exceeded popular tolerance for the ideology of equality before the law. "The Gypsy's Triumph" (fig. 12.4) casts Gascoyne as the king of the gypsies: adorned with a crown, he is credited with saving "the Sovereign of the Lapland race." It was not unusual for magistrates in the seventeenth and eighteenth centuries to try to track down

Figure 12.4. "The Gypsy's Triumph" (Copyright Trustees of the British Museum)

distant witnesses and evidence,[62] but in this case the distances involved called further attention to far-flung networks, real and imagined, and the mobility of those women (and men) who seemed to traverse such large spaces unimpeded. The image of Gascoyne, lord mayor of London, as king of the gypsies demonstrates dramatically perhaps the most threatening anxiety that runs through the narrative of these moving subjects, the permeable, unstable, shifting line constantly crossed by insider and outsider; empowered and disempowered; perpetrator and victim.[63]

The Moral Geography of Eighteenth-Century Britain

The stories surrounding Elizabeth Canning are marked by anxieties about sexuality, race, and nation, the geographical mobility of the protagonists insistently drawing attention to a fissured metropole as well as Britain's imperial project. At the local level we have the story of Elizabeth Canning, who claimed she was dragged eleven or twelve miles from Moorfields, along the Hertfordshire Road, to the home of Susannah Wells in Enfield. During her trial witnesses placed Mary Squires in Abbotsbury, while at her sentencing, Squires claimed that between the end of December 1752 and January 10, 1753, she had been at Coombe, Stoptage, Basingstoke, Bagshot-heath, and Old Brentford, traversing at least 140 miles before arriving at the home of Susannah Wells. The anxiety associated with sexuality and mobility resurfaced after Canning's conviction in 1754, when her supporters feared she would be raped while on board the ship carrying her to the colonies to serve her sentence of transportation.[64]

From a global perspective, the case can be seen within the eighteenth-century myth of geography that divided the hardy, disciplined north from the wanton and effeminate south.[65] The British often cast their imperial enterprise as their national destiny: a civilizing process, providing northern virtues abroad while defending against the threat of degeneration posed at home by the barbarity of southern peoples. Their belief in their distinct and superior northern attributes empowered the British to claim Rome's imperial mantle while replacing Rome's southern luxury and tyranny with British law and liberty.[66] This British conception of the south carried with it a racial ideology that touted British potency over the weakness ascribed to the Mediterranean.[67] Fear of southern influences meant that Britain had to protect itself from the weaknesses of the south even while laying claim to them.

This moral geography had a physical parallel mapped onto the individual and collective female body: while English women were considered civilized, domestic, and sexually contained, women from warmer climates were represented as prone to excessive carnal desires and unrestrained sexual behavior. Felicity Nussbaum argues for the mutually constitutive character of these sexual profiles in which the colonized English woman's civility and virtue relied on the invention of the excesses of the "other" woman. Nussbaum's analysis allows us to see the scandal that was the Canning case: the "other" woman—a member of a group from two possible southern sites, Egypt in the early modern imagination or the real origins of the Romany in India—moved seemingly unimpeded between London and Dorchester, threatening the chastity of at least two white working-class Englishwomen, Elizabeth Canning and Virtue Hall. Like the journeys of Angelique Langlade and her family detailed by Michael McDonnell (chapter 7 here), Squires traversed the countryside in pursuit of her living impervious to regional and national boundaries or the conventions of English respectability.

The assumptions reflected in the representations of Canning, Hall, and Squires produced a sharp definition of Englishness in which the native born, "white" woman emerged as a virtuous and honest victim. This scenario demanded quite a leap of faith in the case of Elizabeth Canning, considering the disdain and suspicion with which servants were regarded in the eighteenth century and the slight credibility of Virtue Hall, a prostitute.[68] But the gypsy, described by Fielding as possessing "scarce even the Appearance of Humanity," and by Hill—Fielding's detractor, who was supposedly sympathetic to her—as having a face "like that of no human Creature," was portrayed as lacking all morality, credibility, or assimilability. Even the mobility that exonerated her did not prove her innocence to readers and jurors in eighteenth-century Britain. Her very presence in England was threatening regardless of whether she had committed any crime against Elizabeth Canning. The *London Evening Post* encapsulated this sentiment with the praise they heaped on the "Public-Spirited and humane Gentlemen" who supported the "poor, injured innocent Girl" and endeavored to "eradicate a Gang of desperate and cruel Villains, of the greatest Danger to a civilized Nation."[69]

In 1753 these portraits of a gypsy underworld did the cultural work of constituting an ephemerally stable national identity. The debate between Fielding and Gascoyne about the Canning evidence demonstrates that national identities are subject to debate and that some versions of Britishness in the eighteenth century were more tolerant of difference than others. The creation or reinvention of difference and foreignness in the courtroom makes this an important site to consider. The legal setting credited circumstantial evidence, rumor, and innuendo with unwarranted authority. With their reputations and their very lives in the balance, the stakes for each woman were tremendously high. The stakes for English law were equally high: to retain its efficacy, this instrument of empire, coercion, and national integration required the preservation of its credibility.[70]

Gascoyne responded to what he perceived as injustice and prejudice when he said of Mary Squires "surely no poor creature ever before appeared at the Bar, more perfectly deprived of the mercy of the law, which presumes guilt in no one before conviction."[71] His ostensible belief in the superiority of English law and liberty (as well as his personal contempt for Henry Fielding) compelled him to defend the alien gypsy, Mary Squires, against Canning's allegations. Paired with Squires as the male sovereign of the Lapland race, Gascoyne paid dearly for his campaign, which led to his defeat in the next election for lord mayor and ultimately cost him his political career. His detractors saw his defense of Squires as a corruption of English law by the imperial project. The Elizabeth Canning case, with its insistence on a multicultural British population, raised doubts about imperial aspiration by disturbing the distinction between colonizer and colonized, citizen and alien, home and away.[72]

Although as foreigners the gypsies had been perceived as a threat and a source of danger since their arrival in England, in 1753 their otherness carried a different resonance. In the eighteenth century, Britain's imperial project and its aspirations abroad put early modern notions of belonging and community defined by common genealogy, shared place, and continuity in tension with the reality of constant mobility and contact with unrelated populations that characterized Britain's colonial reach. The early modern markers of difference ascribed to gypsies, Jews, and other diasporic populations now seemed to apply to Britons. Familiarity with migration and movement and comfort in many changing spaces were precisely the attributes simultaneously spurned in an English setting and embraced in a British one. The scandal surrounding Canning and the controversy over the Jewish Naturalization Bill, which unfolded contemporaneously, revealed widespread unease with Britain's emerging imperial character, international trade networks, and cosmopolitanism.[73] Even those who touted Britain's international presence provided a coherence and interconnectedness to this experience by rooting it in an English territoriality defined by a racial, religious, and cultural homogeneity that implied purity and stability. The presence of outsiders in England exposed the fictive nature of this imagined community and the futile attempt to distinguish those who belonged from those who did not. The vilification of the gypsy and the Jew in the contemporaneous scandals of 1753 may have been an attempt to clean up the glaring contradictions in the ideology made so obvious in each case.

Notes

A version of this essay was presented at the North American Conference on British Studies, Denver, October 8, 2005. I would like to thank Tony Ballantyne, Antoinette Burton, Craig Koslofsky, and Amy Masciola for their generous and insightful comments.

1. Allan Ramsay, *"A Letter to the Right Honorable the Earl of—" (1753)* reprinted in *The investigator. Containing the following tracts: I. On ridicule. II. On Elizabeth Canning. III. On naturalization. IV. On taste.* (London, 1762), 38. More than fifty pamphlets and broadsides with either Canning or Squires in the title are listed in the British Library catalogue. The case has been the subject of several retellings for popular audiences including Josephine Tey, *The Franchise Affair* (London, 1948), and John Treherne, *The Canning Enigma* (London, 1989). Academic examinations include Amy Masciola, "'The Unfortunate Maid Exemplified': Elizabeth Canning and Representations of Infanticide in Eighteenth-Century England," in *Infanticide: Historical Perspectives, 1550–2000,* ed. Mark Jackson (London, 2002), 52–72, and Judith Moore, *The Appearance of Truth: The Story of Elizabeth Canning and Eighteenth-Century Narrative* (Newark, N.J., 1994).

2. Kristina Straub, "Heteroanxiety and the Case of Elizabeth Canning," *Eighteenth-Century Studies* 30 (1997): 296–303.

3. My interpretation follows on the pioneering work of Ann Stoler, *Carnal Knowledge and Imperial Power: Race and the Intimate in Colonial Rule* (Berkeley, 1995); Kathleen Wilson, *A Sense of the People: Politics, Culture and Imperialism in England, 1715–1785* (Cambridge, 1995); Wilson, *The Island Race: Englishness, Empire and Gender in the Eighteenth Century* (New York, 2003); and Wilson, ed., *A New Imperial History: Culture, Identity, and Modernity in Britain and the Empire, 1660–1840* (Cambridge, 2004).

4. The discomfort with empire manifested itself in a series of scandals and court cases in the eighteenth century. See Michael Ragussis, "Jews and Other 'Outlandish Englishmen': Ethnic Performance and the Invention of British Identity under the Georges," *Critical Inquiry* 26 (2000): 773–97; P. J. Marshall, "Empire and Authority in the Later Eighteenth Century," *Journal of Imperial and Commonwealth History* 15 (1987): 105–22; and Marshall, "A Nation Defined by Empire, 1755–1776," in Alexander Grand and Keith Stringer, eds., *Uniting the Kingdom: The Making of British History* (London, 1995), 208–22.

5. For the contemporary definition of gypsy, see the *Oxford English Dictionary (OED)*. The reality of early modern mobility is documented in Lee Beier, *Masterless Men: The Vagrancy Problem in England, 1560–1640* (London, 1985); Paul Slack, "Vagrants and Vagrancy in England, 1598–1664," *Economic History Review* 27 (1974): 360–79; and Slack, *Poverty and Policy in Tudor and Stuart England* (London, 1988). For migration in early modern England, see Peter Clark and David Souden, eds., *Migration and Society in Early Modern England* (London, 1987). For more on gypsies, see David Mayall, *Gypsy Identities 1500–2000: From Egipcyans and Moon-Men to the Ethnic Romany* (London, 2004). For place, honor, crime, and community, see Anthony Fletcher and John Stevenson, *Order and Disorder in Early Modern England* (Cambridge, 1985); Robert Shoemaker, "The Decline of Public Insult in London, 1660–1800," *Past and Present* 169 (2000): 97–131; Garthine Walker, *Crime, Gender and the Social Order in Early Modern*

England (Cambridge, 2003); and Keith Wrightson, "Two Concepts of Order: Justices, Constables and Jurymen in Seventeenth-Century England," in John Brewer and John Styles, eds., *An Ungovernable People: the English and their Law in the Seventeenth and Eighteenth Centuries* (New Brunswick, N.J., 1980), 21–46.

6. This discussion of the cultural meaning of place relies of Doreen Massey, *For Space* (London, 2005), esp. 9–15 and 64–68.

7. *London Evening Post*, February 15–17, 1753, 4.

8. *The Case of Elizabeth Canning* (London, 1753), in Ramsay, *Investigator*, 25.

9. Straub, "Heteroanxiety," 296. Scholarship on race and nation in the eighteenth century includes Suvir Kaul, *Poems of Nation, Anthems of Empire: English Verse in the Long Eighteenth Century* (Charlottesville, Va., 2000); Roxann Wheeler, *The Complexion of Race: Categories of Difference in Eighteenth-Century British Culture* (Philadelphia, 2000); and Wilson, *Sense of the People, Island Race*, and *New Imperial History*.

10. Straub, "Heteroanxiety," 299. The ideology of equality before the law is examined by Douglas Hay in "Property, Authority, and the Criminal Law," in Douglas Hay, Peter Linebaugh, John G. Rule, E. P. Thompson, and Cal Winslow, eds., *Albion's Fatal Tree: Crime and Society in Eighteenth-Century England* (New York, 1975), and E. P. Thompson, *Whigs and Hunters: The Origins of the Black Act* (New York, 1975), esp. 258–69.

11. *London Daily Advertiser*, January 31, 1753, 2. For more on newspapers, see Michael Harris, *London Newspapers in the Age of Walpole: A Study of the Origins of the Modern English Press* (Cranbury, N.J., 1987).

12. *London Daily Advertiser*, January 31, 1753, 2. Stays are "a laced underbodice, stiffened by the insertion of strips of whale-bone (sometimes of metal or wood) worn by women (sometimes by men) to give shape and support to the figure: a corset"; *OED*.

13. *London Daily Advertiser*, January 31, 1753, 2.

14. *Canning*, in Ramsay, *Investigator*, 25.

15. Ibid., 26.

16. John Hill, *The Story of Elizabeth Canning considered by Dr. Hill* (London, 1753), 9.

17. Publications skeptical of Canning's veracity included *The Truth of the Case, or, Canning and Squires fairly opposed* (London, 1753); Ramsay, *Investigator*; and the ballad *The Devil Outdone* (London, 1753).

18. Hill, *Story of Elizabeth Canning*, 13–14.

19. Hill was the first to suggest that Canning had been with a lover, *Story of Elizabeth Canning*, 13. The author of *The Imposture Detected; Or, the Mystery and Iniquity of Elizabeth Canning's Story Displayed* (London, 1753) outlines other likely alternatives, 23–33.

20. *Daily Advertiser*, January 6, 1753, 3. Mrs. Canning placed at least two other ads on January 4 and 20, 1753.

21. James Solas Dodd, *A physical account of the case of Elizabeth Canning* (London, 1753), 14. According to Dodd, the obstruction was caused by "her sleeping great Part of a Night, in a damp Stone Kitchen."

22. Daniel Cox, *An appeal to the public, in behalf of Elizabeth Canning* (London, 1753), 16.

23. Straub, "Heteroanxiety," 296–97. For more on reading the body in the eigh-

teenth century, see Barbara Duden, *The Woman Beneath the Skin: A Doctor's Patients in Eighteenth-Century Germany* (Cambridge, Mass., 1991).

24. David Mayall, "Egyptians and Vagabonds: Representations of the Gypsy in Early Modern Official and Rogue Literature," *Immigrants and Minorities* 16 (1997): 62.

25. *London Evening Post*, February 1–3, 1753, 4. An equally brief mention of Squires was made in the *London Evening Post*, February 8–10, 1753, 4.

26. Henry Fielding, *A Clear State of the Case of Elizabeth Canning* (1753), in *An Enquiry into the Causes of the Late Increase of Robbers and Related Writings*, ed. Malvin Zirker (New York, 1988), 299–301.

27. *London Evening Post*, February 15–17, 1753, 4.

28. Ibid.

29. Lou Charnon-Deutsch describes gypsies as Europe's "quintessential other residing problematically on 'home ground.'" *The Spanish Gypsy: The History of a European Obsession* (University Park, Pa., 2004), 4.

30. Trial of Mary Squires and Susannah Wells, February 1753 (t17530221-47), Old Bailey Proceedings Online, www.oldbaileyonline.org.

31. David Mayall, "The Making of British Gypsy Identities, c. 1500–1980," *Immigrants and Minorities* 11 (1992): 26.

32. Trial of Mary Squires and Susannah Wells, February 1753 (t17530221-47), Old Bailey Proceedings Online.

33. Ibid.

34. Lawn is a kind of fine linen, resembling cambric; *OED*.

35. Trial of Mary Squires and Susannah Wells, February 1753 (t17530221-47), Old Bailey Proceedings Online.

36. Ibid.

37. Thomas Dekker gave a lengthy account of gypsy apparel in *Lantern and Candle-light* (1608), reprinted in Arthur F. Kinney, ed., *Rogues, Vagabonds and Sturdy Beggars* (Amherst, Mass., 1990).

38. Trial of Mary Squires and Susannah Wells, February 1753 (t17530221-47), Old Bailey Proceedings Online.

39. Ramsay, *Investigator*, 3–4.

40. Ibid., 20–21.

41. Fielding, *A Clear State*, 294, 309.

42. Chiromancy is "divination by the hand; the art of telling the characters and fortunes of persons by inspection of their hands; palmistry"; *OED*.

43. *London Evening Post*, February 15–17, 1753, 4.

44. Ann Stoler, *Haunted by Empire: Geographies of Intimacy in North American History* (Durham, N.C., 2006), introduction, esp. 4.

45. Trial of Mary Squires and Susannah Wells, February 1753 (t17530221-47), Old Bailey Proceedings Online.

46. Ibid. Randolph Trumbach, *Sex and the Gender Revolution*, vol. 1, *Heterosexuality and the Third Gender in Enlightenment London* (Chicago, 1998), 136–53, and Mayall, "The Making of British Gypsy Identities," 26–27.

47. Trial of Mary Squires and Susannah Wells, February 1753 (t17530221-47), Old Bailey Proceedings Online. For more on prostitution, see Tony Henderson, *Disorderly Women in Eighteenth-Century London: Prostitution and Control in the Metropolis, 1730–1830* (London, 1999).

48. *Publick Advertiser*, February 10, 1753, 2.

49. The events surrounding the scandal are reconstructed in Zirker, general introduction to Fielding, *An Enquiry into the Causes*, xciv–cxiv.

50. Fielding, *A Clear State*, 296.

51. Salt is referred to only by his last name. He may be Samuel Salt (d. 1792), a lawyer, admitted at the Middle Temple in 1741, admitted at the Inner Temple in 1745, and called to the bar in 1753; *Oxford Dictionary of National Biography*. By March 13, Salt was replaced by John Miles.

52. Fielding, *A Clear State*, 298.

53. Ibid., 301.

54. Ibid.

55. Ibid.

56. Ibid., 302.

57. Ibid.

58. Ibid.

59. Ibid., 306.

60. Sir Crisp Gascoyne, *An Address to the Liverymen of the City of London* (London, 1754), 9.

61. Ibid., 10. Fielding's tactics were made public by Virtue Hall on March 8, 1753. Hall's response on March 8 was made in front of Gascoyne, several aldermen, other onlookers described as "people of fashion," and Canning. Gascoyne included the account of Hall's confession in his *Address to the Liverymen of the City of London* (London, 1754), 11.

62. John Styles, "Sir John Fielding and the Problem of Criminal Investigation in Eighteenth-Century England," *Transactions of the Royal Historical Society* 33 (1983): 127–49.

63. Virtue Hall, too, shifts from prostitute to credible witness to lying whore. The porous nature of these categories stands in contrast to the more strict division described by Stoler in *Haunted by Empire*.

64. *A refutation of Sir Crisp Gascoyne's Address to the liverymen of London: By a clear state of the case of Elizabeth Canning, in a narrative of facts* (London, 1754), 29.

65. Pat Rogers, "North and South," *Eighteenth-Century Life* 12 (1988): 101–11.

66. Kaul, *Poems of Nation*, 28.

67. Wheeler, *Complexion of Race*, 35.

68. Although she did not benefit from the same imperial opportunities enjoyed by Samuel Hudson as described in Kirsten McKenzie's essay, Canning's status as a white Englishwoman allowed her to shape the narrative of events to her benefit, to proclaim her sexual virtue, and to achieve notoriety despite her occupation as a servant maid. For more on service and servants, see Carolyn Stedman, *Master and Servant: Love and Labour in the English Industrial Age* (Cambridge, 2007).

69. *London Evening Post*, February 15–17, 1753, 4.

70. Thompson, *Whigs and Hunters*, 258–69.

71. Gascoyne, *Address*, 3.

72. Michael Fisher, *Counterflows to Colonialism: Indian Travelers and Settlers in Britain, 1600–1857* (New York, 2004), demonstrates the diversity of Britain in the eighteenth century.

73. The Jewish Naturalization Bill (26 Geo. II, c. 26) would have allowed Parliament to naturalize individual Jewish men if they secured the passage of a private Act of Parliament. The Bill passed on May 22, 1753, and was repealed in November of the same year due to popular outcry. For more on the so-called Jew Bill, see my article *"The Jew Bill of 1753: Masculinity, Virility, and Nation,"* *Eighteenth-Century Studies* 39 (2006): 157–71.

13 *Social Mobilities at the Cape of Good Hope*

LADY ANNE BARNARD, SAMUEL HUDSON,
AND THE OPPORTUNITIES OF EMPIRE,
C. 1797–1824

In 1799, during a period of unprecedented British imperial expansion, Lady Anne Barnard (a small but eloquent cog in the wheels setting this enterprise in motion) had a number of pressing concerns in her life at the Cape of Good Hope. Not least of these were the fleas, who showed scant respect for her aristocratic flesh. The continual catching and killing of fleas, she complained in the pages of her diary, was "a most vile degrading Hottentotish business."[1] "I was often obliged to undress two or three times in the course of the day & when I have not time to devote half an hour to Les Plaisirs de la Chasse [the pleasures of the hunt], I change my linnen."[2] Then there was the problem of her own and her husband's social position and political power (two inseparable issues) in a highly factionalized and competitive British administration. As wife to the colonial secretary, Lady Anne[3] dismissed this jockeying for position as "the little politicks of our *Lilliput* court"[4] in a letter to her old flame, Henry Dundas, secretary of state for the colonies. Yet her private diaries reveal that she took it with a deadly seriousness.[5] Finally there was the vexed question of her domestic responsibilities, a realm about which this sometime society hostess was profoundly ambiguous.

274

Among the upper ranks of the Barnard servants was Samuel Eusebius Hudson, similarly tormented by the fleas and bedbugs that evidently swarmed through Cape mattresses.[6] If the vermin showed a democratic spirit, preying on masters and servants alike, the Barnards and Hudson were obsessed with social status and with rank: with ordering their world and with improving their own place within it. The need to protect civilized European flesh from the mortifications of life in the colonies spurred a constant war of attrition in the domestic realm. Ranged on the one side (to extrapolate from Lady Anne's account of life with fleas) were those able to change into clean linen when required. On the other were the servants and (more commonly) the slaves who had to launder it. Control over the body and its domestic environment, interaction with the servants whose labor sustained that environment, and the relationship between social status and political power were all profoundly interconnected in the overlapping worlds of Hudson and of his master and mistress.

It might be tempting to cast the characters of Lady Anne Barnard (1750–1825) and Samuel Hudson (1764–1828) as mistress and servant in a kind of upstairs/downstairs tragicomedy of imperial manners. Alternatively, their voluminous private writings and letters could be situated within an analysis of British elites in a racially hierarchical and oppressive colonial regime. The complexities presented by their racial, class, and status situations as they moved between Britain and the Cape, however, serves to problematize both these scenarios in suggestive ways. Tony Ballantyne and Antoinette Burton remind us that even elite stories can be used as a reminder of "the complexities of power, status, and identity in the context of imperial world systems."[7] Both the earl's daughter and the grave digger's son were on the make in the fluid and competitive social world that linked Britain with its imperial outposts. Both were wracked by status anxiety, an anxiety in which the most intimate relationships of the domestic and the political world were intertwined. Hudson's and Lady Anne's geographical mobility from Britain to its newest imperial outpost, the Cape Colony, was undertaken with the calculated intent of upward social mobility. As a consequence, their writings demonstrate a complex interplay between identity and locality in ways that illuminate the physical and imaginative ways the British Empire was bound together.

In examining the lives of these two diarists at the Cape, I take on the question of intimacy, not in its (more commonly employed) conjugal or sexual sense, but as it pertains to two themes—domestic service and political patronage. These themes manifest themselves in ways that speak to Ann Stoler's twinned concerns of how "intimate domains . . . figure in the making of racial categories and in the management of imperial rule."[8] Intimacy implies "close acquaintance, association or familiarity,"[9] and sexual intimacies, as Mary A. Renda argues in her response to Stoler's formulations, should not be privileged in defining the private realm or in determining racial boundaries and political power.[10] In this case study, racial categories (and status hierarchies) were both confounded and confirmed within the domestic realm.[11] Hudson's ambiguous position of being white, male, and in domestic service (although of a privileged rank) at the Cape was resolved by his leaving the Barnards' employ relatively soon after reaching the colony. The opportunities of empire, for Hudson at least, were quite literally embodied in the enslavement of others. This allowed him to transform himself (both psychologically and economically) from English servant to colonial master. Yet intimate domains could discomfort as well as underline dichotomies of race and class, and Lady Anne's engagement with domestic life in Africa both sustained *and* eroded her status.

With regard to Stoler's second concern, the "management of imperial rule," the lives of Lady Anne and Hudson shed light on the changing place of patronage and close personal connection in imperial governance. As Zoë Laidlaw has recently argued, interpersonal networks, in which patronage played such a vital role, were (and were acknowledged as) central to the administration of the British Empire after 1815. In the 1820s and 1830s, however, pressures within both metropole and colonies led to a bureaucratic revolution in which reliance on the information provided by these personalized networks was dismantled in favor of new statistical forms of knowledge. This transition coincided with altered possibilities for colonial political representation.[12] The demands for new models of both colonial and metropolitan politics made by men like Hudson, and focused on a language of "independence," undermined the personal and patronage relationships of imperial rule in which women (and men) like Lady Anne participated. As an aristocratic woman and as a man leaving service to enter into (and later desperately cling to) the ranks of the middle class, the two diarists had widely divergent ideas about the importance of patronage, about the conduct of politics, and about its relationship to gender. These differences were not just personal but also symptomatic of a transition between what we might distinguish as an eighteenth-century model of patronage and aristocratic influence to a nineteenth-century model of bourgeois public sphere politics dependent on a very particular version of masculinity. It was, in part, out of this shift in political culture, a shift through which the intimate ties of patronage came to be seen as politically illegitimate, that the ideas emerged that became, as Stoler calls them, "cherished assumptions: that the intimate is located primarily in the family, that the family is a ready model for, and microcosm of, the state, and that affective ties are inherently tender ones."[13] The two intimacies I examine in this essay—one very private and domestic, one very public and administrative, and *both* very deeply political—are connected in ways that, as Stoler would argue, demonstrate shifting "regimes of truth" about race and difference.[14] Domestic intimacy and political intimacy in the lives of Hudson and Lady Anne shed light not only on "the competing logics of those who ruled and the fissures and frictions within their ranks"[15] but also on developments that would make whiteness an increasingly stable sign of social and political power as the nineteenth century progressed.[16]

As the eighteenth century gave way to the nineteenth, Britain and its colonies were being mutually transformed by an expanding empire that opened up economic, social, and political opportunities for some at the very moment it curtailed the freedoms of others. At issue in the wider transformative debates taking place in this period over the possession and practice of liberty was a changing culture in which the domestic and political were inextricably connected.[17] If the writings of Lady Anne and Hudson at the Cape demonstrate these connections among domestic intimacies, the culture of political power, and the nature of status, they also speak to the extreme difficulty of disentangling lines of influence between metropole and colony and the relational connection between identity and space.[18] Both diarists were British, and Lady Anne was a self-consciously temporary sojourner at the Cape. This is an important caveat in understanding the way writings shed light on the workings of imperial systems. Lady Anne and Hudson were surrounded by the localized specificities of Cape society, yet they thought of themselves in terms that erode a dichotomy between the local and the global. Like the settlers of Nova Scotia and New Zealand discussed (chapters 3 and 4 here) by Elizabeth Vibert and Charlotte Macdonald (and arguably like many in British settler societies into the twentieth century and beyond) Hudson and his mistress were adept at living in two places at once. They both acknowledged (and sometimes railed against) the particularity of their local circumstances, but they also showed a tendency to situate themselves in an imaginary geographic and social space distinct from the one in which they were physically writing. The social structure within which they fitted themselves thus transcended locality or geography. Having left Britain to improve their social circumstances, they both invoked British models in which to situate their own identities. For Lady Anne this focused on questions of British rank and hierarchy. For Hudson this found expression in evocations of British liberties and the "rights of Englishmen." The writings of Hudson and of Lady Anne thus point to the existence of an extended imperial public sphere. Yet the way their writings are situated in a kind of doubled space make the directional lines of influence between local and metropolitan conditions and circumstances more than usually challenging to separate.

Geographic and Social Mobilities

The presence of Hudson and the Barnards at the Cape of Good Hope (a Dutch imperial outpost since 1652) was the direct result of Britain's seizure of the colony in 1795 in the context of the Napoleonic Wars. This so-called first British occupation would last until 1803. A three-year interlude of control by the Dutch Batavian Republic ended in 1806 with the start of the second British occupation.[19] The Cape was, therefore, a society with an overlapping and often mutually hostile system of Dutch and British imperial governance and a polyglot community of slaves (many of whom traced their descent to the Indian Ocean possessions of the Dutch empire), indigenous African groups in a variety of free or semibonded labor conditions, and Europeans.

When Lady Anne Barnard entered this world, she had good reason to be obsessed with her own status, which was more precarious than her title might suggest.[20] As Lady Anne Lindsay, the eldest child of the impoverished fifth earl of Balcarres, she had married Andrew Barnard, a man twelve years younger than herself, and widely regarded as her social inferior, in 1793. The marriage was a strategic change of direction in Lady Anne's evident search for economic and social security. As prominent hostess to some of London's most powerful men in the 1780s, an intimate of the Prince of Wales and of Mrs. Fitzherbert, she had been courted by men of wealth and influence. It all came to naught. Marriage to Andrew Barnard came after being jilted first by William Windham and then by Henry Dundas (both of whom would later fill the post of Britain's secretary of state for war and the colonies). Aged forty-three, she now accepted the man whose suit she had previously deemed beneath her, a soldier on half pay, the son of the bishop of Limerick, a man without private means. Like many others of his class in the 1790s, Andrew Barnard was looking for preferment—in Europe, if possible, within the expanding empire if not. Lady Anne now called in what she felt to be her emotional and political debts. Through her influence with Henry Dundas she was able to secure for her husband an appointment in the new British administration of Cape Colony. She made pointed allusions to her past relationship with Dundas—"*You owe me some Happiness—in Truth you do*"—in these protracted negotiations.[21] Lady Anne's repeated insistence that Dundas secure her husband a post with sufficient "patronage and rank" received a sharp rebuke from Dundas.[22] Nevertheless, he did eventually deliver on his promise to help the Barnards, and what was settled on was the position of colonial secretary, accompanying the new governor, Lord Macartney, to the Cape of Good Hope. As Lady Anne admitted in the pages of her journal, the Barnards hoped to use Andrew's appointment to return to Britain with improved monetary and career prospects.[23] They arrived at the Cape in 1797 with a miscellaneous party of dogs (which contributed to their flea problems), servants (including Hudson), and dependant relatives. The Barnards' stay at the Cape lasted some five years, ending when the colony was handed back to the Dutch in 1803. When the British assumed control of the colony once more, Andrew Barnard took up a position in the administration, this time leaving his wife in Britain. He died in 1807 during this second period of service at the Cape. Lady Anne largely withdrew from public life after the death of her much younger husband, whom she outlived by eighteen years.

The life of Samuel Hudson remains far less well known than that of his socially prominent employers.[24] Born in Coleshill, Warwickshire, the son of the local sexton, Hudson appears to have had little formal education, although his lifelong writings reveal an overpowering thirst for knowledge about the world. At age twenty-eight, Hudson married Hannah Stopford in 1792, but the marriage appears not to have lasted very long. A daughter, Mary Ann, whom Hudson repeatedly mentions in his journals, was born to them, and subsequently (it seems) brought up by relatives. By 1795 Hudson had a position in service at Wimpole Hall, Cambridgeshire, the seat of the third earl of Hardwicke. He also indulged in a significant act of reinvention—adding the imposing-sounding "Eusebius" to his name for the first time.[25] It was through his position at Wimpole that Hudson came to join the Barnards on their voyage to the Cape. The countess of Hardwicke was sister to Lady Anne Barnard, and Hudson is described in Lady Anne's journals as "a footman of Lord Hardwicke [who] begged hard to be of the party."[26] Recent research by Edward and Raymond Hudson suggests this may have been somewhat disingenuous. Hudson appears to have left England under something of a cloud. Lord Hardwicke later accused his footman of stealing prints from the books at Wimpole's library and demanded that Andrew Barnard arrest Hudson. Without any evidence to support the accusation, Andrew Barnard sent his brother-in-law a tactful refusal.[27] Edward and Raymond Hudson argue, however, that Samuel's hasty removal from Wimpole Hall may have stemmed from a far more intimate theft.[28]

Whatever the reasons for his inclusion in their party, Hudson's hopes of the Cape were no less connected to status than were those of the Barnards. Hudson was a man obsessed with independence, a concept he deemed incompatible with servitude. Among his ambitions seems to have been a desire to rise from the ranks of the servile classes. [29] On board ship, Lady Anne wrote, he was "the Greatest Man in the World! . . . being out of livery for the first time!"[30] Once at the Cape, Hudson only lasted five months in the employ of the Barnards. His relationship with their other servants became increasingly fraught, and he was eventually dismissed after hosting an illicit party at which Lady Anne's best poultry ended up in pies. [31] Andrew Barnard found him a position in the customs service from which he was promoted a year later to first clerk. Hudson left government service and went into partnership with his brother, Thomas, who arrived at the Cape in 1799. The "independence" of the Hudson brothers was bought with the servitude of others, and slave labor enabled them to amass a fairly considerable property. When Hudson returned to Britain in 1807 (for reasons that remain obscure) he owned fifteen slaves, a house in Cape Town where the brothers had run a hotel, and a small farm.[32] As Lady Anne dryly put it, "He soon established a good Hotel on the beach to be in fortunes way and by a turn of her whimsical wheel I believe is now a rich man & perhaps rather more respected than he is quite entitled to."[33]

This marked the height of Hudson's financial success at the Cape. His return there in 1814 was far less happy. He arrived to face the collapse of the family business and the suicide of Thomas: "That independence, which I had with painful industry cultivated, is gone in the general ruin."[34] Hudson tried to recoup his fortunes in the eastern districts of the colony, to no avail; his bankruptcy was declared in 1822.[35] Protracted battles with the Sequestrator's Office to wind up his affairs went on for years,[36] while Hudson's diary reveals him living in increasing poverty in Cape Town, scraping by on what he could earn by copying old masters for the local art market. He was never able to repeat the success of the first decade of the nineteenth century, and had to endure an uncomfortable life in the boardinghouses of Cape Town. In his final years he was reduced to eking out a living on the edges of respectability, desperate to keep up appearances. In 1824, four years before his death, he confided to the pages of his diary: "must have a new suit of Black when the needful comes in my Garbs are getting seedy and to be poor and seem so is the very devil."[37]

If Lady Anne frequently railed against her descent into "Hottentotish" savagery and longed for an idealized British model of domesticity, she was under no illusions as to the benefits a move to Africa offered to

her social mobility. In 1800, she meditated on the opportunities of empire at some length in her diary: "That which is least agreeable to my
lot is certainly more done away in Africa than it could be in England.
. . . I am married to an amiable good man, but he is neither a nabob or a
peer—in Africa I am not reminded of this by any thing which brings my
influence to the test of comparison, I am almost the first woman here."
In Britain, she had "sometimes tho not very painfully felt myself more
secondary than I woud have wished, & regreted that my dear B. was not
one of a groupe of men all richer, greater & more powerfull than himself." Her unassailable position at the apex of the Cape's social world
allowed her the freedom to deny an interest in her own rank.[38] She was
deeply ambivalent about the status opportunities presented by moving
from Britain into the empire. She might sneer at others who exploited
the opportunities of empire, for example Lady Maria Anstruthers, passing through the Cape as wife of the chief justice of Bengal (and whose
"taste of Supremacy" earned her the racially inflected nickname "the
Begum").[39] Yet she also showed a sympathetic realism toward more lowly
women "courting independence" by going out "to market" in search of
husbands in India.[40]

The Barnards were never in the same danger of losing caste as Hudson, with his precarious hold on independence and respectability. Yet
the role of the British imperial administration in shoring up a variety of
faltering social statuses is clearly evident in the merciless social competition that pervaded its ranks. From sneers at the Barnard family silver
(plate) to sniffs about the pay of bishops, a hundred small barbs were
daily loosed in battles over personal status and political precedence.[41]
Hudson's private diaries were even more withering in their scorn of the
ceaseless one-upmanship and sycophancy of the British administrators
than were Lady Anne's. In 1798 he mocked Andrew Barnard for finding
"a new way to pay old debts" by means of "the advantages arising from
connections with antiquated dowagers."[42] Andrew Barnard owed his
appointment to his socially prominent wife. The "accident of having a
wife to whose train a Ladyship is pinn'd"[43] was a constant issue for the
couple's social status: on board ship, among the British administration,
and in their relations with the Dutch.

As he rose in status and wealth at the Cape, Hudson, it seems, never
quite forgave the Barnards for their knowledge of his past life in servitude.
Once he left their employ, he refused to acknowledge them socially: "to
us he owes what he is, but he hates us as he cannot forget how lately he
has been our servant," wrote Lady Anne, when her social overtures were
snubbed.[44] The racial hierarchies of the colonial realm were a central un-

derpinning of these definitions of status. Lady Anne would later comment on some recently arrived slaves from Madagascar: "I did not find . . . that they lookd upon Slavery as the hard lot we regard it, they are Habituated to consider it as belonging to their rank as much as a livery is to an English footman."[45] The issue here is less the relative material condition of African slaves and English servants than the demeaning implication that servitude had for social status, particularly in the colonies. As with Lady Anne's insight into Hudson's great delight and pride in abandoning his livery, we get a sense of the mortification that servitude could be for the socially ambitious.

Once at the Cape, Hudson clearly chafed at his bonds and made trouble with the Barnards' other servants. Lady Anne complained that her husband's Belgian manservant (who later gave frequent trouble of his own) "would have considerable reason to revolt under the flag of Supremacy which Hudson was hoisting over him."[46] Hudson may have felt that whiteness and servitude in the colonial setting of a slave society presented an untenable contradiction. Certainly this was very evident to Lady Anne, who complained at having to deal with racial tension among her servants, with whites objecting to being made to sleep alongside black slaves.[47] She also recorded the near-impossibility of taking white upper servants into the interior of the colony, considering that they fell between the only two available categories of society there: white masters and black bonded laborers.[48] The Cape experiences of Hudson and the Barnards in the first years of the nineteenth century, while they are isolated incidents and need to be seen in the light of their recent arrival from Britain, do seem suggestive in the light of historians' arguments about how race was conceptualized at the Cape in the early nineteenth century.[49] Both Hudson's move out of domestic service and the trouble the Barnards had with the servants they brought out from Europe hint at a direct articulation of clear racial boundaries by both elite and servile whites long before the aftermath of slave emancipation, a moment that has been identified as solidifying thinking about race.[50]

In 1799 Hudson took the ultimate step across the geographical and social gulf between English servant and colonial master. He bought another human being. Having "Reconciled myself to the Idea of purchasing a slave, a traffic my whole soul condemned," Hudson comforted himself that "when we can rescue a poor wretch from a cruel servitude with a determination to render him those comforts to make slavery bearable it becomes an act of charity and which humanity need not blush at. Such is my intention by this Boy who I hope will feel with gratitude and repay my care with fidelity."[51] When Hudson wrote an unpublished essay on

slavery at the Cape,[52] he showed particular interest in the way slaveholding allowed owners—both black and white—to accumulate increased
wealth.[53] There is no doubt that Hudson embarked on slaveholding as
part of his ambition to rise in the world, or that it was an integral part
of the means by which Thomas and Samuel accumulated their wealth at
the Cape. Yet Hudson's diary entry suggests that he felt that the status
of master involved not only material wealth but also a particular brand
of patronage. As such, the purchase of a slave involved both material and
nonmaterial status advancement, allowing him to make a significant role
reversal. It is in the light of his *own* status transformation that we should
most usefully consider Hudson's insistence on the paternalistic bonds
that linked him to those he referred to as "My family": "I treat them as
my Children and they return it with gratitude and affection."[54]

Intimacy, Status, and the Domestic Sphere: Lady Anne Enters the Kitchen

The paternalistic utterances both Lady Anne and Hudson made about
their slaves were underpinned by an uneasy current of fear regarding
slave violence.[55] On a more mundane level, both diaries were profoundly
aware of being embroiled in daily wars of attrition in the intimacy of the
domestic sphere. The experiences of both the Barnards and of Hudson
(particularly in his boardinghouse existence of the 1820s) show what it
could mean that slaves in the urban circumstances of Cape Town had
access to membership in a broader underclass community that undercut
slaveholder authority.[56] Domestic slaves' incessant petty theft, absence
without leave, and drinking punctuates both accounts. Both diarists assured themselves that theft among slaves was endemic.[57] "There is no
looking for principles, truth Honesty Sobriety or chastity amongst the
slaves," Lady Anne wrote; "if Nature has not been sparing of them of
qualitys, the early terrible practices they see corrupts them thoroughly."[58]
"How I shall enjoy my private station in old England, my quiet joint, my
clean table cloth & honest folks about me when I go back," she claimed,
at the height of one of these domestic disputes.[59]

Lady Anne's relationship with the female slaves within her household was particularly vexed: "the women Slaves in this country are in no
respect so good as the men, they are greater Drunkards, thieves, lyars—
rakes & more indolent except in the performance of these dutys."[60] Their
presence within her home was a palpable and embodied anxiety: "one
of the worst points of slaves particularly of women is the dreadful smell
which they leave behind them—a fox is a rose to it."[61] Lady Anne, with

aristocratic sangfroid, made frequent (if oblique) references to the mistresses men of the British administration took at the Cape, including women of color. She was silent on her own husband's activities, but after his death she had his natural daughter, who had been born at the Cape around 1803, sent to her in England. Lady Anne formed a close relationship with her "Protegée of a darker complexion" and seems to have persuaded herself that the relationship from which the child had been conceived had occurred only when she had left Andrew alone at the Cape.[62] Sexual relationships between European men and slave women are an undercurrent in the text of both writers. That both Lady Anne, and in particular Hudson, distanced themselves from the resulting métis culture emerging at the Cape is testament to the definitions of whiteness and Britishness emerging there.

The white mistress's constant surveillance was required to keep control of the unruly domestic situations of the colonial world.[63] This presented problems for Lady Anne's sense of her own rank. Formerly valued as a society hostess for the "Stores of [her] mind,"[64] she was deeply equivocal about playing the housewife. "*Je me flatte* [I flatter myself] that I am now become a famous good Housekeeper, perhaps you will say 'Ah poor Anne! autrefois [formerly] as pretty, and prettier than *some* of your neighbours, imagined to be clever, with a sort of Ignus fatuus [will-o'-the-wisp] about you, which tho' *unreal* yet misled ones belief, light, gay & sparkling do *you* boast of being a good *Housekeeper!*"[65]

As elsewhere in her journal, Lady Anne slips into a voice that confides in her sisters and friends in Britain, yet in doing so she vividly conveys a fractured self, in which the society hostess peeps out from beneath the housewife's coif. Her italicized speech, her Latin and French turns of phrase, evoke the world of the fashionable salons she left in London. Part of her frustration with domestic duties stemmed from the fact that they were a distraction from her unofficial, yet influential, position within the administration. At the Cape she expanded the role she had played in London of the politically influential aristocratic woman. The British position at the Cape in the 1790s was a politically and militarily sensitive one, with no security of long-term colonial occupation. Lady Anne was busily engaged, under Dundas's direct instructions, in cementing an alliance between the British and the Dutch elites through carefully mediated social interactions and in acting as an unofficial eyes and ears for the secretary of state.[66] This placed her in a difficult position, because she had to play these roles while simultaneously avoiding, as far as possible, accusations of overt political interference.[67] The decades of the late eighteenth and early nineteenth centuries were a period of acute anxiety about the role of elite women in British political life.[68] Sustaining the delicate juggling act required by being a woman both within and outside politics was the best means by which Lady Anne could secure her own and her husband's future. Yet the domestic circumstances of the Cape blurred the edges of this elite persona, just as the incessant fleas risked her body's descent into "Hottentotish" savagery.

Lady Anne's anxiety about her role in the domestic sphere was heightened by incessant arguments with her husband's cousin about elite women's place in the home. This cousin, also confusingly named Anne Barnard, accompanied Lady Anne and her husband to the Cape in 1797. Whether or not this move was made explicitly in search of the economic security of marriage, Anne Barnard met and married Colonel James Crauford in the colony. Presented with a variety of suitors, she chose personal attraction over wealth,[69] and the young couple's limited income could not support their delusions of social grandeur. For Lady Anne, the solution to their inability to pay for good servants was for Anne Crauford to practice economy and learn as much as possible of the domestic skills Lady Anne herself had perforce acquired. Twenty-six years younger than Lady Anne, Anne Barnard had very different ideas. She was impatient of the older woman's instruction, and determined to go her own way.

The arguments over an elite woman's role in the domestic sphere that took place between Lady Anne and her cousin, and between the Craufords themselves (both before and after their marriage) punctuate the diary repeatedly in 1799 and 1800. "I know well," Lady Anne wrote, "that it is not Elegant to go to the Kitchen."[70] Yet it was impossible, particularly at the Cape, to "have dinner well dressd" or "linnen incomparably washd at home" without constant personal surveillance over the domestic realm.[71] Part of the problem, Lady Anne claimed, was Colonel Crauford's own contradictory notions of status, which made him both sneer at housewifely activities and require (in the absence of the servants they could not afford) that his wife involve herself in them.[72] His own ambiguity of social position—being illegitimate and unable to inherit his father's wealth—was clearly a related issue. "[T]heir High & Mighty-nesses," wrote Lady Anne of the Craufords, "suppose they can have more luxurys & conveniencys out of their Income than they really can."[73]

It was precisely in this period that extensive discussions were being conducted in Britain about the relationship between social status and material wealth. Aristocratic women might be prompted to give self-conscious performances of domesticity precisely in order to disassociate themselves from contemporary attacks on dissolute elites.[74] These attacks included the charges of female political interference mentioned earlier. It was in the late eighteenth century that the term "vulgarity" took on the meaning familiar today: "a measure of disparity between social actions and station."[75] There was an explosion of British popular literature in this period on the theme of new wealth, with the dangers of social mobility directly linked to the opportunities of empire. Both West Indian planters and East Indian nabobs featured prominently as stock figures of the *arriviste* type.[76]

Intimacy, Status, and the Political Sphere: Samuel Hudson Attacks Patronage

Some twenty years after Lady Anne Barnard and the Craufords were debating the merits of proper housekeeping, Samuel Hudson's domestic travails, as he endured life as an impecunious boarder, were far more serious. Hudson's writings in 1824 are consumed by the twinned frustrations of domestic and political liberty. Hudson had come "out of livery," and as the extracts from his diary that follow indicate, he yearned to exercise the rights of independent masculinity. In order to take up the proper role of a middle-class man, Hudson needed to be in control of both his domestic life and his political destiny. He needed to hold sway within his own household, rather than being subjected to the vagaries and "impudence" of his fellow boarders,[77] his landlord, and his landlord's slaves. The economic disaster of bankruptcy (exacerbated, he claimed, by government mishandling) made Hudson a dependent in a world in which the political rights of middle-class men were increasingly coming to be conceived as predicated on the dependency of wives, children, and servants.[78] Furthermore, Hudson considered that corrupt patronage rather than the "proper" rights of public men held sway at the Cape. Hudson's marginalization from political power was, therefore, paralleled by his lack of control over intimate domestic life in both concrete and conceptual ways.

These obsessions over personal and political liberty came from a man who had clawed his way out of servitude and into independence only to lose it again. The slaves of the boardinghouse ("compleat nuisances their constant study is mischief")[79] and what Hudson considered the landlord's ill management of them were a continual irritation. Daily domestic humiliations (dining with uncongenial fellow boarders, having his precious supply of gingerbread stolen by the servants or gnawed at by mice, being the butt of scorn of his landlord's children) punctuated his rants on the political situation of the colony. His repeated attempts to calculate whether he could afford to live in his own house rather than in lodging make for poignant reading. The day Hudson discovered a "complete rent in my small cloaths" in the presence of a "young Lady" visiting the house, so that "all that nature had given me was staring the damsel in the face," must have been a low point for the self-consciously dignified sixty-year-old.[80] "I must put up with it for a time," Hudson wrote of his domestic circumstances, "till golden opportunity enables me to act more independently."[81]

Hudson's meditations on independence took place in a year of political upheaval at the Cape. The autocratic administration of Governor Lord Charles Somerset was under attack from two fronts. In the first place, the attempt to establish a free press in Cape Town was indicative of the rising political ambitions of the city's middle classes.[82] In the second place, the 1820s saw a broader shift in imperial governance, with increased metropolitan authority being asserted over local administrations.[83] The presence of a Commission of Enquiry into the conduct of the Cape government fueled an atmosphere of speculation and rumor. Arrests were made, presses were sealed, houses were searched, and the streets were daily papered with squibs and placards. The notorious agent provocateur Oliver the Spy (who had been exposed as a government informer on radical British political mobilization and subsequently shipped off to the Cape) was said to be active on the governor's behalf.[84] "Oliver the Spy seems to have engaged the attention of the Public," Hudson noted, "his name being chalked up at the corners of most of the principle streets in Cape Town."[85] Whatever Oliver's role at the Cape (officially he was employed as a builder by the government) it is likely that Somerset used a system of paid informants. On an annotated list of names of those who signed a petition for a free press, transmitted by Somerset to the secretary of state in London, appears "Hudson, S. E.—A Bankrupt late Van Buuren & Hudson Uitenhage."[86]

The newly established press was shut down for reporting the cases against government corruption orchestrated by lawyer William Edwards. For Hudson, Edwards was a hero of a new model of antiaristocratic politics: "Edwards must triumph in thus humbling the pride and arrogance of these degenerate sprigs of the Patrician Class."[87] Hudson breathlessly followed Edwards's legal challenges to the Somerset regime, and chronicled Edwards's arrest, his dramatic escape, and his recapture in his diary. Hudson's diary does not record the discovery by the authorities that Edwards was in fact one of the more extreme examples of the advantages imperial mobility held out for self-reinvention. After his arrest Edwards was exposed as escaped convict Alexander Lockaye, who had made his way to the Cape from New South Wales. Although Edwards always denied this, an investigation conducted in Sydney was considered to have proven his real identity.[88]

In the pages of his diary, Hudson railed incessantly against the operation of patronage, aristocratic privilege (Somerset was the second son of the fifth duke of Beaufort), and favoritism in the political life of the Cape. He had nothing but contempt for Somerset, "sheltering himself under the Patrician influence of the Beaufort name."[89] He was similarly dismissive of Somerset's favorites, variously describing them as "the dishonorable Court of Gothamites,"[90] the "catterpillars who are gnawing into the bowels of the constitution,"[91] and the "Spanish Inquisition":[92] "how miserable must be the people under a domination so servile so wickedly malignant the very lowest slave is more estimable in the Eye of God and Man than such stumbling block in the way of Morality and goodness."[93]

The language of servitude was contrasted to that of independence, and despite his financial distress, Hudson was determined never to stoop so low as to accept government patronage: "that free Independence which every Englishman considers requisite must be first completely done away ere he would descend to act with them in their ruinous schemes of Tyranny and oppression and this I feel confident I could not do."[94]

Part of Hudson's disaffection toward the government was clearly linked to his reduced circumstances, in part the result of the administrative bungling and delay that followed his filing for bankruptcy in 1823. But the insistence of this former servant (and former slaveholder) on the importance of personal and political "independence"—a word he used repeatedly in relation to both his personal circumstances and his political convictions—went beyond this. It was part of a more general attack on aristocratic privilege whereby middle-class men across the British imperial world were asserting the values of the public sphere and claiming political rights on the basis of a distinctly antipatrician model of masculine identity—one with important links to the domestic realm. These claims were not only gendered but also racialized. Domestic service was incompatible with this model of masculine citizenship, and as such, servants were excluded from extensions of the franchise in British parliamentary reforms until the twentieth century. Hudson had used the enslavement of others to leave personal service and to raise himself to the ranks of the middle-class, independent man in the colonies. With the demise of bonded labor, freed slaves at the Cape would make similarly interlocking claims of personal independence and political citizenship in a postemancipation world.[95] They would have less lasting success than would most of Hudson's compatriots, another indication of how his story feeds into the solidification of barriers of race in the nineteenth century.[96]

Changing Status, Changing World

Whether Somerset was really assisted by "his Jackall Oliver"[97] in resisting the demands for changes in the Cape political system remains unknown. Yet the presence of the former spy at the Cape, a man notorious for his role in exposing British radicals, is illustrative of the connections that existed in Hudson's mind in the wider battle for liberty that was being fought out in both Britain and the colonies. Hudson was drawing on a popular and nationally inflected idea of particular rights and privileges that, as Dana Rabin argues (chapter 12 here), belied the internal diversity and inequalities existing within Britain itself. Hudson's claims for "independence" should be seen within the wider changes in political culture taking place as the eighteenth century gave way to the nineteenth, including the rise of a bourgeois public sphere and demands for an extension of the franchise. What was under attack in disgust at so-called Old Corruption was the idea of public office as private property, an idea that was central to the untrammeled operation of patronage and to governance by personal network.[98] After 1815, Zoë Laidlaw argues, an increasing climate of hostility toward corruption and the need to reduce expenditure stimulated metropolitan interference in the absolute power of colonial governors in the 1820s.[99] In the following decade, personal networks, and the more overt styles of patronage associated with them, declined. In 1835, all private correspondence from governors to officials in Britain, with the exception of that directed to the secretary of state, was banned. A more depersonalized and bureaucratized method of governance gained ground, one that "embraced statistical over narrative information."[100] The reorganization of imperial governance, then, undercut the intimate relationships encompassed in patronage and devalued exactly the kind of information exchanges that took place between Lady Anne Barnard and the secretary of state in the 1790s. It mirrored the attack on aristocratic political influence (which could be exerted by elite women) by the manly independence of the (white) bourgeois voter. And it underlined what would become a "cherished assumption": that "the intimate is located primarily in the family."[101]

This essay speaks to the question of how social status and the domestic labor that sustained that status were connected for Europeans at a time when models of political influence and political culture were changing across the British imperial world. When Hudson arrived at the

Cape with the Barnards, patronage was still pervasive within contemporary political culture. Empire was a crucial source of such patronage, but
being a second-tier option for those seeking personal preferment, it was
also an especially fruitful manifestation of contemporary status anxieties.
Patron and client might not be directly known to one another, but they
were still bound together in a web of personal reciprocity that pervaded
government, the church, the armed forces, and public office great and
small.[102] This was a model of politics that created an intimacy between
client and patron, an intimacy that would increasingly come under attack as the eighteenth century came to an end. Hudson might not have
lived to see the enfranchisement of middle-class men in Britain (1832) or
the Cape (1854), but his assertion of a particular model of social status,
and of the kind of political rights associated with it, would prevail over
the values of his erstwhile masters, the Barnards. In the intertwined
lives of Hudson and Lady Anne Barnard we can see the nexus between
the personal and the political in the transformations of social status and
political culture as the eighteenth century gave way to the nineteenth.

Notes

I am grateful to Robert Shell and to Edward and Raymond Hudson for their generosity in sharing with me their work (both published and unpublished) on Samuel
Hudson and to Tony Ballantyne, Antoinette Burton, Alan Lester, Penny Russell,
and Pamela Scully for their comments on earlier drafts.

1. Lady Anne Barnard, Diary, 25 March 1799, in Margaret Lenta and Basil le
Cordeur, eds., *The Cape Diaries of Lady Anne Barnard, 1799–1800*, 2 vols. (Cape
Town, 1998–99), 1:84

2. Ibid., 6 February 1799, 1:37.

3. While a feminist reader (and certainly this feminist writer) might feel more
comfortable with the name Barnard, my use of her title is intended to prevent
confusion between Lady Anne Barnard, her husband, Andrew Barnard, and Andrew Barnard's cousin Anne Barnard (later Crauford).

4. Lady Anne to Henry Dundas, 14 December 1799, in A. M. Lewin Robinson,
ed., *The Letters of Lady Anne Barnard to Henry Dundas from the Cape and
Elsewhere, 1793–1803, Together with Her Journal of a Tour into the Interior and
Certain Other Letters* (Cape Town, 1973).

5. Lady Anne's Diary, which survives for 1799–1800, is far more confessional
and unguarded than her 1797–98 Journal, which she revised and edited from the
original diary for a selected private readership. The original diary (1797–98) was
then destroyed.

6. Diary of Samuel Hudson, 15 October 1824, 19 December 1824, Hudson Papers, vol. 3, A602, National Archives, Cape Town, South Africa (CA). Neither
Lady Anne's nor Hudson's writings were published in their lifetimes. We have
almost no information on the purpose of most of Hudson's writing. While some

of his observations (known to historians as his essays) have been edited by Robert Shell, Hudson's diaries remain unpublished. I quote from his manuscript diaries in the National Library of South Africa, Cape Town (SAL) and the National Archives, Cape Town, South Africa (CA).

7. Tony Ballantyne and Antoinette Burton, "Postscript: Bodies, Gender, Empires: Reimagining World Histories," in Ballantyne and Burton, eds., *Bodies in Contact: Rethinking Colonial Encounters in World History* (Durham, N.C.), 415.

8. Ann Laura Stoler, "Tense and Tender Ties: The Politics of Comparison in North American History and (Post) Colonial Studies," *Journal of American History* 88, 3 (2001): 829.

9. Ann Laura Stoler, *Carnal Knowledge and Imperial Power: Race and the Intimate in Colonial Rule* (Berkeley, 2002), 9.

10. Mary A. Renda, "'Sentiments of a Private Nature': A Comment on Ann Laura Stoler's "Tense and Tender Ties," *Journal of American History* 88, 3 (2001): 884. Stoler's response in the same issue also asserts that "sex is not what intimacy is fundamentally about" and that what is at issue is rather "the making of the private and the managing of the intimate in the making of imperial rule." "Matters of Intimacy as Matters of State: A Response," 895. Nevertheless, there is a tendency to focus on sexual themes in "intimacy studies."

11. Stoler, "Tense and Tender Ties," 831.

12. Zoë Laidlaw, *Colonial Connections, 1815–45: Patronage, the Information Revolution and Colonial Government* (Manchester, England, 2005).

13. Ann Laura Stoler, "Intimidations of Empire: Predicaments of the Tactile and Unseen," in Stoler, ed., *Haunted by Empire: Geographies of Intimacy in North American History* (Durham, N.C., 2006).

14. Stoler, "Tense and Tender Ties," 831.

15. Stoler, "Matters of Intimacy as Matters of State," 895.

16. On the *instability* of whiteness in the colonial and metropolitan realm see Catherine Hall, "Of Gender and Empire: Reflections on the Nineteenth Century," in Philippa Levine, ed., *Gender and Empire*, Oxford History of the British Empire Companion Series (Oxford, 2004), 49–50.

17. Antoinette Burton, "Who Needs the Nation? Interrogating 'British' History," in Catherine Hall, ed., *Cultures of Empire: Colonizers in Britain and the Empire in the Nineteenth and Twentieth Centuries* (Manchester, England, 2000); Catherine Hall, "The Nation Within and Without," in Catherine Hall, Keith McClelland, and Jane Rendell, *Defining the Victorian Nation: Class, Race, Gender and the British Reform Act of 1867* (Cambridge, 2000); Catherine Hall, *Civilising Subjects: Metropole and Colony in the English Imagination, 1830–1867* (Chicago, 2002); Kathleen Wilson, *The Island Race: Englishness, Empire and Gender in the Eighteenth Century* (London, 2003).

18. Doreen Massey, *For Space* (London, 2005), 10.

19. On the first British occupation at the Cape, see H. B. Giliomee, *Die Kaap tydens die eerste Britse Bewind, 1795–1903* (Cape Town, 1975), and M. Boucher and N. Penn, *Britain at the Cape, 1795 to 1803* (Johannesburg, 1992).

20. On Lady Anne Barnard, see *The Dictionary of National Biography*; the introductions to the editions of her writings quoted here; and A. W. C. Lindsay, Earl of Crawford, *The Lives of the Lindsays* (London, 1849). Lady Anne's elite status (and popularity among antiquarian writers) has until recently denied her the se-

rious scholarly attention her writings deserve. See Margaret Lenta, "Degrees of Freedom: Lady Anne Barnard's Cape Diaries," *English in Africa* 19 (1992): 55–68, and Dorothy Driver, "Lady Anne Barnard's 'Cape Journals' and the Concept of Self-Othering," *Pretexts* 5 (1995): 46–65.

21. Lady Anne to Henry Dundas, July 12, 1794, in *Letters*, 15. Original emphasis.

22. Ibid.

23. Lady Anne, Journal, January 1797, in A. M. Lewin Robinson, Margaret Lenta, and Dorothy Driver, eds., *The Cape Journals of Lady Anne Barnard 1797–1798* (Cape Town, 1994), 23.

24. See Edward Hudson and Raymond Hudson, "The English Background of Samuel Eusebius Hudson: The Central Enigma in His Life and the Key to His Mentality," *South African Historical Journal* 52 (2005): 32–59, on Hudson in England, and Kirsten McKenzie, *The Making of an English Slave-Owner: Samuel Eusebius Hudson at the Cape of Good Hope, 1796–1807* (Cape Town, 1993), on Hudson at the Cape.

25. Hudson and Hudson, "English Background," 38.

26. Lady Anne, Journal, January 1797, 27.

27. Lady Anne, Diary, 2:256, September–December 1800. Andrew Barnard to Hardwick, Add MSS 35644, fols. 48–51v, British Library, quoted in Hudson and Hudson, "English Background," 44–45.

28. As the Hudsons admit, their theory that a sexual relationship between Hudson and Lady Hardwicke led to the removal of the footman to the Cape, while intriguing, remains inconclusive.

29. Memorandums made in the course of the voyage to the Cape of Good Hope in the *Sir Edward Hughes,* April 10, 1796, MSB 253, SAL.

30. Lady Anne, Journal, January 1797, 2–28.

31. Ibid., undated, 229.

32. McKenzie, *Making of an English Slaveholder,* 20–21.

33. Lady Anne, Journal, undated, 229.

34. Diary of Samuel Hudson, 12 August 1814, CA.

35. Master of the Supreme Court, Cape Town, Insolvency Branch, Records of Insolvent Estates (MOIB), vol 2/248, no. 1068, CA.

36. Colonial Office, Memorials Received (CO) vol. 3928, no. 224, 1825; vol. 3929, no. 515, 1825, CA.

37. Diary of Samuel Hudson, 19 May 1824, CA.

38. Lady Anne, Diary, 22 August 1800, 2:113.

39. Lady Anne, Journal, undated, 272–73.

40. Ibid., undated, 239; Diary, undated, 1800, 2:228.

41. Lady Anne, Journal, 3 March 1797, 78 (on the pay of bishops); Lady Anne, Diary, 18 June 1799, 1:162 (on the silver).

42. Hudson, Diary, 20 December 1798. Diary of Samuel Eusebius Hudson, chief clerk in Customs, Cape Town, November 1798–April 1800, MSB 252, SAL.

43. Lady Anne to Henry Dundas, 14 December 1799, in *Letters,* 215.

44. Lady Anne, Diary, undated, 1800, 2:256.

45. Ibid., 10 March 1800, 2:71.

46. Lady Anne, Journal, undated, 191.

47. Lady Anne, Diary, 30 May 1799, 1:148.

48. Lady Anne, Journal, undated, 297.

49. Andrew Bank, "Losing Faith in the Civilizing Mission: The Premature Decline of Humanitarian Liberalism at the Cape, 1840–60," in M. Daunton and R. Halpern, eds., *Empire and Others: British Encounters with Indigenous Peoples, 1600–1850* (London, 1999).

50. I am grateful to Alan Lester for his comments in pointing out this possibility. See Alan Lester, *Imperial Networks: Creating Identities in Nineteenth-Century South Africa and Britain* (London, 2001).

51. Hudson, Diary, 1 February 1799, SAL.

52. Like Hudson's other essays, this is undated, but was largely written in Hudson's first visit to the Cape, between 1797 and 1806.

53. Robert Shell, "Introduction to S. E. Hudson's 'Slaves,'" *Kronos* 9 (1984): 44–70, 67.

54. Ibid., 47. On the power structures connecting the family, slaves, slaveholders, and the state, see Pamela Scully, *Liberating the Family? Gender and British Slave Emancipation in the Rural Western Cape, South Africa, 1823–1853* (Oxford, 1997). A detailed discussion of the historiography on paternalism at the Cape is impossible within the constraints of this chapter. See also Andre du Toit and Hermann Giliomee, eds., *Afrikaaner Political Thought: Analysis and Documents*, vol. 1, *1780–1850* (Cape Town, 1983); J. E. Mason, "Paternalism under Siege: Slavery in Theory and Practice during the Era of Reform, c. 1825 through Emancipation," in Clifton Crais and Nigel Worden, eds., *Breaking the Chains* (Johannesburg, 1994), 45–77; Robert Ross, "Paternalism, Patriarchy and Afrikaans," *South African Historical Journal* 32, 1 (1995): 34–47; and Robert Shell, *Children of Bondage: A Social History of the Slave Society at the Cape of Good Hope, 1652–1838* (Hanover, N.H., and London, 1994).

55. Shell, "Introduction to Hudson's 'Slaves,'" 65; Lady Anne, Diary, 20–23 April 1799, 1:107.

56. Andrew Bank, *The Decline of Urban Slavery at the Cape, 1806 to 1843* (Cape Town, 1991); Patricia van der Spuy, "Slave Women in the Family in Nineteenth-Century Cape Town," *South African Historical Journal* 27 (1992): 50–74.

57. Lady Anne, Diary, 25 March 1799, 1:86, and 6 April 1799, 1:97. Hudson, Diary, 20 August 1824, CA.

58. Lady Anne, Diary, 16 April 1799, 1:105.

59. Ibid., 5 August 1799, 1:220.

60. Ibid., 25 March 1799, 1:86.

61. Ibid., 25 March 1799, 1:86.

62. Ibid., undated, 2:293.

63. On the role of white women in policing the boundaries of colonial domesticity and keeping the white body "civilized," see Ann Laura Stoler, *Race and the Education of Desires: Foucault's "History of Sexuality" and the Colonial Order of Things* (Durham N.C., 1995), esp. chaps. 4 and 5, and *Carnal Knowledge and Imperial Power*, esp. chap. 3. Area studies include Claudia Knapman on Fiji, *White Women in Fiji, 1835–1930: The Ruin of Empire?* (Sydney, 1986), and (particularly pertinent to the Cape situation) Jean Gelman Taylor on Batavia, *The Social World of Batavia* (London, 1983).

64. Lady Anne, Journal, undated, 185–86.

65. Ibid.

66. Andrew Barnard to Henry Dundas, 23 August 1797, in *Letters*, 65.

67. Lady Anne, Diary, 3 May 1799, 1:126.

68. Anna Clark, *Scandal: The Sexual Politics of the British Constitution* (Princeton, 2004); Cindy McCreery, *The Satirical Gaze: Prints of Women in Late Eighteenth-Century England* (Oxford, 2004).

69. Lady Anne, Diary, 7 March 1799, 1:65.

70. Ibid., 7 March 1799, 1:64.

71. Ibid., 8 March 1799, 1:67.

72. Ibid., 23 March 1799, 2:83.

73. Ibid., April 1800, 2:91.

74. Ruth M. Larsen, "Dynastic Domesticity: The Role of Elite Women in the Yorkshire Country House, 1685–1858" (Ph.D. diss., University of York, 2003).

75. James Raven, *Judging New Wealth: Popular Publishing and Responses to Commerce in England, 1750–1800* (Oxford, 1992), 138.

76. Ibid., 231.

77. Hudson, Diary, 8 December 1824, CA.

78. Leonore Davidoff and Catherine Hall, *Family Fortunes: Men and Women of the English Middle Class, 1780–1850* (London, 1987); Catherine Hall, *White, Male and Middle Class: Explorations in Feminism and History* (New York, 1992).

79. Hudson, Diary, 12 November 1824, CA.

80. Ibid., 23 September 1824.

81. Ibid., 12 June 1824.

82. Kirsten McKenzie, "'Franklins of the Cape': The *South African Commercial Advertiser* and the Creation of a Colonial Public Sphere, 1824–1854," *Kronos* 25 (1998–99): 88–102.

83. Laidlaw, *Colonial Connections*, 47.

84. See H. C. Botha, *John Fairbairn in South Africa* (Cape Town, 1984); A. K. Millar, *Plantagenet in South Africa: Lord Charles Somerset* (London, 1965); J. Thomas Meiring, *Pringle: His life and Times* (Cape Town, 1968); T. Keegan, *Colonial South Africa and the Origins of the Racial Order* (Cape Town, 1996); and McKenzie, "Franklins at the Cape."

85. Hudson, Diary, 3 April 1824, CA.

86. Government House (GH), Enclosures to Dispatches, vol. 28/10, no. 103, Somerset to Bathurst, 3 July 1824, CA.

87. Hudson, Diary, 5 April 1824, CA.

88. GH, Papers Received from Secretary of State, London, General Dispatches, vol. 1/57, no. 823, CA.

89. Hudson, Diary, 20 November 1824, CA.

90. Ibid., 4 May 1824.

91. Ibid., 24 May 1824.

92. Ibid., 1 May 1824.

93. Ibid., 13 March 1824.

94. Ibid., 6 May 1824.

95. Pamela Scully, "Masculinity, Citizenship, and the Production of Knowledge in the Post-emancipation Cape Colony, 1834–1844," in Diana Paton and Pamela Scully, eds., *Gender and Slave Emancipation in the Atlantic World* (Durham, N.C., 2005); Robert Ross, *Status and Respectability in the Cape Colony, 1750–1870* (Cambridge, 1999).

96. On the shifting definitions of race, and what Robert Ross calls the associated "tragedy of manners" fought out in the Cape context in the wake of the nonracial masculine franchise of 1854, see Ross, *Status and Respectability.*

97. Hudson, Diary, 11 December 1824, CA.

98. Philip Harling, *The Waning of "Old Corruption": The Politics of Economical Reform in Britain, 1779–1846* (Oxford, 1996), 3–4.

99. Laidlaw, *Colonial Connections,* 51–52.

100. Ibid., 161.

101. Stoler, "Intimidations of Empire," 16.

102. Bourne, *Patronage and Society,* 16.

14 *Islands of Intimacy*

COMMUNITY, KINSHIP, AND DOMESTICITY, SALT SPRING ISLAND, 1866

Nestled between Vancouver Island and the Pacific coast of North America, Salt Spring Island was one particular venue in the complicated and necessarily overlapping set of human movements and displacements that defined the nineteenth century. Local indigenous peoples were on the move in response to a variable resource economy, a wide-ranging trading network, and shifting political and military relationships. Indigenous peoples also moved in response to the changes that accompanied the region's gradual incorporation into what an earlier generation of scholars might have called the world economy: resettlement, epidemic disease, wage labor, missionization, and the expansion and redirection of trade. New layers of human movement came to Salt Spring Island in the 1850s and 1860s. The island became a different kind of home to the British settlers who were officially sought by the colonial government, African Americans who were moving north in hopes that "British justice" would be an improvement on Californian, Hawaiians who were putting down roots after wage work in the Pacific maritime economy, and a residuum of the polyglot, mobile, and overwhelmingly male population who were drawn by the usually hollow promises of successive gold rushes.

On Salt Spring Island these peoples met in the manner of political abstractions, the particulars of which are well recounted in local scholarship: the Hudson's Bay Company's charter to Vancouver Island granted in 1849, the colony of British Columbia established in 1858, the Pig War and the fixing of the border dividing American from British territory in 1859. As a new generation of historians are arguing, these shifting and at times volatile relationships were also lived and in no small part constituted at the level of the intimate, the proximate, and the bodily. This historiographical move is perhaps less startling in northern North America than elsewhere. Since the 1980 publication of Sylvia Van Kirk's and Jennifer Brown's respective monographs on relationships and families created by European men and Aboriginal women in the western Canada fur trade, the intimacies of empire have held a comparatively secure spot in regional historiography.[1] High school students and visitors to Canada's officially sanctioned and explained historic sites routinely learn of how *marriage a la façon du pays* bound newcomers to natives and provided the bedrock for the emergence of a métis nation.[2] It has been in the last five years that the category of intimacy has grown more global and sustained scholarly legs. Ann Laura Stoler's work has been crucial here, though like so many germinal heuristic devices, the rubric of intimacy appears to have multiple points of emergence.[3]

This essay explores intimacy, movement, and empire on Salt Spring Island in the shifting ground of the mid–nineteenth century. It does so via an examination of a complicated set of relationships revealed around the alleged poisoning of an Irish settler, James M.[4] The trial that prosecuted his adolescent daughter and her cousin for this crime provides historians with a revealing window into a dense and highly charged web of intimate relationships that spanned indigenous and settler worlds. In step with the rest of this collection, I treat these relationships as constituent of rather than exterior to the politics of colonialism and, in the case of Salt Spring Island, setter colonialism. As a feminist scholar, I am committed to exploring how intimate relations are a critical terrain of gendered power relations in general and patriarchy in particular. Queer scholarship pushes both of these imperatives in slightly different and, to my mind, welcome directions. Queer history demands not a recuperation of the homosexual past, but a radical decentering of heterosexuality, domesticity, and monogamy from our historical vision.[5] Reading this case through the cumulative insights of these literatures makes clear that heterosexual coupling was simply one among a range of colonial intimacies that included affect, acrimony, dependence, and mutuality between parents, children, neighbors, friends, workers, bosses, and coworkers.

In the 1860s, Salt Spring Island was both remarkably cosmopolitan and profoundly local. The island is the largest of the Gulf Islands chain located off North America's Pacific coast, in the midst of Cowichan and Stó:lō territory. This region was densely inhabited by the standards of northern North America.[6] Cowichan and Stó:lō peoples were both fishing peoples whose political life was structured around kinship and household and ordered by social hierarchies.[7] Colonialism, both informal and formal, arrived in these territories relatively late in global terms. It came first indirectly, as part of the wider Pacific exploration and trade in the eighteenth century.[8] James Cook's visit to nearby Vancouver Island in 1778 introduced the region to European reading publics, and the Canton-based trade in sea otter pelts inserted it into the eighteenth century's emergent world market. Over 170 separate ships from Russia, the United States, Spain, France, and Britain traded in the wider region in the years between 1785 and 1825.[9]

The question of what colonial power would control this trade was at the heart of the international struggle over the territory. The Nootka Convention of 1794, as Dan Clayton explains, did not assert formal colonial control as much as it reorganized practices of exploration and commercial contact into European legal and geopolitical codes.[10] Britain's interests in the region were shored up by the arrival of land-based fur trade early in the next century, effectively knitting the territory around Salt Spring Island into a wider web of British-controlled North America. The Oregon Treaty of 1846 severed the Pacific fur trade region into national spheres of influence,[11] and Britain formalized theirs with the creation of the British colony of Vancouver Island in 1849, and the mainland colony of British Columbia in 1858. Despite an increasingly baroque colonial state and the promises of a string of gold rushes, the number of settlers of both colonies probably never broke the ten thousand mark and certainly never neared the number of the indigenous population.[12]

Like the colony it was a part of, Salt Spring Island's path into European geopolitics, imagining, and settlement was a late and wandering one. It was not until the 1820s that the Gulf Islands were acknowledged in a European explorer's map.[13] Archaeological evidence reveals that generations of indigenous peoples had used Salt Spring Island before the middle of the nineteenth century.[14] As in so many other parts of North America, Aboriginal depopulation wrought by warfare and more particularly epidemic disease preceded or coincided with the onset of sustained European colonization.[15] Thus when settlers began to take up land on Salt Spring in the late 1850s, they found it conveniently "empty." Chris Arnett's stinging local history argues that the claim that Salt Spring Island was only occasionally used by local peoples reflects settler's instrumental belief that "hunter-gatherer societies represented an idle, wandering way of live when in fact the exploration of seasonal resources owned by specific families were essential parts of the hwulmuhw indigenous economy."[16]

James M., sometimes called Jemmy, was one of the individuals whose prosaic decisions to cross oceans and form relationships and families cumulatively transformed so much of the nineteenth-century world in general and places like Salt Spring Island in particular. By the standards of a settler world, where the slimmest of newcomer claims could be constituted as evidence of longstanding claims to the local, James M. had lived on the island for a long time by 1866.[17] Like many of the region's first settlers, he began his local career with the fur trade, working as a laborer at the Hudson's Bay Company's Fort Langley from 1852 to 1853.[18] A rough census of indigenous people taken in 1860 listed James M. as one of a handful of "white residents met with" on Salt Spring Island.[19] A year later he preempted land alongside a handful of other former Hudson's Bay Company employees.[20] The census taker did not mention that James came from Ireland or that he had an indigenous family. But late in 1866 he was described as a widower with "three boys and two girls," the eldest of them thirteen-year-old Mary Ann.[21] Elsewhere the children's mother was identified as a "a full-blooded Fraser River Indian woman," whom he presumably met while working at Fort Langley, the place Mary Ann was born in 1853.[22] Two of James's sons, John and William, were both baptized in a Victoria Roman Catholic church in 1865, and may have had a different mother.[23]

In October 1866 a complicated string of events catapulted this family and their neighbors into the courts and the newspapers, two institutions that were critical to the colony's public sphere and, in turn, historians' usual source base. Like so many of the experiences that placed nineteenth-century plebeian people into the archives of the colonial state, these were likely distressing ones for the people involved. On October 12, James was working digging potatoes and minding cattle for his neighbors, Sarah and Richard B. After drinking coffee prepared by his daughter, James "was seized with awful pain in the stomach and fell on my knees and began to vomit." A week later, Henry S., James's neighbor and the island's police constable, convinced James that he had been poisoned by his daughter working in collusion with Henry's wife. Henry's wife was also named Mary Ann, and she was the cousin of James's daughter, presumably on the maternal side. Mary Ann S. was only fifteen or sixteen but had adult status by virtue of her marriage to the English-born, middle-aged constable.

Henry threatened to bring his concerns to the law unless James did so himself. In response James began the complicated procedure of engaging the legal mechanisms of a state that was, by any reckoning, thin on the ground. After waiting for a magistrate who failed to show up, James traveled by boat to the town of Nanaimo, where the Crown charged Mary Ann M. with being a principal and Mary Ann S. with being an accessory to "poisoning with an intent to murder."[24] That this case ever went to trial tells us something about local enthusiasm for the colonial state's legal mechanisms. People in mid-nineteenth-century British Columbia used the highly theatrical and public medium of the trial to reckon with conflicting meanings and practices of gender, race, respectability, and identity just as they did in Red River colony.[25] And lucky for historians. As Ruth Sandwell has argued, the documents created by this particular case provide us with a revealing window into Salt Spring Island in the middle of the nineteenth century and, I think, to the work of intimacy in it.

Within the wider local context of nineteenth-century British Columbia, these families were not unusual in spanning indigenous and settler communities. Intimate ties of marriage, partnership, and parenthood across racial lines both symbolized and helped to constitute the fact that Britain's claim to this chunk of northern North America never easily translated to some simple model of colonial control. The pervasive character of heterosexual partnership and domesticity stood as a sharp reminder of the extent to which the rigid racial separation on which nineteenth-century colonialism was premised were complicated and challenged in lived colonial space. An English observer who arrived in Victoria in 1850 wrote that there was "No town or any approach to civilization" beyond the Hudson's Bay Company's fort. Around it, he explained, were a "few log shanties occupied by half breeds Iroquois, French Canadians and Kanakas who risked their lives outside relying upon the woman influence most of them living with Native women." The fur trade officers he found "in as crude a state, and were only one degree removed, they had a white skin."[26]

The first settlers to take up land on Salt Spring in the 1850s were Canadian and British men with female indigenous partners, often veterans of the fur trade. As David Haines's study of the shore whaling industry in New Zealand (chapter 2 here) makes clear, particular configurations of capitalism produced particular configurations of mixed-race intimacy. Canadian historians have long acknowledged the economic and political work of intermarriage in the fur trade, but scholars are less sure about how to characterize the relationship between settlement and intermarriage. Within the local context of Salt Spring Island, Arnett argues that settler men gained access to indigenous lands by marrying women with hereditary rights to the land and its resources. Sandwell sees the transfer in nearly opposite terms, arguing that it was through intermarriage that First Nations people reasserted their claims to the island.[27]

That mixed-race intimacies were imbricated in the process of Salt Spring Island's settlement was clear. Few of the European observers who committed their opinions to print saw this in a positive light. Ebenezer Robson, a visiting Methodist missionary, called relationships between settler men and indigenous women "adultery" and named them one of the "great sins of this place." Of the nine settler men resident in the island's North Settlement, five lived "with Indian women in a state of adultery" and, to make matters worse, "Some have families from such connexion." One of them had "commenced this degrading course since I was here last. He is a young man who was Educated, in Wesley College England, for the bar & passed his examination for this profession. His father is an old & wealthy methodist. His son, poor now, is far gone in the way to hell."[28] When the Anglican bishop visited the island, he made a similar note and preached a special sermon on "the prodigal son" in response.[29] Colonial intimacies persisted in spite of these views. The census of 1881 and 1891 found that more than half of heterosexual partnerships on Salt Spring Island were between Aboriginal women and non-Aboriginal men.[30]

These households and families could and did cut across a number of lines. The mobilities of empire created a community that was not simply either Aboriginal or settler but hybridized, North American, and Pacific.[31] Between 1859 and 1869 some twenty African American families would settle on Salt Spring.[32] In the 1870s, Hawaiians prevented from taking up land in U.S. territory arrived, showing up as "Kanakas" in the records and forming families with local indigenous peoples.[33] Inasmuch as islands have borders, the nearest border was with the U.S. Washington Territory. Networks of shipping, trade, and mobility linked the island to a wider maritime world that included San Francisco, Victoria, and Hawai'i, and from there Canton. Sandwell, the island's most prolific and astute historian, has noted that in the maritime world of the nineteenth century, living on an island did not connote isolation but rather proximity and connection.[34] Salt Spring Island was a northern branch of what we might call the brown Pacific, one forged not by the proclamations of governments but by the informal intimacies of empire, the pulls of wage labor, and the possibilities of resettlement. It was highly localized but not sui generis. Jean Barman's work on the families of Whoi Whoi, Kanaka Ranch, and Brockton Point offers us another example of an indigenized, plural, markedly Pacific colonial community knitted together by kin ties, especially female ones. Patterns of settlement make clear that these communities could and did overlap, but could also function as contained if not wholly separate nodes.[35]

The indigenous female kin ties that so often knitted together communities like this were severed or at least bent in this particular family. James M. seems to have had children with two women, but he was described as a widower in the local press, and as single by the census of 1881.[36] The mothers of his children are unnamed in the documentary archive, just like the women in the Indian archives studied by Dhurba Ghosh.[37] James explained in court that he had been an intermittent presence in his daughter Mary Ann's early life. She was "brought up on Fraser River," and he "did not superintend the bringing up" because he "had no time" and had been "absent from her a long time, close on five years."[38]

The colonial newspapers that covered the trial read James and his family through the racial imaginary of the "half-breed." British Columbia produced enumerable people of both indigenous and settler origin but without the durable political identity of Métis that emerged east of the Rocky Mountains and is discussed by Michael A. McDonnell (chapter 7 here). During the years around this trial, global ideas of mixed-race people as a distinct, damaged, and dangerous people came to take an ominous local shape. One pundit mused about the fate awaiting those he called "the unhappy offspring" of indigenous women and European men. They were, he argued, "Born, as it is generally the case in mixed races, with the worst qualities of both predominant, and unredeemed by the virtues of either, totally uneducated, deprived of what little guidance the presence of a father might have been, without religion, without morality."[39] Sitting in the prisoner's dock, Mary Ann M. fit all too easily into these explicitly racist and implicitly misogynist fantasies. "She is a bright-eyed girl and rather prepossessing in appearance," a local journalist opined, "but seems to have sadly lacked the careful moral training of a good mother."[40] Here Mary Ann M. emerges as a female version of the colonial fantasy of the vengeful mixed-blood child.[41]

Ideas of racialized respectability also colored the settler society's view of James M. By the 1860s, settler-Aboriginal heterosexual partnerships had come to function as a symbol of British Columbia's apparent backwardness. Popular settler discourse held that mixed-race relationships deracinated white men, stripping them of the very civilization they hoped they embodied but desperately feared they did not.[42] The term "squaw-man," which circulated throughout the late nineteenth and early twentieth centuries, was entrenched in the local lexicon by 1861.[43] As in the Australian context, mixed-race intimacies signaled both the supposed depredations of indigenous womanhood and the dubious morality of settler men, especially working-class ones.[44] Thus when a young improving Scotsman and scientist accessed the perceived failure of Salt

Spring's settlers, he chalked it up to the fact that their "only ambition (it is no use mincing matters by refined Language) seems to be 'a log shanty, a pig, a potato patch, Klootchman (Indian woman) and a clam bed!'"[45] It was men like James M. he was describing. James had left wage labor in the fur trade to become what the local newspaper called a "farmer in a small way."[46] To what extent James continued to rely on wage labor is made clear by a homestead application he made a few years later. He wrote: "I have got no money at present" and promised to pay for his application "as soon as my Job of work is done."[47]

When the case was tried in March 1867 in the colonial capital of Victoria, James M. became a spectacle of poor, backwoods manhood, unable to control his mixed-race children or maintain their loyalty. That on the day in question he had breakfasted on country foods—the "heart and liver of a deer, and a piece of rabbit pie . . . a basin of wine . . . potatoes and badly baked bread"[48]—was taken as an especially telling sign of his class status and associated racial liminality. When a physician testified that James M.'s illness had not been caused by poison but by "the breakfast partaken of; the unbaked bread and the berry wine," the audience at court found a white, rural man harmed by local foods and his mixed-blood daughter's poor cooking hilarious. They laughed openly.[49] Nobody noted that a father raising five children under the age of thirteen seemingly alone disrupted well-cherished notions of the irresponsibility of settler fathers for the children they shared with local women. Scripts of gendered and racial respectability could be and were unsettled by the messy presence of colonial lives, but they were hard and sometimes impossible to dislodge.

The intimacies revealed by the poisoning case stretch well beyond a narrow conception of kinship and alert us to the dense web of community within which James and his children lived and worked. James had his own farm, but did paid work "by the month" for the family of Richard and Sarah B. On the day in question he had his first breakfast at Mary Ann S.'s father's house, and his second at Richard and Sarah's.[50] Material resources were shared alongside food and labor. Strychnine, used for killing nuisance birds, was co-owned by the B. family and another settler family. On the day in question Lucy, an "Indian woman," had come by that house to borrow flour.[51] There is evidence here of webs of female exchange and reciprocity that crisscrossed households, not to mention what goods were scarce and valued in an environment rich in natural resources but poor in manufactured goods. James M. would be remembered by a settler who grew up on nearby Galliano Island as a kindly and experienced neighbor who shared milk with her family when they needed it.[52]

The supposed boundaries of private and public had little meaning here. Children did not necessarily live with their parents. At the time of the alleged poisoning James had, in his words, "surrendered" Mary Ann to his neighbor and sometime employer Sarah B. She was in her early twenties and one of the few settler women on the Island.[53] Mary Ann S. also lived with them and not, presumably, with her husband. Whether the young women functioned as servants, family members, or something in between is unclear, though they did do the B. family's laundry. The biological family was not the only way of reckoning who should live with whom or should wash whose clothes. Sandwell's reading of census materials from later in the century found that a significant number—over 30 percent in 1891—of households sheltered people with no obvious kin relationship.[54] Many people visited Richard and Sarah's house on that day in October 1866. The presence of Lucy, who as Mary Ann S. explained, "lived with my husband before I was married to him," made clear that layers of heterosexual partnerships could and did live alongside each other in a world where lifelong monogamy was not the only possible option for domestic and sexual life. Henry S. would return to Lucy after this case, and by the time the census taker came knocking in 1881, they shared a large family.[55] We catch other layers of intimacy and friction in the written archive, including the possibility of a grudge between James M. and Mary Ann S. and Lucy's possible malevolence toward the young Mary Ann, who had replaced her in Henry's family.[56] The lives of these two families would be intertwined for generations.

Men and women and children and adults did not inhabit separate worlds, but they did inhabit unequal ones. Mary Ann M. made breakfast *for* her father, whether as his daughter or the B. family servant. Her material dependence on him was unavoidable. When James accused Mary Ann M. of having tried to poison him, he not only spoke to her about the seriousness of her actions and threatened to whip her but invoked the alarming prospect of "what would become of her if I had gone."[57] These records evoke a social world where women and children were overwhelmingly Aboriginal and the adult men overwhelmingly settlers. James M.'s command of the written word was limited, and none of the historical actors discussed here left written archives that I am aware of beyond the snippets gathered by the state, employers, and media. But Jemmy could and did write and so was able to take a more active role in the legal process that unfolded around him. Both Mary Ann M. and Mary Ann S. signed their depositions with a single X. Salt Spring Island was a hybrid milieu that blended diverse indigenous and settler ways, but the legal system brought into play in times of crisis was that of Britain. Two very young women whose literacy was oral rather than written were at a disadvantage.

Working together was a palpable intimacy, one that put bodies in proximity to one another on a daily basis. Work groups spanned generations but rarely genders. James M.'s son was helping him dig potatoes on the day of the alleged poisoning.[58] Men labored alongside one another outside the house, minding livestock, superintending crops, and, we might imagine, hunting and fishing for the foods that constituted so much of the local diet. We know from Sandwell's detailed microhistory of Salt Spring that women and girls fished, gathered, grew crops, and prepared food, labor that was enabled by indigenous women's knowledge of the local environment.[59]

The archive produced around this case reveals women working largely within households, doing laundry, preparing food, borrowing. Like men's work, women's work created relationships of mutuality, a context for trading, complaining, sharing, and planning. Indigenous kin ties animated this story, the putative absence of the Aboriginal mother from the M. home notwithstanding. The two Mary Anns were cousins, a particularly close relationship in the society they came from. The young women worked alongside one another and tried to imagine a better life. Escaping the odious authority of settler fathers and husbands—who were not always clearly differentiated in the snippets of conversation paraphrased in court—seems to have been their central motivation or the one they thought most convincing to tell in court. Sarah B. reported that Mary Ann S. had told her younger cousin that "when her father was dead she could run round where she liked."[60] Their shared maternal territory was ever-present in their plans alongside the charms of modernity, urban space, and consumer culture. Mary Ann S. allegedly convinced her cousin to poison her father by promising her a trip to Victoria, a new dress, and an eventual escape to Fraser River together.[61] When suspicion was first placed on her, Mary Ann S. promptly ran there.[62]

Violence animated these colonial intimacies. Physical force was part of James M.'s parenting. This was at odds with local indigenous practices, which tended to reserve force for conflicts outside the kinship group and, to a lesser extent, between adult men and women.[63] It was very much in keeping with the fur trade world that introduced James M. to North America and to the settler world that was developing around him. The fur trade, as Tina Loo explains, ran on "club law."[64] The settler world that followed it on North America's Pacific has been characterized by David Peterson del Mar as a masculinized frontier world where the use of force was normalized as a means to control others, children included.[65] Mary

Ann S. had a vested interest in stressing conflicts between James M. and his children in her testimony to the court, but her report that William M. preferred to live apart from his father "because he whips him" and that William "would like to see his father die" does not stand out as anomalous.[66] James M. admitted that it was his threat to whip Mary Ann M. rather than his "natural authority over her as her father" that prompted his daughter to confess that she had added strychnine to his coffee.[67]

That incest might explain Mary Ann M.'s behavior was not out of the question for contemporary observers of this trial. Sarah B. adhered too closely to codes of female respectability to mention the possibility of incest in her disposition and was prevented from testifying in court by her pregnancy. Yet her husband was willing to give indirect voice to the possibility by relaying a conversation between women to the courts: "My wife said she asked the girl if her Father had illused her and she said no."[68] The newspapers covering the case made a special effort to note that Mary Ann M. claimed that "she was always treated kindly by her father," making clear that they and their readers might well have entertained another possibility.[69]

As much as these records speak to the imbrication of violence in the daily intimacies of empire, they also speak to profound ambivalence about men's violence against children and to children's capacity to resist and survive. Mary Ann and William M. both found ways to resist James and his authority. The court would side with them in this respect. The presiding judge ultimately instructed the jury that there was no case to try here, since Mary Ann M.'s confession was compelled by her father's threat, and thus not "of the voluntary sort which the law allows."[70] The intimate ties of kinship could outlast familial violence and the anger it sometimes engendered. The trial ended with James promising to forgive a penitent Mary Ann M.[71] Fifteen years later, the census reported that William, now an adult, still lived and worked on his father's island farm.[72]

Power worked within as well as outside these households and communities. Three decades of feminist analyses of the family and its histories have conclusively challenged the self-serving image of the family as a haven from a heartless world, especially for women and children. The intimacies of empire were shot through with violence, pathology, and power just as were the intimacies of the metropole. Historians have paid attention to bonds of affection and mutuality in hybrid colonial spaces and to the work that sexual violence and rape played in colonial conquest,[73] but we have done less well with the petty inequities and violations that structured the ordinary intimacies between men, women, and children the colonial world over. Stressing consent, affect, and mutuality within hybrid relationships and families is a predictable response to the lingering nineteenth-century discourse that positioned mixed-race families and people as necessarily debased and pathological but is an inadequate response to the analytic complexities of intimacy, not to mention the persistence of violence against indigenous women in settler societies.[74]

This is the range of relations brought into view when historians look for intimacy rather than marriage or family. The idea of intimacy helps us further down the road early traveled by Martha Hodes's remarkable collection on love and sex across the American color line(s),[75] and that is to move beyond a narrowly defined and even fetishized idea of sexuality toward one that includes domesticity, child-care, love, friendship, and company.[76] Yet too much recent scholarship persists in equating intimacy with sexuality and more particularly heterosexual marriage. To some extent, this implicit connection between the colonial and the narrowly heterosexual is merited. The politics of nineteenth-century imperial sexual relations can seem, as they do to Robert Young, to be essentially reproductive.[77] Read from this vantage point, colonial administrators, missionaries, and observers feared not so much sexual acts, feelings, and thoughts as much as they dreaded the children that could be produced by them. Yet there is more to the fretting and legislating about intimacy between native and newcomer than the fear of mixed-race children. In British Columbia, and I suspect elsewhere, such politics were motivated by deep fear of what the loaded intimacies of home, children, love, and companionship did to colonial subjects' identities, allegiances, and practices. This was not simply about reproduction, but about creating and sustaining the identities, categories, and privileges that could either buttress or challenge colonial projects.

Putting heterosexual practice within a wider framework of familial and affective life also prompts us to better consider where same-sexuality fits within the historiography on empire and intimacy. Gay and lesbian history began to flourish in the 1980s, just as did the feminist scholarship on imperialism. Both literatures have roots in feminist critical practice and share a sometimes strained relationship to mainstream historical practice. For all this common ground, only a small handful of notable exceptions bridge the genres. There is much to be said about colonialism and same-sexuality beyond the facile celebrations of the empire as a venue for European men's latent or situational homosexuality.[78] The little we do know makes clear that same-sexuality was a part of the imperial economy of intimacy from the American West to the Sierra Leone.[79] Lee Wallace's work on the Pacific makes a compelling argument that the historiographical silence around the intimacies between men and between women not only silences a range of human relationships but forecloses the kind of more complicated reading of the development of hetero- and homosexualities through colonial encounters.[80] Such findings only hint at what the conversation between colonial historiography and sexuality studies that Anjali Arondekar calls for might produce.[81] This is not to suggest that the archive produced out of the by this case contains a rich record of evidence of same-sex sexuality: it does not. That said, it yields nothing direct about heterosexual practice either.[82] What these records do reveal is a dense world where dependence, emotion, and connection was not limited to relations between men and women.

The court found the older Mary Ann responsible for the events of the preceding autumn. The younger Mary Ann was given a morals lesson by the judge and returned to the custody of her father.[83] Some time later she married Thomas C., and by 1881 they lived with their three children and a laborer on a local farm. The next time the census taker came calling, Mary Ann's life had changed. Now thirty-seven, she was enumerated as a widow and "farmer" living with seven children in a four-room, wooden house.[84]

Mary Ann S. was sentenced to two years of hard labor for being an accessory to administering poison, apparently the first woman to be convicted of a serious crime in the colony. A settler society attenuated to bourgeois ideals of womanhood, her youth, and the fact she was pregnant turned conventional ideals of indigenous womanhood on their head and demanded her release. The grand jury, the "women of Victoria," and her husband petitioned separately for her pardon.[85] The press commented that "the half-breed girl" was depressed, and called attention to the fact that she was the only woman in the jail, and that hers was solitary confinement as an unintended result. The newspapers quoted "settlers on Salt Spring" and argued that she was "something of a heroine":

> Before marriage she was the mainstay of her father's house; she can plough a furrow and sow an acre of ground with as much skill as regularly trained husbandman. When the family were in want of meat she would don pants and shirt, shoulder a rifle, and away into The woods in search of game, and woe befell The hapless deer or bear that came within range of her unerring aim. She was also a first-rate horsewoman, bestriding the animal like "any other man"; a capital cook, good housekeeper, and her husband (who ought to know) says that she made him an excellent wife.[86]

Thus Mary Ann S. was rematerialized as a vulnerable young woman, a good daughter and a better wife. As Adrian Carton argues in his study of

"Portuguese" women in early colonial India (chapter 11 here), discourses of racialized womanhood could be fluid. That settlers recuperated Mary Ann S. by stressing her departure from models of bourgeois womanhood suggests how the intimacies of mid-nineteenth-century British Columbia could and did work in unexpected ways.

Empire was bound together by intimate contacts, and the trial of two young women both named Mary Ann on Salt Spring Island offers us an unusual window into the work and experience of intimacy in one mid-nineteenth-century colonial setting. Historians can tend to equate intimacy with heterosexual coupling, but the stories that were narrated in the courts in 1866 and 1867 reveal a world where friendship, community, and conflict encompassed but stretched well beyond partnerships between men and women. Anne Marie Plane points out that marriage was not necessarily the primary or most significant social unit in indigenous North American societies, where lineage and kinship ties weighed more heavily than those of adult heterosexual unions.[87] Historians of creole North American and Métis ethnogenesis have stressed the centrality of indigenous women to family, household, and community life, but no woman like Angelique Langlade (see chapter 7 here) is present in this narrative.[88] James M. was a seemingly lone, working-class father of a mixed-race household, and the world he lived in was animated by relationships between parents and children, coworkers, friends, neighbors, and cousins. That the case against Mary Ann M. and Mary Ann S. occurred at all reminds us not to romanticize colonial intimacies as a space apart from the inequalities, pathos, and pain that structured the nineteenth-century world here and elsewhere. There were many kinds of colonial intimacy, and we miss something important about them when we define them too narrowly or separate them from their place within the politics that gave them meaning and weight.

Notes

I would like to acknowledge the Social Sciences and Humanities Research Council of Canada and the Canada Research Chairs Programme for their support of this work. I would also like to thank the Groupe d'Étude sur l'Histoire des Amériques, Universite de Montreal, and the Law and Society Research Cluster at the University of Manitoba for the opportunity to present preliminary versions of this work. Mora Gleason and Tamara Myers provided long-distance assistance. Jean Barman was, as always, a model of scholarly generosity and knowledge, and Tony Ballantyne, Antoinette Burton, and Karen Dubinsky provided critical and valued interventions.

1. Sylvia Van Kirk, *"Many Tender Ties": Women in Fur Trade Society in Western Canada, 1670–1870* (Winnipeg, 1980); Jennifer S. H. Brown, *Strangers in Blood:*

Fur Trade Company Families in Indian Country (Vancouver, 1980). Work that followed includes: Susan Sleeper-Smith, *Indian Women and French Men: Rethinking Cultural Encounter in the Western Great Lakes* (Amherst, Mass., 2001); Jacqueline Peterson and Jennifer S. H. Brown, eds., *The New Peoples: Being and Becoming Metis in North America* (Winnipeg, 1985); Jean Barman, "Invisible Women: Aboriginal Mothers and Mixed-Race Daughters in Rural Pioneer British Columbia," in Ruth Sandwell, ed., *Beyond the City Limits: Rural History in British Columbia* (Vancouver, 1999); Jean Barman, "Taming Aboriginal Sexuality: Gender, Power, and Race in British Columbia, 1850–1900," *BC Studies* 115–16 (1997–98): 237–66; Jay Nelson, "'A Strange Revolution in the Manners of the Country': Aboriginal-Settler Intermarriage in Nineteenth-Century British Columbia," in John McLaren, Robert Menzies, and Dorothy E. Chunn, eds., *Regulating Lives: Historical Essays on the State, Society, the Individual and the Law* (Vancouver, 2002); Sylvia Van Kirk, "From 'Marrying-In' to 'Marrying-Out': Changing Patterns of Aboriginal/Non-Aboriginal Marriage in Colonial Canada," *Frontiers* 23, 3 (2002): 1–11; Renisa Mawani, "In Between and Out of Place: Mixed-Race Identity, Liquor, and the Law in British Columbia, 1850–1913," in Sherene H. Razack, ed., *Race, Space, and the Law: Unmapping a White Settler Society* (Toronto, 2002); Carol J. Williams, *Framing the West: Race, Gender, and the Photographic Frontier in the Pacific Northwest* (New York, 2003); Jean Barman, "Aboriginal Women on the Streets of Victoria: Rethinking Transgressive Sexuality during the Colonial Encounter," in Katie Pickles and Myra Rutherdale, eds., *Contact Zones: Aboriginal and Settler Women in Canada's Colonial Past* (Vancouver, 2005).

2. See the website of the Batoche National Historic Site of Canada, www.pc.gc.ca/lhn-nhs/sk/batoche/natcul/hist01_e.asp.

3. Ann Laura Stoler, "Intimidations of Empire: Predicaments of the Tactile and Unseen," and "Tense and Tender Ties: The Politics of Comparison in North American History and (Post) Colonial Studies," both in Ann Laura Stoler, ed., *Haunted by Empire: Geographies of Intimacy in North American History* (Durham, N.C., 2006). Also see her earlier "Genealogies of the Intimate: Movements in Colonial Studies, in Stoler, *Carnal Knowledge and Imperial Power: Race and the intimate in Colonial Rule* (Berkeley, 2002). For relatively early uses of the "intimate" in an imperial frame of reference see Ann Marie Plane, *Colonial Intimacies: Indian Marriage in Early New England* (Ithaca, N.Y., 2000); Lynn Zastoupil, "Intimacy and Colonial Knowledge," *Journal for Colonialism and Colonial History* 3, 2 (2002): paras. 1–61.

4. I have decided to use initials instead of last names in an effort to address some of the questions of privacy, voice, and authority that researching this story has produced. Published authors and personae who were public in their own context will be named in full. See, for a model of this technique, Karen Dubinsky, *Improper Advances: Rape and Heterosexual Conflict in Ontario, 1880–1929* (Chicago, 1993).

5. See, for the potential of queer studies for the history of colonialism, Anjali Arondekar, "Without a Trace: Sexuality and the Colonial Archive," *Journal of the History of Sexuality* 14, 1–2 (2005): 10–27.

6. Olive Dickason, *Canada's First Nations: A History of Founding Peoples from Earliest Times*, 2nd ed. (Toronto, 1997), 8.

7. Keith Thor Carlson, ed., *You Are Asked to Witness: The Stó:lo in Canada's Pacific Coast History* (Chilliwack, British Columbia, 1996).

8. See Alan Frost and Jane Samson, eds., *Pacific Empires: Essays in Honour of Glyndwr Williams* (Melbourne, Australia, 1999).

9. Jean Barman, *The West beyond the West: A History of British Columbia* (Toronto, 1991), 23.

10. Daniel W. Clayton, *Islands of Truth: The Imperial Fashioning of Vancouver Island* (Vancouver, 2000), 183, 188.

11. Richard Somerset Mackie, *Trading beyond the Mountains: The British Fur Trade on the Pacific, 1793–1843* (Vancouver, 1997).

12. These years are best dealt with in Cole Harris, *The Resettlement of British Columbia: Essays on Colonialism and Geographical Change* (Vancouver, 1997).

13. Mackie, *Trading*, 49–50.

14. R. W. Sandwell, *Contesting Rural Space: Land Policy and Practices of Resettlement on Saltspring Island, 1859–1891* (Montreal and Kingston, 2005), 4. The website "Who Killed William Robinson?" produced by Sandwell and John Lutz, is also revealing: http://web.uvic.ca/history-robinson.

15. Harris, *Resettlement*, chap. 1.

16. Chris Arnett, *The Terror of the Coast; Land Alienation and Colonial War on Vancouver Islands and the Gulf Islands, 1849–1863* (Vancouver, 1999), 15.

17. In December 1862 the "British Columbia Pioneer Association" was formed, declaring anyone who had been in the colony some six months earlier eligible to claim the status of a pioneer. See *British Columbian*, 31 December 1862.

18. See "Employees," Web site of the Children of Fort Langley, www.fortlangley .ca/employee.html. Many thanks to Jean Barman for this and more.

19. George William Heaton to W. A. G. Young, colonial secretary, 16 June 1860, Colonial Correspondence, GR 1372, reel B-1333, file 748/24a, British Columbia Archives, Victoria (BCA).

20. Charles Kahn, *Salt Spring: The Story of an Island* (Madeira Park, British Columbia, 1998), 37.

21. "A Daughter Attempts to Destroy Her Father by Mixing Strychnine with His Tea," *British Colonist*, 28 November 1866.

22. "The Assizes," *British Colonist*, 22 March 1867.

23. For the records of the baptism, see Baptismal Records, vol. 109, record 1, file 214, BCA, bcarchives.gov.bc.ca. Their mother was identified as Bella Bella.

24. "The Assizes." Mary Ann M.'s place and date of birth are listed on her death certificate, GR 2951, vol. 512, registration 1771, BCA.

25. See Erika Koenig-Sheridan, "'Gentlemen, This Is No Ordinary Trial': Sexual Narratives in the Trial of Reverend Corbett, Red River, 1863," in Jennifer S. H. Brown and Elizabeth Vibert, eds., *Reading beyond Words: Contexts for Native History*, 2nd ed. (Peterborough, Ontario, 2003); Van Kirk, "*Many Tender Ties*," chap. 9; Frits Pannekoek, *A Snug Little Flock: The Social Origins of the Riel Resistance of 1869-1870* (Winnipeg, 1991).

26. Charles Bayley, "Early Life on Vancouver Island" [1878?], transcript, E/B/ B34.2, 2, BCA.

27. Arnett, *Terror of the Coast*, 53; Sandwell, *Contesting Rural Space*, 4. Peter Carsten's study of Okanagan people suggests how intermarriage legitimated settler men's occupation of indigenous lands. Ambitious settler Cornelius O'Keefe, for instance, appeared relatively benign to indigenous peoples because "he was, after all, one of the family." See his *The Queen's People: A Study of Hegemony,*

Coercion, and Accommodation among the Okanagan of Canada (Toronto, 1991), 73.

28. Ebenezer Robson, "Diary," microfilm, reel 17A, n.p., entry for 25 March 1861, BCA.

29. George Hills, Diary, transcript, MS 65a, PSA 57, 469, Archives of the Diocese of New Westminster/Ecclesiastical Province of British Columbia, Vancouver School of Theology.

30. Sandwell, *Contesting Rural Space,* 134. This point is echoed in Megan Vaughn, *Creating the Creole Island: Slavery in Eighteenth-Century Mauritius* (Durham, N.C., 2001)

31. Jean Barman, *Stanley Park's Secret: The Forgotten Families of Whoi Whoi, Kanaka Ranch and Brockton Point* (Vancouver, 2004)

32. Sandwell, *Contesting Rural Space,* 47. See also Crawford Killian, *Go Do Some Great Thing: The Black Pioneers of British Columbia* (Vancouver, 1978).

33. Jean Barman, *Maria Mahoi of the Islands* (Vancouver, 2004), 16–7; Sandwell, *Contesting Rural Space,* 1.

34. Sandwell, *Contesting Rural Space,* 228.

35. I thank Jean Barman for reminding me of this point.

36. 1881 Canadian Census, District Vancouver, Sub-district Cowichan and Salt Spring Island, family 155; www.//vihistory.ca.

37. Durba Ghosh, "Decoding the Nameless: Gender, Subjectivity, and Historical Methodologies in Reading the Archives of Colonial India," in Kathleen Wilson, ed., *A New Imperial History: Culture, Modernity, and Empire in Britain and the Empire, 1660–1840* (Cambridge, 2004).

38. "The Assizes."

39. I.D.C., "'A Man's a Man for a' That,'" *British Columbian,* 4 June 1862.

40. "A Daughter Attempts to Destroy Her Father."

41. Vaughan, *Creating the Creole Island,* 247.

42. Perry, *On the Edge of Empire,* chaps. 2 and 4; Barman, "Aboriginal Women."

43. See "A Disorderly Neighborhood, *British Colonist,* 14 October 1861.

44. See, for instance, Marilyn Lake, "Frontier Feminism and the Marauding White Man: Australia, 1890s to 1940s," in Ruth Roach Pierson and Nupur Chaudhuri, eds., *Nation, Empire, Colony: Historicizing Gender and Race* (Bloomington, Ind., 1998). The best analysis in Canada is Sarah Carter, *Capturing Women: The Manipulation of Cultural Imagery in Canada's Prairie West* (Montreal-Kingston, 1997), chap. 5.

45. "Journal of the Vancouver Island Exploring Expedition 1864," in John Hayman, ed., *Robert Brown and the Vancouver Island Exploring Expedition* (Vancouver, 1989), 122.

46. "A Daughter Attempts to Destroy Her Father."

47. M. Preemption Files, British Columbia Department of Lands & Works, GR 766 box 7, file 81, BCA.

48. "An Extraordinary Case," *British Colonist,* 23 March 1867.

49. "The Assizes."

50. Ibid.

51. Deposition of Mary S., 17 December 1866, Attorney General Files, GR 419, box 6, file 1866/24, BCA, hereafter AG files.

52. Margaret (Shaw) Walter, *Early Days among the Gulf Islands of British Columbia* (Victoria, 1946), pp. 7–8.

53. "Deposition" of James M., 13 November 1866, AG files.

54. Sandwell, *Contesting Rural Space*, 144.

55. Ibid., 204.

56. The former was suggested by the article "A Daughter Attempts to Destroy Her Father," and the latter by Mary Ann S. in her deposition.

57. "The Assizes."

58. "Deposition" of Mary Ann S., 17 December 1866, AG files.

59. Sandwell, *Contesting Rural Space*, 132–37.

60. "Deposition" of Sarah B., 13 November 1866, AG files.

61. "The Assizes."

62. "A Daughter Attempts to Destroy Her Father."

63. David Peterson Del Mar, *Beaten Down: A History of Interpersonal Violence in the West* (Seattle, 2002), 19.

64. Tina Loo, *Making Law, Order, and Authority in British Columbia, 1821–1871* (Toronto, 1994), chap. 1.

65. David Peterson Del Mar, *What Trouble I Have Seen: A History of Violence against Wives* (Cambridge, Mass., 1996).

66. "Deposition" of Mary Ann S., 17 December 1866, AG files.

67. "The Assizes."

68. "Deposition" of Richard B., 20 December 1866, AG files. See, on the work of incest rumors in a different colonial context, Kirsten McKenzie, "Women's Talk and the Colonial State: The Wylde Scandal, 1831–1833," *Gender and History* 11, 1 (1999): 30-53.

69. "A Daughter Attempts to Destroy Her Father."

70. "The Assizes."

71. "A Daughter Attempts to Destroy Her Father."

72. 1881 Canadian Census, District Vancouver, Sub-district Cowichan and Salt Spring Island, family 155; www.//vihistory.ca.

73. On sexual violence, see Antonia I. Castañeda, "Sexual Violence in the Politics and Policies of Conquest: Amerindian Women and the Spanish Conquest of Alta California," in Adela de la Torre and Beatríz M. Pasquera, eds., *Building with Our Hands: New Directions in Chicana Studies* (Berkeley, 1993).

74. See Anne McGillivray and Brenda Comaskey, *Black Eyes All of the Time: Intimate Violence, Aboriginal Women, and the Justice System* (Toronto, 1999).

75. Martha Hodes, ed., *Sex, Love, Race: Crossing Boundaries in North American History* (New York, 1999).

76. This is my definition. As Stoler has recently remarked, there is no common working consensus on what intimacy means. See Stoler, "Intimidations of Empire," 15.

77. Robert J. C. Young, *Colonial Desire: Hybridity in Theory, Culture and Race* (London, 1995), 26.

78. See here Ronald Hyam, *Empire and Sexuality: The British Experience* (Manchester, England, 1990).

79. See Nayan Shah, "Between 'Oriental Depravity' and 'Natural Degenerates': Spatial Borderlands and the Making of Ordinary Americans," *American Quarterly* 57, 3 (2005): 703–25; Richard Phillips, "Heterogeneous Imperialism

and the Regulation of Sexuality in British West Africa," *Journal of the History of Sexuality* 14, 3 (2005): 291–315. Also see Ross G. Forman, "Randy on the Rand: Portuguese African Labor and the Discourse on 'Unnatural Vice' in the Transvaal in the Early Twentieth Century," *Journal of the History of Sexuality* 11, 4 (2002): 570–609.

80. Lee Wallace, *Sexual Encounters: Pacific Texts, Modern Sexualities* (Ithaca, N.Y., 2003).

81. Anjali Arondekar, "Without a Trace: Sexuality and the Colonial Archive," *Journal of the History of Sexuality* 14, 1/2 (2005): 10–27.

82. On the differing standards of evidence for questions of heterosexuality and homosexuality, see Martha Vicinus, "Lesbian History: All Theory and No Facts or All Facts and No Theory?" *Radical History Review* 60 (1994): 57–75.

83. "The Assizes."

84. Thanks to Jean Barman for some critical assistance here. See 1881 Census, Cowichan and Salt Spring Island, family 217, http://vihistory.ca/. Here she is enumerated as Mary. The 1891 data comes from 1891 Census, Sooke and Goldstream Sub-District, Family 38.

85. "The Poisoning Case," *British Colonist*, 25 March 1867

86. "The 'Wild Huntress,'" *British Colonist*, 26 March 1867.

87. Plane, *Colonial Intimacies*, 6.

88. Langlade's story sits at the center of McDonell's analysis in chapter 7 here. More generally, see Lucy Eversveld Murphy, "Public Mothers: Native American and Metis Women as Creole Mediators in the Nineteenth-Century Midwest," *Journal of Women's History* 14, 4 (2003): 142–66; Jennifer S. H. Brown, "Woman as Centre and Symbol in the Emergence of Metis Communities," *Canadian Journal of Native Studies* 3 (1983): 39–46.

MICHELLE T. MORAN

15 *Telling Tales of Ko'olau*

CONTAINING AND MOBILIZING DISEASE
IN COLONIAL HAWAI'I

In the months following the overthrow of Queen Lili'uokalani of Hawai'i in January 1893, a newly formed provisional government—comprised primarily of white settler businessmen—sought to consolidate its control over the islands and their inhabitants. Public health policy provided a useful tool for displaying and exercising moral and civil authority, and the government Board of Health embarked on an intensive campaign during this period to round up all Hawaiians with leprosy who had hidden themselves within communities throughout the islands. When health agent and deputy sheriff Louis Stolz attempted in June 1893 to remove several Hawaiians from the remote Kalalau Valley on the island of Kaua'i, a small group refused to comply and encouraged others to resist. Stolz and his assistants planned an ambush of a man named Ko'olau, a Hawaiian with leprosy who they presumed acted as the leader of the resisters. The trap failed when Ko'olau shot and killed the deputy sheriff and eluded capture with his wife and son.[1] The incident prompted Sanford Dole, head of the provisional government, to send troops to the Kalalau Valley to arrest Ko'olau and to transfer approximately twenty Hawaiians with leprosy to the Kalawao leprosy settlement on the island of Moloka'i. After a two-week siege, the new government could declare only a partial victory. Health agents took into custody most valley residents suspected of having leprosy, but they failed to contain either Ko'olau and his family or the written and spoken tales of their successful resistance.

The multiple retellings of the story of Ko'olau reveal contests among health officials and Hawaiians over the management and movement of bodies with leprosy in colonial Hawai'i. Hawaiians' ability to draw on familial and communal networks and to circulate information in defiance of white settlers' attempts to immobilize and isolate them helped shape a Hawaiian identity that constantly destabilized colonial visions of authority and mechanisms of control. The first part of this essay explores how growing anxiety among Euro-Americans over the mobility of diseased island residents led public health officers in the decades before 1893 to begin removing people with leprosy to the Moloka'i settlement. The provisional government sought to refashion affective ties among the islands' original inhabitants under the guise of protecting the Hawaiian "race" from its own poor health habits. This entailed not the interracial unions that Kerry Wynn describes (chapter 8 here), in which marriages between U.S. citizens and American Indians encouraged the incorporation of Indian bodies (and lands) into the United States through an implicit severing of Cherokee domestic ties. This study instead recognizes a different type of domestic disruption, enacted under a similar aim to "civilize" and incorporate, with state officials seeking to remove and contain supposedly contaminated indigenous bodies. In both contexts, however, the policies intervened in intimate relations to gain control of territory, a goal understood and resisted by many Cherokee and Hawaiians. Domestic networks among Hawaiians provided comfort to those with leprosy and allowed them to circulate freely, and government officials believed such practices threatened their attempts to present Hawai'i as a timeless island paradise.

The provisional government wanted to impose a history on this space that saw civilization beginning with the arrival of Euro-Americans who brought salvation to diseased Hawaiians, but Hawaiians circulated their own histories that linked locations to celebrations of their own families and communities. Health officials and English-language newspapers portrayed Ko'olau as a murderer whose flight was an act of cowardice that threatened everyone. Euro-Americans used this story as a justification for their intervention in Hawaiian lives. Many Hawaiians, however, would come to present Ko'olau as a heroic figure who protested the practices of removal and restriction on the grounds that they unjustly separated him from his family. The second part of this essay explores two contrasting accounts of Ko'olau's defiance that challenged the government's version of events. Jack London's 1912 short story "Koolau the Leper" emphasized Ko'olau's bravery, but it also unleashed to an international print audience a distorted and grotesque view of diseased Hawaiians that health officials had hoped to repress. A retelling of the incident by Pi'ilani, Ko'olau's wife, challenged white settler accounts by valorizing Ko'olau as a devoted husband and father able to fight colonial restrictions through the assistance of family and community members. The multiple stories of Ko'olau and the controversy they generated thus reveal the precarious nature of colonial rule, as health officials could neither assert complete control over the mobility of patient bodies nor contain the trajectories of stories carrying visions of Hawai'i that ran counter to official territorial accounts.[2]

Western medicine in Hawai'i engaged in ongoing dialogues with local forms of knowledge that often centered on intimate ties, a process that complicated the implementation of imperial policies and the creation of colonial identities.[3] Warwick Anderson has sought to expand scholarly conceptions of the intimate to incorporate "the expert and habituated benevolence of the state." He draws attention to the ways colonial officials justified as public health measures their intrusive handling, probing, and relocating of indigenous bodies, a process that often reshaped domestic habits and affective ties.[4] Public health policy in Hawai'i certainly provided the provisional government with a means of ameliorating the potential danger that arose from crosscultural contacts unfolding in marketplaces, plantations, and communities among presumably healthy Euro-Americans and potentially diseased Hawaiians. At the same time, public health officials drew on the authority of Western medicine to contend that their knowledge of the body and its diseases could offer a supposed backward and reckless colonized people a path to civilization and survival. In this way, Western medicine played a critical role in what David Arnold refers to as the "colonization of the body."[5] But as Ramón Gutiérrez has argued, the power of colonial governments was never complete, "always providing oppositional spaces for resistance and political possibilities that end[ed] in rebellion and revolt."[6] The rebellion of Ko'olau demonstrates how medical policy shaped contested spaces in "intimate arenas," as Western visions of health imposed on bodies from without clashed with Hawaiian understandings of healing unfolding within familial and community networks. The multiple accounts of the struggle over the right to separate families or to defend them offers a window into the process by which competing narratives of Western domination and Hawaiian endurance continued to shape and destabilize Euro-American rule in the islands long after Ko'olau's struggle ended.

––––––––––

Brought to the islands some time after Captain James Cook established Western contact in 1778, leprosy became intimately identified with

Hawai'i by the late nineteenth century. Foreign settlers, particularly those from the United States, used the spread of the disease among the islands' inhabitants to justify intervening in the Hawaiian government and linking the nation's interest more closely to Western powers. White settlers began to assume official responsibility for governance under the Hawaiian monarchy in such agencies as the Board of Health. Euro-American officials working for the board recognized that the Hawaiian population had decreased precipitously in the hundred years following Western contact, due in large part to diseases brought by outsiders, but they chose to interpret this decline as evidence of Hawaiians' inability to adapt to the rigors of Christian civilization.[7] Doctors knew that tuberculosis, influenza, cholera, venereal diseases, and smallpox posed greater threats to Hawaiian lives than leprosy, but it was this disease that inspired the most attention. Health agents argued persuasively that the Hawaiian government should adopt a policy of compulsory removal of people with leprosy to a settlement on the island of Moloka'i.[8]

Under the influence of Western advisors eager to contain the effects of a highly stigmatized disease, King Kamehameha V urged the Hawaiian legislature in 1865 to pass "An Act to Prevent the Spread of Leprosy." The law strengthened the power of the government's Board of Health by granting its members the authority to establish places to isolate people with leprosy and to create a system that mandated the arrest and inspection of any person "alleged to be a leper."[9] Although the law required the isolation of any person found to have leprosy, its actual implementation fell most harshly on native Hawaiians, who soon discovered that the new regulations required them to send friends and relatives away to either the Kalihi Hospital and Detention Center in Honolulu on O'ahu (which served as a sorting station and treatment center for less advanced cases) or the Kalawao settlement on Moloka'i.[10] By the early 1870s, the board was sending about one hundred patients to Kalawao annually, almost all of them Hawaiian and all showing physical manifestations of the disease.[11]

Responses to leprosy among Hawaiians and white settlers highlight the contentious nature of the state's use of Western medicine to intervene in the intimate lives of the colonized. Despite determined efforts by health officials to provide one fixed and scientific understanding of the disease, Hawaiians constructed their own ideas about leprosy from their evolving encounters with the series of illnesses white settlers had brought to the islands' populations. Indeed, they came to identify leprosy by the curious insistence among white settlers that this disease required unique treatment to arrest its spread. Hawaiians sometimes referred to it as "ma'i ho'oka'awale," or the "separating sickness." For Hawaiians, caring for the sick was a communal effort in which the healthy and ill intermingled and family and friends provided care for one another. Many Hawaiians found the Euro-American practice of forcibly isolating the sick from their communities a disturbing and peculiar policy that exacerbated suffering rather than ameliorating it.[12] Foreign administrators, for their part, condemned Hawaiians for accepting people with leprosy and willingly living among them. Such acceptance contrasted sharply with Western religious traditions of separating and stigmatizing people with leprosy in their communities. Western colonizers interpreted Hawaiian failure to adopt these Christian practices as a cultural weakness that left Hawaiians vulnerable to extinction.

Euro-American health officials enjoyed some success in convincing Hawaiians to forgo what they characterized as a misplaced island spirit of aloha and to comply with the mandate that people with leprosy be contained at isolated settlements. Even as some Hawaiians accepted containment, however, they rejected efforts to completely sever affective ties and relinquish traditional health practices. Health officials argued that Hawaiians in leprosy settlements and hospitals would have to adapt to the strictness of institutional life and abandon such practices as sharing a common *poi* bowl and sleeping on grass mats. Hawaiians often refused to accept such intrusions into their intimate lives as unnecessary to prevent the spread of disease. They instead sought to develop policies that would enable family and friends closer contact with those who had leprosy, and they petitioned for regional facilities on all the islands, treatment by community healers, and more open visitation policies.[13] While Western health regulations demanded the strict isolation of contagious bodies and stringent policing of personal contacts, Hawaiians continued to maintain intimate connections between the segregated sick and their own communities throughout the islands.

To Euro-American physicians and health administrators, enacting a properly "civilized" treatment meant ending the Hawaiian practice of communal support for the ill and replacing it with intrusive surveillance and closely monitored incarceration. Medical officials accordingly drew on contemporary understandings of contagion and the germ theory of disease to resuscitate and update the model of the medieval Christian lazaretto as a Western imperial medical institution. They thus transformed leprosy from a divine scourge of the sinful into a disease of the "primitive."[14] Many Hawaiians with leprosy, recognizing that condemnation to Kalawao represented a lifelong separation from kin and communities, flouted the new laws. Relatives and friends hid those with leprosy from health investigators, while people sent to Kalihi or Kalawao frequently escaped from those sites to transact business or to contact loved ones on "the outside." White settler administrators condemned Hawaiians for failing to follow Western moral and medical advice. Dr. Arthur Mouritz, a physician who attended to patients at the Moloka'i settlement, warned that "until such time as the Hawaiian mind is impressed with the necessity of social ostracism being practiced toward all lepers," the islands would fail to realize "the true advantages of public segregation in chosen sites."[15] Colonial authorities sought to cast those who refused to accept intervention in their domestic arrangements as impediments to scientific medicine's goal of remolding the islands into their conception of a healthy and civilized space.

Efforts to round up those suspected of having leprosy intensified as Westerners increased their control over the Hawaiian government at the end of the nineteenth century. In 1887, a group calling itself the Hawaiian League, comprised primarily of foreign businessmen and the descendants of missionaries, forcibly imposed what came to be known as the Bayonet Constitution on King Kalakaua. This document effectively removed power from the Hawaiian monarchy and placed it the hands of Westerners—mainly Americans—determined to protect their own property and business concerns.[16] With a new legislature came new appointments to the Board of Health and changes in the bureaucracy, both of which improved the board members' ability to round up those they suspected of having leprosy.[17] Segregation of leprosy patients remained the centerpiece of the Board of Health's policy, and the number of people incarcerated for having the disease rose dramatically. The resident population at Kalawao almost doubled in seven years, rising from 590 in 1886 to 1,155 by the end of 1893.[18]

The Board of Health still lacked the ability to direct police officials, however, which meant it could not compel Hawaiians to notify public health authorities about leprosy cases. People with leprosy and their family members saw little reason to comply voluntarily with such rules. In some communities, Hawaiians with the disease carved out small, relatively hidden enclaves, remaining beyond the reach of health officials and in contact with loved ones who could provide them with food and other necessities.[19] Board of Health officials contented themselves with periodic raids on such leprosy strongholds, which they saw as both a threat to public health and an affront to Western authority. Since friends and family members warned those with leprosy when health agents planned to investigate an area, these raids were usually unsuccessful.

The power of the Board of Health increased dramatically in 1893, after a group of Americans deposed Queen Lili'uokalani and declared Hawai'i an independent republic under the control of white settlers.[20] With the establishment of a new provisional government, public health policy became a means for officials to mobilize, display, and exercise their moral and civil authority. Board of Health president William O. Smith also held the position of attorney general, thereby consolidating medical and civil authority and enabling the new government to use health policy as an avenue for maintaining order and gaining control over Hawaiian bodies. Health agents dispatched to various localities throughout the islands now worked with local police to identify, collect, and incarcerate those suspected of having leprosy. In some cases, public health representatives were granted policing authority; such was the case with health agent and deputy sheriff Louis Stolz. In May 1893, he requested an expansion of his territory on the island of Kaua'i to incorporate the Kalalau Valley, where numerous people with leprosy maintained contacts with friends and family while remaining hidden from government officials. Stolz vowed to "round up" peaceably all people with the disease who had been evading the law and to bring them to the Moloka'i settlement.[21]

Reaction to Stolz's plan among Kalalau Valley residents tempered the health agent's initial confidence that Hawaiians with leprosy would succumb to what press accounts labeled the "kind yet firm" hand of the Board of Health.[22] Stolz notified his superiors that he had placed the valley under quarantine to weed out the "leprous" from the "non-leprous" residents. His efforts to encourage people with leprosy to leave their homes or their hideaways met with mixed success. Some people offered to go, others proved less willing, and the younger and stronger—those most capable of physically resisting health officials' decrees—openly challenged him. The board offered to send in troops to assist Stolz in removing patients who had headed deeper into the valley to escape incarceration, but the health agent insisted that he wished to handle the matter "peacefully."[23]

Stolz and other white settler officials believed Hawaiians to be an inherently passive people and did not anticipate strong opposition to the roundup and deportation. They decided that capturing and containing a visible leader would be sufficient to halt the promiscuous intermingling of healthy and unwell bodies and to end the open defiance of the board's policies. Identifying a cowboy foreman named Ko'olau as the ringleader of the resisters, Stolz planned an ambush to capture him. Instead, Ko'olau shot and killed the deputy sheriff and escaped deep inland with his wife and son and other Hawaiians with leprosy.[24] Ironically, on the same day that officials in Honolulu learned of Stolz's death, the *Daily Pacific Commercial Advertiser*, the white settler newspaper most supportive of the

Board of Health's enterprise, had reported that the Hawaiians of Kalalau Valley would raise no serious objections to forced removal. The paper contended that only "two or three" residents showed "any disposition to resist the orders" and confidently asserted "there will be little or no trouble in effecting their removal."[25] The casual underestimation of the number of residents opposed to the colonial directive displayed Euro-American blindness to the strength of the intimate ties that connected individuals such as Ko'olau to broader networks of resistance.

Stolz's death at the hands of Ko'olau illuminates the Kalalau Valley as a contested space and a true "meeting-up" place as described by Doreen Massey.[26] The provisional government depicted the valley as a territory trapped in a timeless state of primitivism, one that it would have to wrestle from a group of recalcitrant "natives" in order to incorporate the island and its people more fully into civilization. The defiant stand taken by Ko'olau and his allies, however, shaped the valley into a site of resistance and opened the space to multiple potentialities. Frances Steel has recast the port as a kinetic site that forged new forms of contact and conflict among diverse "mobile men" (chapter 5 here), and the tale of Ko'olau suggests that the heart of the island may benefit from a similar reconceptualization. This new perspective would allow such spaces as Kaua'i's Kalalau Valley to act as dynamic fields of interaction among competing visions of colonial power. Rather than forming a bounded space temporarily lying beyond the reach of conquest, or acting as a haven that could momentarily shield an indigenous population from outside forces, the valley itself served as a site of connection, forging networks among health workers and resisters, healthy and sick, contained and mobilized, settlers and subjects, even as all these groups challenged such distinctions.

Press coverage following Stolz's death revealed a new government struggling to legitimate its authority in Honolulu and to undermine defiance of its policies by stringently enforcing the relocation of Hawaiians with leprosy against their will. Republic president Sanford Dole proclaimed a state of martial law in the districts surrounding the Kalalau Valley, ordering all those suspected of having leprosy to "surrender" within twenty-four hours. The government also dispatched a brigade of thirty-five armed men to a beach near the valley. Although the *Advertiser* announced Dole's intention "to remove the lepers without further bloodshed," it also made clear the government's commitment to "clean out every leper from the valley either dead or alive."[27] Thus, a policy that ostensibly aimed to provide humane treatment became wedded to a drive to cleanse the islands of the menace of leprosy by the forcible and potentially violent removal and segregation of Hawaiians with the disease. The shooting incident bolstered the perception among Western settlers that all persons with leprosy who refused removal were criminals on the run and a threat to public health and safety until their arrest and detention by the state.

Board members viewed the shooting as a dangerous act of defiance and a sign that some Hawaiians still failed to grasp the enormity of the risk that leprosy posed to their islands. In their public statements, health officials attempted to portray the incident as the hostile action of a lone man, but they struggled to make sense of the fact that Ko'olau and the other resisters had the cooperation of communities throughout the islands whose members told stories of the fugitives' exploits, aided their escape, and refused to assist officials in providing information about their whereabouts.[28] One newspaper account admitted that in the Hanalei district of Kaua'i, "it was difficult to get any information regarding Kalalau or the movements of the murderous lepers."[29]

As days passed without the surrender of Ko'olau or the other resisters, the government response assumed a more pointedly militaristic tone. The small armed force sent to Kaua'i enlisted several Hawaiians to contact the renegade group and warn them that "war would be declared on them" if they failed to surrender within two days. At the mouth of the valley, soldiers set up military quarters, which they christened Camp Dole. The threat of armed violence convinced eight people with leprosy to submit to health authorities and accept their removal to Kalihi or Kalawao.[30] The increased military threat only solidified Ko'olau's resolve to remain at large, however, convincing him that his life and those of his wife and son remained in jeopardy. When Ko'olau failed to surrender, soldiers fired shells at the base of the cliff where he and his family remained hidden. As the standoff continued, five other valley residents with leprosy escaped into the Hanalei Mountains, where troops were dispatched to track them down.[31]

Euro-American politicians and businessmen characterized the resisters as dangerous outlaws and labeled leprosy as a "national curse" that would threaten the future of the young nation if left unchecked. Reporters for the *Daily Pacific Commercial Advertiser* portrayed Ko'olau and his family as an army unto themselves, claiming that they possessed three thousand rounds of ammunition and identifying each family member—including the nine-year-old son—as a skilled sharpshooter.[32] Such exaggerated portrayals of the threat posed by Ko'olau and the other Hawaiians with leprosy who remained at large helped to justify for white settlers the extraordinary steps taken by the provisional government in the Kalalau Valley. On July 4, fifteen soldiers moved up the mountain toward the location of the sequestered family. As they approached, Ko'olau shot and killed two soldiers, and a third accidentally shot himself in the melee.[33] One editorial writer placed the blame for the bloodshed squarely on Ko'olau rather than on the military intervention that precipitated the confrontation. This journalist called for the "re-established and purified" government to conduct a full-scale effort to locate and remove all people with the disease.[34] The account drew on what Warwick Anderson has called the "poetics of pollution" to cast uncooperative Hawaiians as dangerous contaminants who needed to be quarantined and subjected to medical discipline.[35]

Despite such press accounts, members of the provisional government came to realize that total segregation could never occur without the full consent of the Hawaiian population, and full consent they did not have.[36] Government officials who viewed Hawaiian domestic arrangements primarily as threats to public health measures came to recognize how such networks also provided effective means of resisting other forms of colonial authority. The fact that the five other resisters from Kalalau Valley surrendered to authorities after the July 4 confrontation did not offset the humiliation of losing Ko'olau or of facing opposition from Hawaiians in raids on other Kaua'i communities. Board of Health physician C. B. Reynolds and a company of soldiers inspected all houses in Hanalei, but residents claimed that people with leprosy had left without telling anyone where they intended to go. When Reynolds, who claimed he "knew the natives were lying," threatened to punish the residents if they failed to cooperate, some of them retorted, "If you want the lepers, go and find them." Arresting selected residents to elicit information regarding the whereabouts of people with leprosy also failed to produce useful results. The deputy sheriff claimed that his Hawaiian officers were "useless" and hampered the removal effort.[37] Ultimately, the government called off the search for Ko'olau and returned to Honolulu.

In the months following Ko'olau's resistance, the Board of Health attempted to recover from the embarrassment of what it termed "the sad experience at Kalalau" by portraying itself as a noble army engaged in a crusade against a dangerous enemy. Refusing to acknowledge the elusive Ko'olau, the board's executive officer claimed, "I think the board can congratulate themselves on the fact that the Islands have not been so free from known lepers at large for the past ten years as at present." Speaking of people stricken with a disease as armed guerrillas, he pointed to health agents' success in removing people from the Kalalau and Wainiha valleys on Kaua'i and from the more remote islands of Ni'ihau and Lana'i, "places that have been undisturbed strongholds of lepers for many years."

Many islanders viewed this as an unnecessarily harsh targeting of native Hawaiians, but the executive officer of the board termed it an "impartial and thorough segregation" crucial to public health.[38] Still, the roundup of other Hawaiians with leprosy could not offset the reality that Ko'olau had successfully slipped away into the forests of Kaua'i with his family and had inspired a widespread tale of Hawaiian resistance to the board's authority. He died three years later, still free.[39]

The story of Ko'olau proved as mobile as the fugitive himself, continuing to spread after his death and assuming new forms in different hands. Journalist and author Jack London heard this tale during his 1907 tour of the Hawaiian Islands.[40] The account inspired him to write a short story, "Koolau the Leper," which was published in 1912. London depicted Ko'olau as a heroic renegade who believed in the justness of his cause, but obscured the intimate bonds that sustained his defiance by casting other Hawaiians with leprosy as oversexed, deranged, and ultimately disloyal. Though it is reasonable to conclude that the Board of Health would have preferred London to have avoided such imagery, the tragic nature of his tale implicitly supported segregation policies and reduced Ko'olau to a romantic figure cut off from both ongoing Hawaiian resistance and colonial visions of progress. Ko'olau's wife, Pi'ilani, and their son do not appear in the story, nor do other members of the valley community, thus removing Ko'olau's original motivation for refusing to enter the Moloka'i leprosy settlement and suggesting that his ability to elude health officials rested entirely on his own resourcefulness. Despite offering a sympathetic portrait of Ko'olau, London's story further sensationalized the disease, marginalized the active resistance among the Hawaiian people, and portrayed Kalalau Valley as a primitive space cut off from the beneficent effects of civilization.[41]

London's tale begins with a strong indictment of imperialism's impact on native Hawaiians. The reader meets Ko'olau as he delivers a stinging rejection of the mandate that those with leprosy be sent to the Moloka'i settlement, painting the policy as an example of illegitimate white colonial domination. Ko'olau asserts that those with the disease were being stripped of their liberty and imprisoned against their will, though they had committed no wrong. As an example, Ko'olau relates the case of one woman who had been sent to Moloka'i seven years earlier, noting that her brother had not seen her since. "Nor will he ever see her," Ko'olau predicts. "She must stay there until she dies. This is not her will. It is not Niuli's [her brother's] will. It is the will of the white men who rule the land." He explains further how white men had assumed control of the islands by having the Hawaiian people act as their servants. "They who had nothing have everything, and if you, or I, or any Kanaka be hungry, they sneer and say, 'Well, why don't you work? There are the plantations.'"[42]

London contrasts this eloquent soliloquy with sensationalized descriptions of Ko'olau's audience. He portrays its members as the most hideous of beings and renders the physical manifestations of their disease in exaggerated and horrifying terms. He literally strips them of their humanity, asserting, "They were creatures who once had been men and women. But they were men and women no longer. They were monsters— in face and form, grotesque caricatures of everything human."[43] To further emphasize the sense of the monstrous, London sketches a gruesome parody of the idyllic Hawaiian night, filling the blossom-fragrant, moonlit evening with diseased men and women swaying to the sounds of a ukulele. "It was a dance of the living dead, for in their disintegrating bodies life still loved and longed."[44] The story conveys to the reader the warning that the seeming paradise of the Hawaiian Islands harbored spaces populated by unknown horrors, creatures who in failing to accept their condition as a threat refused to be safely contained.

In London's account, the standoff between Ko'olau and colonial officials becomes a final spasm of defiance among Hawaiians before their inevitable submission to the provisional government. The story expands the encounter into a full-scale battle, with shells and bullets unleashed by the soldiers shattering the bodies of Ko'olau's followers. The cowboy himself guns down four policemen and the sheriff in an initial confrontation before proceeding to shoot an unidentified number of soldiers in "a massacre, in which one man did the killing."[45] Despite his disease, Ko'olau emerges as a skilled and terrifying marksman capable of standing down an army. Throughout this account, Ko'olau shows himself to be a man of valor and principle, frequently reiterating his innocence and his simple request to be left alone, but London's story takes the form of a tragedy. Ko'olau eludes capture, but all of his surviving followers abandon him by handing themselves over to officials, cursing him as they go. He is forced to conclude that there is "No gainsaying that terrible will of the haoles," because "They never knew when they were beaten. It was where his own kind lacked."[46] Ko'olau dies alone, with only his rifle for company. The account erases family and community, and it offers no sense that Ko'olau's story would live on as Hawaiians continued to share, spread, and retell his tale of heroic struggle.[47] London might strike a note of regret for what Hawaiians had lost, but his story suggests that a decimated population had no real chance of halting the spread of a more persistent and dominant people whose triumphant entry into the islands' interiors was inevitable.

Before writing his account, London had sought official permission to visit the leprosy settlement on Moloka'i, explaining that he and his wife were "keenly interested" in the subject of leprosy. Aware that territorial health officials worried about public portrayals of the settlement and its residents, the author assured the president of the Board of Health that he did not intend to write "any sensational newspaper writing, and I doubt if, after my visit, I should write a line upon said visit." He did indicate, however, that he sought "atmosphere" for a short story he planned to write about "the celebrated case of the leper of Kauai."[48] Board president L. E. Pinkham hoped London's writing would help him offset what he viewed as "sentimental and sensational" accounts circulating abroad about the settlement. In the board's annual report, Pinkham presented the pending visit by the Londons as a potential counterpoint to previous misrepresentations, concluding "I trust his promised account of their experience may be placed before the reading public."[49] London convinced health officials of his good intentions, and they welcomed him and his wife to the settlement on Moloka'i in July to join in Independence Day celebrations.

London did write a 1911 chronicle of his experiences at the Moloka'i settlement that portrayed those with leprosy in less sensationalized terms, emphasizing their humanity and depicting conditions at the settlement in a positive light.[50] However, the publication of "Koolau the Leper" and other tales involving leprosy in London's short story collection *The House of Pride* one year later unleashed a storm of protest in the English-language Honolulu newspapers, as readers objected to London's depiction of the disease within the islands.[51] The grotesque images that haunted the stories threatened the portrait of an island paradise promoted by the Hawaiian Board of Tourism.[52] Frustration among white islanders matched the concern of Board of Health officials, who continually sought to demonstrate that leprosy was a health issue they had firmly under control. They found themselves unable to contain the images circulated by London, though they sought to effect tighter controls on information leaving the Moloka'i settlement.[53] Still, the sensationalized accounts of leprosy in London's stories inadvertently reinforced the fundamental assumption that underlay the territorial government's policy of incarcerating those with leprosy: the belief that circumscribing the mobility of those with the disease and separating them from family and friends was necessary for the good health and financial strength of Hawai'i. While London's story of Ko'olau unleashed distorted and grisly images of the disease, linking it firmly to Hawai'i in the imaginations of his readers, he also reiterated the colonialist assumption that the territorial mandate of isolating those with leprosy in sites far removed from familial and communal connections proved a better policy than any efforts at health care practiced by Hawaiians.

Yet Hawaiians themselves continued to contest this understanding of leprosy, in part by circulating their own accounts of Ko'olau. Pi'ilani had told her version of the story to other Hawaiians following her return from hiding after her husband died. In 1906, she offered her depiction of events to journalist John Sheldon, who transcribed the account and published it in the Hawaiian language.[54] Pi'ilani relates a story of family and kinship, offering background on the births of Ko'olau and herself, their marriage, the birth of their son, and the onset of the disease in her husband and child. In her account, the confrontation with soldiers occurred only after public health officials refused to allow her to accompany her husband to the settlement on Moloka'i. In direct contrast to London's theme of individualism, Pi'ilani details the contributions of community members who sustained the family during their years of hiding in the Kalalau Valley. She reveals the heartbreak of caring for their son as he weakened and died. She describes how she remained by Ko'olau's side during his final days, ultimately fulfilling his final request by burying him in the land that had hidden them from the provisional government.

Pi'ilani's story ends not with the death of Ko'olau, however, but with one final challenge to the territorial government. After returning to her family, she faced the health officials who had sought to imprison her husband. Buoyed by the support of her relatives, Pi'ilani related to officials her version of what had happened in the Kalalau Valley. She thereby staked her right both to tell her own story and to reclaim her own freedom. After receiving the officials' assurances that she was absolved of all wrongdoing, she asserted, "On this day I triumphed over my doubts as to the effects of the government's power over me."[55] Her freedom and her telling of the "true story of Kaluaiko'olau" demonstrated that the colonial government's plan to contain completely the mobility of Hawaiians and the trajectory of their counternarratives proved not only elusive but also illusory.

Government officials justified the extreme provisions of their strict segregation policy by portraying it as a humanitarian arrangement that employed public health measures to save what they viewed as a primitive and irresponsible Hawaiian "race" from extinction. More practically, they saw the policy as a means of protecting Western business interests from the taint of leprosy and of exerting physical and moral control over Hawaiians. Hawaiians thwarted the goal of total segregation, however, and thereby revealed the tenuous nature of colonial authority. The story of Ko'olau emerged as a narrative space on which various interests could map out their own version of the appropriate ordering of Hawaiian society. Christine Skwiot has shown how Western interests sought to appropriate Hawaiian royal genealogies as a means of naturalizing U.S. rule in the islands, even as Hawaiians actively challenged these Western interpretations to contest the legitimacy of American governance (chapter 9 here). The story of Ko'olau proved to be a different kind of "intimate history" that competing interests sought to mobilize in support of their claim to manage the domestic affairs of Hawaiians. Western officials depicted Ko'olau as a dangerous renegade and contaminant who threatened both the stability of a new legitimate republic and the health of all who lived in Hawai'i. Hawaiian accounts of Ko'olau reflected resentment of the restrictive Western leprosy policies that sought to interfere in their most intimate relations. In Pi'ialani's account, Ko'olau escaped through his ability to draw on familial and community networks, and his exploits served as a symbol of Hawaiian defiance. His act of resistance, along with those of other Hawaiians with leprosy who thwarted health authorities, called into question the legitimacy of foreign intervention as a whole. Even after the Board of Health sought to strengthen its authority through the passage of new rules and regulations in 1893, Hawaiians found ways to recognize and manipulate fractures in the system to secure their freedom to move and to challenge foreign dominance.

Rather than view this period as the Hawaiians' final attempt to check the growth of a dominant and ultimately triumphant Western presence, the end of the nineteenth century should be seen as the beginning of a new phase in an ongoing series of negotiations between colonizer and colonized. Writing in 1916, former settlement physician Arthur Mouritz professed to having heard Hawaiians remark: "Hawaii is our country, it belongs to us, or at least it did until the haole got possession of most of it. If the haole is afraid of leprosy let him go back to where he came from."[56] While Hawaiians could neither eject Westerners nor prevent the incorporation of their islands into the United States by the end of the century, they did continue to undermine white settler leprosy policies by evading health officials, escaping incarceration, and manipulating institutional rules. They also mobilized their own stories of Hawaiian encounters with and challenges to colonial authority, as evidenced by Ko'olau's emergence as a Hawaiian hero. The spread of this epic of defiance highlights what Doreen Massey calls "the real import of spatiality, the possibility of multiple narratives" that Western histories of modernity sought to foreclose.[57] The story of Ko'olau did not represent a last stand of Hawaiians so much as it provided a tale of Hawaiian mobility and intimate ties that paralleled Western stories of conquest and civilization and continually undermined colonial authority. This tale thus provides a counterhistory of colonialism, one coexisting with and thereby challenging a modern history that insisted on the inevitability and beneficence of Western rule.

Notes

1. The most extensive account of this incident was provided by Ko'olau's wife, Pi'ilani, recorded by John G. M. Sheldon and published in Hawaiian in 1906. Frances N. Frazier published an English translation as "The True Story of Kaluaiko'olau, or Ko'olau the Leper," in *Hawaiian Journal of History* 21 (1987): 1–41. Both versions have been republished as *The True Story of Kaluaikoolau, as Told by His Wife, Piilani*, trans. Frances N. Frazier (Lihue, Hawai'i, 2001).

2. For traditional histories, see Ralph Kuykendall, *The Hawaiian Kingdom*, vol. 3, *1874–93, The Kalakaua Dynasty* (Honolulu, 1967); Gavan Daws, *Shoal of Time: A History of the Hawaiian Islands* (Honolulu, 1968); Sylvester K. Stevens, *American Expansion in Hawaii, 1842–1898* (New York, 1945; reprint, 1968); and Lawrence H. Fuchs, *Hawaii Pono: An Ethnic and Political History* (Honolulu, 1961). Recent scholarship has directly addressed the issue of American imperialism in Hawai'i. See, for example, Haunani-Kay Trask, *From a Native Daughter: Colonialism and Sovereignty in Hawai'i*, rev. ed. (Honolulu, 1999), 113–22; Sally Engle Merry, *Colonizing Hawai'i: The Cultural Power of Law* (Princeton, 2000); and Noenoe K. Silva, *Aloha Betrayed: Native Hawaiian Resistance to American Colonialism* (Durham, N.C., 2004).

3. For discussions of colonial medicine, see, for example, Megan Vaughan, *Curing Their Ills: Colonial Power and African Illness* (Stanford, 1991); Sheldon Watts, *Epidemics and History: Disease, Power, and Imperialism* (New Haven, Conn., 1997); Philippa Levine, *Prostitution, Race, and Politics: Policing Venereal Disease in the British Empire* (New York, 2003); and Warwick Anderson, *The Cultivation of Whiteness: Science, Health and Racial Destiny in Australia* (New York, 2003).

4. Warwick Anderson, "States of Hygiene: Race 'Improvement' and Biomedical Citizenship in Australia and the Colonial Philippines," in *Haunted by Empire: Geographies of Intimacy in North American History* (Durham, N.C., 2006), 97–98.

5. David Arnold, *Colonizing the Body: State Medicine and Epidemic Disease in Nineteenth-Century India* (Berkeley, 1993).

6. Ramón Gutiérrez, "What's Love Got to Do with It?" *Journal of American History* 88, 3 (2001): 866–70.

7. Conservative estimates place the population of native Hawaiians at 250,000 in 1779; by 1890, that number had dropped to 40,622; see Eleanor C. Nordyke, *The Peopling of Hawai'i*, 2nd ed. (Honolulu, 1989), 174–78. For alternate population figures, see David E. Stannard, *Before the Horror: The Population of Hawai'i on the Eve of Western Contact* (Honolulu, 1989), 3–31.

8. A. W. Crosby, "Hawaiian Depopulation as a Model for the Amerindian Experience," Terence Ranger and Paul Slack, eds., *Epidemics and Ideas: Essays on the Historical Perception of Pestilence* (New York, 1994), 190–91.

9. Arthur A. M. St. Mouritz, *The Path of the Destroyer: A History of Leprosy in the Hawaiian Islands and Thirty Years Research into the Means by Which It Has Been Spread* (Honolulu, 1916), 33.

10. Excerpt from the 1865 "Act to Prevent the Spread of Leprosy," as quoted in St. Mouritz, *Path of the Destroyer*, 63–65.

11. *Report of the Board of Health for the Biennial Period Ending Dec. 31, 1897* (Honolulu, 1898), 166.

12. For discussions of Hawaiian rituals of healing, see O. A. Bushnell, *The Gifts of Civilization: Germs and Genocide in Hawai'i* (Honolulu, 1993), 64–67; and Mary Kawena Pukuai, E. W. Haertig, and Catherine A. Lee, *Nana I Ke Kumu (Look to the Source)*, (Honolulu, 1972), 1:38, 64, 74–75.

13. Pennie Moblo, "Leprosy, Politics, and the Rise of Hawaii's Reform Party," *Journal of Pacific History* 34, 1 (1999): 81; Michelle T. Moran, *Colonizing Leprosy: Imperialism and the Politics of Public Health in the United States* (Chapel Hill, N.C., 2007).

14. Watts, *Epidemics and History*, 71–76. For a discussion of medieval leprosy, see Saul Nathaniel Brody, *The Disease of the Soul: Leprosy in Medieval Literature* (Ithaca, N.Y., 1974), 104–6.

15. "Report of Arthur Mouritz," in *Appendix to the Report on Leprosy of the President of the Board of Health to the Legislative Assembly of 1886* (Honolulu, 1886), lxxix–lxxx.

16. Ernest Andrade Jr., *Unconquerable Rebel: Robert W. Wilcox and Hawaiian Politics, 1880–1903* (Niwot, Colo., 1996), 44–52.

17. Moblo, "Leprosy, Politics, and the Rise of Hawaii's Reform Party"; Moran, *Colonizing Leprosy*.

18. *Report of the Board of Health of the Territory of Hawaii for the Eighteen Months Ending December 31, 1902* (Honolulu, 1903), 13.

19. See, for example, *Biennial Report of the President of the Board of Health to the Legislature of the Kingdom of Hawaii*, (Honolulu, 1890), 13.

20. Silva, *Aloha Betrayed*, 123–63.

21. Board of Health Meeting, May 17, 1893, 5:45, Minutes of the Board of Health, Hawai'i State Archives, Honolulu (hereafter HSA).

22. Editorial, "Board of Health," *Daily Pacific Commercial Advertiser* (hereafter *DPCA*), June 9, 1893, 2.

23. Board of Health Meeting, May 31, 1893, 5:47; Board of Health Meeting, June 16, 1893, 5:52, Minutes of the Board of Health, HSA.

24. *The True Story of Kaluaiko'olau*; for contemporary press coverage, see "Shot by a Leper: The Shocking Fate of Deputy Sheriff Stolz of Waimea," *Daily Bulletin*, June 29, 1893, 3.

25. "The Kauai Lepers: Preparations Being Made to Remove Them to Molokai," *DPCA*, June 29, 1893, 3.

26. Doreen Massey, *For Space* (London, 2005), 4.

27. "Dead or Alive: Lepers to Be Removed from Kalalau," *DPCA*, June 30, 1893, 3.

28. Board of Health Meeting, July 1, 1893, 5:57, Minutes of the Board of Health, HSA.

29. "At Bay: Koolau and His Backers Will Make a Stand," *DPCA*, July 5, 1893, 2.

30. Ibid.; "Return from Kalalau: S.S. Waialeale Brings a Number of Surrendered Lepers," *Daily Bulletin*, July 5, 1893, 3.

31. "The Pele Arrives: The Situation Not Changed at Kalalau," *DPCA*, July 8, 1893, 3.

32. "Stronghold of the Lepers: An Impregnable Fastness Where Koolau Will Die before Yielding," *Daily Bulletin*, July 8, 1893, 3; "Pele Arrives," *DPCA*, July 8, 1893, 3.

33. "Taste of Real War: Three Soldiers Killed in the Kalalau Expedition," *Daily Bulletin*, July 10, 1893, 3; "Killed by Koolau! Two Soldiers Shot by the Leper Bandit," *DPCA*, July 10, 1893, 5.

34. "Notes and Comments," *DPCA*, July 10, 1893, 3.

35. Warwick Anderson, "Excremental Colonialism: Public Health and the Poetics of Pollution," *Critical Inquiry* 21 (Spring 1995): 640–69.

36. "They All Came Back: The Troops Return from Kalalau without Koolau," *Daily Bulletin*, July 13, 1893, 2; "Koolau Provisioned," *Daily Bulletin*, July 18, 1893, 2.

37. "Flight of Koolau," *DPCA*, July 14, 1893, 5.

38. *Report of the President of the Board of Health for the Nine Months Ending December 31, 1894* (Honolulu, 1895), 60.

39. "The True Story of Kaluaiko'olau," 36–41.

40. A. Grove Day, introduction to Jack London, *Stories of Hawaii*, ed. A. Grove Day (Honolulu, 1994), 3.

41. Jack London, "Koolau the Leper," in London, *Stories of Hawaii.* The story first appeared in 1912 in a collection entitled *The House of Pride*.

42. London, "Koolau the Leper," 39. For an interpretation of London as critical of Western imperialism, see James Slagel, "Political Leprosy: Jack London the Kama'aina and Koolau the Hawaiian," in Leonard Cassuto and Jeanne Campbell Reesman, eds., *Rereading Jack London* (Stanford, 1996).

43. London, "Koolau the Leper," 40.

44. Ibid., 43.

45. Ibid., 51.

46. Ibid., 52.

47. See John R. Eperjesi, "Becoming Hawaiian: Jack London, Cultural Tourism, and the Myth of Hawaiian Exceptionalism, " in Eperjesi, *The Imperialist Imaginary: Visions of Asia and the Pacific in American Culture* (Lebanon, N.H., 2005), 117–20.

48. Jack London to L. E. Pinkham, President of the Board of Health, June 18, 1907, Kalaupapa Settlement, DOH4–49 Correspondence, Board of Health Records, HSA.

49. *Report of Board of Health*, 1907, 17.

50. Jack London, *Cruise of the Snark* (London, 1911; reprint, 1971).

51. Day, introduction, 9–10; Eperjesi, "Becoming Hawaiian," 118.

52. This threat was perhaps most pronounced in London's story "Good-by, Jack," in which a white multimillionaire has an affair with a beautiful Hawaiian woman, only to find her later bound for the leprosy settlement on Moloka'i.

53. For an example of continuing interactions between the Board of Health and the Hawaiian Chamber of Commerce, see Board of Health Meetings, January 11, July 19, and August 16, 1922, Minutes of the Board of Health, HSA.

54. See Frazier, foreword to *The True Story of Kalauaikoolau*, vii–viii.

55. *The True Story of Kalauaikoolau*, 45.

56. Mouritz, *Path of the Destroyer*, 58–59.

57. Massey, *For Space*, 71.

TONY BALLANTYNE AND
ANTOINETTE BURTON

Epilogue

THE INTIMATE, THE TRANSLOCAL,
AND THE IMPERIAL IN AN AGE OF MOBILITY

In 1998, Sonia Ryang, an anthropologist of Korea and Japan, published an essay in the British-based collective *Feminist Review* entitled "Love and Colonialism: Takamura Itsue's Feminism," in which she argued for the possibility that when love—a very particular form of affective expression, a very contingent articulation of intimacy—was used as an analytical category it had the power to subvert, if not transform, conventional understandings of colonial gender relations. If the twinning of love and empire was jarring as recently as a decade ago, it is not so now. There has been a wave of scholarship produced at the intersection of a variety of disciplines—anthropology, history, sociology, feminist theory, queer studies, cultural studies, and colonial/postcolonial studies—in ensuing years that has aimed to put emotion on the table as the right and proper object of post-Enlightenment scrutiny. This, together with the torrent of work on love and hate and what Raymond Williams perspicaciously called "structures of feeling," means that everywhere one turns, it seems, students of the past and of the present are critically engaged in creating accounts of why and how the political economies of emotion, intimacy, and friendship shape state formations, political movements, and the materialities of culture—and, as Ryang argued in her prescient article, the interiorities of racism and imperialism as well.[1] To borrow from the language of the *fashionistas,* affect is the new black. This would appear to be especially the case in post-colonial studies, where Vincente Rafael's

335

White Love, Ann Stoler's edited collection *Haunted by Empire* and not one but two monographs on the subject of *Empire of Love* (by Matt Matsuda [historian] and Elizabeth Povinelli [anthropologist]) represent just a few of the recent titles with which we are in dialogue in our attempts to historicize the work of intimacy in global imperial histories.

It is beyond the scope of our project to diagnose this preoccupation. Nor would we like—in light of the wide variety of emotional possibilities offered in the essays in this collection—to reduce intimacy or affect to love per se. Given the rich and exponentially growing literature on emotion and empire in the last decade (not to mention the high stakes of recent forms of affective rationality undergirding a new century of imperial aggression), we make a case for tighter, more nuanced connections to be made between "love" as a sign of liberal governance (or social practice) and the place of empire as one of its territorializing technologies. *Moving Subjects* operates from the premise that empire has historically been an intimate project and that modern Western empires are indebted to the presumption that the intimate couple is the humanizing ground of all legitimate subjects (whether of the state or of history). Along with Povinelli, we suggest that the "intimate events" that produce the normative conjugal couple—or that fall short of that ideal—are produced by the collision between the foundational logic of the civilizing mission as a rationale for empire and the instabilities of the constantly moving ground of imperialism in situ.[2] In so doing we recognize that the circuits of reproductive desire, of the kind that modern empires routinely engendered, need to be more fully countenanced, especially in this, the newest age of Anglo-globalization and Anglo-imperial war.

Our contribution to this enterprise has been, on the one hand, to push beyond the parameters of the category of "migration" to try to capture the less aggregate but nonetheless historically consequential force of "mobility": to emphasize, in other words, the instability of imperial territoriality as much as the movement of subjects per se. As we suggested in the introduction, this framing reflects our desire to strive toward a more dynamic set of understandings of the dialogic historical relationship between space and body. We seek an analytical toolkit that acknowledges, in short, the power of individuals (both as subjects and objects of imperial power) to harness the kinetic energies of that power at the site of intimacy and affect. We have aimed to do so without privileging the agency of those subjects or their powerlessness as absolutes; the work of the contributors to this collection points to these relationships and the patterns of agency they throw up as the effects of translocal history itself. On the other hand, we have sought both to draw attention to and to diminish, by specifying in historical terms, the effect of putatively global processes on what were indubitably globalized and globalizing imperial spaces. Our invocation of the "translocal" is one attempt to rematerialize not just the ideological and structural work of local and regional people and space, but to insist, with Lisa Rofel, that that the global is always already an act of positioning, used, if not designed, as a "signifier . . . of difference."[3] Given the ways in which some of the "locales" in this book may seem off-center to North American readers accustomed to empire in the British context meaning Africa and India—and especially given the ways in which their apparently "minor" location is both invoked as evidence of their statistical insignificance in global terms and of the putative normativity of the Euro-American center—this seems a point worth underscoring. Many of the essays collected here convey both historical configurations of affect and recent debates over the legacies of imperial intimacies that may well appear unusual to readers or students of empire raised on Niall Ferguson or even William Dalrymple. But these stories remind us that neither our contemporary period of globalization nor the age of the "new imperialism" fashioned homogenous or seamless worlds. Rather, ages of empire produce cultural formations riven by conflict and disjuncture that are, in turn, unevenly connected to global forces that emanate from a variety of "global centers."[4] To use Fiji, Australia, New Zealand, and Hawai'i to reimagine the operation of empire through questions of intimacy— to insist on sites that have historically been both minor and "other" in the context of modern Western regimes of rationality and social science discipline–making—is to stake a double claim about the centrality of colonial bodies and imperial mobilities as moving targets as well as moving subjects for "global" analysis and critique.

Moving Subjects, then, offers a distinctive angle of vision on the question of empire and intimacy. As a set of reflections primarily grounded in the Pacific and the American West but reaching out to southern Africa, to Portuguese India, to Britain itself, this collection illuminates new topographies and redirects our attention to white settler colonies in an attempt to suggest that imperial histories also need to be re-territorialized so they take full account of all the geographies of intimacy sponsored by modern imperial systems. Like the recent collection *Haunted by Empire,* edited by Ann Laura Stoler, the multi-sited perspectives offered here are deeply invested in convergence and connection as well as comparison.[5] In an effort to "carve out a common ground of conversation between United States history and postcolonial studies," Stoler's collection foregrounds the divergent place of intimacy within various empire-building projects in North America and offers a range of case studies from the borders and littorals of the developing United States to call the self-evidence of that nation into question.[6] While the essays gathered here share Stoler's concern with the "geography of intimacy," they are less committed to reimagining the history of a single nation-state than they are in charting the shifting place of the intimate within a modern world that was characterized by accelerating mobility *and* a new insistence on the "rootedness" of national identity—as well as by the global reach of imperial systems and new efforts to define, inscribe, and police the boundaries of the local. Imperial and colonial subjects were undoubtedly on the move, but it was not always intimacy that rooted them. In many instances, intimacy was a motor and a moving subject itself, reminding us equally of the capacity of feeling to transform the geopolitics of territoriality and of the risk to all kinds of histories of that power. If nothing else, the stories that moving subjects tell testify not just to the impossibility of the nation or the local as a fixed and stable ground, but to the indispensability of the intimate as a metaphor, a structural reality and a material resource for those looking to exceed the limits of "home" and those seeking refuge in the kinetic spaces of empire.

Notes

1. See Sonia Ryang, "Love and Colonialism in Takamure Itsue's Feminism: A Postcolonial Critique," *Feminist Review* 60 [Special issue on Ethics and the Politics of Love], (1998): 1–32, and her *Love in Modern Japan: Its Estrangement from Self, Sex, & Society* (London, 2006).

2. Elizabeth Povinelli, *The Empire of Love: Toward a Theory of Intimacy, Genealogy and Carnality* (Durham, N.C., 2006).

3. Lisa Rofel quoted in Tze-lan D. San, *The Emerging Lesbian: Female Same-Sex Desire in Modern China* (Chicago, 2003), 10. For the original, see Lisa Rofel, "Qualities of Desire: Imagining Gay Identities in China," *GLQ* 5, 4 (1999): 456. We are grateful to Emily Skidmore for this reference.

4. Arjun Appadurai, *Modernity at Large: Cultural Dimensions of Globalization* (Minneapolis, 1996), 32–33.

5. Ann Laura Stoler, "Intimidations of Empire: Predicaments of the Tactile and Unseen," *Haunted by Empire: Geographies of Intimacy in North American History* (Durham, N.C., 2006), 5–7.

6. Ibid., 1.

CONTRIBUTORS

TONY BALLANTYNE is an associate professor of history at Washington University, St. Louis. His publications include *Orientalism and Race: Aryanism in the British Empire* and *Between Colonialism and Diaspora: Sikh Cultural Formations in an Imperial World.*

ANTOINETTE BURTON holds the Bastian Chair in Global and Transnational Studies at the University of Illinois, Urbana-Champaign. Her publications address empire, women, gender, and colonialism; the most recent is *The Postcolonial Careers of Santha Rama Rau.*

ADRIAN CARTON is a lecturer in cultural and social analysis at the University of Western Sydney in Australia. He is at work on a book on the imperial politics of hybridity in British and French India.

DAVID HAINES works at the Bodleian Library, Oxford University. Until recently, he was a historian in the Office of Treaty Settlements for the New Zealand government. His personal research focuses on the history of whaling and of Ngai Tahu Whanui in nineteenth-century New Zealand.

KATHERINE ELLINGHAUS is a Monash Fellow at the School of Historical Studies, Monash University, Clayton, Victoria. Her publications include *Taking Assimilation to Heart: Marriages of White Women and Indigenous Men in the United States and Australia, 1887–1937.* She is at work on a book about Native Americans of mixed descent, blood quantum, and assimilation policy.

CHARLOTTE MACDONALD is a lecturer in history at Victoria University, Wellington/Te Whare Wananga o Te Ika a Maui, New Zealand. She edited *New Zealand* in the series *Women Writing Home: Female Correspondence across the British Empire* (Klaus Stierstorfer, gen. ed.) and is at work on a chapter on sport and society for the *Oxford History of New Zealand.*

MICHAEL A. McDONNELL is a senior lecturer in history at the University of Sydney. His publications include *The Politics of War: Race, Class, and Conflict in Revolutionary Virginia* (2007) and numerous articles on the American Revolution. He is at work on a book on the Langlades, the Ottawa, and the métis communities of the Great Lakes.

KIRSTEN McKENZIE is a senior lecturer in history at the University of Sydney. Her work includes *Scandal in the Colonies: Sydney and Cape Town, 1820–1850,* and she is at work on a book about social climbing and imposture in the British Empire.

MICHELLE T. MORAN is an associate professor of history at Montgomery College, Rockville, Maryland. Her publications include *Colonizing Leprosy: Imperialism and the Politics of Public Health in the United States.*

FIONA PAISLEY is a senior lecturer in cultural history at Griffith University, Brisbane, Australia. Her publications address settler colonialism in transnational context, empire and masculinity, childhood, gender, and modernity and include *Loving Protection? Australian Feminism and Aboriginal Women's Rights, 1919–1939* and, as coeditor, *Uncommon Ground: White Women in Aboriginal History.* Her forthcoming book is titled *Glamour in the Pacific: Cultural Internationalism and the Women's Pan-Pacific Association, 1928–1959.*

ADELE PERRY is Canada Research Chair in Western Canadian Social History at the University of Manitoba, Winnipeg. Her works include *On the Edge of Empire: Gender, Race, and the Making of British Columbia, 1858–1871,* and she is at work on a book about intimacy, kin, and migration in the British Empire in the nineteenth century.

DANA RABIN is an associate professor of history at the University of Illinois, Urbana-Champaign. She is at work on a book about race, gender, and topographies of empire in eighteenth-century Britain.

CHRISTINE M. SKWIOT is an assistant professor of history at Georgia State University. She is at work on a book about U.S. tourism and empire in Cuba and Hawai'i.

RACHEL STANDFIELD is a doctoral candidate at the University of Otago, Dunedin, New Zealand. Her earlier research focused on the position of indigenous peoples and immigrants in postwar Australia. She is at work on a study of the development of racial thought in the early Australasian colonies.

FRANCES STEEL is a lecturer in Pacific history at the University of Otago, Dunedin, New Zealand. She is at work on a study of the history of the Union Steam Ship Company of New Zealand.

ELIZABETH VIBERT is an associate professor of history at the University of Victoria, Canada. Her publications include articles on colonial identities in British North America in the early 1800s, *Traders' Tales: Cultural Encounters in the Columbia Plateau, 1807–1846,* and, as coeditor, *Reading beyond Words: Contexts for Native History.*

KERRY WYNN is an assistant professor in the Department of History, Washburn University. Her dissertation is "The Embodiment of Citizenship: Sovereignty and Colonialism in the Cherokee Nation, 1880–1920."

INDEX

The University of Illinois Press
is a founding member of the
Association of American University Presses.

Composed in 9.5/12.5 Trump Mediaeval
by Jim Proefrock
at the University of Illinois Press
Manufactured by Sheridan Books, Inc.

University of Illinois Press
1325 South Oak Street
Champaign, IL 61820-6903
www.press.uillinois.edu